THE AFRICAN EXPERIENCE
Volume II: Syllabus

THE AFRICAN EXPERIENCE

Volume II: Syllabus

by
JOHN N. PADEN
and
EDWARD W. SOJA

Northwestern University Press
Evanston 1970

Library of Congress Catalog Card Number: 70–98466
Cloth Edition SBN 8101–0306–0
Paper Edition SBN 8101–0307–9
Copyright © 1970 by Northwestern University Press
Printed in the United States of America

JOHN N. PADEN is Assistant Professor of Political
Science at Northwestern University.
EDWARD W. SOJA is Associate Professor of Geography
at Northwestern University.

Book design by Elizabeth G. Stout.
Cover design by Edward Hughes.
Photograph by Russell Kay.
Chi-Wara antelope headdress, worn by Bambara (Mali) dance society,
from the collection of Robert Plant Armstrong.

Contents

LIST OF FIGURES

Acknowledgments

THIS SYLLABUS originated as part of the African Curriculum Project, sponsored by the Office of Education, U.S. Department of Health, Education and Welfare. In 1967 USOE contracted with the Program of African Studies, Northwestern University, to develop a three-volume set of teaching materials on Africa for college use. The set was to include a syllabus, a computerized bibliography, and an anthology of original essays. Since the completion of the contract in 1968–69, and after receiving comments from readers of the USOE edition, work was begun to revise and enlarge the three volumes with the intention of producing an interdisciplinary introduction to African studies that would be available to a wider readership. *The African Experience, Volume I: Essays; Volume II: Syllabus;* and *Volume III: Bibliography*, are the product of these efforts. It should be noted, however, that the content of both the African Curriculum Project materials (which were produced with the encouragement and financial support of the U.S. Office of Education) and the three volumes of *The African Experience* (which have built upon these original curriculum materials) does not necessarily represent official Office of Education position or policy, but rather the professional and personal judgments of the co-authors.

For its assistance in all aspects of the preparation of this volume, we would like to express our deep appreciation to the Program of African Studies, Northwestern University; and particularly to Professor Gwendolen Carter, Director of the Program, who took time out from her exceedingly full schedule to provide detailed comments on many portions of the manuscript. Major aid in reworking parts of this volume was also supplied by Ronald Cohen, Frank Willett, Margaret Priestley Bax, George Dalton, Remi Clignet, Thurstan Shaw, Ivor Wilks, Roland Young, Jack Berry, Robert C. Mitchell, Ibrahim Abu-Lughod, and Pat McGowan. These individuals, in the extremely short time available to them, made comments, corrections, and suggestions which have greatly improved the text. We are very grateful for this help.

In addition, we would like to thank Tom and Phyllis Lewin for the basic preparation of the chronology; Debbie Pellow and Frank Jordan for their assistance on several of the topic summaries; Vaughan Bishop and Oscar Beard for their day-to-day assistance; Anne Potter, Pat Miller, and Barbara Teising for their typing and ability to adjust to the erratic schedules of the authors; and the innumerable colleagues (faculty and graduate students) who have become involved in one way or another with the African Curriculum Project and the subsequent production of the three volumes of *The African Experience*, which in its many months of gestation managed to involve what appears to be a sizable portion of Northwestern University. Special thanks are due to Diana Cohen for her continuing help on administrative aspects of the syllabus preparation and to Hans Panofsky, Curator of Africana at Northwestern, for the consistent co-operation we have received from him and the Africana Library.

Because of the necessary scope of this syllabus and the consequent limitations of the authors, the conventional caveats exonerating all but the authors for any problems in accuracy, balance, or viewpoint must be emphatically repeated. Although in some ways this syllabus is the product of a cooperative effort on the part of members of the Program of African Studies, the authors have been the only ones to examine thoroughly the finished product, and we take full responsibility for any errors or shortcomings. We also invite substantive corrections and any comments on the utility of the volume for teaching purposes.

Finally, our appreciation to Northwestern University Press: to all the staff for their practical and substantive help, their patience and prodding, and their continuing good judgment on editorial matters; to Russell Kay especially for his editorial and organizational assistance; and to Ann Paden for her editorial—and domestic—skills. And while on the subject of the authors' wives, Maureen, thank you too.

Introduction

It does not seem necessary in this introduction to stress the importance of African studies. Given the growing presence of independent Africa in world affairs, the developments within American education aimed at recognition of an increasingly integral global society and the clear relevance of the African heritage to all Americans, it is evident that the continent of Africa demands attention from teacher and student, scholar and layman, black and white. This volume is a syllabus designed for the teacher and the student interested in the African experience: African responses to the challenges which face all mankind. As such, the syllabus not only explores the uniqueness of the African experience but also attempts to illustrate the global relevance of Africa, especially to highlight its distinctive importance to American society.

This *Syllabus* constitutes Volume II of a three-volume set of teaching materials with the general title *The African Experience.* These materials are exploratory and suggestive rather than exhaustive or definitive. They provide a gateway and guide to the study of Africa but are not intended to cover the totality of the African experience—a virtually impossible task. The particular perspectives which have guided the selection, organization, and presentation of materials are made explicit in this introduction, and readers are urged to bear these perspectives in mind when they use the volumes.

The Syllabus consists of 100 topic summaries, or modules, organized for use in a one-year interdisciplinary course in African studies at the undergraduate college level. (With modifications, it might be used at the advanced high-school level.) Five of the modules are composed of study questions which can be used for discussion, examination, or review. In addition, there are three appendixes: (1) an alternative organization of topic summaries and a selected list of about 150 books which are keyed to the modules; (2) a selected chronology of African history; and (3) a guide to pronunciation of African terms and names.

Volume I of *The African Experience* contains 31 *Essays* which represent attempts by specialists in African studies to synthesize existing information about a wide range of African themes and to present this synthesis within an intellectually provocative and interdisciplinary framework. As such, it forms a basic textual accompaniment to the *Syllabus.*

Volume III of *The African Experience* is in two parts. The *Bibliography* contains about 4,000 references which may be used in conjunction with the other two volumes. References are organized to parallel the 100 modules of the *Syllabus,* to fit within a country-by-country case-study approach to the 42 independent African states, and alphabetically by author. The *Guide to Resources* consists of a supplementary set of articles and bibliographic notes on more specialized aspects of Africana resource materials.

The three volumes are organized around a single framework which serves as the primary means of integrating essays, modules, and bibliographic references into a coordinated curriculum. This framework consists of five parts: "African Society and Culture"; "Perspectives on the Past"; "Processes of Change"; "Consolidation of Nation-States"; and "Africa and the Modern World." There are approximately six essays, about twenty syllabus modules, and a balanced number of bibliographic references for each of these parts. For each of the 100 syllabus modules, the *Bibliography* provides introductory references (with full annotations), further references (useful to teachers and for more detailed research projects such as student term papers), general theory sources (not necessarily dealing directly with Africa), less accessible sources (including French-language sources), and case-study materials. A diagrammatic summary of this coordinated framework can be found in the pages preceding each of the five parts of the *Syllabus* and, in a slightly different form, in Appendix A.

THE AFRICAN EXPERIENCE:
INTERPRETIVE PERSPECTIVES

There is an inevitable subjectivity in any interpretation of the African experience. All human experience is a reservoir from which individuals, societies, and cultures draw in particular ways. We make no claim that the interpretation of the African experience which appears in this syllabus would be identical to the interpretation that might be made in a black studies course or in a conference of African leaders, although there may be some similarities. Nevertheless, the production of this syllabus has been guided by a set of perspectives of sufficient generality to assure an applicability which extends beyond the particular perceptions of the authors.

1. The Teaching Perspective

We have been guided in the preparation of this syllabus first by our role as teachers. The selection of subject matter and the way in which it is organized and presented reflects what we, *as teachers,* consider appropriate and helpful. We recognize that course outlines tend to be matters of personal preference and background, and rare is the syllabus which can be comfortably adopted by some-one other than the initial author. Consequently, we have attempted to make this syllabus as flexible as possible with respect to the ways it can be used by teachers and students.

One means of achieving some degree of adaptability to individual differences in approach and methodology is the bare-boned topic outline, a sequential list-ing of lecture topics and subheadings accompanied by lists of readings and reference sources. This is the standard type of syllabus given by college teachers to their students. But this form provides flexibility only through the absence of information. Twenty different teachers can teach twenty different courses using basically the same outline. This can be very advantageous, of course, but it is not very useful when, as is the case here, the objective is to guide inquiry into a broad body of information upon which lectures or discussions can be built. The skeletal outline does not help the teacher who may be relatively unfamiliar with some of the topics to be discussed (except by sending him to the library, which would be expected in any case). It also does not help the student to an-ticipate the content of future lectures, to evaluate the readings prior to classroom discussion, or to obtain a more detailed overview of the materials to be covered. We have chosen, therefore, to construct a syllabus of topic summaries in the form of short, expository discussions. Additionally, in order to avoid some of the rigidity which comes with tightly ordered sequences, we have designed these topic summaries as modules.

The term *module* was originally used in electronics to denote a self-contained unit which can be grouped with any number of similar units to create a variety of wholes. In recent years, the term has been adopted by educators in reference to units used to permit flexible scheduling in secondary-school curriculums. Many high-school syllabuses and schedules are now based on modular course-structures which allow greater flexibility and freedom for the individual student (and, to some extent, for the teacher) than would normally exist. The student, for example, can select from a large number of modules (course units of varying length) a variety of combinations to suit his interests and fulfill basic require-ments.

The 100 modules of the *Syllabus* consist, in most cases, of short interpretive statements briefly elaborating three or four central themes. The full set of modules, used in conjunction with the *Essays* and *Bibliography* (Volumes I and III of *The African Experience*), provide the basis for a one-year interdisciplinary introduction to African studies. In addition, however, several different com-binations of modules can be used for courses of shorter duration or as com-ponent African units in other courses which do not deal entirely with Africa. It is also possible to reorganize the modules to suit African courses within particular disciplines, some modules providing background reading in related disciplines and others supplying more directly relevant syllabus materials. More will be said of these possible permutations later in this introduction.

Certain special needs of teachers of African studies are accommodated in the three appendixes at the end of this volume. *Appendix A* restructures the 100 modules into a course outline which assumes that the teacher will organize his course entirely around the volume of *Essays*. We have also included in this appendix a list of one or two key bibliographic references for each module—in essence, a basic book-list of approximately 150 items. *Appendix B* gives a selective chronological summary outlining African history. The chronology contains nearly all major dates mentioned in the syllabus, as well as others to fill in particular gaps. It is more than a simple time-chart, however, in that it attempts to identify the major processes which together provide a dynamic and interconnected framework for studying African history and social change. Finally, *Appendix C* provides a pronunciation guide, giving what the authors consider acceptable or standard American pronunciation of African words and names. The form and content of this appendix, like the others, are designed to be of maximum practical use to the student and teacher.

2. The Social-Science Perspective

Whereas the general form and structure of this syllabus reflect our experience as teachers, its substantive content derives primarily from our role as social scientists. The African experience, therefore, is interpreted from the distinctive perspective of social science. This perspective has guided the selection of materials and the way in which these materials are treated in each module. Our definition of social science is relatively broad and is discussed in greater detail in Modules 98, 99, and 100.

Nearly all of the materials covered in the syllabus are drawn from the fields of political science, economics, geography, sociology, anthropology, psychology, and history, although attention is also given to the arts and humanities. The various modules dealing with the arts and humanities are, however, treated primarily from a social-science point of view. Thus, for example, special attention is given to the importance of the social context in the discussion of traditional art and music and of modern African literature. African religion and conceptual thought are interpreted, in large part, either as components of ethnic society in Africa, as forces in and reflections of the processes of social change, or as important factors in contemporary politics. Even the modules that are explicitly historical do not purport to present history in precisely the same way that a historian, particularly one who is oriented to the humanities, might do. Instead, these modules attempt to select and highlight important *processes* or *concepts* which have special relevance to contemporary Africa (e.g., state-formation, interethnic and interracial relations, migration and diffusion, the continuity of social change).

This emphasis on the perspective of social science also lends itself to an alternative, although complementary, use for the three volumes of *The African Experience*. In addition to providing introductory materials for the study of Africa, the syllabus can be used as a contextual steppingstone to more intensive work in any of the social sciences. Important concepts in each of the social sciences are introduced within the specific African context, general works not necessarily dealing with Africa are given in the *Bibliography*, and special attention is given to social-science methodology and research emphasis in many of the modules and in an epilogue to each of the first two volumes.

Finally, as teachers and as social scientists, we have chosen to organize the 100 modules into a particular intellectual framework which is identical in broad outline for each of the three volumes of *The African Experience*; this framework has been discussed earlier. Although this order of presentation was carefully and purposefully selected to convey what we consider to be a cohesive way of organizing the materials, the particular ordering should not be considered as definitive. Like the modules themselves, the ordering represents an evaluative judgment designed to aid, not restrict, the teacher in the development of course materials and lectures in African studies. Indeed, the whole question of how to organize a course in African studies should be an open one and might provide an initial focus for interpretation and discussion between teacher and students. The imposition of an organizational structure may, to some extent, reduce the full flexibility of independent, self-contained modules; but it is felt that this loss of flexibility is more than balanced by the greater clarity derived from the identification of closely related modular clusters.

3. The Interdisciplinary Perspective

Proceeding from the above discussion is the clear direction of the syllabus toward an interdisciplinary social-science perspective. Many courses in African studies are taught cooperatively, with members of the various disciplines sequentially presenting their distinctive perspectives and subject matter. Although it is possible to restructure the syllabus to permit such a compartmentalized presentation, a major focus throughout the three volumes of *The African Experience* has been to encourage a coordinated, interdisciplinary approach in which the individual can encompass and integrate a wide range of disciplinary perspectives. All too often, the tightly compartmentalized course leaves the student without effective means of bringing together the enormous variety of approaches to African studies. Courses which involve a large number of specialists, each presenting his own field, frequently can be very effective, particularly when there is opportunity for review, comparison, and synthesis. In practical terms, however, there are few universities in this country which have an interdisciplinary staff of African specialists. We feel that a coordinated interdisciplinary approach by a single teacher (or small team) can not only be effective but may also more adequately reflect current developments in both the social sciences and African studies.

The major problem areas and research themes of both African studies and social science clearly cut across disciplinary boundaries. Economic development in Africa, for example, is not the exclusive prerogative of the economist but necessarily involves the political scientist, the linguist, the geographer, the anthropologist, and other social scientists, as well as many natural scientists and professionals. Similar conclusions can be made for other major subjects in the syllabus: nation-building, modernization, urban problems, international relations, apartheid in South Africa, political instability, African-American relations, the relevance of Africa to black and white America, African art and music, African religion and social thought, the psychological stresses of rapid social change, the problems of population growth.

Accordingly, in both the *Syllabus* and the volume of *Essays*, there is an emphasis on the interrelationships between particular topics and approaches. A large proportion of the individual modules are cross-referenced to other modules and to the *Essays*. Many general themes are repeated throughout the syllabus. The presentation of detailed lists of facts is sacrificed in favor of the discussion of important concepts. Some of the gaps in our knowledge of Africa are clearly identified, and where disagreement or controversy exist over a particular subject, this is generally noted.

4. The Perspective of Cultural Pluralism

If one central substantive theme can be said to thread through all three volumes of *The African Experience*, it is the theme of cultural pluralism. There are probably 1,000 to 2,000 distinct ethnic and/or linguistic groups in Africa, each differing (to various degrees) from the others in traditional social and cultural patterns as well as in the degree to which it has experienced the forces of social change. These differences, however, are balanced by a common experience with the challenges of ethnic and cultural pluralism.

The problems of creating and maintaining cohesive and productive pluralistic societies from an amalgam of heterogeneous peoples are woven through the entire fabric of African history. Pluralism has characterized the pattern of interethnic relations for the full range of African societies, from the relatively small noncentralized ethnic communities to the large pre-colonial states and empires, from colonial Africa to the contemporary mosaic of independent states.

In pre-colonial Africa even the smaller scale noncentralized societies did not exist in isolation but were constantly confronted with the need to adapt their ethnic identity to meet changes in the larger situation. These dynamic patterns of ethnicity are given detailed attention in several modules in Part I, "African Society and Culture." Community boundaries of identity and territory in pre-colonial Africa were not rigid and impermeable. As mentioned in Module 6, "cohesive communities were appearing and disappearing, blending and breaking off, as a result of . . . changes in intergroup relations." Trade, competition for land and animals, urbanization, the growth of states and empires, migration, the diffusion of Islam, warfare, and other developments tended to draw or force unlike peoples together, creating the need for new mechanisms of societal integration. The interethnic contact developing from such situations often resulted in a form of cooperative interaction in which distinct ethnic groups maintained their identities but effectively worked together in a variety of ways.

The larger-scale states and empires of pre-colonial Africa were faced with an even more formidable challenge in maintaining the cohesion of ethnically pluralistic societies. One of the most important mechanisms of societal integration for many of these states, especially those in the Sudanic belt (e.g., Ghana, Mali, Songhai, Kanem-Bornu, the Hausa states) was Islam, which has continued to play a major role throughout Africa. Throughout Part II, "Perspectives on the Past," the patterns of fission and fusion which characterized the growth and decline of African states and empires are discussed, while several of the *Essays* (especially Holden, chap. 10) provide more specific detail on this subject.

Africa during the colonial period continued to be faced with the problems of ethnic pluralism, and continued to react flexibly by restructuring ethnic identities within a multiethnic context. The initial imposition of rigid administrative and territorial boundaries over societies which may never have been rigidly bounded resulted in many changes. Some of the dynamics of interethnic relationship, both peaceful and nonpeaceful, were stabilized as the colonial powers sought to establish effective administrative control over the variety of peoples within the artificially created territories they controlled. At the same time, however, new contexts were introduced which stimulated a wider scope of interethnic relations than had probably ever existed before in Africa. The colonial territories themselves encompassed within their boundaries groups of people who would, in the traditional context of interethnic relations, probably never have voluntarily joined together. Urbanization, Western education, the expansion of a money economy, and the sharing of a single colonial administration planted the seeds of the new multiethnic states which were to emerge in the period of African independence.

The ethnic pluralism which developed during the colonial period, however, involved a clearly defined dominant-subordinate relationship. Instead of promoting the cooperative interaction upon which ethnic or cultural pluralism is based, the colonial system maintained order primarily through bilateral relations between the central government and the ethnic groups individually. Linguistically related groups which had never been effectively united in the past (e.g., the Kikuyu and Luhya in Kenya, the Ewe in Ghana and Togo, and many others) often restructured their ethnic identities to establish larger units within the colonial context. But it was extremely difficult for a colony-wide pattern of interethnic cooperation to develop, in large part because of the administrative policies of the colonial powers. The drive toward independence temporarily created a common anti-colonial focus which clearly cut across ethnic lines, but once the colonial system was removed a vacuum was created at the center which could not easily be filled by indigenous leaders because of their individual ethnic identities. As mentioned in the *Essays* (chap. 1),

whereas mechanisms were developed during the colonial period to govern relationships between ethnic groups and the colonial power, similar mechanisms for
conflict resolution between ethnic groups themselves were virtually nonexistent.
Independence, therefore, created a situation of competition for power largely
between ethnic units, since other forms of group identity at the national level
usually were not sufficiently developed to provide a wide basis of support.

The new states of contemporary sub-Saharan Africa, with the possible exceptions of Somali, Lesotho, and Botswana, are all ethnically heterogeneous,
and it is likely that some form of cultural pluralism will be the basis of national
political integration for some time to come. In essence, this situation underlies
virtually all the modules in Parts III and IV of this syllabus, "Processes of
Change," and "Consolidation of Nation-States."

Many of the contemporary problems in Africa reflect the challenges of creating
a pluralistic order in multiethnic societies. It is this challenge and the African
experience in dealing with it that to a great degree underlies the relevance of
Africa—and African studies—to the modern world and, in particular, to the
United States. Owing in part to a powerful Western ethnocentrism, a remarkable
lack of knowledge about Africa, and an underlying element of historical racism,
there has been a tendency for the bulk of the American population to consider
African problems as being rooted primarily in "tribalism," a rather primitive
and pejorative concept which is thought to have little relevance to the developed
Western countries. This point of view is reinforced in the United States by the
concept of the "melting pot," in which the American nation is seen as a cohesive
blend of peoples who have submerged their (or their forebears') ethnic and
national identities under the broader mantle of American nationalism. Recent
history in the United States—and in the United Kingdom, Canada, Belgium,
and Czechoslovakia—has shown that even in the most developed countries
cultural and ethnic pluralism may more accurately describe the foundation of
national society than the more holistic concept of a homogeneous nation.

Perhaps the most powerful indication of ethnic pluralism in the United States
has been the emergence of an Afro-American, or black, identity. Although this
syllabus on Africa has not been designed to be relevant primarily to the Afro-
American or to Afro-American studies, this critically important theme has influenced the selection and treatment of module topics, and a detailed description
of how many of the modules can be structured to suit an emphasis on Afro-
American studies is provided later in this introduction. But the relevance of
Africa to the United States does not rest solely on the powerful African legacy
in black America and the increasing influence of Africa on the Afro-American
population. Contemporary America, black and white, North and South, rich
and poor, urban, suburban, and rural, faces many of the same challenges as the
new states of Africa. Indeed, the whole world shares the challenge of pluralism,
whether it be based on national, ethnic, or cultural identities, religious convic-
tions, ideology, wealth, or color. For this reason, the African experience with

cultural pluralism has provided a central conceptual perspective throughout this syllabus.

5. *The Individual Perspectives of the Authors*

Another issue which affects the entire set of teaching materials in *The African Experience* involves the point of view of the two authors. As already mentioned, we have attempted to coordinate an interdisciplinary set of summary materials for use in courses on African studies. As this project developed, it became clear that there were many knowledge gaps not only with respect to our own backgrounds and experience but in the African studies literature as well. But rather than limit ourselves only to topics for which there is a wealth of scholarly material, we have often chosen to give interpretive overviews of topics selected for this syllabus. We have tried, however, to indicate where we are summarizing accepted knowledge and where we are trying to identify broad areas where little or no research has been done.

If our examples seem to be drawn primarily from East and West Africa, this is a reflection of our own major research experiences. If many of the specific illustrations tend to be from Hausa society and culture, this derives not only from the fact that Hausa speakers form one of the largest linguistic communities in Africa but also from the two years during which one of the authors lived within the Hausa community in Kano. Similarly, despite the fact that both authors have spent extensive periods in Nigeria (including a year of teaching at the University of Ibadan), whatever Nigerian emphasis may exist in the syllabus is also related to the size and importance of Nigeria. It must be remembered that one out of four black Africans is a Nigerian, that Nigeria has probably the tenth-largest population in the world, and that the Hausa and Yoruba populations each outnumber the population of Norway and Sweden combined. Similarly, important attention is given to Islam in Africa, both reflecting the interests of the authors and as a corrective to the fact that Islam is frequently omitted in discussions of Black Africa. About one-fourth of the independent states of Africa are predominantly Muslim. In West Africa, approximately half the population is Muslim, and four of the major vernacular languages in Africa (Hausa, Fulani, Swahili, and Arabic) are all associated with Islamic cultures. Seventy per cent of the world's Arabs live in Africa. Our personal experience, however, does extend beyond the sixteen West African states. One of us has traveled in much of North Africa, and the other has traveled throughout East Africa and done research there on communications and modernization.

The limits of our personal knowledge, however, were extended by the opportunity to draw upon the extraordinary cluster of Africana resources available at Northwestern University's Program of African Studies. Northwestern University has one of the finest Africana libraries in the world, and the Program of African Studies itself has associated with it over thirty professors with African experience in more than a dozen disciplines. Virtually all have aided in some way in the production of this syllabus. As is discussed in the introduction to the *Bibliography*, the production of the three volumes of *The African Experience* has also involved the participation of scholars and others outside the North-western community, especially those who contributed to the *Essays*.

We have not hesitated to insert our own value judgments when we considered them appropriate. But in our writing and topic selection there has been no attempt to undermine the old orthodoxies in African studies only to replace them with new ones, recognizing clearly that even in our lifetime the African experience will probably be modified beyond the range of our present imaginations. We have tried to give a balanced view of the problems and contemporary perspectives involved in studying the African experience. We have tried to suggest that not all the answers are known and, in fact, that not all the appropriate questions have yet been asked. Perhaps most important, we have tried to present our materials in a way which will encourage all readers — teachers, students, and anyone else interested in Africa — to discover for themselves the integrity and the scope of the *human* experience as it is acted out in all its complexity on the African continent.

USING THE SYLLABUS MODULES

As noted earlier, the modular structure of the syllabus is designed to permit a maximum of flexibility in its use. Those who wish to organize courses in African studies using the *Essays* as a text will find the existing ordering of modules appropriate. Alternatively, Appendix A supplies an arrangement of the modules which somewhat more closely parallels the *Essays* and provides a selection of a few key reference books drawn from the *Bibliography* for each module.

It was decided not to include detailed case studies in the syllabus but to keep the topic summaries as broadly based and as interdisciplinary as possible. We are by no means opposed to case studies. Indeed, we feel that their use should be strongly encouraged as a necessary supplement to the curriculum materials and as a further means of "individualizing" the *Syllabus*. Accordingly, a major portion of the *Bibliography* is devoted to the case-study approach. In the introduction to the *Bibliography*, there is a detailed discussion of the selection and use of case studies. For all of the appropriate modules, case-study references are provided. This will be of particular use to teachers wishing to illustrate specific modules with one or two case-study examples. For those who wish to emphasize the case-study approach throughout, especially to stress a country-by-country comparative analysis, Part II of the *Bibliography* contains, for each of the 42 independent African states and for the remaining colonial areas, a list of case studies arranged according to the major five-part structure of the syllabus. The five parts are further subdivided into the following categories: ethnic groups and culture, history, social change (general), elite development (including writings by political leaders), urbanization, national integration, politics, economics, international relations, literature (and social thought), general materials and bibliographies.

A wide range of possible alternative uses of the syllabus can be developed by a selective restructuring of the modules to conform to a specific theme or problem-area. Some of these possibilities are elaborated below to illustrate the process of module restructuring.

1. Afro-American Studies

A selection of modules from this *Syllabus* can be used to provide background and suggestions for discussion of the African component in courses dealing with Afro-America. The core of this modular structure would consist of the three modules concerned with *Afro-American Linkages:* 94, "Africa and Afro-American Identity"; 95, "Africa and Afro-American Social Change"; and 96, "African Interpretations of Multiracial America"; along with Module 30, "The African Legacy in the New World." From this core, one may wish to expand in several different directions. A unit on the Afro-American cultural heritage might include the eight modules on *Aspects of Ethnic Culture* (8 through 15), the six modules on *The Growth of African States* (21 through 26), and perhaps the three modules on *Personality and Change* (39 through 41). A special subunit would include three of the modules on *The African Slave Trade* (27 through 29).

Another direction could involve discussion of cultural pluralism and black-white relations in Africa. This would involve Modules 31, 32, 88, and 89 on the problem of South Africa, Modules 57 through 60 on *Nation-Building*, Modules 33 through 35 and 87 on *The Impact of Colonialism*, and Module 79 on "Pan-Africanism and Continental Unity." A related unit on the contemporary role of Africa would include Modules 90 through 93 on *Creativity in Contemporary Africa*, 81 through 84 on *Africa and the Major Powers*, 85 and 86 on *Africa and the Third World*, and 65 on "The Implications of Nigeria-Biafra." This modular structure is outlined in the following diagram and reference is made to the relevant sections of the *Essays*. Readings for each module are, of course, included in the *Bibliography*.

2. Islam in Africa

A unit on the history and influence of Islam in Africa could include the following modules:

21. The Impact of Islam in Africa
22. Empires of the Western Sudan
23. Coastal States of East Africa
24. States of the Central Sudan
38. Social Change and Modernization in Africa

POSSIBLE MODULAR STRUCTURE FOR AFRO-AMERICAN STUDIES

The Afro-American Cultural Heritage

8. Family and Kinship
9. Traditional Political Systems
10. Traditional Economic Systems
11. Language and Linguistic Systems
12. Literature and Oral Tradition
13. Conceptual Systems and Religion
14. Visual Arts
15. Traditional Music
20. Early Culture and State Formation
21. The Impact of Islam in Africa
22. Empires of the Western Sudan
23. Coastal States of East Africa
24. States of the Central Sudan
25. Indigenous Kingdoms of East and Central Africa
26. Forest States of West Africa
39. The Concept of African Personality
40. Characteristics of African Personality
41. Personality and Social Change

Essays: Cohen, Willett, Wachsmann, Holden, LeVine, Albert, Berry

Cultural Pluralism and Black-White Relations in Africa

31. White and Black Migrations in Southern Africa
32. African Reactions to European Settlement
88. Race Relations in Southern Africa
89. Politics and Race in South Africa
33. The Scramble for Africa
34. African Resistance and Reaction
35. The Nature of Colonial Systems
87. The Remnants of Colonialism
57. Interethnic Integration
58. Mass-Elite Integration
59. Territorial Integration and Boundaries
60. The Role of Ideology in Nation-Building
79. Pan-Africanism and Continental Unity

Essays: Mbata, Carter, Paden

Core Cluster: Afro-American Linkages

30. The African Legacy in the New World
94. Africa and Afro-American Identity
95. Africa and Afro-American Social Change
96. African Interpretations of Multiracial America

Essays: Turner, Hammond

The African Slave Trade

27. Early Western Contact
28. Origins and Growth of the Slave Trade
29. Abolition and States for Freed Slaves

Essays: Hammond

The Contemporary Role of Africa

90. Contemporary African Literature
91. Contemporary Social Thought
92. Urban Design and Architecture
93. Visual Arts and Music
81. Africa at the United Nations
82. Africa and the Former Metropoles
83. Africa and the United States
84. Africa and the Communist Countries
85. Africa and the Third World
86. Africa and the Middle East
65. The Implications of Nigeria-Biafra

Essays: Cartey, Mazrui, Abu-Lughod

52. Islamic Reformation Movements
65. The Implications of Nigeria-Biafra
66. Legal Systems in Africa
86. Africa and the Middle East
Essays: Abu-Lughod, Holden

3. The Role of Ethnicity

A clearly identifiable core cluster exists for this topic, including:

3. The African Ethnic Mosaic
4. The Nature of Ethnicity
5. On the Concept of "Tribe"
6. The Changing Nature of Ethnic Boundaries
7. Modern Variants of Ethnicity
Essays: Soja (Introduction), Cohen

Supplementary modules would cover:

8. Family and Kinship
9. Traditional Political Systems
11. Language and Linguistic Systems
13. Conceptual Systems and Religion
39. The Concept of African Personality
40. Characteristics of African Personality
41. Personality and Social Change
43. Education and Elite Recruitment
46. The Nature of Urban Life
54. Concepts of Nationalism
57. Interethnic Integration
58. Mass-Elite Integration
59. Territorial Integration and Boundaries
65. Implications of Nigeria-Biafra
77. Concepts of Supranationalism
78. Emergent Patterns of Regionalism
79. Pan-Africanism and Continental Unity
Essays: Albert, Levine, Clignet, Mabogunje, Paden, Zolberg, Crawford Young

4. The Problem of South Africa

A modular structure on the problems of race and politics in South Africa would focus around five modules and two essays:

31. White and Black Migrations in Southern Africa
32. African Reactions to European Settlement

87. The Remnants of Colonialism
88. Race Relations in Southern Africa
89. Politics and Race in South Africa
Essays: Mbata, Carter

Additional modules to supplement this core cluster would include:

27. Early Western Contact
33. The Scramble for Africa
51. Innovation, Synthesis, and Independency
69. An Assessment of Resources
79. Pan-Africanism and Continental Unity
81. Africa at the United Nations

5. The Arts and Humanities

Modules and essays dealing with this subject are:

12. Literature and Oral Tradition
13. Conceptual Systems and Religion
14. Visual Arts
15. Traditional Music
90. Contemporary African Literature
91. Contemporary Social Thought
92. Urban Design and Architecture
93. Visual Arts and Music
94. Africa and Afro-American Identity
Essays: Berry, Albert, Willett, Wachsmann, Cartey

6. Economic Development

This interdisciplinary theme could be discussed using the following sources:

10. Traditional Economic Systems
43. Education and Elite Recruitment
44. The New Elites of Africa
45. The Development of Urban Society
46. The Nature of Urban Life
47. Problems of Urbanization
48. Spatial Aspects of Transportation and Communications
49. New Modes of Communication
69. An Assessment of Resources
70. Agricultural Reorganization
71. The Industrialization Process
72. Planning for Development

73. Development of Economic Systems
74. Population Pressure and Social Factors in Development
75. Technology and Nation-Building
78. Emergent Patterns of Regionalism
79. Pan-Africanism and Continental Unity
80. International Organizations in Africa
81. Africa at the United Nations
82. Africa and the Former Metropoles
83. Africa and the United States
84. Africa and the Communist Countries

7. *In Conclusion*

Additional permutations of the syllabus modules are possible and the teacher and student are encouraged to experiment with recombinations to fit particular needs (and, in fact, to design new modules). This syllabus has not intended to imply a single way of organizing a course in African studies. It is meant to be suggestive, selective, and evaluative—not to be exhaustive. Indeed, all three volumes of *The African Experience* are essentially experimental as curriculum materials rather than definitive; they provide guidelines to the study of Africa rather than a complete synthesis of existing knowledge. It is worthwhile stressing again that these materials have been selected and presented in a way which hopefully will encourage anyone interested in Africa to discover for himself the drama, integrity, and scope of the *human* experience as it has evolved and continues to unfold on the continent of Africa.

Bibliographic Note

ALL REFERENCES GIVEN in this *Syllabus* are presented in abbreviated form. References are to the *Essays,* the *Bibliography,* and the *Guide to Resources,* Volumes I, IIIA, and IIIB of *The African Experience.*

References to the *Essays* volume are of the form (Zolberg, *Essays,* chap. 21). For the reader who may not have the *Essays* in hand, essay titles are given in this volume on the part-opening pages.

References to the *Bibliography* normally give only the author's name and the date of publication (Bohannan, 1964), along with a page number when applicable. When the possibility of confusion exists, the title is also given (Crowder, *The Story of Nigeria,* 1962). The complete citation is, of course, found in the *Bibliography.*

References to the *Guide to Resources* have no special form, but generally list only the author's name after mentioning the *Guide to Resources.*

The African Experience

Modules	Suggested Reading in *Essays*
1 African Society, History, and Social Change 2 African Nation-Building and the Modern World	1 Introduction to the African Experience (*Soja*)

African Society, History, and Social Change

THIS SYLLABUS ON THE AFRICAN EXPERIENCE has been divided into five major parts: "African Society and Culture," "Perspectives on the Past," "Processes of Change," "Consolidation of Nation-States," and "Africa and the Modern World." The intellectual structure of the *Syllabus* and the logic of sequential development are not something to be taken for granted in an introductory course on African studies for American students. Does one begin with the contemporary scene, hoping to gain some criteria of relevance for the study of the past? Does one begin with the past, building up through time to the present? Or does one first try to gain some insight into the core of African culture and society before trying to approach either the present or the past?

1. AFRICAN SOCIETY AND CULTURE

We have decided to begin with the topic of African society and culture. There are probably over 1,000 ethnolinguistic communities in Africa at present, ranging from small-scale groups of less than 50,000 persons to ethnic nations of more than 18,000,000. These communities continue to form the backbone of African cultural life. It is important to stress that Africa comprises a wide variety of peoples and cultural patterns. Marriage customs vary throughout the continent. Patterns of social structure range from completely egalitarian communities to some of the most elitist states in the world. Creativity in the visual arts includes the merely functional as well as some of the finest sculpture ever created by man. Nevertheless, it is possible to identify cultural elements which African communities share with one another. The family-oriented nature of society is surely one such feature. In the modules which follow there will be an attempt to "take apart" these societies according to different criteria, including family and kinship systems, political authority systems, economic systems, linguistic systems, literature and oral tradition, conceptual systems and religion, and visual and musical arts. It must be realized, however, that in practice these sectors intertwine and blend together more closely than is common in European and American society. Political, economic, and social roles tend to overlap, and the same individuals find themselves responsible for a broad range of functions in society. Hopefully, by the end of Part I, students will have some idea of the nature of ethnicity, the ways in which ethnicity changes, the primary patterns of social

3

organization within ethnic communities, and the way in which these patterns might affect modern life.

2. PERSPECTIVES ON THE PAST

In Part II of the *Syllabus*, we focus on the historical patterns which seem most relevant to a balanced view of the development of the continent. There are five component sections. The first deals with the earliest history: the geological up-heavals which have shaped the continent; the evolution of mankind in what is now eastern and southern Africa; the development (in a much later period) of techniques of food production and their diffusion throughout Africa; the migration of Bantu-speaking peoples into central and southern Africa; the growth of the earliest states, Axum and Kush, in northeast Africa; and the de-velopment of the distinctive Nok culture in West Africa.

The second section deals with the growth of centralized states in Africa south of the Sahara: the impact of Islam after the seventh century A.D. on both North and West Africa; the development of the large-scale empires of Ghana, Mali, and Songhai during the tenth through the fifteenth centuries A.D.; the emer-gence of coastal states in East Africa (Kilwa, the Swahili-speaking complex, Zanzibar) partly as a result of contact with Arab civilizations; the development of states in the Central Sudan (Kano, Sokoto, Bornu) with their close links across the Sahara to North Africa; the indigenous kingdoms of East and central Africa (Buganda, Luba/Lunda, and the peoples of Zimbabwe, whose stone acropolis still stands); and the forest states of West Africa (Ashanti, Benin, and Yoruba). All these states were large and complex, and often were based on cultures as sophisticated as those of pre-industrial Europe. The selection of particular states is intended to suggest both the wide geographical distribution of the early states of Africa and their regional variations. The discussion also illustrates the degree to which Africa has, since earliest times, been in cultural and economic communication with the rest of the world.

In the third section we try to sketch the major elements of the African slave trade: the initial trading contacts at forts such as Elmina; the nature of domestic slavery in Africa; the origins and growth of the slave trade; the abolition of the slave trade by Britain in 1807 and the subsequent dwindling of trade throughout the nineteenth century; and the establishment of states in West Africa for freed slaves (notably Liberia and Sierra Leone). A final module evaluates the African legacy in the New World and the cultural continuities which have established linkages between Africa and both North and South America since the "black diaspora." We recognize the sensitivity of these topics in American society, but we have tried to summarize the core elements of slavery and the black diaspora as historical phenomena, without ignoring their significance as moral issues.

The contemporary issue of race and politics in South Africa is placed in its historical context in the fourth section. The major topics discussed include the early patterns of black and white migrations, the violent confrontations which have characterized black-white relations since the seventeenth century, and the historical origins of—and African resistance to—the contemporary South African policies of apartheid. The moral implications again are not ignored, but the emphasis is placed mainly on the historical background, leaving the reader to draw his own conclusions.

In the fifth section we deal with the impact of colonialism on Africa: the "scramble" for African territory by European powers in the late nineteenth century (approximately 1885–1914); the nature of African resistance to this conquest (which was largely unsuccessful, because of lack of technological resources); and colonial rule during the twentieth century (approximately 1900–1960). Colonialism is also recognized as a moral issue, but is dealt with primarily as a series of political relationships. We have not been able to explore in detail the economic aspects of colonialism, although many of these are discussed in later sections. Similarly, the psychological impact of colonialism is dealt with in the section on *Personality and Change* in the next part of the *Syllabus*.

3. PROCESSES OF CHANGE

The third part of the *Syllabus* focuses on the processes of social change. Here we have tried to imply a constant process of change both with regard to the ethnic communities of Africa and in the course of historical events. Social change is dealt with as a historical process in order to underscore the fact that Africa had experienced change long before it came into contact with the West. In this part we focus on specific aspects of social change, beginning with a brief theoretical overview of the nature of change and modernization. After this general introduction, there are five additional sections.

The first deals with individual personality, considering the argument that there is an "African personality" and discussing the types of changes in personality characteristics which may be occurring in the contemporary context. Attention is also given to such themes as achievement motivation and the psychology of colonialism.

The second section deals with education and elite formation, the pre-colonial and Islamic patterns of education, the nature of the colonial educational systems (which were often very meager), the way in which educational recruitment tends to determine the next generation of elites in society, and, finally, a discussion of contemporary elites in Africa (their education, outlook, and tendency toward social cohesion). In general, the twentieth century in Africa has been a period of rapid social mobility. There has not yet developed a rigid class system based on wealth or education, although related patterns of social stratification have begun to emerge.

In the third section the topic of urbanization is discussed. Urban society has developed in parts of Africa from very early times, and urban life in Africa today may be regarded as basically similar to urban life anywhere; there is a division of labor and an interdependence of persons which allows for high-density living. But the speed of urban growth in Africa, which has been greater than that of any other continent over the last hundred years, and its distinctive relationship to traditional ethnic society have created a range of particular patterns and problems which are perhaps more acute in Africa than elsewhere. Accordingly, the relationships between urbanization and other dimensions of social change are also explored.

The growth of transportation and communication systems and their impact on social change provides the focus for the fourth section. An approach to the study of social change and modernization using the spatial perspective of geography is briefly outlined, with particular emphasis on the process of diffusion. The contemporary status and future potential of the mass media—the press, radio, television, and the cinema—are also evaluated.

The final major section is concerned with religion and change: the impact of Christianity, the innovations by local African communities who rejected European versions of Christianity, and the patterns of Islamic reform in both a traditional and a modern sense. Religion has been a key factor in mobilizing African communities to social change, whether that change is in the realm of family life or political organization.

2
—

African Nation-Building and the Modern World

THE TWO REMAINING PARTS to the *Syllabus* will be discussed in this module. It would be possible for a teacher to add a sixth part on contemporary problems which could be updated each year. An excellent source of materials on current issues is Legum and Drysdale (1969), a detailed review of developments in Africa during 1968–69. This volume is the first of a series of annuals entitled *Africa Contemporary Record.*

1. CONSOLIDATION OF NATION-STATES

In Part IV, we deal with the way nation-states have been created and how they function as the major contexts of African social, economic, and political life. There were thirty-six independent states in sub-Saharan Africa by the beginning of 1970, including Madagascar and the small island of Mauritius but excluding white-dominated South Africa and the illegal white government of Rhodesia. In all of Africa there are forty-two sovereign states, constituting approximately one-third of the entire membership of the United Nations. The problems of consolidating the populations of these states into viable national systems, of creating national identities and integrated political, economic, and social organizations are the major focus of this part.

The first section deals with nationalism and independence: concepts of African nationalism prevalent at the time of independence (ranging from Pan-Africanism to negritude); patterns of African nationalism in the attainment of independence (ranging from violent revolution in Algeria and Kenya to peaceful transition in most of the continent); and the phenomenon of independence itself, including the formal transfers of power and the informal reorientations which occurred. African nationalism emerged primarily after World War II and reached its peak about 1960, when most of the continent achieved independence from the European colonial powers. This pre-independence period was one of intensive political organization, formulation of ideologies, and establishment of new symbols (such as the names of new states—Ghana, Mali). It was also the period in which the colonial powers, primarily Britain and France, set up political institutions to parallel the Westminster model and the Fifth-Republic model, respectively. These political institutions were to be adapted considerably in the post-independence period.

The second section deals with the problems of nation-building in the post-colonial era. The three major dimensions involved in creating unified national communities within the inherited states are identified as interethnic integration, mass-elite integration, and territorial integration. African states have an average of four or five major ethnic groups within their boundaries. It is necessary in some way to work out linkages between these groups in terms of a common language, a common set of economic interests, and a common agreement as to how decisions in government should be made. At the same time, there has developed in many countries a gap between the educated elites, who are in control, and the masses, who are part of a different cultural framework. Ironically, the increases in educational facilities have only widened this gap. Social mobilization of the masses is necessary for economic development and for the consolidation of the nation-state, particularly linkages at the grass-roots level. In most cases, political parties (or at least the dominant political parties) have tried to organize themselves so that a two-way system of communications is established with the people. In cases where this was not successful, political tensions have mounted. Finally, it is necessary to bind together those geographical sections of the country which had not thought of themselves as part of a single unit. Fragmentation has existed between coastal and inland regions, and between parts of the country which have been linked through transportation systems and parts which have not. A unified system of transportation and communication (or infrastructure) is thus necessary to achieve territorial integration. As a means of linking all segments of a country into a cohesive whole, African statesmen have tried to develop ideologies which could mobilize people and at the same time bind them together. Various concepts of African socialism have emerged, along with ideologies identified with major African leaders (e.g., Nkrumahism, Zikism), as frameworks for nation-building.

The third section deals with political systems development: with the specific types of civilian regimes, with institutions and bureaucracy, with the patterns of participation and mobilization, and, finally, with the breakdown in political systems and the establishment of military rule (in approximately one out of three African states). In the immediate post-independence period, the inherited political systems based on French or British models were in most cases modified into some form of single-party system. There have been problems inherent in single-party systems, however, and many of them have succumbed to military takeovers. Military regimes have frequently tried to arbitrate the establishment of new types of political systems which are perhaps more appropriate to the African context than either the inherited models or the modified forms which developed in the first major period after independence. Because of its general significance to the problems of nation-building and political integration throughout Africa, the situation in Nigeria-Biafra is evaluated in detail in the last module in this section.

The fourth section deals with legal systems development: with a survey of legal systems in Africa (customary, Islamic, civil, common law), with the problem of the integration of legal systems, and with the growth of constitutional law. To a large extent, the development of political and economic sectors in Africa will depend on the degree to which an acceptable legal code can be worked out within each of the countries. Such codes will probably incorporate much of traditional customs with regard to family and civil law and will turn more to Western models in the fields of corporate, administrative, and criminal law.

The final section is concerned with economic and technical systems development. The topics covered include an assessment of African mineral and energy resources, the problems of agricultural reorganization and industrial development, development planning, the institutional growth of economic systems, the population and social factors which affect economic growth, and the attempts to apply modern technology to accelerate the development process. Economic development in Africa is closely associated with increased agricultural production and the growth of light industry which will substitute locally produced items for costly imported ones. The rate of economic growth, in terms of increased income per capita and expanding industrial production, has been disappointing in most of Africa and has been frustrating to many African people, who have hoped for a more dramatic increase in the standard of living. It is clear, however, that it is still too early to evaluate effectively the patterns of economic growth since independence. Africa, with its late start, is attempting to achieve economic goals which the developed countries took centuries to attain.

2. AFRICA AND THE MODERN WORLD

In Part V of the *Syllabus*, Africa is viewed within a global context; its role in international relations, in the development of the arts and humanities, and in the specific context of Afro-American interests are evaluated.

The first section deals primarily with interstate relations in Africa, charting the growth of regionalism, the continued interest in Pan-Africanism, the emergence of the Organization of African Unity as an important continental institution, and the development of other international organizations concerned with Africa. The new states of Africa have become more nationally introspective since independence, with the challenges of nation-building receiving more attention than the older established goal of continental unity. But while attempts at formal political grouping have met with little success, there are indications that economic and technical cooperation have been increasing in recent years. The present pattern of regional economic groupings is described.

The second section covers the relations between Africa and the major powers: the increasing African role in the United Nations, African relations with the former colonial powers, African relations with the United States, and African relations with the Communist countries. Some of the major international issues which Africa has become involved in—the U.N. operations in the Congo, the problem of race and discrimination, and the continued efforts against colonial-ism throughout the world — are discussed.

In the third section, Africa's role in the Third World is examined, including African relations with Latin America and with the Indian subcontinent, the linkages between Africa and the Arab and Islamic areas outside the continent, and African reactions to such issues as the Arab-Israeli conflict.

A fourth section covers certain specific problems in Africa of an international character. These include the last remnants of colonialism in Africa, the pattern of race relations in southern Africa, nationalist movements in the Portuguese territories, the status of Rhodesia since its illegal declaration of independence from the British, and the critical problems of race and politics in the Republic of South Africa. All these problems have become issues with major international implications.

In the fifth section, developments in African literature, social thought, art, and music are viewed from the perspective of human culture. The continuities of African creativity and their global relevance are stressed.

The complex set of relationships between Africans and Afro-Americans is opened for interpretation in the sixth section. Afro-American perspectives on Africa and African interpretations of multiracial America are examined as is the role of Africa in Afro-American identity formation and social change.

In the "Epilogue," the role of social science in Africa is discussed. It is hoped that to conclude with the theme of social science will encourage further study of African topics whatever the primary disciplinary interests of the student. An argument is made for the contribution of such understanding to the enrichment of human society as a whole.

African Society and Culture

The Nature of
Ethnic Community

3

The African Ethnic Mosaic

THIS MODULE WILL INCLUDE a broad overview and classification of ethnolinguistic groups in Africa and an introduction to ethnic terminology and concepts. An ethnolinguistic group is one which shares a distinct language, common cultural patterns, and a sense of identity. In the remainder of this module we will refer to such groups as *ethnic* groups, although in Modules 4, 5, 6, and 7 the idea of *ethnicity* will be further explored.

1. ETHNIC DISTRIBUTION AND COMPLEXITY

Of the 2,500 to 3,000 distinct and mutually unintelligible languages in the world, Africa has at least 800 to 1,000 (i.e., 33 per cent of the world's languages, with only 10 per cent of the world population). One ethnic classification (Murdock, 1959) identifies 49 culture "provinces," 112 "tribal" clusters, and 850 "tribes." The large number of relatively small-scale ethnic communities tells much about the extent and intensity of social communications in traditional Africa and, in addition, is suggestive of the great difficulties of nation-building facing many of the new African states today. Contemporary Nigeria, for example, contains 200 or more distinct ethnic groups, and Cameroon and Congo-Kinshasa close to 100, depending on the level of classification selected. Although there are certain broad similarities among many of these groups (discussed below), there are just as many differences — in social structure, economy, language, political organization, etc. — due in part to ecological differences (e.g., forest *vs.* grassland), migration patterns, and the uneven geographical impact of innovations in technology and in economic, social, and political organization.

It is important to note, however, that Africa contained many large-scale centralized societies. That sub-Saharan Africa was able to create and maintain these larger entities (some with populations in the millions)—and in many cases without the aid of written communications or other mechanisms which permitted the growth of large states elsewhere in the world (e.g., the administrative organization associated with large-scale irrigation)—is one of the great accomplishments in African history.

Larger-scale groups developed in Africa primarily in response to such forces as increased trade and agricultural productivity, population growth, the establishment of centralized authority, the indigenous elaboration of technology, migration and diffusion, including the spread of organized religions such as Islam. The framework for most of African history, therefore, is neither the small-scale unit generally called the "tribe," nor the broader cultural and linguistic groups discussed later in this module, but the *state*. Hence the emphasis on states and state formation in Part II, "Perspectives on the Past." Nevertheless, to understand the historical processes of state formation in Africa and to grasp the nature of traditional African society, one must have some basic knowledge of ethnic-group distribution and the broad cultural similarities which can be identified on an ethnic map of Africa.

2. ETHNIC CLASSIFICATIONS

For general teaching purposes, it is extremely valuable to introduce the student to some of the attempts by various scholars to find order and pattern in the complex African ethnic mosaic. The following classifications are probably the most widely used, although several others are available (see Murdock, 1959; Baumann and Westermann, 1962).

a. Culture Areas

Herskovits (1962; chap. 3 includes a map) provides one of the simplest and most useful classification schemes. He groups together peoples whose traditional ways of life have a high degree of similarity, while attempting to balance a range of factors, especially those relating to ecology and institutions. He works at a·broad level of generalization, sacrificing detail for the larger perspective. His culture areas (and criteria) include: (1) Khoisan (Bushman hunters and gatherers, Hottentot pastoralists); (2) East African Cattle Area (the role of cattle, mixed agriculture); (3) Eastern Sudan ("residual" area, great heterogeneity, a transition zone); (4) East Horn (pastoralism, religion, and external contacts); (5) Congo (agriculture, markets and village life, the arts); (6) Guinea Coast (urbanization, economic specialization, high population density); (7) Western Sudan (Islam and herding, cultural crossroads); (8) Northern Areas (desert, North Africa, Egypt). A superimposition of the Herskovits map over one showing major vegetational zones can be found in the frontispiece to Gibbs

(1965). (For a criticism of the culture-area concept, see Bohannan, *Africa and the Africans,* 1964, chap. 8.)

b. Language Areas

Until recent years, there had not been many attempts to classify African languages purely on the basis of linguistic critera. Many of the older classifications were frequently distorted by racial stereotypes, as, for example, with regard to what has been called the "Hamitic myth." It was widely presumed that many powerful and dominant groups, especially pastoralists, must speak Hamitic (i.e., "white") languages to signify the source of their power and domination. Thus the Fulani, who have provided the ruling aristocracy in the Hausa society of northern Nigeria, were usually classified as Hamitic speakers, while the Hausa language was grouped with supposedly more "primitive" African languages. Due in large part to the work of Joseph Greenberg (1955 and 1963), it has been found that Hausa is actually part of what used to be called the Hamito-Semitic language family (which includes Arabic), while Fulani is grouped in the Congo-Kordofanian family, which includes Bantu and West African languages. Moreover, neither Fulani nor Hausa can be identified in origin with "white" populations.

Building upon and extending the earlier works of Meinhof and Westermann, Greenberg's African linguistic classifications of 1955 and 1963 — which are discussed and mapped in Berry (*Essays,* chap. 5) — did much to dispel the racial biases which flavored linguistic writings of the past. Based upon a study of "critical" words and their meanings, similarities in grammatical structure, and other key linguistic features, Greenberg in his 1963 classification identifies four major language families (a simplification of the twelve families he identified in 1955). These may be regarded as somewhat equivalent in generality to a category such as the Indo-European language family (which includes English, Sanskrit, Italian, etc.), although the proven degree of unity within the African language families is probably less than that for Indo-European. The identification of verifiable historical linkages between the various components of African language families remains an important research problem. The Greenberg categories are as follows.

The *Congo-Kordofanian* family encompasses the Guinea Coast, Congo, and most of the East African culture areas. Bantu languages are included here, but only as an offshoot of Benue-Congo languages (indicative of the relatively recent evolution of Bantu as a distinct set of closely related languages). Nevertheless, Bantu speakers cover a larger part of the area of Africa and form a larger proportion of the total population than any other equivalent linguistic group. (For a discussion of Bantu migrations, see Module 19.) The West Atlantic subfamily of Congo-Kordofanian includes the Fulani, who were formerly classified as "Hamitic" because of their role as pastoral conquerors and their European-like features.

The *Nilo-Saharan* family groups together a wide variety of languages, from Songhai (along the middle Niger) to the languages of the savanna regions of the Eastern Sudan and northern East Africa. Note on the map in Berry (*Essays,* chap. 5) the great complexity of languages in the Eastern Sudan, indicative of its important role as a corridor for the movement of people and ideas throughout African history.

The *Afro-Asiatic* family was formerly called "Hamito-Semitic," but this term was discarded by Greenberg, in part because of the racial connotations often associated with its use. This family interpenetrates with Nilo-Saharan in the Eastern Sudan, reflecting the two-way flow of culture contact in this area. It includes Arabic (Semitic) and Hausa (Chadic), two of the largest speech communities in Africa (especially since most Bantu languages are not mutually intelligible).

The *Khoisan* family is primarily composed of Bushman and Hottentot languages, with two small outliers in Tanzania (which reflect the greater areal extent of these peoples in the past). Most Khoisan languages include "clicks" as an integral part of words. Some nearby Bantu speakers (e.g., the Xhosa) have also adopted these click sounds.

It should be noted, in conclusion, that a great deal of research is currently being conducted in the field of African linguistics and that major modifications in the Greenberg classification may develop in the near future. Although the 1963 classification by Greenberg is considered the standard linguistic reference work by most of the social sciences, it has been less readily accepted by African linguists. (See Mfoolou, 1969.) See Module 11 for a discussion of linguistic systems.

The relationship between language criteria and cultural criteria in the formation of "ethnicity" is discussed further in Modules 4, 5, 6, and 7.

4

The Nature of Ethnicity

THIS MODULE SERVES as an introduction to the concept of ethnicity and to the range of aspects of ethnic society in Africa. For a broader introduction to traditional society in Africa, see Cohen (*Essays,* chap. 3).

1. WHAT IS AN ETHNIC GROUP?

This question, which is not as simple as it sounds, may be approached by examining first the various subethnic categories which (together with the ethnic group) form primary units of human culture and identity. The most basic unit is the nuclear family, consisting of a married couple and their children (see Module 8). Beyond the nuclear family, the following groupings can be identified.

a. The Extended Family

The extended family consists of two or more nuclear families, joined vertically (e.g., parents and offspring) and/or horizontally (e.g., cousins). A married adult may be linked to his brothers and sisters, his children, his parents, and his parents' parents as well. Thus three or four generations, including the nuclear families of fathers and sons (as well as unmarried children) may live under the same roof or in a cluster of adjacent dwellings or may act in other ways as a cohesive unit.

b. The Lineage

The lineage refers to a social group based upon common unilineal descent (generally limited to three to five generations but in some cases up to twenty generations) and traceable genealogically through either the father (in a patrilineal society) or the mother (in a matrilineal society). To a variable extent, the lineage can hold property as a unit and/or act as a political unit, a marriage unit, or even an economic unit (i.e., it is often a corporate group). It usually has a name (e.g., the name of a progenitor, perhaps the great-grandfather), and each member can trace his or her genealogical relationship to all others. Lineages can be joined or subdivided by genealogical relationships into larger and smaller groups, so that in some African societies there are minimal, minor, and major lineage segments, which include progressively more people and progressively greater numbers of generation levels.

c. The Clan

The clan consists of a number of lineages, among which it is impossible to identify exact genealogical relations although members nevertheless consider themselves descended from a common ancestor. A clan may be scattered over a wide area, may or may not act as a corporate group, and may have quite vague notions of common ancestry, although this belief is always present to some extent.

d. The Ethnic Group

The ethnic group is a broad extension of community identity based on an individual and communal acceptance of joint membership in, and identification with, a society and its culture. It is therefore associated with a whole series of cultural correlates, the most common of which are language, specific descent patterns, social structure, and shared values. But since it is based on a "feeling" of identity rather than on precise genealogies or clan memberships, and may be changeable over time (closely interacting with its human and physical environment), an ethnic group is not always easily identifiable nor is it always based on exact kinship principles. Also, it is not necessarily stable in size, membership, or degree of identification.

2. ETHNICITY AND GROUP IDENTITY

Ethnicity, which may be defined at this stage as identification with one's ethnic group, is one of the most fundamental categories of human loyalty and organization. In recent years, the term "ethnicity" has come to replace "tribalism" with reference to societies in which kinship or kinshiplike relations provide the basis of group identity. The notion of "kinshiplike" relations refers to the existence of generalized obligations, some core set of values, and a distinct "we-they" feeling, all of which are similar to the paradigm of "family" in terms of the quality of relationships. (Note the use of such terms as "father," "brother," etc., in many religious or nationalist movements.) In other words, kinship terms and attitudes form an idiom and a behavioral model for non-kin relations. Several additional points should be made about ethnicity.

1. Human beings organize themselves in a variety of ways, and each individual, anywhere on earth, usually has a wide range of loyalties and/or identities. An American, for example, may identify in varying degrees with his family, his religious group, his country, his home city or region, and so on. Moreover, the relative strength of these loyalties differs from person to person, from place to place, and from one time period to another. Indeed, "American" itself may be an ethnic identity for some people.

2. Most—but certainly not all—traditional societies in Africa were ethnically based, that is, they shared a common culture and generated common loyalties and identity. It should be stressed that ethnic societies still exist in Africa, as in most parts of the world, and that they exist as positive as well as negative

factors with respect to the contemporary problems of new African states (see Wallerstein, 1960; Mercier, 1965; Mazrui, 1969).

3. The adaptive and changeable character of ethnicity must be emphasized (see Module 6). Ethnic identity, whether for the African of A.D. 1500 or the African of A.D. 1970—or, for that matter, the contemporary American or Japanese—is a constantly changing "syndrome" which blends together many different identities.

4. Although ethnicity serves many functions, one primary purpose seems to be "to permit people to organize into social, cultural or political entities able to compete with others for whatever goods and services [are] viewed as valuable in their environment" (Skinner, 1968, p. 173). Thus, as competitive environments change, ethnic identities may change. The following statement by Skinner summarizes some of the contemporary relevance of ethnicity and may stimulate further discussion:

> Some of the names which are now used as symbols for group identity do refer to distinct socio-cultural entities in the past. However, many of the so-called "tribal" groups were creations of the colonial period. But even those groups for which continuity with the past could be claimed have lost so many of their traditional characteristics that in fact they must be viewed as new entities.
>
> The various groups in contemporary African societies are not competing for ancestral rights or privileges, but for the appurtenances of modern power. In most cases they seek to control the nation-state where they find themselves, or at worst seek to prevent being dominated by other groups within the state. Even when groups do try to secede from a nation-state, it is not because they prefer small-scale organization *per se,* but because they believe that a separate organization, or unity with members of the same group across state borders would bring with it a better life.
>
> One of the reasons why Africans rally around descent groups, fictive or otherwise, is that the colonial situation did not provide sufficient scope for the growth and development of those secondary associations which historically have appeared in societies with complex political organizations. The social orders within the more complex traditional African polities decayed during the colonial period. And the incipient classes which began to emerge within the mainly pluralistic colonial society were not strong enough to provide the group identity around which Africans, fighting for political power, could rally. Many an African leader with universalistic values found that he had to appeal to group identity based on descent, if he would galvanize his followers to seek political power, and thus the opportunity to build a modern society (Skinner, 1968, p. 183).

(For a general discussion of ethnic identity, ethnic symbols, ethnic stratification, and ethnic change, see Shibutani and Kwan, 1965).

5
—

On the Concept of "Tribe"

BECAUSE OF ITS AMBIGUOUS DEFINITION, analytical deficiencies, and pejorative connotations in both popular and scholarly literature, the term "tribe" is being discarded by many social scientists in favor of such less "loaded" terms as "peoples" or "ethnic units," or even "nationalities." Similarly, "tribalism," with its connotations of primitiveness, atavism, and traditionalism, is being superseded by the more rigorously defined and analytically more useful concept of "ethnicity" to describe the patterns of identity being used by groups competing for power and status in contemporary Africa (and elsewhere). To reinforce this trend, neither "tribe" nor "tribalism" will receive much usage in this syllabus. But lest "ethnic" and "ethnicity" be construed as mere euphemisms for "tribe" and "tribalism," the weakness of the "tribal" concept must be examined in detail.

1. THE AMBIGUITY OF "TRIBE"

As a vague referent to peoples among whom kinship or blood ties form the major basis of group identity, the notion of "tribe" may have some value. But this general definition has several faults.

1. It fails to view this form of ethnic identity as a *dynamic* pattern which can adjust to its immediate position vis-à-vis other organized units and its own local environment. Whatever the "tribe" may be, it is not a constant, immutable unit; it thus becomes nonsense to speak of Africans "reverting to tribalism." Ethnic identities have always been changeable, and therefore it is misleading to think of a contemporary identity group as necessarily representing some sacred primordial unit.

2. Then there is the problem of universality. There is no apparent justification for the use of a concept of tribe in Africa which is not similarly applied in Europe. Blood ties, real or imagined, and other types of ethnicity are an important basis for societal integration nearly everywhere in the world. Are the Serbians, Polish, Danish, or Welsh to be considered tribes? In Africa, there have been no clear guidelines as to what scale unit should be called a "tribe," and thus the term has been applied indiscriminately. To say that the Yoruba, Hausa-Fulani, and Ibo are the three major "tribes" of Nigeria may not only be uninformative but may also be misleading. Thus, "The Ashanti, Baganda, Bakongo, Hausa, Mossi, Ngoni, Songhoy, Yoruba and other societies represented the end product of political and other socio-cultural processes by which different ethnic groups have been welded together. All of these societies were internally differentiated, even though class and associations often had a kinship base or were expressed in kinship terms" (Skinner, 1968, pp. 172–73).

3. Also confusing has been the tendency to define African "tribes" by socio-cultural characteristics. Such sociocultural criteria may include any combination of the following: common territory; language; common cultural values; genealogical relationship; cooperation in ceremonial, economic, or political organization. But there is no reason to assume coincidence of these features either with one another or with the unit of ethnic identification. These characteristics are important and usually are closely associated with ethnicity, but they do not in themselves identify a "tribe." These criteria appear to be hypotheses rather than "real-world" social boundaries (see Fried, 1968; and Dole, 1968).

2. POPULAR MISCONCEPTIONS REGARDING "TRIBE"

Some of the difficulties which have developed around the concept of "tribe" and "tribalism" include the following:

1. "Tribe" has come to be a pejorative term, synonymous with primitive, atavistic society which resists all change, particularly that associated with "modernization." This connotation has proved highly insulting to Africans, particularly when applied to all African societies prior to colonial conquest.

2. Related to the above is the view that prior to the colonial period most Africans lived in mutually hostile small groups. This fails to take into account the extremely wide range of organized political societies that existed in Africa prior to European penetration, as well as the very complex processes of change and development initiated by Africans themselves or by non-European outsiders (see Modules 37 and 38).

3. Finally, "tribalism" is sometimes viewed as responsible for most contemporary problems in Africa. This view both belittles the significant changes which occurred prior to and during the colonial period and oversimplifies the reasons for the struggles going on in Africa today. It also fails to recognize the positive contributions of ethnic groups to modern African politics as well as the existence of multiple identities (e.g., national and ethnic) that are not necessarily incompatible. It should be noted that the term "tribalism" is widely used by Africans in Africa to mean rivalry between ethnically based constituencies for scarce resources in the new nation-state. These ethnically based constituencies, however, may or may not correspond to traditional units.

3. ANALYTICAL DEFICIENCIES OF "TRIBE"

a. Problems of Political Evolution

The "tribe" has often been considered a necessary stage between the hunting band and the centralized state in the evolution of political organization. This view is most associated with the work of M. D. Sahlins (1961) and E. R. Service (1962). More recent views (see especially Fried, 1967; and Helm, 1968) have challenged the use of the term "tribe" in this context, suggesting that the larger-scale ethnic units called tribes are the product of contacts with more complexly organized state-based societies and therefore not part of the evolutionary schema. (See Module 6.)

b. Problems of Ethnic Unit Classification

Anthropologists have become increasingly interested in cross-cultural analysis, and this has required the identification of comparable units (see Naroll, 1964; Fried, 1968). The concept of "tribe" has thus far proved to be of little or no use in this respect because of the logical inconsistencies involved in its definition and usage (e.g., the lumping together of religious groups, language groups, urban groups, and territorial locations).

c. Relevance to the Contemporary World

Perhaps the most serious deficiency in the concept of tribe from the viewpoint of social science is the inadequacy of "tribalism" in dealing with contemporary ethnic and even modern identity groups, especially those identities which are emerging in the large urban centers of Africa. Ethnicity seems a more appropriate concept than tribalism, detribalism, supertribalism, or retribalization in dealing with urban phenomena.

6
—

The Changing Nature
of Ethnic Boundaries

1. THE DYNAMIC NATURE OF ETHNICITY
IN TRADITIONAL AFRICAN SOCIETIES

AMONG OTHER THINGS, ethnic identification is an adaptive mechanism which reflects both internal and external perceptions of group membership at a particular point in time. The African communities which engendered such identity were frequently in a state of flux — cohesive communities were appearing and disappearing, blending and breaking off, as a result of an almost continuous series of changes in intergroup relations, including trade, competition for land and animals, migration, and warfare. Conflict and fighting took place not only between ethnically unrelated groups but also within groups that shared a common cultural and even genealogical background. This does not mean that there was no underlying framework of relatively stable community boundaries. Social boundaries were generally constant within the short run, and clearly identifiable, but they were also sufficiently permeable to permit peaceful absorption of outside groups when the situation arose. Clusters of related peoples developed a veneer of unity based upon sets of linkages that cut across kinship lines; although these linkages did not always prevent internal conflict, they did provide a structure for cooperative action against external adversaries. The key feature was an adaptability which permitted relative autonomy for small-scale communities in times of peace but also allowed for a complex system of combination and cooperation between groups when there was stress (Turnbull, 1964). The volume edited by Cohen and Middleton (1969) explores these patterns of ethnic boundary change in more detail.

2. ETHNICITY AND POLITICAL EVOLUTION

Certain social scientists have viewed political evolution as a progression from hunting band to "tribe" to chiefdom to state, with the major transformation taking place when society shifts from being kinship-organized to being territorially organized and expressed. This transformation, which produces the "state" as a form of sociopolitical organization, is illustrated by the changes, for example, in the title of French kings from the Merovingian "King of the Franks" to the Capelian "King of France." The equivalent in Africa might be the emperor of Ethiopia who is still regarded as "King of Kings," signifying his role as head of the Amharic community and as leader of all the other kingdoms in Ethiopia. Sahlins discusses this subject of state formation in detail and elaborates on the shift from "kinship to territory." According to Sahlins:

> The critical development was not the establishment of territoriality in society, but the establishment of society *as* a territory. The state and its subdivisions are organized as territories — territorial entities under public authorities — as opposed, for instance, to kinship entities under lineage chiefs (Sahlins, 1968, p. 6).

This view has been reshaped in recent years, particularly in the seminal works by Fried and others (Helm, 1968). This challenge has not been directed against the "kinship to territory" shift per se but instead has focused on two points: first, the role of "tribal" organization as a necessary step in political evolution; and second, the tendency to view kinship-based organization as a static phenomenon rather than an adaptive reaction which persists throughout the entire evolutionary process. According to Fried:

> Tribes as political structures are ad hoc responses to ephemeral situations of competition . . . tribes seem to be secondary phenomena in a very specific sense: they may well be the product of processes stimulated by the appearance of relatively highly organized societies amidst other societies which are organized much more simply. If this can be demonstrated, tribalism can be viewed as a reaction to the formation of complex political structure rather than a necessary preliminary stage in its evolution (Fried, 1968, p. 15).

In this view, therefore, the "tribe" is primarily a *reaction formation* by a people to external forces. There is no reason, however, not to include internal forces as well. The important point is that this process of solidification, consolidation, and fusion as well as fission is a continual one and is not erased with the formation of the state. This further supports the avoidance of the terms "tribe" and "tribalism" which too often form part of an oversimplified dichotomy. Ethnicity, in contrast, provides a more analytical perspective on the overall process and allows for the persistence of kinship-based organization as one of several forces which promote group identity in both the ancient and modern worlds. Furthermore, if Fried is correct, the simple progression of band to tribe to chiefdom to state is much more complex than it has hitherto been believed to be.

Examples of ethnic change are found in all parts of Africa. One good example are the Hausa of northern Nigeria. With the introduction of Islam in Hausaland in the fifteenth century, those peoples who accepted Islam were called Hausa, and those who did not remained Maguzawa. This process of "fission" essentially divided the community into two ethnic societies. On the other hand, in the nineteenth century, after the Fulani conquest, the merger of the urban Hausa and Fulani produced or "fused" a new group which has been called Hausa-Fulani. In more recent times, the Hausa-Fulani have absorbed many other northern ethnic groups into a "northern" (sometimes called "Hausa" in a broad sense) ethnicity, as a result of competition and confrontation with "southern Nigerians" (see Paden, 1969; Melson and Wolpe, 1970).

It is clear that ethnic boundaries are not constant but change to accommodate or react to a given situation. In "ethnic Africa," group identity was and is fluid, and it is frequently difficult to clearly distinguish one group from another because of their "transitional" nature. It should be stressed very strongly that new vehicles for group identity and sociopolitical integration had appeared well before the colonial period. Large-scale states and empires developed throughout Africa from earliest times. The factors of Islam, organized trading systems, language spread, etc., acted to create new frameworks for identification long before the initial imposition of colonial boundaries acted to freeze temporarily the dynamism of African ethnicity.

3. PLURAL SOCIETIES AND NATIONAL PLURALISM

We have stressed above the importance of interethnic contact in the formation and adaptation of ethnic boundaries. It is important to recognize, however, that this process of adaptation did not always result in a blending of one group with another, and that in many cases distinct ethnic groups retained their identities and interacted with each other in a variety of limited ways. This interethnic contact has occurred in traditional nonstate contexts, in traditional state contexts, and in modern nation-state contexts.

In traditional nonstate contexts, the most frequent form of cooperative interaction was trade and economic division of labor. This could occur within a particular location, where several ethnic groups shared a common market, or it could occur between two separate functional areas, as between pastoralists and agriculturalists.

Within a traditional state system, the interaction was usually economic and political. A common market system was shared, and there was some linkage between the political decision-makers of all relevant ethnic groups (even between the Fulani and Hausa in the Sokoto caliphate, or the Tutsi and Hutu in Rwanda). In some cases there was also social contact (e.g., intermarriage or breakdown of residential segregation), but in most cases there was not, since this tends to be related to "assimilation" rather than to "pluralism."

Contemporary events in Africa may lead to the relative submergence of ethnic ties beneath the broader umbrella of the national state (see Module 57). This was true in an earlier period of European history (e.g., the unification of the Teutonic ethnic groups into Germany) and to some extent is still occurring in Europe (e.g., the breaking down of barriers between various cultural-linguistic groups in Spain). However, many states in Africa and elsewhere have not attempted to break down the identity groups which constitute the contemporary polity. Rather, they have sought to accommodate a multiethnic, or multi-national, or "pluralistic" national state. This topic will be discussed in detail in Part IV, "Consolidation of Nation-States."

In all three types of multiethnic contexts mentioned above (traditional non-state, traditional state, or modern national state), the variety of types of inter-ethnic interaction is perhaps similar. An interesting diagrammatic presentation of the varieties of response to intersocietal contact, ranging from peripheral contact to pluralism to full integration, can be found in Banton (1968, chap. 4). Although this study deals primarily with race, the diagrams are equally appli-cable to the present discussion of ethnicity (Figure 1).

Several points should be made about these diagrams:

1. The circles are themselves highly variable, reflecting the adaptive nature of ethnicity.

FIGURE 1
TYPES OF INTERETHNIC CONTACT
(AFTER BANTON)

	a. Peripheral Contact—for example, "silent trade" in which people presumably exchanged goods without actually meeting.
	b. Institutionalized Contact—largely a peripheral contact based upon some institutionalized meeting point (e.g., trade, conflict).
	c. Acculturation—a partial merging, with the weaker society making more adjustments than the stronger and accepting some of the outward manifestations of identity of the dominant group.
	d. Domination—a "single" society with two categories distinguished primarily by nonethnic characteristics (e.g., income, education, religion).
Metropolitan Society Colonial Society Colonized Society	*e. Paternalism*—a specialized form of institutional contact which, unlike domination, involves the retention of distinctiveness among the interacting societies.
	f. Integration—a reduction in ethnic identity and stratification and the establishment of larger unity based upon associational ties.
	g. Pluralism—ethnicity far more important as an indicator of roles and behavior than in an integrated situation. Nevertheless, a larger order exists—but without the clear dominant-subordinate relation of *d.*

2. The relationships described may be helpful in the modules on nation-building, but should not be regarded as the only way to conceptualize ethnic relations, nor even the primary way which will be used or suggested in other sections of this syllabus.

3. No implied directionality should be attributed to the sequence or development of interethnic contact from one "stage" to another.

7

Modern Variants of Ethnicity

As ALREADY EMPHASIZED, ethnicity is a dynamic form of human group identity. The following is a very brief overview of same variants of ethnicity in contemporary Africa.

1. URBAN ETHNICITY

The rate of urbanization in Africa is among the highest in the world (see Modules 45, 46, and 47). As part of this process, rural migrants from many different ethnic backgrounds often find themselves in a context in which not only are their cultural values under pressure to adapt to the new environment (see Wallerstein, 1960) but also their ethnic identities are perceived differently, both by themselves and by others. Thus, migrants to the copper-mining towns of Zambia, who came originally from Nyasaland (now Malawi) found that they were considered as a single ethnic identity group (regardless of their original ethnicity) by the inhabitants of the urban areas (see Epstein, 1958 and 1967).

Since the urban context frequently contains ethnic residential groupings, an urban migrant would find that he might be ascribed one ethnic identity during his working hours and another during his evening hours at home. This illustrates the idea of *situational ethnicity,* which is critical to understanding modern patterns of ethnic identity. Thus, depending on the situation in which a person found himself, his ethnicity might change. Needless to add, if a migrant returned to his original home outside the city his "original" identity would probably be ascribed to him. It is important to recognize that multiple or situational identities do not necessarily indicate a particular pattern of cultural or personal values, for there are significant differences between identities, values, and loyalties.

The idea of multiple identities, especially in an urban context, will be illustrated later in this module using examples from northern Nigeria. In brief, people from Kano City are called Kanawa (perhaps equivalent to Bostonian);

at the same time, a person may be identified as a member of a particular lineage such as the (Fulani) Sullubawa (perhaps equivalent to being a Kennedy) or as a speaker of a certain language such as Hausa, which is primarily a language group (perhaps equivalent to being part of the Spanish-speaking community in an American city). He may also be identified by his rural home town (e.g., Shirawa are people from the village of Shira).

2. REGIONAL ETHNICITY

Just as the urban context can provide the basis for situational ethnicity, so may the regional context. Regional ethnicity, however, is complicated by the fact that regionalism is territorially defined and in its purest form may go well beyond even putative ethnic ties. The relationships between regionalism and ethnicity provide an exciting, but very complex, field of current social-science research. Much of what is usually called "tribalism" in Africa is often a non-ethnically-based regionalism or at least a form of identity which goes well beyond ethnic ties. Contemporary politics in Nigeria, Ghana, Uganda, Kenya, and in fact in most African states, are filled with constant reference to "Northerners," "Southerners," "Easterners," "Middle-belters," or "Midwesterners." Much of the "tribal" politics in Congo-Kinshasa, as another example, is more accurately regional in nature. Skinner notes:

> Interestingly enough, *"regionalism"* rather than "tribalism" is turning out to be the object of group identity and exclusiveness below the national state level in many African countries. Perhaps this appears to be so, since Africans, often ashamed of "tribalism," readily accept the "region" as the basis of group loyalty and identification (Skinner, 1968, pp. 180–81).

This notion may be interesting to explore and discuss in greater detail.

3. LANGUAGE AND ETHNICITY

A mutually intelligible language is usually one of the strongest foundations of ethnicity. But whereas ethnic groups are usually language groups, language groups need not be ethnic groups (for examples from southern Nigeria, see Wolff, 1959 and 1967). The relation between language and ethnicity, while being very close, is also highly variable. In fact, language groups undergo processes of fission and fusion similar to those of ethnic groups. Hymes (1968) comments on this relationship in general, and his examples (largely non-African) are very useful. Ethnic identity may be built around language similarity, as seems to be happening in the Arab world, or language may be a symbol of ethnic cohesion, as perhaps in Yorubaland.

As has been pointed out in several of the *Essays*, the colonial impact in Africa often created units of subnational identity of a larger scale than had traditionally existed. Groups such as the Ewe of Ghana or the Kikuyu of Kenya came to think of themselves as single units during the colonial period. Language similarity frequently provided the outer "boundary" of this expansion; that is, formerly autonomous units grouped together (due to both internal and external influences) within broad linguistic limits. It should also be noted, however, that this process was generated not only by colonial contact but by other factors as well. The Hausa, the Swahili, the Bangala, and many other "ethnic" groups in Africa are really conglomerations of peoples who have adopted the same language, and secondarily may share other characteristics such as religion. Although a strong Hausa identity, for example, may exist (in certain situations), it would be more accurate to refer to "Hausa-speaking peoples" than to a Hausa ethnic group. Alternatively, it becomes rather absurd to speak of the Hausa as a "tribe."

4. SITUATIONAL ETHNICITY

It becomes clear from the preceding discussion that ethnicity in both traditional and contemporary Africa is highly situational in that it can be reshaped to fit a great variety of conditions and contexts. Beyond the fluid traditional milieu and the interrelationships between language and ethnicity, contemporary variants of ethnicity may be associated with different contexts and/or criteria. This may be illustrated by taking the example of the late premier of the Northern Region of Nigeria—the Sardauna, Alhaji Ahmadu Bello—and showing how his ethnicity might have varied with context.

There are at least nine different ethnic identities which have been ascribed to the Sardauna. When he was operating within a Fulani context, he would have been identified as a member of the *Toronkawa* clan. When he was operating within "Hausaland" he would have been identified as a *Fulani*. Within a Hausa-Fulani context, particularly in situations where the traditional rivalries between the cities of Kano and Sokoto were germane, he would have been identified as one of the *Sakkwatawa* (people from Sokoto). When he was traveling in Bornu Province (in the north) or even in parts of Southern Nigeria, he would have been regarded as *Hausa*. While conducting Islamic conversion tours of the Middle Belt, he would have been considered essentially as a *Muslim*. With respect to Southern Nigeria he would have been regarded as either Hausa, or *Yan Arewa* (northerner). When he was on pilgrimage in Mecca, he would have been regarded as *Takrur* (i. e., black West African). While traveling in Britain or in other parts of Africa, he would have been considered *Nigerian*. When he came to the United States, most of the students he met regarded him as *African*. Each of the above identities is legitimate, and appropriate to a particular situation. This may be summarized in Figure 2 on the following page.

One of the inferences to be derived from these observations is that ethnicity, in its many forms, is not simply a premodern basis of human group identity which must be erased in the modernization process. Indeed, one of the exciting challenges facing Africa is how to use ethnic identity most effectively as a means of creating and maintaining stable political units able to encourage and sustain rapid economic development.

FIGURE 2
SITUATIONAL ETHNICITY:
THE EXAMPLE OF AHMADU BELLO

Sample context	Criteria of identity	Sample identity name	Explanation
1. Interlineage context	Lineage	Toronkawa	Members of a particular Fulani clan
2. Local pluralistic society	Language/origin/culture	Fulani	A major language/descent group
3. Interurban context	Residence or origin with reference to a particular city or city-state	Sakkwatawa	Persons from Sokoto
4. Outside the individual's language zone, but within adjoining areas	Language/culture in broadest sense	Hausa	People who speak Hausa, and who assume Hausa culture.
5. Bireligious context	Adherence to a religion	Muslim	Persons who identify with Islam
6. Within a national context where regionalism exists	Region of origin	Yan Arewa	People from the North (within Nigerian context)
7. Within a biracial context, outside region of origin	Skin color and geographical origins.	Takrur	Black-skinned people from West Africa (term is common in Arab countries)
8. Outside national state, but in areas where nationality is recognized	Nationality	Nigerian	People from the state of Nigeria
9. Within a biracial context (usually but not always outside area of origin, where other identities are not known, or are less relevant)	Race in broadest sense plus continent of origin	African	People from Africa

Aspects of Ethnic Culture

8

Family and Kinship

IN TRADITIONAL AFRICAN SOCIETY, with its emphasis on social relations, kinship is often the predominant principle of local organization. Kinship, as the criterion for relating individuals, is based upon a recognition either of common ancestry or linkage through marriage. Like marriage, genealogical ties between people must be socially recognized; this introduces the concept of "fictive" kinship, as in the case of a formerly unrelated person who is incorporated into a particular category of kinship and who therefore behaves in an appropriate manner. For example, a boy may be brought into a man's house as an apprentice, with the father-son relationship ensuing as a natural and enduring consequence which is recognized as such by "real" kin and society at large.

Kinship is most easily discussed by breaking it down into three main dimensions: family, marriage, and descent. In many respects the mother-child bond is the basis of the kinship network and forms the nucleus of the family, whose specific type is determined by the rules of marriage and descent. As such, the distinction between family, marriage, and descent is somewhat artificial as the three are interdependent and overlapping. An excellent introduction to the broad spectrum of kinship terminology and concepts can be found in Murdock (1956), and Goody (1969).

1. FAMILY

A family may be either *nuclear*—a married couple and their children—or *extended*—a married couple, their children, their parents, their children's spouses and children, and other horizontally proximate kin. The nuclear family consists of two bonds—the *affinal* (husband-wife) and *consanguineal* (blood relationship, i.e., sibling and parent-child). As pointed out in Cohen (*Essays*, chap. 3) most African families are organized around the *household*, which may or may not be based exclusively on kinship, but which is usually based on some combination of nuclear and extended families. A household is a domestic group—it shares residence and food—and its cycle follows the life cycle of its members. In its expansionist phase, the household may be augmented by the birth of *real* members or by the incorporation of outsiders; the latter may include *foster children*, who either retain their genealogical tie to their natural kinship relations or who are incorporated in the fictive manner into the fostering family (see Goody, 1969).

Family residence location is of considerable social importance, and usually follows definite rules. The majority of African societies are *patrilocal* (living with the husband's family); some are *matrilocal* (living with the wife's family); and a few are *duolocal* (with either family) or *neolocal* (taking up new residence). Residence rules are usually contingent upon environmental factors, economic patterns, descent rules, and marriage practices. Once again, households may expand as the result of rules of residence or other social behavior; for example, in societies with formal *age-grades* (i.e., a clearly prescribed set of functions and obligations associated with particular age groups) as among the Nuer, Nyakyusa, and others where boys move in and out of different residences at prescribed times.

2. MARRIAGE

Traditional African marriage may be viewed from two vantage points—that of the married pair and that of the community, with the two perspectives generally linked closely together. A particular society may attach great value to *polygynous marriage* (the man having more than one wife) rather than *monogamous marriage* (one man, one wife). In Africa, the majority of societies in fact do accept polygyny, and their members generally endorse the practice whenever it is economically feasible. Although it may appear as an extravagance, for a relatively important individual who maintains a busy schedule of entertaining it may be cheaper in the long run to have the extra help and the option of parceling-out household and economic chores. Still, many marriages in Africa, even within polygynous societies, are monogamous.

Furthermore, not only number of marriage partners but the categories from which they are selected may reflect a distinction between individual behavior (or options) and societal preferences. Thus, an individual (usually termed "ego") may either marry *endogamously* (within a stipulated group) or *exogamously* (outside of a stipulated group). A given community may reflect an exogamous rule of marriage yet make allowances for individual preferences. Both perspectives are important and tie in to each other through the generally accepted principle of marriage as alliance formation.

In traditional African society, marriage is less a linkage of two people than it is an alliance of two groups. As mentioned previously, African societies tend to favor polygynous marriage; where this is not of the *sororal* type (marriage to sisters, successively), it institutes an association of at least three separate groups of kin, thereby increasing the number of people one can count on in time of need. By the same token, since in most African societies a man can make demands upon group members, to marry endogamously duplicates or reinforces these ties, whereas to marry exogamously increases one's circle of support.

Closely tied in with this concept of alliance is the exchange of goods or services which in effect seal the bargain. Thus, for example, in the East African cattle-culture area, cattle ownership is prestigious, and the animal has not only economic but symbolic value. Where cattle are so highly prized, giving a stipulated number of head as bridewealth provides sanctions against marriage dissolution and, by extension, the cutting of ties.

3. DESCENT

Genealogical relationships are calculated on a basis of biologically traceable links. However, certain blood links (or even putative blood linkages) may assume a special importance in the perception and social organization of *descent*. It is through the rules of descent that possessions, rights, and obligations are passed from generation to generation.

Traditionally, there are two main types of descent rules. (1) *Unilineal* descent is reckoned through relationship to one parent. This can be either *matrilineal* (uterine), with the relationship network operating through female links, as with the Ashanti of Ghana, or *patrilineal* (agnatic), with the relationship network operating through male links, as with the Yoruba of Nigeria. Patrilineal descent is predominant in Africa. A few African societies are *bilineal* in that they reckon descent through membership in two unilineal descent groups, usually a patrilineal one through the father and a matrilineal one through the mother. This relates ego to two grandparents for descent purposes. An example would be the Yaku of Nigeria (see Forde, 1964). (2) *Bilateral* descent relationships, which are less common in Africa, are based not on a single line of descent (either patrilineal or matrilineal) but through both parents (and through them to all four grandparents). Here, ego traces kinship to all of his genealogically reckoned kin. (Examples include the Hausa and Kanuri of Nigeria; see Cohen, 1967.)

In short, descent groups are comprised of those people who share the same inherited rights and duties. Returning to the principle of fictive kinship, descent groups may also include those who have been incorporated from outside. Thus, for example, among the Nuer of Sudan there is a practice of absorbing stranger Dinkas into the lineage structure, and they and their descendants are recognized as full-fledged members with accompanying rights and duties (see Evans-Pritchard, 1953).

A *lineage*—a unilineal descent group which generally is localized and which can trace its genealogical links—not infrequently forms the core of a new community. Among the Yao of Mozambique and Tanzania, a brother and his sisters (a branch of the matrilineage) set up their own village, which is known by the name of the matrilineage, even though it eventually takes on a different character through absorption (i.e., through affinity and fictive kinship) of others.

9

Traditional Political Systems

1. BASIC CHARACTERISTICS

TRADITIONAL POLITICAL SYSTEMS in Africa cover a very wide range, from the small-scale, family-structured hunting band (e.g., Bushmen) to the large-scale states and empires. (See Cohen and Holden, *Essays,* chaps. 3 and 10). Since many of the larger kingdoms and states are discussed in Modules 21 through 26, focus here will be on the smaller-scale societies.

a. Lack of Differentiation of Political Sector

Characteristic of most traditional political systems was the lack of clear distinctions between political roles and functions and economic, social, or religious activities. Specialized "politicians" were rare, since political leadership was often inextricably associated with economic, social, and religious leadership as well. This relative lack of differentiation (or specialization) is one of the most important aspects of traditional society all over the world.

b. The Role of Kinship

Kinship is the basic social and political fabric of traditional society in most of Africa (as noted in Modules 5 through 8). One might, however, consider kinship along with other important factors affecting the nature of political systems such as ecology and settlement patterns (Cohen, *Essays,* chap. 3); territorial identification (Sahlins, 1968); population density (Stevenson, 1968); and the role of "associational" ties not based on ethnicity in the emergence of the state (Krader, 1968).

c. Non-Centralization

Although historians have generally given less attention to the so-called stateless societies in Africa than to centralized states and kingdoms (Collins, 1968), the former have been a common subject for political anthropologists, (see Fortes and Evans-Pritchard, 1940; Middleton and Tait, 1958). These societies had few or no specialized institutions or roles of a specifically political nature (e.g., chiefs, courts, or councils). At first, these societies were thought to have no system of government at all (especially vis-à-vis the African kingdom or state). Later, new questions were asked about how certain political *functions* were carried out, and it was realized that political activities were indeed being performed — the resolution of conflict, the distribution of scarce resources, decision-making regarding sustenance activities. Some interesting questions to investigate regarding these societies include: (1) How are law and order and security from external attack maintained? (2) How are problems discussed and decisions reached on matters concerning the whole society or a large part of it? (3) Who are the leaders (formal or informal)? (4) What is the nature of leadership, influence, authority, and succession to authority? These questions might be examined using some of the many available case studies from Africa (for example, Cohen and Middleton, 1967; Fortes and Evans-Pritchard, 1940; Middleton and Tait, 1958). Fried (1967) provides a more general introduction in his chapter on "Rank Societies."

2. TYPES OF AFRICAN POLITICAL SYSTEMS

There have been numerous typologies of African political systems (most are cited in the *Bibliography*). There is by no means a universal agreement on any one typology, and the composite categorization outlined below must be viewed as a heuristic outline rather than an authoritative conclusion. (To put the African context in wider perspective, see Wiseman, 1966; and Fried, 1967.)

a. Hunters and Gatherers

Hunting and gathering groups in Africa (e.g., Bushmen, Pygmies) consist primarily of egalitarian bands ranging in size from about 35 to perhaps 250 members. Group boundaries, social as well as territorial, are relatively open, permitting great flexibility in group size and membership. Although today very small in numbers and occupying some of the most marginal environments, hunting and gathering bands provided man's basic social milieu for 99 per cent of his history on earth. For an extremely interesting scientific analysis of *Man the Hunter*, see Lee and Devore (1967).

b. Acephalous Communities

Dependence upon agriculture and/or pastoralism contributes to a larger scale community, wider economic and political activities, and the beginnings of a functional differentiation of society. Kinship, however, remains the basic glue holding such societies together. Like bands, the acephalous (i.e., "leaderless") communities lack formal centralization and are basically egalitarian, although certain elements of ranking become important, and in some groups an incipient structure of authority and leadership can be identified. Among the many varieties of acephalous ethnic communities are the following.

1. Those which feature age-set systems, varying in the degree to which the age-set organization cuts across the various subgroupings of the society. Examples include the Kikuyu and many other groups in East Africa and the Mende of Sierra Leone. With a large population and an organization cutting across many village groups or clan units, as among the Nyakyusa of Tanzania, these societies often approximate certain aspects of centralized political systems. Eisenstadt (1964) provides a detailed analysis of age-groups throughout the world.

2. Those which are based on a village or council ward, such as the Yaku and Ibo of Nigeria. These vary with the degree of authority at the village as distinct from the ward level, which in turn is usually related to the amount of inter-village hostility in the local area. When hostility is high, it is likely that the village rather than the smaller ward will be the center of political life.

3. Those which are based on segmentary lineage systems. These vary according to the depth of genealogical reckoning and the degree of physical mobility. Generally, the more mobile groups (e.g., pastoralists like the Somali and such groups as the Tiv of Nigeria and Nuer of Sudan) depend most heavily upon lineage ties to keep the society together. Less mobile groups such as the Tallensi of Ghana can depend more on residential or locality ties.

c. Chiefdoms

The chiefdom is one of the most controversial types of political system. The existence of a category of chiefdom distinct from the state and other centralized systems has been challenged by many political anthropologists (see, for example, Cohen and Middleton, 1967). Within this category, when it has been separately identified, kinship still remains the most powerful unifying factor. But society is centralized and at least partially stratified along functional (rather than kinship) lines—that is, specialized groups of rulers, such as "bureaucrats," or religious and military leaders, begin to emerge. Several anthropologists (e.g., Fried, 1967) consider these societies to be the most "fragile" of political types, tending to move either in the direction of acephalous society or toward the fully centralized state. Many scholars (e.g., Service, 1962; Fried, 1967) consider the need for more coordinated control and direction growing out of trade and increased interaction between ethnic groups to have been a major factor in the genesis of the chiefdom. Examples include the Nyamwezi and many other groups in Tanzania, and, according to some scholars, the Fanti of Ghana.

d. Centralized States

Many of the characteristics of African state formation are discussed in Modules 20 through 26 and in Holden (*Essays*, chap. 10). An excellent survey of this

subject can also be found in Lloyd, "The Political Structure of African Kingdoms" (1965), which could provide the basis for further class discussion. Lloyd
stresses both the variety and complexity of African kingdoms and introduces
criteria by which kingdoms may be characterized. The two major dimensions
he uses to differentiate African kingdoms are as follows: (1) the degree of
autonomy of local groups (which generally decreases with social complexity,
thereby increasing the number of levels of superior/subordinate relations); and
(2) the mode of recruitment into politically relevant roles (which is a central
focus in the Lloyd article).

10

Traditional Economic Systems

TRADITIONAL ECONOMIC SYSTEMS in Africa, as outlined in Dalton (*Essays*, chap. 4),
reflected the basic nature of ethnic society. Economies were generally small in
scale and relatively undifferentiated in that economic functions were neither
very specialized nor distinct from other societal functions (e.g., religious or
political). Yet an enormous diversity existed in types of economic organization,
levels of technology, dependability of production, and in nearly all facets of
economic life. There was an absence of machine technology and applied science,
an overwhelming emphasis on subsistence production, and, with very few exceptions, no large-scale resource or product markets beyond the local level
(see Bohannan and Dalton, 1965). Whereas market exchange is the major
mechanism integrating modern capitalist economies, traditional economic
systems in Africa were held together by a socioeconomic form of transaction
called "reciprocity," defined by Dalton as "two-way transfers (gifts and counter-
gifts) of goods, money, and services induced by a social relationship between the
gift partners." It is with this form of reciprocal exchange and its changing role
under the impact of modernization that much of the study of economic anthropology is concerned. For more detail on this subject, see the works of Karl
Polanyi, especially those in Dalton (1968). In this module, several additional
aspects of traditional economies will be discussed.

1. ECOLOGY AND AGRICULTURE

African agriculture has always suffered from rainfall problems—too much,
too little, or too variable and undependable. In addition, the general poverty of
tropical African soils has hindered agriculture. Most tropical soils are very low in

humus (due to the rapid decomposition of organic material), are easily leached (thus reducing their mineral content), and are thin and rapidly exhausted. In most savanna and rainforest areas the relatively insoluble minerals, such as iron and aluminum, frequently become compacted into what is called "laterite," which is more a rock than a soil (although as such it may be used as an "adobe" for building houses). Pure laterite has been called a "pedological leprosy" and "utterly infertile." Faced with these conditions, African farmers outside the few favored areas (e.g., certain volcanic highlands, river valleys, and areas such as southern Uganda) practiced a form of shifting agriculture or bush-fallowing. A piece of land would be cleared and usually burned, the ashes providing some extra fertilization, and then farmed for several years until exhausted. The plot was then left fallow for from five to thirty years, with the farmers moving on to another plot. In most cases, the first plot would be returned to after the fallow period. This is a land-exhausting system and has been frequently criticized as a form of "robber economy." Many scholars today, however, consider this system to be a suitable, if not inevitable, adjustment to environmental conditions, given a low level of technology.

2. PATTERNS OF MOBILITY

Cohen (*Essays*, chap. 3), drawing from a large sample of African societies, provides a useful categorization of settlement patterns and mobility in Africa. The variations he identifies are associated not only with different economies but also with differences in kinship systems, political organization, and other aspects of ethnic society. Cohen estimates that about three-fourths of African societies have been locationally stable communities, the rest being partially or wholly mobile. A more detailed breakdown is given in Figure 3.

FIGURE 3
DISTRIBUTION OF SETTLEMENT PATTERNS
IN AFRICA (AFTER COHEN)

Description	Percentage
Fully nomadic migratory groups with no permanent settlements	10
Seasonally nomadic groups; some fixed settlements	8
Groups which shift between alternative fixed settlements	4
Groups with fixed but impermanent settlements; movement after a period	2
Dispersed settlements; fixed, permanent, but not concentrated	27
Small settlement clusters forming local communities	9
Larger, village-type communities, ethnically organized	36
Complex urban communities with some hierarchization in size and function	4

3. LAND AND TERRITORY

African attitudes toward the land and legal arrangements regarding land tenure are among the most widely misunderstood aspects of traditional Africa. Here, as has often been the case with respect to European interpretations of traditional African patterns, the confusion arises out of an attempt to apply Western attitudes to the African context. Perhaps the best general statement on this problem can be found in Bohannan (1964, chap. 11). Bohannan points out that, whereas in Western societies land is considered a "thing" or commodity which can be bought and sold like other marketable commodities, most Africans regard space and land as a basis for regulating social relationships. The organization and "ownership" of space is viewed in terms of social relationships and the positioning of social groups. Most Africans did not partition their space into parcels but considered it a reflection of their social system. In some cases, specific locations were given particular recognition and either economic or ritual meaning—rain shrines, ancestors' or saints' graves, wells, and so forth. This provided the key link between social and territorial organization. In other cases, the social-territorial link was more direct. In contrast to the rigidly partitioned, precisely bounded Western map, most Africans mapped space genealogically rather than in terms of property and values. Rights to use particular pieces of land depended upon the kinship structure and were constantly changing. This flexibility occurred not only at the local level but also for entire ethnic groups. Because of constantly changing territorial "boundaries," it is extremely difficult to map (in the Western sense) the distribution of ethnic groups in Africa.

Land "ownership" as known in the West was extremely rare in Africa, if it existed at all. Because of their distinctive perspective toward space, Africans tended to be more flexible in the way they organized and allocated rights to use land. There was no "contractual" basis to rigidify the system. Frequently, the term "communal ownership" (as opposed to individual ownership or title) has been applied to African land-use systems, but, as Bohannan notes, even this is inaccurate because it does not specify which of several types of tenure arrangements based on ethnic affiliation is being referred to. "Communal" is used simply to denote something unlike Western commercial arrangements through land and real-estate markets. In nearly all African societies, nobody "owned" land in an absolute sense, but a man was given rights to use land as part of his position within a kinship system. This right of usage (or *usufruct*) to a farm sufficient to support his immediate dependents was inalienable, but only insofar as he was part of the social-territorial group in that area. Land, therefore, could not be "sold" in most of traditional Africa for it was not a commodity but an integral part of the whole social structure. As one might imagine, these contrasting views toward the land caused enormous misunderstandings during the colonial period. In certain parts of eastern and southern Africa, European settlers thought they had "purchased" huge tracts of land, while African leaders believed they had simply granted the Europeans temporary rights of usage for pieces of territory that they were not then using themselves. Some contrasting views of land tenure in Africa are given in Jomo Kenyatta (1964); Meek (1957 and 1949); Ronald Cohen, *The Kanuri of Bornu* (1967, pp. 79–80); Bentsi-Entschil (1964); and Biebuyck (1963). These studies properly explain the widespread conceptual simplification of "communal" land tenure and illustrate the extent to which ideas of land tenure in parts of Africa formed a continuum of rights ranging from usufruct on the one hand to more Western notions of individual ownership on the other. There is little attention given in these studies, however, to the varying perceptions of space and territory in most of Africa.

11

Language and Linguistic Systems

THE THREE MAJOR INTERESTS of contemporary linguists working in Africa are clearly represented by Berry (*Essays*, chap. 5): (1) to make statements about language classification and diversity; (2) to describe specific languages in terms of their linguistic components; and (3) to examine language-use situations, including multilingualism. Since language classification is discussed in Module 3 (and follows, primarily, the work of Greenberg, 1963) this discussion will concentrate on other features of African languages and linguistic systems. (For further references to classification, see Guthrie, 1967; Voegelin, 1964; Fodor, 1968; and Westermann and Bryan, 1952). It is worthwhile to note, however, that the two major approaches to the classification of African languages seem to be based on (1) similarity of language components, including morphology and phonology (represented in the work of Greenberg and Voegelin); and (2) historically traceable linkages between languages within a language family (represented in the work of Westermann and Guthrie). It is clear, however, that two languages may be considered similar (e.g., Hausa and Kanuri) because of the incorporation of loan-words due to proximity rather than because of common etymologies. This is often a source of complication in both these approaches.

1. LANGUAGE DIVERSITY

Because of the disagreement among linguists as to the criteria of language classification, it is difficult to state precisely the number of African languages. It is generally agreed, however, that around one-third of all the distinct languages in the world (not including dialects) are found in Africa. In the larger

African states, such as Congo-Kinshasa, Sudan, and Nigeria, there are probably well over 100 languages spoken in each country. The number of languages in Nigeria, for example, is conservatively estimated at about 125, but recent estimates have ranged up to 400. Figure 4 provides some contemporary estimates and indicates the major language for each of the tropical African states.

2. DISTINCTIVE SOUNDS, MORPHOLOGY, AND SEMANTICS

Among the distinctive sounds (phonology) which characterize many African languages are the several varieties of "clicks" in the Khoisan languages and others in southern Africa (interestingly exemplified on a popular record, "The Click Song," by Miriam Makeba); the labiovelar (*kp*, *gb*); the simple vowel and consonant systems, in which each vowel or consonant can be sounded in only one way (i.e., they resemble Italian or French in this respect rather than English or Dutch in having "pure" vowels and very few diphthongs); the widespread use of initial sounds combining a nasal with either a voiced stop (*N*gola, *M*boya) or unvoiced stop (*Nk*rumah); and the very extensive use of tone. In tonal languages, two words may be spelled exactly the same but differ entirely in their tone patterns and therefore in their meaning. One word in Twi, the language of the Ashanti in Ghana, means "show me" when the tone rises on the final syllable, but means "leave me alone" when the tone drops. This tonality is the operative principle of the "talking drum." The drummer, by altering the tones of his drumming, can imitate the sequence of tones in familiar phrases and sentences, thereby communicating with his audience. For a fuller discussion of sounds, see Greenberg (1962).

With regard to morphology and semantics, it is difficult to make general statements. Complex noun classifications, with root terms modified in meaning by adding various prefixes and suffixes, are a common morphological characteristic of Bantu languages. For example, in the Ganda language *Buganda* is the country (Uganda is the Swahili form of *Buganda*); *Baganda*, the people; *Muganda*, an individual; *Luganda*, the language, etc. Bantu is actually *Ba-ntu*, the generalized plural form of *ntu*, or *mtu*, meaning person. Greenberg (1962) also discusses the many idioms and metaphorical terms distinctive to African languages.

3. MULTILINGUALISM AND LANGUAGE USE

Most Africans speak more than one language. Berry (*Essays*, chap. 5) briefly reviews some of the reasons why Africa is the most multilingual area in the world—the spread of lingua francas as a means of fostering wider communication among diverse linguistic groups being perhaps the most important. Apart from European languages, some of the major regional languages of Africa (i.e., languages spoken by a large number of people from different ethnic

FIGURE 4
LANGUAGE PLURALISM IN TROPICAL AFRICAN STATES

Country	Predominant European language[a]	Number of major African languages[b]	Major African language[c]	Number of major-language speakers, as percentage of total population[c]	Greenberg (1963) classi-fication[a]	Other major languages (and lingua francas)[c]
1. Botswana	E	2	Tswana	90	IA5	Shona
2. Burundi	F	2	Rundi	95	Composite of Hutu (IA5) and Tutsi (IIE1)	Swahili (lingua franca)
3. Cameroon	F, E	50	Fang	18	IA5	Bamileke, Fulani, Kirdi, Bassa, Baya
4. C.A.R.	F	41	Banda	31	IA6	Sango (lingua franca), Baya, Mandjia
5. Chad	F	22	Arabic	55	IIIA	Sara
6. Congo-Brazzaville	F	7	Kongo	50	IA5	Toke, M'bochi, M'bete
7. Congo-Kinshasa	F	61	Kongo	30	IA5	Lingala and Swahili (lingua francas), Mango, Luba, Lunda
8. Dahomey	F	15	Fon/Ewe	58	IA4	Bargu, Yoruba
9. Ethiopia	E	63	Amharic	50	IIIA	Galla, Sidamo, Somali
10. Equatorial Guinea[e]	S	–	Fang	60	IA5	–
11. Gabon	F	15	Fang	50	IA5	Eshira, M'bete, Kota, Omyene
12. Gambia	E	2	Mandingo	50	IA2	Fulani, Wolof, Diola
13. Ghana	E	37	Akan (Twi)	44	IA4	Mole/Dagbani, Ewe, Ga-Adangbe
14. Guinea	F	22	Mande	48	IA2	Fulani, Kissi
15. Ivory Coast	F	57	Akan (Twi)	25	IA4	Kru, Mande, Senufo, Lobi
16. Kenya	E	22	Kikuyu	38	IA5	Swahili (lingua franca),

19. Malawi	E	5	Nyanja	IA5	46	Ngoni, Yao, Tumbuka
20. Mali	F	15	Malinke-Bambara	IA2	43	Fulani, Senufo, Sarakole, Tuareg
21. Mauritania	F	2	Arabic	IIIA	90	Fulani, Berber
22. Niger	F	14	Hausa	IIIE	75	Djerma-Songhai, Fulani, Tuareg, Kanuri
23. Nigeria	E	125	Hausa	IIIE	50	Yoruba, Ibo, Tiv, Fulani, Ibibio, Kanuri
24. Rwanda	F	2	Rwanda	Composite of Hutu (IA5) and Tutsi (III E)	90	Swahili (lingua franca)
25. Senegal	F	8	Wolof	IAI	42	Fulani-Tukulor, Serere, Diola, Mandingo
26. Sierra Leone	E	8	Temne-Limba	IAI	45	Mende, Mande
27. Somali	E, I	2	Somali	IID3	95	Arabic
28. Sudan	E	171	Arabic	IIIA	51	Nilotic, Darfur, Nuba and Beja clusters
29. Swaziland[e]	E	2	Swazi	IA5	95	Zulu
30. Tanzania	E	56	Nyamwezi	IA5	17	Swahili (lingua franca)
31. Togo	F	16	Ewe	IA4	44	Kabre, Moba, Kotocoli, Gurma
32. Uganda	E	24	Ganda	IA5	33	Nilotic cluster, Karamajong, Gisu
33. Upper Volta	F	27	Mossi	IA3	55	Mande, Senufo, Grunsh, Fulani
34. Zambia	E	69	Bemba	IA5	15	Tonga, Nyanja, Lunda, Barotse

[a] E = English, F = French, S = Spanish, I = Italian.

[b] Jan Knappert, "Language Problems of the New Nations of Africa," *Africa Quarterly*, V. no. 2 (1965), 95–105.

[c] Donald G. Morrison, Robert C. Mitchell, John N. Paden, and H. Michael Stevenson, *Black Africa: A Handbook for Comparative Analysis* (New York: Free Press, 1970).

[d] Joseph H. Greenberg, *The Languages of Africa* (The Hague: Mouton, 1966).

[e] Information derived from various other sources.

groups and often with varying first languages) include Swahili (Tanzania, Kenya, and parts of Uganda, Rwanda, Burundi, eastern Congo-Kinshasa, northern Zambia, Malawi, and Mozambique); Hausa (northern Nigeria and throughout West Africa); Arabic (throughout northern Africa); Amharic (Ethiopia); Pidgin English (along the Guinea Coast of West Africa); Mande (Western Sudanic belt); Lingala (Congo-Kinshasa); Sango (Gabon and C.A.R.); and Zulu (South Africa).

It should be mentioned that several of the lingua francas in Africa are composite languages. Swahili, for example is based on Bantu structure but with much of the vocabulary coming from Arabic and some from other languages such as Portuguese. The Arabic influence is probably strongest in the main coastal areas such as Mombasa and Zanzibar, where Swahili emerged as a trading language for Arabs and Africans. Pidgin English, in West Africa, is similarly based on local sentence structures, but with most of the words being English. (A pidgin is distinct from a creole in that a creole language is spoken as the *first* language by a particular group rather than as the second or third language. Thus, the English-based creole of Sierra Leone or the French-based creole of Haiti may sound like Pidgin English and Pidgin French but they serve as native tongues for their speakers.)

Patterns of language use and multilingualism have been important both in traditional African societies and in present times. In the early empires and forest states of Africa, there were frequently groups of professional interpreters in the courts of kings whose job consisted of interpreting correspondence with other kingdoms. In the multiethnic states of the Western Sudan (e.g., Ghana, Mali, Songhai), some form of multilingualism must have been evident in the military (and other) sectors. For a discussion of multilingualism and language policies in contemporary Africa, see Fishman *et al.* (1968).

Sociolinguistics is the study of the social usages of language. It includes the study of multilingual situations (such as in the pluralistic urban centers, among migrant groups, or in trade). But it also includes the study of language use within a relatively homogeneous linguistic area: the variations between men, women, and children, in language use; the language patterns which characterize superior-subordinate status relationships; the difference between language use in religious institutions and economic institutions. There is much research that remains to be done in all of these areas. (See Berry and Greenberg, 1966.)

12
‾‾

Literature and Oral Tradition

HISTORICAL TALES, MORAL PARABLES, king-list recitations, and social anecdotes form major categories in African traditional literature. Their motifs are often expressed through mythic figures and personified animals. Although such tales, usually told by elders to children, serve to amuse, instruct, admonish, and recall, their major functions are entertainment and socialization. The telling of the tale is an art in itself. The dramatic impact is heightened by the fact that recitation usually takes place at night. All societies socialize their young to the beliefs and values of the society. In Africa these are verbalized largely through stories. According to Herskovits: "Animal tales which offer explanations of natural phenomena, or account for accepted modes of behavior, or point morals, are regarded by natives themselves as important educational devices . . . 'we teach our children through our stories' " (in Ottenberg, 1960, p. 454).

1. THE IDEA OF ORAL TRADITION

In many areas of Africa (as where Arabic, Hausa, Amharic, and Swahili are spoken and written) some of the literature may be recorded in writing. Even in parts of Africa where there is no tradition of writing, a formalized lore may still exist. There is usually a system of professional folklorists, or "rememberers," who keep track of the traditions. Past events are recounted, with contemporary happenings linked in through the art of improvisation. As with written literature, oral lore may be transmitted in a consistent manner; there are special methods to maintain its faithful representation (for further discussion, see *Essays:* Berry, chap. 5; Rowe, chap. 9; and Holden, chap. 10).

Frequently, specialists entrusted with the oral traditions are trained through long apprenticeships. Among the Rwanda of Rwanda, there are still schools for instruction in the classical tradition. Here, oral tradition is used in Vansina's sense to mean all verbal testimonies which are reported statements concerning the past, as distinct from eyewitness account and rumor (Vansina, 1961). The Rwanda also support other specialists who are employed as a sort of walking library, transmitting their knowledge only to direct successors. Among African peoples with centralized governments, the phenomenon of the official whose duty it is to recite the history at the ruler's court is common. (For examples of such literature among the Ankole, Zulu, and Fulani, see Morris, 1964; Stuart, 1968; and Sow, 1968.) Among the Rwanda there are genealogists to remember lists of kings and queen mothers, memorialists to remember the most important events of the various reigns, rhapsodists to preserve panegyrics on kings, and *abirru* to preserve secrets of the dynasty (see Coupez and Kamanzi, 1969).

Where a society pays particular attention to preservation of the tradition and there is no writing to record it, mnemonic devices are often used. For example, material objects are used, such as the Ashanti king's "stool," the history of which represents the history of the kingdom.

2. SYMBOLS IN LITERATURE

In African folklore, symbolic references often emerge from free association or play-on-words. For example, the Bushongo word for *abyss* is sometimes used to mean *king*. The explanation for this is that *abyss* is an antonym for *hill*, and the king's highest title is *God of the Hills*. Myths and tales are forms of African folklore which draw heavily on symbolic representation. (For examples from the Zande, Limba, and Ibo, see Evans-Pritchard, 1967; Finnegan, 1967; and Umeasiegbu, 1969).

African animal tales are probably best known in the Americas due to their infinite variety and number and the popularity of the Br'er Rabbit stories. According to Herskovits: "These tales are in many cases regarded as the type forms of the Negro animal-trickster tale, and reference is frequently made to them in identifying a given story found in the folklore of various peoples of Africa itself" (in Ottenberg, 1960, p. 445). Within African ethnic society, a group of tales may be regarded as a unit in which a whole cycle of adventures is acted out by well-known figures. In the cycle, action centers about a protagonist of outstanding importance; for example, "the Dahomean group includes animal-trickster cycles centering about Tortoise and Hare, a cycle having as its central character a trickster of gross undisciplined appetite called Yo, a cycle of tales concerning the adventures of the twins," etc. (*ibid.*).

Rattray discusses the adoption of tales as reinforcements of ways of thought and as means of political commentary. The names of animals, and even that of the sky-god himself, were substituted for the names of real individuals whom it would have been very impolitic to mention. Later, no doubt, such a mild exposé in the guise of a story often came to be related qua story. The original practice is still resorted to, however, to expose someone whom the offended party fears to accuse more openly.

3. THE CONTENT OF ORAL LITERATURE

Each culture has characteristic norms which dictate how one should behave. Proverbs and riddles prove useful in this respect, as they reflect morality to a greater extent than most other forms of folklore. That proverbs are significant throughout the African continent is evident from the great number identified with each society. For the Hausa alone over 2,000 have been collected, and this is felt to be only a portion of those in existence (see Kirk-Green, 1966; Skinner,

1969). Proverbs are used to inculcate children with the given morality; they are cited as evidence in legal cases; they may be used when subtlety is advantageous. Some good examples are provided in Hausa proverbs: "Even if the lion comes down in the world he doesn't consort with the pig"; "Whoever catches a hyena should know how he's going to release it" (cited in Johnston, 1966, p. 103).

Another important category of African literature is the myth-of-origin. Stories may give a cosmological account of the creation of the world (including arrival of the gods or nature-deities, functions of the gods, and how they interrelate with man) as well as accounts of the origins of clans, lineages, and even the ethnic society itself. Such stories may indicate the ontology of a people, explain the non-comprehensibility of nature, validate ritual beliefs, and give a sense of time perspective. (Middleton, *Myth and Cosmos*, 1967, contains many African examples of this type of oral literature.) In addition to morality, cosmology, and ontology, African literature may deal specifically with the spirit world, including both major and minor deities. As mentioned in Module 13, the family of deities in many African societies is comparable in complexity to the Greek and Roman views of the spirit world.

4. CONCLUSIONS

African folklore as a whole is primarily oral. Even in Swahili and Hausa areas, many of the stories and legends were not put to writing until the beginning of this century. Yet these stories do maintain their uniformity and continuity over time, despite the large number of raconteurs, and the large bodies of literature.

Currently, there is an Oxford University Press series of publications of African traditional literature (for examples of Yoruba and Somali literature, see Babalola, 1966, and Andrzejewski, 1964, respectively). Other anthologies of African stories are also becoming available (see Radin and Sweeney, 1969). The art of the raconteur seems to be flourishing, even in contemporary Africa, perhaps because of the inherent feature of improvisation. It is also clear that much of the cultural heritage of Africa is embodied in its oral tradition. Although this module has not dealt with the tradition of written literature in Africa, there is a special article in the *Guide to Resources* on published literature in African languages (Getso *et al.*).

13
———

Conceptual Systems and Religion

A CONCEPTUAL SYSTEM is described by Albert (*Essays*, chap. 6) as "a pattern of beliefs and values that define a way of life and the world in which men act, judge, decide, and solve problems." Religion may be used in the broad sense of ultimate concern (Bellah, 1966, p. 227) or in the more narrow sense of belief in a deity or deities which give meaning to life. It is often difficult, as mentioned by Albert, for Western students to comprehend pre-scientific conceptual systems. The difference between scientific and pre-scientific intellectual activity, however, is not a matter of complexity but of focus. According to Lévi-Strauss, it "lies not in the quality of the intellectual process, but in the nature of the things to which it is applied. . . . The improvement of scientific thought lies, not in the alleged progress of man's mind, but in the discovery of new areas to which it may apply its unchanged and unchanging powers" (Lévi-Strauss, 1967, p. 227). The prevailing Western stereotype of "primitive" conceptual systems and religions in Africa may be modified when students examine both the internal complexity and societal use of religion in the African context. For an excellent analysis of African conceptual systems and their relationships with Western "scientific" philosophy, see Horton (1967).

1. RELIGIOUS AND CONCEPTUAL SYSTEMS IN AFRICA

A conceptual system does not exist apart from other cultural expressions in society but may be regarded as the beliefs which give consistency to the different aspects of daily life. For this reason, it may be useful for students to let the patterns of African conceptual systems emerge from those case studies which examine religion as part of the entire society, such as those of the Nuer (Evans-Pritchard, 1956); the Ndembu (Turner, 1969); the Maguzawa (Greenberg, 1969); the Bété (Holas, 1968); the Mende (Harris and Sawyer, 1968); the Dinka (Lienhardt, 1961); the Tallensi (Fortes, 1959); the Nupe (Nadel, 1954); the Kono (Parsons, 1964); and others.

Even in the case studies, however, scholars may find primarily what they are conditioned to look for, and the debate over the appropriate conceptual framework for the study of African religions and philosophy may remain as intense as ever (see Fabian, *Essays*, chap. 19). A number of articles and volumes do explore the problem of approaches to non-Western religious and conceptual systems: e.g., Horton (1967), Geertz (in Banton, 1966); Spiro (in Banton, 1966); Glock and Stark (1965); Weber (1963); Wallace (1966); Evans-Pritchard (1965); Bellah (1966); Durkheim (1965); Malinowski (1948); and Middleton (1967). In addition, the international meetings at Bouaké on African traditional religion (1965), the depth of concern of the *Présence Africaine* writers (e.g., at the Abidjan Conference, 1961), the continuing African controversy over Tempel's *Bantu Philosophy* (1961; originally published in 1946), and the writings of scholars such as Ba (1966) and Mbiti (1969, 1970) are a testament to the intense interest of African scholars in these questions. It is also significant that almost every African leader insists that African traditional life is essentially religious (see, for example, Senghor, 1964; and Nkrumah, 1969).

2. THE SENSE OF COMMUNITY

The relationship of cultural concepts, religion, ethnic identity, and a sense of community are closely interwoven within most African societies. Some scholars, such as Turnbull, even argue that:

> The tribe is nothing if it is not a religious unit, just as much as it is domestic, economic and political. From this derives the power of its morality. . . . The tribe is, in a sense, then a church; it is a community bound together in common allegiance to a common ancestor in whom its members believe. It would scarcely be worthy of its continued existence, indeed it would probably cease to exist, if it did not uphold its beliefs. But belief, for the African tribe, does not merely emerge in times of crisis; it permeates and motivates everyday life (Turnbull, 1964, pp. 25, 29).

According to Middleton (1967) the Lugbara of Uganda have a sense of community which includes members who have died, mythical beings, and living members. The basic distinction in Lugbara society is between "close" people — consisting primarily of the above-mentioned "members" — and "distant" or "inverted" peoples, who fall outside the sphere of social relations, mythology, and genealogical tradition. A non-Lugbara group ten miles away may be "distant" while a related Lugbara group at a greater physical distance may be regarded as "close." According to Middleton:

> These categories form a framework in which are set the relations of individuals and groups. But concepts of time and space denote extension in different directions. For Lugbara there are no fixed scales and no directions in this system of categories. Differentiation in time of the myths of origin and of the coming of the Europeans is irrelevant: the units or themes of each corpus of myth are arranged in the same pattern. Analogously the units of social distance are arranged in the same pattern, round a focal point, but this arrangement is not expressed in terms of a common scale of distance measured in miles, nor is it oriented directionally or topographically (Middleton, 1967, pp. 59–60).

Within segmental societies, such as the Logoli, the Tallensi, or the Nuer, the sense of community does not require a strong chiefship. In other societies, the chief, as head of the "religious" community, is regarded as divine. (For a discussion of divine aspects of kingship in West Africa, see Crowder and Ikime, 1970.)

Within the "close" community, whether hierarchical or segmental, the interpersonal relations of the members are usually regulated through an elaborate set of codes, which, in turn, are usually justified in terms of a conceptual system or religion. As mentioned by Cohen and LeVine (*Essays*, chaps. 3 and 15), African children learn, at an early age, complex modes of appropriate behavior which differ with respect to the child's relationship to different members of his family and different sectors of his society.

But the very closeness of some African societies (especially those which are segmental and endogamous rather than exogamous) may result in interpersonal tensions which require some "release." One way of displacing such tensions seems to be through the belief in witchcraft, (see Evans-Pritchard, 1951), which in its basic form is found in every part of the world (see Mair, 1969). Among African societies, the belief in witchcraft (the ascription to a particular individual of powers to do evil) is common. As a system of ideas, it has definite implications for social relations and in turn is influenced by the social structure. For example, as Evans-Pritchard (1951) has pointed out, Zande witchcraft often provides an explanation for illness and death. As a system of thought, witchcraft answers questions of "why?" Furthermore, it provides a means for alleviating stress by pointing out a course of action and terminating doubt (see Middleton and Winter, 1963).

3. THE SENSE OF DESTINY

Closely related to the concept of witchcraft as an explanation of evil, is the notion of spirit involvement in the destinies of individuals (see Beattie and Middleton, 1969). Spirits may protect against evil, or may cause evil. Spirits must be placated and appeased, usually through material offerings.

But underlying the concepts of spirit involvement in human destinies is the common belief in some form of predestination or predetermination. Albert (*Essays*, chap. 6) discusses the concept of fatalism. Belief in fatalism does not prevent the individual from trying to alter the actual impact of fate, but it does suggest the ultimate causal impotence of man on the one hand and the superiority of superhuman forces on the other.

Man acts, but despite good performance he may suffer and/or fail. By and large, fatalism is a self-consistent, faithful reflection of actual human existence, with its unpredicted ups and downs and its often outrageous injustices and undeserved strokes of luck. Among the Tallensi of northern Ghana, fatalism takes the form of belief in a prenatal destiny which becomes an innate determinant of an individual's life history. Before birth, a child's wishes are declared to Heaven, and these wishes are presumed to shape his future. Such a doctrine, in its context, gives an explanation which defies ordinary knowledge; it also relieves society of responsibility if the sufferer is a misfit in the social situation or in his psychological or physical mien (Fortes, 1959).

4. THE SENSE OF WORSHIP

Because of the importance of spirits in the determination of individual and group destinies, there is a sense of reverence and fear which blends into a sense of worship. While the patterns of worship vary with most ethnic groups, there is in general a pattern of a high god (who is relatively unapproachable) and several lesser deities, some of whom are private, and some of whom are public (see Herskovits' study of Dahomey, 1967). There is also a common pattern of reverence, or worship, for the deceased ancestors who are present in spirit, and for the life force which is a part of all living and material entities.

Reverence for the dead and belief that the dead are alive in spirit are common in Africa. (It should be noted that both Christianity and Islam hold this belief in varying degrees.) This belief plays an important role in the living community: ancestors are invoked and propitiated because their influence is not terminated at death. For example, among the Tallensi "the ancestor cult is the transposition to the religious plane of the relationships of parents and children," i.e., the ritualization of filial piety (Fortes, 1959). Tallensi religious institutions are incomprehensible without reference to the social organization, especially the segmentary system of authority and emphasis on the agnatic (male) line of descent. A man's destiny, which manifests benevolence, "consists of a unique configuration of ancestors who have of their own accord elected to exercise specific surveillance over his life-cycle and to whom he is personally accountable" (Fortes, 1959, p. 46).

The belief in animism (ascription of life forces to material objects, such as trees and earth) is prevalent, especially in agrarian societies where a high value is placed on fertility. This can be likened to sympathetic magic; the African knows that beyond his labor and efforts are powers over which he has little if any control. To ensure the optimum sunshine and rainfall, and a bountiful crop, the forces of nature are personified and appealed to for benevolent intervention. For example, the earth has the image of the giving mother, whose yield is so important to the society. She is dealt with as a personality who can be cajoled and invoked.

Similarly, in those few African societies that are still dependent upon the forces of nature for hunting and gathering, as, for example, the Mbuti Pygmies, animism takes an active role in daily life. The Pygmies are totally dependent upon the forest for their diet, clothing, and shelter. When they have a good supply of subsistence materials, they are grateful to the forest for its generosity; when, however, the hunt is unsuccessful, they believe that they have in some way insulted the forest and, through propitiatory means, attempt to rectify the situation.

Just as a group's conceptual framework provides the *raison d'être* for a particular way of life (including secular affairs), the group's religious beliefs represent the spiritual forces under which its members live. In the worship of these forces, a society's sense of community and destiny is confirmed.

14

Visual Arts

THERE IS A CONTINUING ACADEMIC CONTROVERSY as to whether traditional African visual art forms (which include sculpture, pottery-making, weaving, metalwork, and, in a few instances, painting) should be considered "art" in isolation, or whether they can only be understood and appreciated with respect to their functions within particular social contexts. Religion and sculpture, for example, are intimately connected. But does the belief that African sculpture is only understood in its religious context underestimate the potential of the art form, the genius of the sculptor, and the aesthetic tastes of the sculpture users?

Broad generalizations about African art are difficult to make since art forms are integral parts of particular ethnic cultures and thus differ accordingly. Few traditional African cultures were sufficiently compartmentalized or differentiated to permit one aspect (such as art) to be isolated from the others (e.g., put in museums). Furthermore, there is great variation in the nature and intensity of interaction between the artist and the audience in the African context (although in nearly all cases the level of interaction is high). Another question can therefore be posed: can one fully appreciate the aesthetic content of African art forms without knowledge of the social context, how the art forms are used, or what relationship is being aimed for between artist and audience?

1. SOCIAL USAGES OF VISUAL ARTS

Willett (*Essays*, chap. 7) addresses himself to the relationship of visual arts to their social contexts. He regards aesthetic appreciation of the visual arts as a blend of form and social content. Similar pieces of sculpture, fashioned in exactly the same manner in two different societies, may not convey the same meaning. There are many items of African material culture which may be viewed in terms of function. In this view, the intricacies of design and the actual carving on an African mask, for example, follow a particular pattern for reasons of social usage; in other words, form follows function. Yet few scholars would deny that a material item may also have an intrinsic aesthetic appeal. The question remains as to whether an aesthetic judgment can be made about African art without reference to social context. Leon Siroto, of the Field Museum of Natural History in Chicago, designed an experiment to examine this issue. He showed several pieces of Congolese art to different audiences (African and American) and solicited comments as to the quality and aesthetic appeal. His interviewees all chose the same items as representing the highest quality, thereby suggesting some universality of aesthetic taste.

Willett suggests that an approach somewhere between the two extremes (social usage *vs.* aesthetics) is desirable. This means heightening the aesthetic experience (art for art's sake) by taking into account the circumstances in which an art object was fashioned or used. For example, a piece of sculpture may be fashioned of bronze, which in a given society is a prestigious metal; hence, the object is artistically appealing as well as serving as a status symbol for its owner. Furthermore, as noted by Willett, a piece of art may serve religious functions in certain circumstances and secular functions in others. It is clear, however, that most African sculpture is related to socioreligious functions having to do with the "life cycle" (i.e., birth, puberty, marriage, death) or with economic necessities, as in agriculture (e.g., fertility ceremonies) or pastoralism (e.g., cattle rituals).

2. VISUAL ART FORMS

In traditional Africa, painting as an art form is rare. In the recent past, it has been used mainly as a decorative device for sculpture, but there are also many cases of rock painting, such as that of the Bushmen and their ancestors (who have only lately ceased to make rock paintings in South Africa) or the prehistoric hunting and pastoralist frescoes in the Tassili and elsewhere in the Sahara. In Islamic areas, where representational art is prohibited, the arts of abstract design and calligraphy have been developed. In the main, however, visual art in Africa most often takes the form of sculpture. The specific materials used generally reflect the environment of the people and may even be used to trace migration movements around the continent. The forms of sculpture generally reflect major cultural values. For example, in the East African cattle area, cattle are a symbol of prestige and are felt to embody cultural values. In most of this area sculptural art consists of clay models of cattle and men, masks for ceremonies, and wooden figurines. As an additional point, one must keep in mind the correlation between complexity of material culture and mode of subsistence. Thus the Bushmen (nomadic hunters and gatherers in the Kalahari

Desert) concentrate their artistic expression on very portable and necessary items, such as engraved ostrich-egg shells used to carry and to store drinking water.

The visual arts may also include (depending on cultural complexity and leisure-time availability) pottery, leatherwork, basketry, textile-weaving, and metalwork (in the main for jewelry, but also for such items as gold weights, as with the Ashanti, or weaponry, as with the Hausa).

3. AFRICAN SCULPTURE

As previously mentioned, sculpture, particularly in wood but also in bronze, iron, cement, gold, ivory, soapstone, and other materials, is probably the most prevalent visual art form in Africa. In addition to playing a vital role in traditional ethnic culture, African sculpture has also had a major impact on Western art forms (e.g., with respect to the revitalization of modern Western art in the works of Picasso, Braque, and Klee). For a long period, it was thought that the Congo Basin was the main center of African sculpture, but work over the past several decades has shifted the focus to West Africa and, in particular, to Nigeria (due in large part to the work of the long-established Nigerian Department of Antiquities). By far the longest continuous period of major artistic creativity can be attributed to Nigeria, starting from the ancient terracotta heads of the Nok culture (see Module 20) through to the famous bronzes of Benin and the brilliant wood and bronze sculpture of the Yoruba. There is no reason, however, to assume that future archaeological investigation will not reveal an equivalent or perhaps greater artistic continuity in other areas of West Africa which already have rich artistic traditions.

The concentration of sculpture in the Congo Basin and West Africa is closely related to the locational pattern of forests in Africa as well as to particular aspects of traditional culture (amount of leisure time, the impact of settled village life, etc.). In the grasslands and savanna of eastern and southern Africa (with some important exceptions) wooden sculpture has understandably been much more meager. Instead, the populations here have focused on other forms of artistic expression including textile-weaving, pottery-making, music, and dance.

4. AESTHETIC FORMS AND CHARACTERISTICS

Given the predominance of sculpture, particularly human figures carved from wood, it may be useful to quote R. P. Armstrong at length on some of the formal and aesthetic characteristics of African wood-figurine sculpture:

> Bodies are not executed with any marked interest in naturalistic depiction, and the
> space which has been exploited for the figure is disrupted with intervals different

from those one encounters in European art. Further, the characteristics of the interrupting volumes themselves are radically different as well. The predominating scheme of spatial interruption is vertical. Length or height is the overwhelming spatial interval, and these linear volumes are divided into the head, large in proportion to the rest of the body; the generally narrow trunk whose length is emphasized to the point where its relationship to reality is in no real sense factual; and the legs, which are shorter than life, are flexed and have bulk incommensurate with their height.

The volumes tend to be developed into strong columns. The head rests upon a columnar neck; the neck in turn rests upon the columns of the trunk, slightly molded ventrally, and dorsally composed of two positive columns and one intervening negative column representing the spine, which is inevitably inverted. Columns constitute the legs, and the arms as well, which frequently are close to the body — at the sides, or resting on the abdomen. But skeletality is not emphasized at the expense of muscularity; although there is no accuracy of muscular detail, there is little doubt that the bones are fleshed or that cavities contain their organs. The sacrifice of horizontality lends thrust to the bodies. They are always forcefully intruded into their space, a dynamic which gives secondary assertion to the force they initially assert by virtue of their purpose with respect to the commemoration or management of power (Armstrong, 1966).

It is clear that a descriptive elaboration of form does not in itself constitute the aesthetic characteristics of an art object. Many scholars, American, European, and African, have suggested a range of aesthetic criteria to evaluate African art (see, for example, Armstrong, 1969; and Nketia, 1964). However, many published photographs of African art are available (see, for example, Willett, 1967; Fagg, 1963 and 1965; and Carroll, 1967 and, for both traditional and contemporary examples, the superb journal *African Arts/Arts d'Afrique,* published at UCLA), and students should be encouraged to draw their own conclusions.

15

Traditional Music

As WITH VISUAL ARTS in Africa, music is integral to the culture of which it is part. This module will stress the social uses of music, the types of music and instruments found in Africa, and some aspects of musical aesthetics.

1. SOCIAL USES OF MUSIC

According to Merriam:

> The separation of the "artist" from the "audience" is not an African pattern—although specialists are always present, music is participative. Almost everyone can and does sing; many people play musical instruments; most people are competent in at least one type of musical expression. African music is functional on two levels—the music itself is integrated into daily life, and it is performed and enjoyed by large numbers of people within the society (Merriam, 1962, p. 56).

In most African societies, however, there are special groups of persons who are associated with particular types of music. In some societies, poetry is recited as music by professional musicians; there may be a wide range of uses of such music/poetry. For example, individuals in Hausa society compose and perform liturgical music (for Islamic prayer meetings), praise-singing music (for use in the palaces), children's lullabies (sung by mothers to their babies), work chants (sung by laborers), and life-cycle songs (for the occasions of marriages or funerals). In addition, many of the women improvise "pre-Islamic" verse for spirit invocation (especially regarding fertility or health). Among the Wolof of Gambia, communal work groups provide a solution to manpower needs in cultivation. The group work is efficient, and monotony is minimized by singing and working rhythmically to drum beats.

Perhaps the most noticeable use of music, however, is in conjunction with dance. There are few African villages or cities where drumming and dancing cannot be found in the evenings after work.

2. TYPES OF MUSIC AND INSTRUMENTS

There is a large variety of instruments in Africa, although this fact is often obscured outside of Africa by the stereotypical emphasis on drums. The range includes wind instruments and stringed instruments, as well as a variety of percussion instruments, including gongs, bells, calabashes, finger pianos, and xylophones. Some of the wind instruments include the small "penny-whistle" of South Africa, various animal horns used for calling cattle, the reeded flutes often used in story-telling and praise-singing, the twelve-foot-long trumpets used to herald the arrival of emirs in the Western and Central Sudan, and a variety of chanter instruments (which sound like bagpipes) found throughout the continent. A similar variety of stringed instruments is also found, including the small open-ended harps of Ethiopia and a whole range of guitar and zither-like instruments. Further description of African instruments can be found in Powne (1968), Nketia (1963), and Ames (1968).

It must be kept in mind that types of music in Africa, as well as instrumentation, tend to be area-specific, corresponding to some extent to the culture areas discussed in Module 3. This specificity is distinguished by the types of instruments used, the social uses of drumming, and variation in musicology. It should be noted that talking drums, essentially a communication device based on tonal variation, are more a linguistic than a musical phenomenon.

The drum, however, is the African instrument par excellence. With reference to the drum, it is clear that the aesthetics and form of music are closely interrelated. According to R. P. Armstrong:

> Aside from the pressure drum which changes tone and is used for specialized purposes, drums are monotonal, so that there are no gradations of tone leading to the definition of an extended simultaneous structure tonally annealed into a wide continuity. What exists, rather, are stratified drum voices, insistent and constant in the structure of successivity. The drum is the trunk-body of a tree, sacrificed to before harvesting, consecrated when completed . . . the trunk of the tree . . . the force of the spirit indwelling . . . the voice of that spirit . . . or its heart, beating. Lighter drums are intercostal murmurs. There are patterns of rhythm throughout, patterns of continuity, on-going, maximizing and analyzing time itself. The beats are there, in dermal layers of time, stretching magically from beginning to ending in an undulating universe of beat. They assert their force, which is death and transfiguration. Dancers, when they dance to it, are trapped in the deluge of excoriating beats, then flayed to freedom (Armstrong, 1966, p. 141).

3. THE INTEGRAL ASPECTS OF MUSIC

Wachsmann (*Essays*, chap. 8) suggests that there are four aspects of music: the cultural system, the musical instrument (including voice) as an extension of the body of the performer, musical time, and language. His essay is devoted primarily to illustrating how these aspects interrelate with one another on an equal basis in African music. Like Willett (*Essays*, chap. 7) Wachsmann is disturbed by the overly stressed dichotomy between "art for art's sake" aesthetics *vs.* art as human behavior in particular social contexts. Going beyond a mere blending of the two viewpoints, he introduces a more comprehensive model which includes the four aspects mentioned above. Each is essential to appreciating African or any other kind of music. All four interweave and interrelate to provide the basis for both aesthetic and contextual interpretation.

A discussion of musical aesthetics is available in Nketia (1964), but if possible students should listen directly to African traditional music. Recordings are now becoming increasingly available (e.g., on the Folkways label), and students and instructors should be encouraged to discuss the characteristics and impact of such music. A brief list of excellent recordings of traditional African music would include the following:

> *Afrique Noire: Panorama de la musique instrumentale.* Edition de la Boite a la Musique, Paris LD 490 (A) Production O.C.O.R.A.
>
> *Ethiopie: Polyphonies et Techniques Vocales.* Disques O.C.O.R.A. 44 (Documents recurillis par Jean Jenkins)
>
> *Bushman Music and Pygmy Music.* Published by the Peabody Museum, Harvard University and Musée de l'Homme Departement d'Ethnomusicologie, Paris
>
> *Musique Kongo (Republique du Congo).* Disques O.C.O.R.A. 35
>
> *Anthologie de la Musique du Tchad.* Disques O.C.O.R.A. 36, 37, 38

Additional recordings are listed by Byrne in the article on audiovisual materials in the *Guide to Resources*; for a comprehensive and annotated discography of African Music on LP, see Merriam, 1970.

Study Questions

16

Study Questions:
African Society and Culture

THE FOLLOWING STUDY QUESTIONS are suggestions only. Some deal with specific modules, while others presume a synthesis of materials from the entire section. Some are analytic and some are matters of judgment.

1. What criteria have been used by linguists and anthropologists to classify African ethnic groups? Have these classifications been useful? How might you account for the large number of ethnic groups in Africa?

2. Which of the following types of groups, if any, do you think might pose the greatest problems in the construction of modern African states: language groups, racial groups, ethnic or kinship groups, religious groups? Why have the term and concept of "tribe" recently been challenged? Does the use of this term have any contemporary relevance?

3. What are some of the ways in which ethnic groups change their boundaries? What is the difference between assimilation, acculturation, ascription, fission, and fusion? How are these concepts related to ethnic social boundaries?

4. Are most of the marriage patterns in Africa monogamous or polygynous? From the societal or the individual point of view? In cases where a man may have more than one wife, does this mean that there are more women than men in the community? How might arranged marriages lead to linkage within or between social communities? Does it matter whether the communities are nuclear families, extended families, lineages, clans, or ethnic groups?

5. In a matrilineal descent system, what would you expect to be the role of women? Would a woman's brother, father, or husband be of most importance in her life? What would happen if a matrilineal and a patrilineal ethnic group became integrated?

6. Does it make sense to speak of ethnic communities having no government? Do all communities need some form of institutionalized decision-making procedure? What have been some of the largest-scale traditional communities in Africa? Are they based on divine kingship? elected representation? Islamic vice-regency? participatory democracy? or some other criteria?

7. Do you think the major economic problems in traditional Africa have to do with poor soil, lack of technology, poor climatic conditions, poor social organization, or some other factors? What is meant by pastoralism? Do most African markets link up different ethnic groups, or are they found only within a single ethnic group?

8. What is meant by "tonal language"? How might this be adapted to "drum language"? How do you think Africans of different ethnic groups communicate, if at all, with each other? What is meant by bilingualism? multilingualism? Do you think that any of the vernacular African languages might (or should) be used at the national level?

9. Are traditional African concepts of fatalism similar to Christian or Islamic concepts of predestination? What is meant by "high god" or "minor deities" in African religions? Do you see any parallel between African traditional religious beliefs and Greek mythology? To what extent does African mythology result in an oral literature dealing with the exploits of the gods? What is meant by "reverence for ancestors"? Are ancestors considered to be alive?

10. What are the major categories of African oral literature? In what situations would one find the telling of stories? What are some of the reasons so many of the African languages are not written? Does this affect the quality of the literature? To what extent does modern African literature draw on traditional oral literature? What is the basis of the animal symbolism in many of the African proverbs or stories?

11. What are the major forms of visual art in Africa? Why? What are the attitudes held by traditional Africans regarding their own sculpture? How is African traditional art utilized by the ethnic community? Why have certain kinds of visual art been less common in the Islamic parts of Africa? How does music play a part of African traditional life? Are musicians professional? Is singing always a part of dancing?

12. What are the features of African society and culture which pertain most widely across the continent? On what features does one find the greatest range

of patterns? Do you think it is possible to speak of "African society and culture"? What features are most (or least) similar to American society and culture? Do you believe that culture is inherited or learned or both? How would you argue your position? What are the major similarities and differences between Islamic and non-Islamic portions of Africa?

13. What aspects, if any, of African cultural life do you think have been omitted from these modules? Does any of the contemporary autobiographical writing by African novelists help provide insights into African culture and society (for example child-rearing)?

14. Do you think that environmental factors are of major importance in shaping cultural patterns? What would be the relevant environmental factors in Africa?

15. What aspects of ethnic society, if any, would you expect to change most rapidly in modern times? (e.g., language shift? modification of marriage patterns? reorientation of economic pursuits? decay of traditional political authority? secularization of conceptual systems?)

II

Perspectives
on the Past

Modules	Suggested Readings in *Essays*
Early Physical and Human Development 17 Continental Origins and Physical Character 18 The Evolution of Man in Africa 19 Ecological Adaptation and Diffusion of Agriculture 20 Early Culture and State Formation	2 The African Setting *(Soja and Paden)* 9 Major Themes in African History *(Rowe)*
The Growth of African States 21 The Impact of Islam in Africa 22 Empires of the Western Sudan 23 Coastal States of East Africa 24 States of the Central Sudan 25 Indigenous Kingdoms of East and Central Africa 26 Forest States of West Africa	27 Africa and the Islamic World *(Abu-Lughod)* 10 Empires and State Formation *(Holden)*
The African Slave Trade 27 Early Western Contact 28 Origins and Growth of the Slave Trade 29 Abolition and States for Freed Slaves 30 The African Legacy in the New World	11 West Africa and the Afro-Americans *(Hammond)*

Early Physical
and Human Development

Continental Origins
and Physical Character

AFRICA IS A CONTINENT of great age and physical stability, consisting primarily of a huge rigid block, higher in the east and almost entirely fringed with escarpments. It is a continent of plateaus, broadly etched by a series of depositional basins of varying size. The basins generally are filled with more recent deposits, are drained by the major river systems, and are surrounded by outcroppings of hard, ancient crystalline rocks which form part of what is called the *Basement Complex.*

This "basin and swell" structure dominates the landform pattern throughout most of the continent. The major physical feature in eastern Africa, however, is the African Rift Valley system, one of the most spectacular features on the face of the earth. The rifts consist of parallel faults enclosing a flat valley averaging 20 to 40 miles in width. The major branch of the African rift system stretches from north of the Dead Sea south to the mouth of the Zambezi, a distance of over 6,000 miles. Note the eastern and western branches in Africa, the string of rift lakes, and the associated volcanic features—Ethiopian Plateau, Kenya Highlands, Mt. Kilimanjaro (see maps in *Essays,* chap. 1).

1. ORIGINS OF THE AFRICAN CONTINENT

Most of Africa was once at the heart of a vast supercontinent called Gondwanaland (composed of most of the present African continent plus the Arabian peninsula, peninsular India, Madagascar, Antarctica, Australia, and South America). Much of this supercontinent was glaciated during an ice age about 250 million years ago. The evidence from this glaciation (boulder clays, striations in rocks)

65

supports the view that the southern continents were at that time most likely part of a single land mass. (Additional supporting evidence for grouping has been found in the patterns of rock structure, fossil similarities, and climatic changes in the geologic past.) Africa at this time had no "coast" and was probably characterized by a series of large depositional basins of interior drainage, many filled with large lakes.

Gondwanaland started to break apart during the Cretaceous Period (about 200 million years ago) and the continents slowly began to take their present shape (although drifting is still an ongoing process). Evidence for continental drifting has always been impressive and theories of continental drift appeared almost as soon as accurate maps of the world were produced. (Note the startling jig-saw-puzzle fit of West Africa and eastern South America—but also note that the edges to fit together are not the present shorelines but the rims of the continental shelves, the true edges of the continents.) A systematic theory of continental drift was presented by Wegener in 1910, but despite the mass of evidence from Wegener and others (especially du Toit), the theory was disregarded since no one could effectively explain *how* the continents drifted apart. In recent years, however, more evidence has accumulated and a mechanism for drifting has been discovered, leading one geophysicist to state that research "should now be turned from the question of whether drift has occurred to the manner in which it has occurred." References to these recent discoveries are found in the *Bibliography* (see Wilson, 1963; Sullivan, 1967; Hurley *et al.*, 1967; and Hurley, 1968).

2. IMPACT OF CONTINENTAL BREAKUP
AND SUBSEQUENT GEOLOGIC CHANGES

As Gondwanaland began to split apart, the marginal blocks drifted away and the African coast came into existence. Rapid erosion occurred along the new continental margins, which were uplifted due to the removal of so much material from alongside them. Existing streams were "rejuvenated" and new marginal streams created. More recent geological activity, not directly associated with drifting, resulted in the tilting of the great African block, most intensely in the east and south, creating the basic division into High and Low Africa. These movements were accompanied by extensive rifting and volcanic activity (see de Blij, 1964); new basins (e.g., for Lake Victoria) were created and existing ones modified. The rejuvenated streams caused both by the continental breakup and by this more recent geological activity resulted in many changes in drainage patterns. Small rivers were often able rapidly to extend their headwaters back from the coast to "capture" portions of interior drainage systems, thus providing an outlet to the sea for these areas and draining many of the old interior lakes. Most of the great river systems of Africa are composites of several streams of the past and are typically characterized by waterfalls and rapids near their ocean outlets, where they plunge over the edge of the African escarpment. These features hindered penetration from the coast into the interior in more recent human history, but at the same time they provide Africa with enormous hydroelectric potential for future development.

3. THE FACE OF MODERN AFRICA

Evidence of these developments in Africa's geologic history can be seen today in the five major river basins which occupy a large proportion of the continent. (See the map of Major Physiographic Features, *Essays,* p. 22).

a. Niger Basin

The Inland Niger Delta above Timbuktu suggests that the Niger River, which today rises in the Fouta Jallon, just 200 miles from the sea, once flowed into a lake or larger swampland in the center of the present basin. This area was drained by a new stream, cutting back from the coast through the rim of the basin, capturing the Upper Niger to form the unusual course of the river today, with its 90° bend at the old delta. The same pattern of "capture" is shown in upper reaches of the Benue, the Niger's main tributary. The Benue has partially captured some of the drainage flowing north to Lake Chad and is probably still doing so. Note also the flow of the Senegal and the Gambia. Both originate close to the Niger, parallel it for some distance toward the center of the basin, then turn abruptly to the Atlantic coast, the Senegal passing through an area of near-desert. Further evidence of these changes is seen in the pattern of great waterless valleys at the southern edge of the Sahara, showing drainage into the Niger during a less dry period in the past.

b. Chad Basin

Lake Chad, which now ranges from about 10,000 to 25,000 square kilometers in size, was once part of a much larger lake which covered about 400,000 square kilometers two to three million years ago and even more recently. The larger lake, traceable today in a series of beach ridges, probably centered on the Bodélé depression, the lowest part of the basin, which is connected to the present Lake Chad by the wadi Bahr el Ghazal.

Despite these changes, however, the Chad Basin today probably has more of its ancient geologic character than any of the other major basins. It still lies at the heart of the continent and has no ocean outlet.

c. Congo Basin

The Congo River, with its narrow outlet to the sea, is studded with a series of rapids and falls that have some of the greatest potentials for hydroelectric development in the world. In the distant geologic past the main stream probably flowed northwest to Lake Chad and the Bodélé depression, but movements contemporaneous with the formation of the Rift Valley created the Congo-Chad watershed and dammed up a vast lake (remnants of which include the present Lac Léopold II). The upper Lualaba once flowed to the Nile but was captured by the lower Lualaba to form the Upper Congo. (The narrow gorge at Portes d'Enfer—"Gates of Hell"—at Kongolo is the site of this capture.) The segments eventually linked up with the Lower Congo, draining the ancient lake, and creating the present course of the river.

d. Nile Basin

The White Nile breaks through the downwarped Lake Victoria basin, moves through the vast swamps of the Southern Sudan, and joins with the Blue Nile near the present city of Khartoum. The Nile then completes its 4000-mile course to the Mediterranean over a series of six cataracts in the Northern Sudan and southern Egypt. The heart of the ancient basin is probably the previously mentioned swampland, called the Sudd (Arabic for "obstruction"), while the famous cataracts mark the exit of the river from the basin and its remarkable seaward journey: over 1,000 miles without a single important tributary through an extremely arid landscape.

e. Zambezi-Kalahari

The Zambezi, navigable in its upper courses, breaks through the rim of its ancient basin in the Victoria Falls and gorge (343 feet as compared to 165 for Niagara) and then flows 900 miles to the sea, with many rapids along the way. Its headwaters in the past probably fed the interior basin now occupied by the Okovango Swamps and Makarikari Salt Flats, but were redirected either through stream capture or blockage by its own alluvium. This pattern is duplicated by the smaller Cunene River, which rises on the plateau, similarly cuts through the plateau edge (in Rio Cuna Falls), and moves away from its former course (which most likely was to Etosha Pan). The fact that the Zambezi flows across the grain of High Africa to the Indian Ocean probably reflects the drifting away of Madagascar which created an opening to the coast. This also explains the unusually extensive (for Africa) coastal plain of Mozambique and the absence there of the characteristic coastal escarpment (which is displaced into the interior along the eastern boundary of Rhodesia). The southern portion of the basin is drained by the Orange River, which breaks through the basin rim at Aughrabies Falls.

18

The Evolution of Man in Africa

FROM EXISTING EVIDENCE, it appears that man's ancestors first became differentiated from the primates in Africa, probably in the wooded savanna areas of eastern Africa. Recent archaeological finds in the Omo Valley of Ethiopia suggest that this occurred at least three million years ago.

But in defining man, where is the line to be drawn between ape and man? Put more appropriately, at what point on the ancestral stem did the Pongid and Hominid branches diverge? (See the top section of Figure 5.) The question is difficult to answer simply from a study of fossil features, since the definition of *man* generally depends more on mental than physical attributes (e.g., man as toolmaker, or as having power of speech). But how can this be determined from archaeological evidence? Today, the most acceptable definition of *man* includes the making of cutting tools; the ability to walk, stand, and run in an upright position without difficulty; a prolonged period of dependency on the parent; and other related characteristics. The precise division between man-apes and apemen is thus likely to remain a rather controversial subject. (Good introductions to human evolution in Africa can be found in Bishop and Clark, 1966; and Howell and Bourliere, 1966.)

1. A CLASSIFICATION OF HIGHER PRIMATES

Several views on this question are depicted in Figure 5. Through natural selection, *Homo sapiens* is all that remains of the Hominid line today. Whether there was a single line of evolution to *Homo sapiens* or one with many branches representing Hominid forms which became extinct is still being debated. The earliest Hominids include the following.

1. Australopithecus Africanus: This very early form was probably omnivorous, small, lightly built, more adapted to life in open country, and possibly a toolmaker in later stages.

2. Australopithecus Robustus: (Often a separate genus, *Paranthropus.*) This Hominid type was much larger, more "robust," and apelike. His huge molars show he was probably a vegetarian, more adapted to a forest environment.

3. Zinjanthropus: Often called "Nutcracker Man" because of the huge size of his molars. (*Zinj* was an early name for East Africa.) Now this type is generally considered another form of *Australopithecus robustus.*

4. Homo Habilis: "Handy Man" existed side-by-side with *Zinjanthropus* nearly two million years ago and, like *Australopithecus africanus* (which some archaeologists consider subsumes *Homo habilis*) in relation to *Australopithecus robustus*, it disappeared earlier than its "cousin," probably after having evolved into a higher form of Hominid. *Homo habilis* was probably the earliest toolmaker.

FIGURE 5

THE EVOLUTION OF MAN

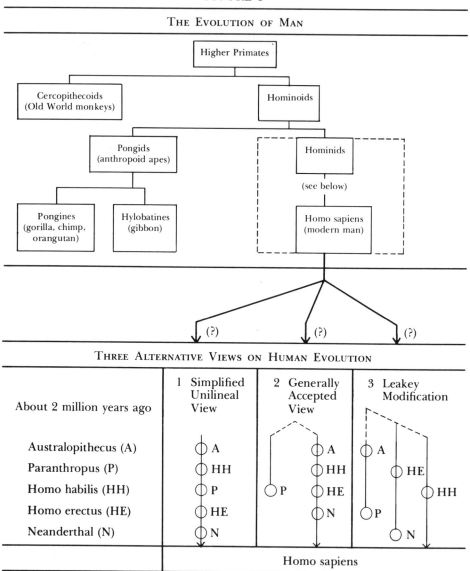

THREE ALTERNATIVE VIEWS ON HUMAN EVOLUTION

About 2 million years ago	1 Simplified Unilineal View	2 Generally Accepted View	3 Leakey Modification
Australopithecus (A)	A	A	A
Paranthropus (P)	HH	HH	HE
Homo habilis (HH)	P	P HE	HH
Homo erectus (HE)	HE	N	P
Neanderthal (N)	N		N
	Homo sapiens		

5. *Homo Erectus:* The hand-ax maker of the Early Stone Age is also called *Pithecanthropus*. This type probably existed around 300,000 years ago in Africa and was the creator of the Acheulian hand-ax culture. He occupied mainly open country, camping near lake shores and rivers. Some areas where remains have been found include Algeria, Morocco, Chad, Tanzania, Indonesia, and China (the Asian examples being somewhat younger). Many of the most important archaeological finds of *Australopithecus robustus* (i.e., *Zinjanthropus*), *Homo habilis,* and *Homo erectus* were made by the Leakeys at Olduvai Gorge in

Tanzania. The gorge, with its exposed beds filled with fossils, provides a virtually unbroken record of human evolution to modern man, including the best and most continuous evidence on the evolution of early tools. It has been called a "reference book to the human past" and remains so despite many recent archaeological discoveries in Africa and elsewhere. (See Leakey, 1961, and his articles in Bishop and Clark, 1966, and Howell and Bourliere, 1966.)

Homo erectus is followed by generalized *Homo*, which gave rise to many offshoots (Rhodesian Man, and probably Neanderthal) and to *Homo sapiens* (around 35,000 years ago). During this evolutionary period of over one million years, *Homo erectus* and his hand-ax culture spread throughout much of the Old World. Although many early Hominid forms have been found outside of Africa, all existing evidence points to the conclusion that Africa, particularly East Africa, was the major center for the physical and technological development of man during at least the first million years of his existence. "And there is little doubt that throughout all but the last small fraction of this long development of the human form, Africa remained [culturally] at the centre of the inhabited world" (Oliver and Fage, *A Short History of Africa*, 1962).

2. THE EARLY EVOLUTION OF HUMAN SOCIETY IN AFRICA

Perhaps reflecting some of the first variations in Hominid ways of life, early man became differentiated very largely by the major type of environment he occupied (especially forest *vs.* grassland). The different demands of each environment are reflected, in part, in man's physical evolution but much more clearly in the development of man's toolkit. These developments took place during the late Pleistocene Period, when wet and dry phases alternated in Africa reflecting the retreat and advance of the great ice sheet covering much of Europe (mainly 50,000 to 25,000 years ago). It was also during this period that modern man distinctly emerged. The following is a brief outline of developments from this period to the arrival of Iron Age technology and agriculture in Africa.

a. Middle and Upper Paleolithic (Old Stone Age)

Stone Age cultures displaced "hand-ax" culture with a wide variety of tools, made in new forms and of new materials. Bows and arrows and even the first cosmetics made their appearance. During this period there were three developments of special importance. First were the *Sangoan toolkits* which reflected man's penetration into the woodland fringe of the rainforest regions of the Congo and Guinea Coast (also near Lake Victoria and the Zambezi). Specialized tools were developed for digging and gathering wild plants. Second, were the *Fauresmith* developments, being a somewhat less specialized evolution from hand-ax culture by those who remained in the open country from Ethiopia to the Cape. Many settled down near permanent streams and became fishermen. Third were the *Aterian* developments, which were found in North Africa and Sahara.

b. Later Stone Age

The Later Stone Age cultures represented a further differentiation between forest cultures and those found in more open country. This period began with the onset of drier conditions throughout much of Africa about 11,000 years ago and lasted until the arrival of an Iron Age technology and agriculture (at different times in different places). This period is noted for the occupation by various hunting groups of a very large area of the continent including widely varying environments (Daniels, 1966). Highly specialized technologies were developed with respect to these environments. Many of these technologies, some scholars feel, were overly specialized and inflexible, and therefore unable to adapt easily to the new technology of agriculture and settled life which was introduced later.

c. The Development of Basic Racial Stocks

Physical anthropologists cannot reliably recognize racial differences simply from examining skeletal remains. Furthermore, it is now evident that different racial features evolve at different rates. There must have been "races" of prehistoric man, for example, but there is insufficient evidence (skeletal or otherwise) to differentiate them. Similarly, although it is generally believed that the major racial differences of contemporary man evolved with the development of *Homo sapiens* from about 35,000 years ago, it is very difficult to discern the exact patterns of development or to link these patterns with the earlier forms of man.

Four broad racial stocks are conventionally identified in Africa. The first is the *Bushmanoid* type, ancestors of the present-day Bushman. They were probably the dominant type to emerge in the Upper Paleolithic Period. They extended from the Sahara through Ethiopia, and from eastern Africa to the Cape, mainly occupying open country. Most scholars feel they evolved in the north and moved south.

Second were the *Negroid* type, whose origins are still obscure. Early Negroid stock probably evolved in the heavily forested regions of western and central Africa but became distinct primarily on the fringes of the forest. As fishermen, they had a more settled way of life than the Bushman or Pygmy types. As with the Caucasoid type, they were well placed to take advantage of later developments in agriculture.

Third were the *Pygmoid* type, which remain a major enigma with regard to origins. Scholars are still undecided whether they evolved from Bushman or Negroid stock or are a totally separate group.

Fourth were the *Caucasoid* type which emerged in North and East Africa about 10,000 years ago. Again, their origins are still obscure (either northeast Africa or southwest Asia). They were closely linked with early Negroid types in the Sudan.

It should be stressed, however, that this typology is now considered far too broad and poorly defined to describe racial differences in Africa. Patterns of migration and intermarriage have created such a mixture of races in Africa (and elsewhere) that the above classification can only have value as an extremely generalized attempt to convey some of the major dimensions of racial differentiation on the continent (see *Essays,* chap. 2; Bishop, 1967; and Hiernaux, 1968).

19

Ecological Adaptation and Diffusion of Agriculture

THE DEVELOPMENT OF AGRICULTURE initiated one of the most significant "revolutions" in human history. It led to major changes in man's relationship with his environment and in his social, economic, and political organization and behavior. The emphasis in this module is on how agriculture evolved in Africa, how it spread throughout the continent, and how this affected subsequent developments in terms of both space and time. Interesting correlations exist, for example, between modern patterns of rural population density and the historical developments described in this module. Also, the spread of major migrations is basic to understanding present patterns of language and ethnic groups. A good population density map should be available to students during the discussion to illustrate these relationships (see, for example, the population map in *Essays,* chap. 2).

1. EARLY CENTERS OF PLANT AND ANIMAL DOMESTICATION

There were probably at least four different centers of early plant and animal domestication. The first was in southwest Asia in the foothills of the Fertile Crescent. This is generally considered to be the oldest center of agricultural development in the world. Radiocarbon dating indicates that Semitic peoples (Afro-Asiatic language family) began to produce wheat and barley as major crops in that area as early as 9000 B.C.

The second area was in southeast Asia, in the well-watered river valleys where Mongoloid peoples developed rice agriculture (along with many other important crops). Very recent evidence suggests that this center may eventually prove to be even older than that in southwest Asia.

The third area was in the New World, between Mexico and Peru. Here the American Indian population developed maize and potatoes.

The fourth area may have been in Africa. This is still very controversial, yet many scholars feel that domestication of certain food crops developed independently among the Mande-speaking peoples of the Western Sudan and possibly in Ethiopia as well. Other scholars feel this development was the result of diffusion from the Nile Valley or North Africa.

2. THE SPREAD OF AGRICULTURE IN AFRICA

a. Phase I

Cereal agriculture was developed in the Lower Nile Valley and the Fayum Depression. The diffusion from southwest Asia (about 5000 to 4000 B.C.) of wheat and barley eventually resulted in Africa's first "population explosion." Probably less than 20,000 hunters and gatherers could have occupied the Lower Nile area before the introduction of agriculture, yet by about 3000 B.C., the labor force for pyramid-building alone exceeded 100,000. Today, Egypt is still one of the most densely populated areas in the world.

Population growth was accompanied by widespread urbanization and the development of more elaborate forms of social, economic, and political organization. Populations spread slowly through Africa north of the Sahara and up the Nile Valley, perhaps as far south as modern Khartoum. The impact of the Sahara desert as a "barrier" or as a "bridge" is still not fully understood. It is generally thought that the Sahara was capable of supporting both agriculture and pastoralism until approximately 2000 B.C., at which time desert conditions had become firmly established. Some feel that interaction between Negroid populations on the southern Sahara fringe and the population of the Nile Valley existed, with innovations flowing in *both* directions. This may have created what one author claims is "the first contact of major cultures in human history," as Egypt succeeded in fusing Negro and Semitic cultures (Wiedner, 1962). Recent radiocarbon dates show that true Neolithic culture had reached the Algeria-Niger border region by 3500 B.C.

b. Phase II

Agriculture was developed in the Sudanic belt from the Atlantic Ocean to the Ethiopian Highlands. The timing is still very controversial. It is often dated 2500 to 1000 B.C. (Oliver, 1966) but may have been much earlier (Murdock, 1959, with relatively little evidence, suggests 5000 B.C.). Basic agricultural knowledge is generally felt to have come from Egypt, although the implementation of these ideas depended upon the domestication of suitable drought-resistant cereals of the savanna grasslands (e.g., sorghums, millets, and, in the west, dry rice). These developments resulted in a second, but much slower, build-up of population in Black Africa. It did not, however, lead to the growth of social and political organizations of a very large scale, as in the Nile Valley, but, in general, took place in small linguistic "compartments" with little mutual interaction. Much of this development was confined to the Sudanic belt, hemmed in on the north by the progressively drying Sahara and on the south by the equatorial forests, where savanna crops were unsuitable. The Nile swamps (Sudd) probably prevented direct spread to eastern African grasslands, but small groups of agriculturists began to appear (after 1000 B.C.) in various localities from present-day Kenya south to Zambia and southern Angola. This was most likely the result of the spread of Ethiopian forms of millet (eleusine) and sorghum. These pockets of agricultural settlement were to play an important role in the next phase of development (Bantu migrations). The more humid regions of Africa (Congo Basin, Guinea Coast, Great Lakes region, parts of the Zambezi Valley) were to remain mainly hunting and gathering areas, with perhaps some form of vegeculture (based on yams and the oil palm), until the beginning of the Christian era. Compared to the African savanna, there has been a general lack of indigenous food plants in the African rainforests. The settlement of the rainforests over the past 2,000 years has therefore depended to a greater extent on the introduction of food crops from outside these areas.

c. Phase III

Bantu migrations and the spread of agriculture to the humid areas are of major significance to present population distributions in Africa. The spread of agriculture to the more humid regions has been linked to a combination of three factors: the introduction of southeast Asian crops to Africa; the growth of an Iron Age technology; and the migration of the Bantu-speaking peoples, who now occupy nearly all of Africa south of the equator. (As noted in Module 11, Bantu is a linguistic term. The people who speak the language, although basically black-skinned, display a wide range of physical and cultural characteristics.) Where the Bantu came from originally and how they spread is still the subject of heated debate among African historians. A widely accepted outline of the stages of Bantu expansion is given in the following section, based on the work of Oliver (1966). As is true of most statements involving African history and prehistory, new information may result in major modifications (see Guthrie, 1962; Clark, 1962; Fagan, 1961, 1963, 1965; Posnansky, 1968; and Hiernaux, 1968).

3. STAGES IN THE MIGRATION OF THE BANTU

a. Pre-Bantu Speakers

Speakers of a language which eventually gave birth to most of the present forms of Bantu probably migrated from central Cameroon or the Ubangi-Shari woodlands into the woodlands south of the Congo forest. Migrants, following the Congo waterways, entered an area very much like their homeland where familiar crops could be grown. The woodland region, in present Katanga, was an excellent hunting and fishing territory and contained abundant mineral resources (iron and copper). This *Bantu nucleus* (Guthrie, 1962) becomes the center of population growth and diffusion.

b. Consolidation of Settlement

Consolidation of settlement and population growth resulted in the establishment of a bridgehead outward from the nucleus to the Atlantic Ocean coast. The ancestral Bantu became much more like their contemporary descendants, basing their strength on a new iron technology and an expanding number of cereal foods adopted from East African agriculturalists. The spread of Iron-Age technology permitted improvements in woodworking and in the production of boats, tools, and weapons, which were especially useful in hunting and fishing. Iron technology probably came either from the Nile Valley (Merowe) or across the Sahara from North Africa and spread first through the Sudanic belt, slowly filtering southward into the forests. (Peoples of the well-known Nok culture, in what is today Nigeria, were smelting iron before the fourth century B.C.)

c. Southeast Asian Influences

The introduction of southeast Asian food crops permitted an expansion from the woodlands into the more heavily forested areas. Contact with the East African coast brought in the banana, the coconut, and the outrigger canoe (A.D. 1 to 500) from Indonesian migrants who had begun to colonize Madagascar (still part of the Malayo-Polynesian language area) and parts of the coast during the first few centuries A.D. East Africa by this time was probably occupied by sufficient numbers of cultivators to absorb both the Indonesian migrants and their crops. Banana cultivation in particular resulted in a rapid population increase in the Great Lakes region from A.D. 500 to 1000.

d. Colonization of Central and Southern Africa

Bantu-speaking populations moved into the highlands and plateaus of present-day Kenya and Tanzania, while pastoral Bantu (e.g., the Zulu) pushed progressively farther south. There was a more gradual colonization of both the very dry and the very humid regions, which today contain the greatest number of remnant populations (hunters, pastoralists, and some agriculturalists who preceded the Bantu but who have been almost totally absorbed). See the linguistic map in Berry (*Essays,* chap. 5) for remnant groups: Pygmies (who speak Bantu languages now), Bushmen, Hottentots, Hatsa, Sandawe, Iraqw, Gorowa, Tatog, and Dorobo. Many of the more recent Bantu migrants in southern Africa also have "clicks" (from Bushman-Hottentot languages) in their languages. In the areas of relatively recent colonization are found a tremendous variety of physical types and cultures, even among people who speak basically the same language.

It should be re-emphasized that this outline is a tentative one which is not necessarily subscribed to by all historians. New evidence and interpretations have already suggested modifications in both the broad framework and in specific details. The African Iron Age remains a robust source of archaeological research interest, and it is likely to spawn many new and challenging discoveries if sufficient funding permits the required field excavations.

20

Early Culture
and State Formation

1. AFRICA AND EGYPT

THE QUESTION OF THE INTERRELATIONSHIPS between ancient Egypt and the rest of Africa has been one of the most tantalizing as well as one of the most perplexing in African history. An effective overview of this problem is given in Collins (1968, pp. 7–62).

For example, who were the ancient Egyptians? There have been strong claims that the ancient Egyptians were Negroes (Diop, 1962), although many scholars feel it is more likely that Egypt was a melting pot of races. To make *any* racial claims (black or white) to the accomplishments of Egyptian civilization is likely to be either irrelevant or inaccurate.

The question of Egyptian influence in Africa beyond the Nile Valley is another controversial subject, but is perhaps a useful way of introducing the question of diffusion *vs.* independent invention in Africa. Some have attributed all early African achievements to the migration of a super-race of "Hamites" (Seligman, 1966, originally published in 1930). This view has now been totally rejected, but it was first replaced by the notion of a diffusion of ideas and institutions (rather than people) from the Nile Valley. More recently, a much greater emphasis has been placed on independent innovation in Black Africa. Collins notes, for example, that:

> Dynastic Egypt was born in the womb of Neolithic Africa. Its ideas and institutions undoubtedly flowed to the south and west against the stream of Negroid, African

culture moving east and north toward the Nile Valley. Independent in origin, syncretic in development, Africa should claim a unique, not a synthetic past (Collins, 1968, p. 10).

2. KINGDOMS OF THE NILE VALLEY

The Nile Valley forms a fertile corridor which cuts across the prevailing east-west grain of environmental zones in Africa, thus linking the Lower Nile and the Mediterranean coast, north of the desert, with the Sudanic belt, stretching from the Atlantic coast to the Ethiopian Highlands south of the Sahara. Whatever the importance of independent invention, these routes (north-south along the Nile, east-west along the Sudanic belt) became the most important early channels for cultural diffusion in Africa. And in or near the area where the two routes meet, the earliest African kingdoms south of the Mediterranean and Lower Nile regions were established.

a. The Kingdom of Kush

During the pharaonic period of Egypt, the Middle Nile region of Nubia (in present-day Northern Sudan and southern Egypt) became vassal to the Egyptians. In about the eighth century B.C., the peoples of this region revolted and established the kingdom of Kush, with its capital at Napata. The rulers of Kush eventually conquered Egypt, ruled for about 100 years (as the Twenty-fifth Dynasty of Pharaohs), and Napata briefly became the capital of the ancient world.

After the Assyrian invasion of Egypt (seventh century B.C.), Kush became reoriented southward and its capital shifted to Merowe, about 100 miles north of Khartoum. The Kushites had learned ironworking by about 500 B.C. (perhaps from the Assyrians) and succeeded in establishing a flourishing trading empire, focused on Merowe, which reached its peak from about the middle of the third century B.C. into the early Christian era. The Kushites developed a distinct alphabet, elaborated advanced architectural forms, and engaged in trade with Africa south of the Sahara, with the Mediterranean basin, and with the Indian subcontinent. The fall of Merowe occurred around A.D. 325, when the armies of the Ethiopian kingdom of Axum invaded.

b. The Kingdom of Axum

The modern kingdom of Ethiopia is derived from an unbroken line of succession from the kingdom of Axum, located in the northern section of the Ethiopian Highlands. Legend records that the first emperor of Ethiopia, Menelik I, was the product of a marriage between King Solomon and the Queen of Sheba. By the seventh century A.D. the commercial interests of Axum ranged as far as India and Ceylon. The conversion of the Axumite kingdom to Coptic

Christianity in about the fourth century A.D. was important in several respects. The culture and civilization of the Amharic people is derived largely from this influence. Also, with the Muslim conquest of the Red Sea area in the seventh century, the Amharic people retreated into the Ethiopian Highlands, from which isolation they were not to emerge until the Portuguese expedition to Ethiopia in 1541. The early kingdom of Axum was notable for its skill in dry-stone building, hillside terrace cultivation, and for the development of written forms of communication.

c. Contacts with the Sudanic Belt

Some African historians feel that after the defeat of Merowe by Axum the royal family of Kush retreated westward along the Sudanic belt, spreading not only their technology but their social and political institutions (e.g., a strongly centralized political structure based on the concept of divine kingship). The following points, however, are important to remember about this view: it has not been entirely accepted by historians; it has often led to the neglect of other important developments, such as independent innovation in Africa south of the Sahara and alternate routes of diffusion across the Sahara from the Mediterranean coast; the political structures supposedly diffused from Merowe are so widespread in Africa that it may be more reasonable to view Kush as merely one local example of a general African phenomenon; and there still are enormous gaps in our knowledge which are only beginning to be filled in (primarily through archaeological research).

3. NOK CIVILIZATION

In 1944, near the tin mines of the Middle Belt region of Nigeria, a terracotta head was discovered. Later excavation in the region revealed further specimens which appear to indicate that a civilization of farmers and probably ironworkers existed in the area from about 500 B.C. to A.D. 200. A comparison between the later bronzes of Ife (in Yorubaland) and the Nok terracotta figures indicates many stylistic and cultural similarities. The origin of the Yoruba kingdoms is still obscure, but there is some speculation that a group who were to become the ruling class of the Yoruba people migrated southward into Nigeria toward the end of the Nok era and established themselves over the people who had produced the Nok terracotta figures. Willett suggests that:

> As yet there is no direct evidence of who these people were, where they came from, or when. They seem to have come from the east or the northeast, possibly from Meroe, which collapsed in the early fourth century. . . . The Yoruba migration legends, both those about their origin and those of diffusion within Nigeria, almost certainly refer only to the ruling group. . . .

Yoruba civilization appears therefore to be the result of a small intrusive ruling class, bringing ideas from outside, with a highly artistic indigenous population. The resulting social pattern seems to have borne some resemblance to that of the City States of Ancient Greece, but the unique achievement of the Yoruba was to have possessed such an evolved urban civilization without the knowledge of writing (Willett, 1960).

There are still many unanswered questions about the Nok civilization. Who were the people? Did they develop agriculture independently? Where did they obtain their knowledge of ironworking? It seems likely that further research in this area will produce some major discoveries on early African history, particularly with respect to early patterns of culture contact—not only with the Nile Valley but perhaps with other areas of Africa and even beyond. For example, it is becoming increasingly evident now that ironworking among Nok peoples almost certainly spread from Carthage across the Sahara. (See Fagg, 1963, for photographs of the Nok figures and the equally magnificent sculpture of Yorubaland which succeeded the Nok culture.)

The Growth of African States

The Impact of Islam
in Africa

1. WHAT IS ISLAM?

THERE ARE SEVERAL POINTS to be noted in summarizing the nature of Islam (for further details, see Gibb, 1961). The first is that Islam was established in the seventh century A.D. by the Prophet Muhammad in what is now Saudi Arabia. A person who follows the religion of Islam is called a *Muslim* (note that the English spelling is often *Moslem*). Essentially, Islam is built on the Christian and Judaic tradition but added a new revelation from God (Allah) to Muhammad, which came to be called the Koran (or *Qur'an*). There are five requirements or pillars of faith in Islam.

The first requirement of Islam is *witness*, i.e., a person must make a declaration of faith in the unity or singleness of God and the prophethood of Muhammad. (Muhammad is regarded as the "Messenger"—*Rasul*—of God). This declaration is sometimes called the *shahada*. It consists of the statement: "There is no god but God and Muhammad is His prophet." ("La ilaha illallahu, muhammadu Rasulullahi.")

The second requirement is *prayer*. There are five ritual prayers which must be said every day while facing toward Mecca. The times set for prayer are daybreak, noon, midafternoon, just after sunset, and the early part of the night. On Friday, prayers are said in a central mosque (church) in all major Muslim towns. On weekdays, prayers are usually said individually, wherever the person happens to be at the appropriate time.

The third requirement is *fasting*. It is prescribed that during one month out of

81

the year, which is called the month of *Ramadan* (the ninth month of the lunar year; Muslims follow a lunar calendar), it is required that there be complete abstinence from food and drink during the hours of daylight. People can eat and drink only at night. Ill persons, travelers, children, and several other categories of persons are exempted from fasting.

The fourth requirement is giving *charity* (alms). Alms are normally given to poor people or to learned religious men (*ulama*) who distribute it to the poor. There are certain obligations as to what portion of your income must go to the poor, normally set at one-fortieth of a person's annual revenue in money or in goods.

The fifth requirement (for those who are able) is to make a *pilgrimage* (called *hajj*) to the sacred mosque of Mecca in Arabia. This is done during the twelfth month (*Zulhajj*) of the lunar year. Muslims from all over the world participate in ceremonies of remembrance and atonement centered around the *kaaba* (a large monument in Mecca) and other sacred places. A person may go on pilgrimage as many times as he is able. (A person who has been to Mecca is frequently called *Al-hajj*.)

In sub-Saharan Africa, the two requirements of Islam that became of central importance were the declaration of faith in God and His Messenger Muhammad, and, secondly, the requirement of prayer. A standard way of asking if a person in Black Africa is Muslim is to ask whether he "prays." It should be noted that there is no "priesthood" in Islam, and every Muslim is regarded as equal in the sight of God.

2. THE SPREAD OF ISLAM TO NORTH AFRICA

Abu-Lughod (*Essays*, chap. 27) details the way in which Islam was carried throughout the whole of North Africa during the first hundred years after the death (A.D. 632) of the Prophet Muhammad. It extended as far west as Morocco and later also penetrated into Spain. The Arab conquest of North Africa meant that Islam was imposed on the indigenous North African people who were primarily of Berber descent. One of the effects of this conquest was an arabization of the Berber areas and, to some extent, an integration of the Arab and Berber communities over the centuries. The extension of Islam into North Africa resulted in the Moorish civilization with its advanced medicine, university systems, and architecture. North Africa soon began to have its impact on West Africa—both through trans-Saharan trade and through direct conquest.

3. THE SPREAD OF ISLAM IN WEST AND EAST AFRICA

As mentioned by Abu-Lughod, in the eleventh century a movement called the Almoravids (a Berber movement based in Mauritania) assumed control of the entire region of northwest Africa and began to spread both into Spain and southwards into the Western Sudan. It conquered the established African state of Ghana in 1076. (The African successor states to Ghana, which were also Islamic-based, are discussed in Module 22. The three successor states included Ghana, Mali, and Songhai. These are also discussed in Holden, *Essays*, chap. 10.) Fuller details on the spread of Islam in West Africa, as well as details on the spread of Islam in North Africa, may be found in Trimingham (1962). The first chapter of Trimingham deals with the expansion of Islam in North Africa, including sections on the Sahara and Sudan before the coming of Islam; the Islamization of the Berbers; and the conversion of the Saharan tribes to Islam and its spread into the Sudan. The second chapter deals with the Western Sudanic states, including the Sudanic state system: the states of the Senegal, the Soninke empire of Ghana, the Mandinka of Mali, and finally the Songhai empire of Kawkaw. The third chapter deals with the Central Sudanic states: the state of Kanem-Bornu, the Hausa states, the state of Bagirmy, and the state of Waday.

For details on the spread of Islam in East Africa, see Trimingham (1964), especially the first two chapters. The first chapter has four sections: early Islamic traders and settlers; Swahili coastal states; the Portuguese interlude and aftermath; and the penetration of Islam into the interior. The second chapter includes discussions of contemporary Muslim communities; of the more recent spread of Islam; and of characteristics of East African Islam. In short, if one looks at the map of Islamic zones contained in Abu-Lughod one can see that Islam spread from northern Africa into western Africa and eastward across the Sudan — from the Western Sudan to the Central Sudan. It also spread from other sources into the Horn of Africa and southward along the eastern coastal zone of Africa.

4. THE IMPACT OF ISLAM ON AFRICAN SOCIETY

a. Legal Systems

In most areas where Islam prevailed, an Islamic legal system (*shariʿa*) was adopted which had a comprehensive range of concerns — from family law to criminal law to administrative law. Within the Islamic legal tradition there are four distinct schools. They are known as *Maliki, Shafi, Hanbali,* and *Hanafi*. Of these four, the Maliki legal system has predominated in northern and western Africa. There are a few scattered Shafi communities in East Africa, but most of the continent adopted the Maliki legal system. Ruxton (1916) has published a translation of one of the major texts in Maliki law, namely the *Mukhtasar* of Sidi Khalil. For a scholarly interpretation of Islamic law in Africa, perhaps the best source is Anderson (1954). The important thing about the Maliki legal system, as distinct from the other Islamic legal systems, is that it tends to be the most traditional and most tolerant of local customary law and practice.

As with all schools of Islamic law, however, the Maliki tradition divides human actions into five legal categories: those actions which are required, those which are recommended, those which are morally neutral, those which are discouraged, and those which are prohibited (*haram*). It should be noted that certain foods (e.g., pork) and drinks (e.g., alcohol) are prohibited by shari'a law.

b. Language and Literature

The language of the Koran is Arabic. The Arab conquest of North Africa established Arabic as the major written and spoken language there. In Islamic areas of both East and West Africa, the written use of the Arabic language (and/or vernacular languages in Arabic script) was important in religious affairs, but also in literary, political, and economic affairs. Sometimes the Arabic language would be learned only so that the Koran could be read in Arabic (translation was prohibited), whether or not it was understood by the local people. Yet in those African societies which used the Arabic script to write their own language (particularly in West Africa; for example, the Hausa, Kanuri, or Fulani) the Arabic script was used to convey the local heritage and literature of the various ethnic societies.

c. Family Structure

Islam tends to be patrilineal, that is, it stresses the male descent line and the prerogatives of the males in inheritance. Also, Islam endorses a system of plural marriage, restricting the number of legal wives to four. These cultural patterns tend to be dominant in Islamic areas. (Only the Yao of Malawi and Tanzania and a few other groups in East Africa have remained matrilineal after accepting Islam.)

d. The Sense of Community

Part of the Islamic conception of the world is a division of peoples into two categories: those who are Muslim and those who are not. The classical Islamic concept of spiritual/political community (*umma*) is based on this distinction. One of the results of establishing an Islamic culture area in Africa may have been to extend the notion of a world-wide Islamic community (*dar-al-islam*) consisting of diverse ethnic groups and people who share certain common beliefs and the ability to communicate (to some extent) in the Arabic language. Abu-Lughod notes that in modern times the concept of *dar-al-islam* may have important consequences in the political and international roles of the new African states.

22

Empires of
the Western Sudan

THERE WERE THREE MAJOR EMPIRES in the Western Sudan during the early period
(ca. eighth to sixteenth centuries A.D.): Ghana, Mali (Melle), and Songhai. Note
that the names of two of these empires, Ghana and Mali, have been taken by
modern African states, and the third, Songhai, was suggested as the name of a
proposed state in Hausaland (Niger Republic and Northern Nigeria).

1. GHANA

Holden (*Essays*, chap. 10) suggests that there is evidence of Ghana's origin as
early as the fourth century A.D. (although the standard date is the eighth
century). During this period, Ghana was a black African (Soninke) empire. However, by the mid-eleventh century (A.D. 1076 is the standard date), the Ghana
empire was conquered temporarily by the Almoravids. At this time, the empire
of Ghana was based on trade. It lay at the crossroads between the trade from salt
deposits of North Africa and the various gold deposits in West Africa. The flourishing of this kingdom is directly attributed to its position on the trade routes.
The conquest of Ghana by the Almoravids (a dark-skinned Berber people) was
important to the flow of culture between North and West Africa. Islamic culture
became established in the Ghana empire. However, for various reasons (some of
which are related to the lessening of the strength of the Almoravids in North
Africa), the empire of Ghana declined in the eleventh, twelfth, and thirteenth
centuries and was finally incorporated totally into the rising empire of Mali.

It is important to mention the assertion that the Akan peoples of contemporary
Ghana (which is more than a thousand miles to the south and east of the old
empire) were descendant from the mixture of peoples which comprised the
empire of Ghana. While the Ghana empire undoubtedly influenced the areas.
to the south, there is no evidence of an actual migration of peoples.

2. MALI

The empire of Mali grew from the small Mandingo (Malinke) state of Kangaba, largely through the efforts of its first great king, Sundiata. In A.D. 1235 he
annexed the Susu empire to the north, and then defeated the Ghana empire.
The Muslim empire of Mali was centered in two main cities, Niane and Kangaba,
but expanded later to include Timbuktu and Jenne. These latter two cities
helped to stimulate the trans-Saharan trade and, by the year 1400, there were

caravan routes of major proportions across the west-central Sahara. (There are reports of a single caravan train of over 12,000 camels.) The wealth of the rulers of Mali became legendary both in the Middle East and in Europe, especially after one ruler, Mansa Musa, made the pilgrimage to Mecca about A.D. 1324. He took thousands of Malians with him and large quantities of gold, which he lavishly gave away to charity. Mansa Musa brought back from Mecca architects and learned men, who helped build some of the mosques and palaces of Timbuktu and other cities. An Arab observer, Ibn Battuta, has written of the advanced state of learning at the University of Sankore in Timbuktu.

After Mansa Musa, the empire of Mali declined, until by the fifteenth century it had lost all its eastern territories, including Timbuktu and Jenne. These cities continued to flourish, however, under the Songhai empire.

3. SONGHAI

By the mid-fifteenth century the Songhai peoples had become well established in the middle Niger region, and had established a capital at Gao. Through a series of conquests, mainly at the expense of Mali (including the cities of Timbuktu and Jenne), the Songhai empire came to dominate the middle Niger region. One of the strongest rulers and builders of the Songhai empire during this early period was Sunni Ali, who ruled from 1464 to 1492. During the sixteenth century, under the leadership of Askia Muhammad I, the system of government and the wealth of the empire became legendary. The University of Sankore, in Timbuktu, continued to be highly advanced, and the police and banking systems were well developed. The Songhai state developed river transportation to a high degree, including the use of artificial linkage canals.

The Songhai empire was finally defeated by an invasion from Morocco in A.D. 1591. However, the Moroccans were unable to keep the empire together, and there was no strong successor state.

4. CONCLUSIONS

It should be noted that empires like Mali and Songhai at their largest were about one-third the size of the present-day United States (approximately one million square miles). Administrative skills, as well as transportation and communications technology, were necessary to the conduct of such empires. Islamic learning was particularly important in this process. The University of Sankore taught many fields of learning, and Arabic literature and sciences were very sophisticated for that time. One observer from the period, Leo Africanus, writes that books were the single largest item of trade in these black African empires.

The empires of Ghana, Mali, and Songhai were also illustrative of the processes of state formation in Sudanic West Africa. Holden (*Essays*, chap. 10) discusses the influences of Islam in all three empires. Islam provided a model for state organization, including the differentiation of bureaucracy into financial, legal, defense, and other types of ministries. Islam also provided the social contacts for the interurban trade which was so important in the growth of empires.

All three empires were dominated by horse-equipped cavalry, and this provided an important element of communication within the empires. (As noted above, Songhai also developed river transportation.) All three empires were also intermediaries on the trade routes which crossed the Sahara from North to West Africa. (Trade included books, gold, salt, other minerals, plus handicrafts.)

The time span of the three empires is also significant: each covered several centuries. Although Holden suggests that Ghana may have begun as early as the fourth century, scholarly evidence at the moment suggests that it flourished during the eighth through eleventh centuries. The empire of Mali rose and fell over the course of almost three centuries (thirteenth through fifteenth). The empire of Songhai spanned almost two centuries (fifteenth and sixteenth). These sustained and sophisticated empires have rightfully become a source of historical pride in contemporary Black Africa.

23

Coastal States
of East Africa

LIKE MUCH OF AFRICAN HISTORY, the history of coastal East Africa is constantly being modified by new research and archaeological discoveries. This module is primarily in the form of a chronological outline so as to provide some feel for the historical continuities in this region. More detailed studies of coastal history can be found in Oliver and Matthew (1963), Coupland (1938), Freeman-Grenville (1963), and Sutton (1966).

1. THE COAST PRIOR TO THE PORTUGUESE CONTACT

Trading ports probably existed along the coast even before the Christian era. The earliest important evidence on this period is found in *The Periplus of the Erythrian Sea*, a traders' handbook to the commerce of the Red Sea, the Gulf of Aden, and the Indian Ocean written, it is generally thought, about A.D. 100 by an Alexandrian Greek. The East African Coast, called Azania, was at that time only a minor backwater of the main trading areas, Arab and Graeco-Roman, but it grew rapidly in the three centuries before Portuguese contact.

a. Fourth to Eighth Centuries A.D.

Very little is known of this period. Perhaps Persia and Axum isolated the coast from the rest of the Indian Ocean trading system. Probably this period witnessed the first major absorption of black-skinned peoples (migrating Bantu). Earlier populations are not described as black.

b. Eighth to Thirteenth Centuries A.D.

Islamic influence began to grow, probably with migrations of Persians, "Syrians," and other Muslim groups. In the latter half of the period, the *Shirazis* migrated from the Persian Gulf area and from other areas along the coast and settled in a string of trading settlements, now clearly identified at such places as Pemba, Mafia, Mogadishu, and, later, Kilwa. Trade by this period was clearly reoriented from southwestern Arabia to Oman and the Persian Gulf, focusing on Baghdad (the capital and leading center of the Islamic world during this period).

c. Thirteenth to Sixteenth Centuries A.D.

This was the height of coastal civilization. The coast was now an integral part of the Islamic world, trading with the entire Indian Ocean fringe and maintaining trade contacts in China and Indonesia. There was interior trade with the African continent at least in the southern Zambia-Rhodesia-Katanga area. Major trade items included ivory, gold from Rhodesia, and copper from Katanga. This period saw the rise of major city-states at Mogadishu and Kilwa (which controlled Sofala, entrepôt to Rhodesia and Katanga). Coins were minted at Kilwa, Mogadishu, and Zanzibar, and gold from eastern Africa may have provided the source of the first English gold coins (although most East African gold went to India). Other important city-states were established at Pate and Lamu. At the end of this period, Mombasa had grown to major importance, and Kilwa was on the decline.

Important historical themes in this period include: (1) the continuity of Islamic trading cities with pre-Islamic settlements or seasonal markets; (2) the nature of Indonesian contacts in pre-Islamic times; (3) the nature of contacts with the interior; (4) the extent of Africanization of the towns by the fifteenth century.

2. FROM PORTUGUESE CONTACT TO 1840

a. The Swahili Culture

There emerged a distinctive coastal culture during the twelfth through sixteenth centuries. A language, called Swahili, developed which was primarily Bantu, with strong Arabic, Persian, and Indian influences. It was written first in Arabic script. Swahili people (a mixture of Arabs and Bantu) become important traders and were Muslims. (They probably absorbed large numbers of indigenous African groups.)

b. Portuguese "Conquest"

In 1505, the Portuguese overran Kilwa and Mombasa. Their main base was at Malindi. The result was a rapid decline of the coast, especially the southern sections. By 1569, Kilwa was almost deserted. Later, in 1593, the Portuguese moved their base to Mombasa and built Fort Jesus. The latter was sacked in 1698 by Islamic groups from Oman (Arabian peninsula), thus ending the period of Portuguese domination.

This was a bleak period in East African coastal history. The Portuguese were unable to supplant the Arabs in trade, but they did introduce new crops such as manioc (cassava) and maize which rapidly became important food staples throughout East Africa. They tried unsuccessfully to exploit the region and left it to stagnate and decay in isolation. They never even governed the coast but merely demanded acknowledgment of their sovereignty.

The Portuguese remained in coastal Mozambique and reoriented their interests to the interior (Zambezi Valley and Zimbabwe area — see Module 25).

c. The Rise of Oman, 1650-1840

The Omani Arabs grew rapidly in power in Arabia. They allied themselves with discontented elements along the East African coast and succeeded in displacing the Portuguese north of Mozambique. (Yet even the Omani Arabs did not act as "rulers" since most city-states remained virtually independent.)

During this period, the interior opened up commercially, with trade primarily in the hands of African middlemen. The major caravan route was in central Tanzania, dominated by the Nyamwezi, but branches and other routes reached Buganda (Lake Victoria region) and Katanga. Trade items included ivory, copper, and slaves. The southern route, from Kilwa to Lake Nyasa (dominated by Yao traders), became a major slaving route. The northern routes from Mombasa, the northern Tanzanian coast (Mrima) and the northern Kenya coast led, respectively, to the Kenya Highlands, the northern interior of Tanzania, and the Tana Valley in Kenya. Trade here was mainly for ivory, with the Kamba as leading middlemen.

Zanzibar emerged during this period as the leading ivory and slave market, a position it was to build upon in the next period.

3. THE RISE OF THE SULTANATE OF ZANZIBAR, 1840-1885

This period is really a prelude to European colonization. It begins with the shift of the Court of Oman to Zanzibar under Seyyid Said in 1840. From this time, the coast was brought more nearly under a unified government than ever before.

a. Growth of Slave Trade

Undoubtedly the slave trade had begun many centuries earlier, but in the nineteenth century the early trickle became a flood. The best short account is found in Alpers (1967). It focused on the Zanzibar market and was linked in part to the development of clove plantations on Zanzibar and Pemba islands. Some historians link the low population density of parts of East Africa (especially southern Tanzania) to Arab slave-trading.

b. Indian Influences

Traders from the Indian subcontinent largely controlled the financing of the slave trade and shipping from Zanzibar. Many Indians settled in Zanzibar and along the coast. (Some had been there for centuries.) In the late nineteenth century they were an important link with Britain, for they claimed British protection and were able to import British goods.

c. Other External Influences

American cotton cloth found a very large market in East Africa. However, the British were most influential, using the Sultan as an ally against the French and, later, in their effort to suppress the slave trade. According to Sutton (1966): "The widening of European interests—commercial, political and humanitarian—was the background for the opening of the later history of East Africa, both coast and interior." By the late 1880s and early 1890s, the European colonial penetration of East Africa had begun.

4. SUMMARY OF THEMES

There was a continued absence of unity, confederation, or solidified external domination of the East African coast. Instead there were a series of virtually independent city-states vacillating between cooperation and conflict. The overall linkage of the area as a trading system was largely based on Swahili and Islamic culture.

24

States of
the Central Sudan

THE MOST IMPORTANT OF THE CENTRAL SUDANIC STATES have been Bornu, the Hausa city-states, and the Fulani empire. All were located primarily in what is now northern Nigeria, and all have continued to exist, in modified form, up to the present day.

Historically, Hausaland consisted of seven major city-states, of which Kano and Katsina were the most important. These city-states were relatively autonomous, highly centralized, and dependent on trans-Saharan trade. By the fifteenth century, members of the Hausa ruling class were converting to Islam; the Hausa states have continued to be organized according to Muslim principles, more or less, since that time. Bornu, to the east, was also Islamic in principle, and a competitor with the Hausa states for trans-Saharan trade. In the early nineteenth century, a revolution of oppressed social classes overthrew the Hausa ruling class (although they failed to conquer Bornu), but much of the governmental organization remained unchanged under the Fulani leadership which emerged. Under British rule there were few basic alterations in the system of government which had existed both in Bornu and the Hausa-Fulani states for a thousand years. All three of the Central Sudanic states were large-scale, were sustained over long periods of time, drew heavily on Islamic culture, and had written forms of communication based on Arabic script or language.

1. THE KANURI EMPIRE OF BORNU

Bornu was founded in about the fifteenth century as a successor state to Kanem. During this period—from the fifteenth century to the present time— Bornu has retained relative autonomy, although it has been part of Nigeria since the turn of the twentieth century. Bornu is one of the kingdoms in contemporary Africa which is distinguished by its longevity. The dynasty may have been founded some time in the first millennium A.D. in the kingdom of Kanem— north and east of Lake Chad. In the fifteenth century there was a split in the kingdom of Kanem, and the royal clan and its followers fled to the area of present-day Bornu. A capital city called Birni Gazargamo was set up. The dominant ethnic group in Bornu has been Kanuri, although the empire at its peak encompassed several ethnic societies. There are particular cultural and language patterns associated with the Kanuri, e.g., a centralized form of government and a bilateral descent system with a powerful patrilineal emphasis.

In the early nineteenth century, the royal dynasty of Bornu was overthrown by Shehu al-Kanemi, whose family has continued to rule Bornu until the present time. Throughout the nineteenth century the Kanuri were primarily concerned with resisting the encroachments of the Fulani caliphate of Sokoto. A cultural history of Bornu is presented by Cohen, *The Kanuri of Bornu* (1967), which deals with the "land and people" of Bornu, the history of Kanem-Bornu during the nineteenth century and the colonial period, the patterns of family and household in Bornu, and other aspects of cultural life, such as political organization. Bornu is significant partly because of its size and longevity but also because it has formed an important link on the north-south routes to Tripoli and other North African towns.

2. THE HAUSA CITY-STATES

One of the best interpretive sources of early Hausa history is by M. G. Smith (1965), who deals with the seven city-states in Hausaland: Kano, Katsina, Zazzau (Zaria), Gobir, Daura, Rano, and Garun Gabas. During the period A.D. 1000 to 1500, these city-states were distinguished by their use of a common language, a common myth of origin, and common cultural patterns, but in other ways they were relatively separate from each other. In this pre-Islamic period, the Hausa were predominately agriculturalists and followed a form of animism called *bori*. Only after the fifteenth century did they begin to accept Islam on a broad scale, come to engage in long-distance trade, and begin to confront their neighboring states (such as Bornu) militarily. During the period 1500 to 1800, the number of North African traders and scholars in Hausaland increased, and cities such as Kano became relatively cosmopolitan.

As mentioned above, the Hausa states came to be dominated by the Fulani, who had come from the west to settle in the towns of Hausaland. The town of Sokoto, however, was created by the Fulani as the center of their empire. (Note: most of the cities in the Sokoto empire, which included most of Hausaland, were Hausa-based towns.) Because of its importance in trade, the Hausa language came to be a lingua franca in the Central Sudan. Town Fulani came to speak Hausa, and peoples peripheral to Hausaland came to use the language and to adopt Hausa cultural patterns. By the mid–twentieth century, "Hausa" had extended beyond a mere ethnic society to become a broad cultural and linguistic zone. Hausa continues to be the major language group in West Africa, and Hausa styles of life have become a model of Islamic culture in various parts of Black Africa. Notable characteristics include a patrilineal family structure, within a generally bilateral descent system, a secondary social role for women, and a hierarchical status system.

3. THE FULANI EMPIRE OF SOKOTO

From the fourteenth century onward, the Fulani began to migrate from the Western to the Central Sudan. They were cattle people and for the most part nomadic. Yet many Fulani clans came to settle in Hausaland during the seventeenth and eighteenth centuries. Relations became strained between the town Fulani and the urban Hausa by the end of the eighteenth century. In 1804 a Fulani religious leader named Uthman dan Fodio called for an Islamic jihad (holy war) against the "nominally" Muslim Hausa city-state rulers. In the course of the next six to ten years the Fulani conquered the whole of Hausaland and many of the adjoining areas. This Fulani theocracy, known as a *caliphate*, was centered at Sokoto and remained strong throughout the nineteenth century. When the British conquered northern Nigeria in the early twentieth century, they ruled indirectly through the existing Fulani elites. A good account of a Hausa city-state within the Fulani empire is given by M. G. Smith (1960) who discusses Fulani government in Zaria. Another book, by D. M. Last (1967), discusses the Sokoto empire in general with particular reference to some of the political offices in Sokoto.

The subsequent significance of the Fulani caliphate has been twofold. (1) Its political leaders and ideas dominated Northern Nigeria during the colonial and much of the post-colonial periods; and (2) the Fulani are one of the largest and most widely distributed ethnic groups in West Africa—occupying areas from Senegal in the west to Cameroon in the east—and hence they tend to have an intrinsic transnational outlook on contemporary nation-building.

The Fulani can be divided into three different categories according to life style: the rural pastoralists who tend cattle; the rural settled agriculturalists; and the urban Fulani who have been closely associated with city-state government, yet assimilated into Hausa culture. In fact, the urban Fulani have absorbed so many of the customs and cultural patterns of the Hausa that today most do not speak Fulani (Fulfulde) but use Hausa as their mother language.

4. CONCLUSION

The city-states of the Central Sudan came into special importance after A.D. 1500 and have continued to flourish to the present time. These states have been Islamic in form and were retained more or less intact during the period of British colonial rule.

25
___

Indigenous Kingdoms of East and Central Africa

THE BROAD SAVANNA AREA fringing the Congo Basin, stretching from the mouth of the Congo River southeastwards through Angola, Katanga, the Zambezi Basin, and then northwards to the Great Lakes region of East Africa has been the site of a complex succession of African states and kingdoms. Many of these were very short-lived, and most could not match the size, power, and complexity of organization of the Western Sudanic empires. But it must be remembered that the history of many of these kingdoms and chiefdoms, particularly those of central Africa, have only begun to be unraveled (in large part through the systematic analysis of oral traditions exemplified in the work of Vansina, 1966). This module attempts to sort out some of the important historical strands of state formation in three main areas: (1) the central African savanna (mainly Congo and Angola), (2) the Zambezi-Limpopo region, and (3) the Great Lakes, or interlacustrine, region of northern East Africa.

1. "KINGDOMS OF THE SAVANNA"

The major states in the Congo zone included Kongo, Luba, Lunda, and Lozi. Vansina (1968) points out that these and other smaller states and chiefdoms in the area shared many general characteristics. All focused almost entirely on the ruler, thus enabling the personalities of particular kings to have enormous impact on the state and its growth, prosperity, or decline. In addition, the nature of political succession in these states, as in the Western Sudan, required a successor to prove his power by overawing or defeating all other contenders; when no one was able to do this, a period of protracted civil strife ensued. Finally, a complex system of territorial control prevailed in which the outer provinces were considered as tributaries but allowed a great deal of autonomy. Provinces could — and did — break off whenever the circumstances were favorable. Alternatively, political control often meant heavy-handed exploitation.

Most of the development of these states took place after A.D. 1500 and subsequently was linked directly or indirectly to early Portuguese contact and the growth of the slave trade, further enhancing the inherent instability of the area. (Additional information on the Portuguese contact is given in Module 27.) In general, the Portuguese first stimulated, and then led into decline, the westernmost kingdoms such as Kongo and Ndongo (most of this territory eventually became part of the Portuguese colony of Angola). In contrast, many of the interior kingdoms (e.g., Luba, Lunda) were able to increase their power and control via the sale of slaves and the purchase of arms. Several of these kingdoms were able to ward off Portuguese and Arab control coming from the east as well. Vansina's conclusion on these states suggests:

> It is possible that, despite the succession problem, the development of the African states would have gone on had there been no influence from the outside. But as it actually happened, the political structures could not cope with the new stresses fostered by the slave trade and tended to collapse during an interregnum, when their power was weakest (Vansina, 1968, p. 248).

2. THE ZAMBEZI BASIN

The Zambezi Basin has been the site of trading in gold and copper from at least A.D. 850 and probably very much earlier. From about 1100 to 1440, the Karanga people migrated into this area and established an important state, centered on a huge stone acropolis or temple to their god, Mwari. This was the *Great Zimbabwe,* the most magnificent of perhaps over 400 stone-building ruins in what is today Rhodesia. (African nationalists in fact now call Rhodesia "Zimbabwe.") It has long been established that these impressive buildings were African creations. Nevertheless, the Zimbabwe buildings have often been attributed, in large part through European racial arrogance, to a variety of sources, from the Phoenicians and Arabs to King Solomon (i.e., his "mines"), and indeed the illegal white government in Rhodesia today still refuses to accept the African origins of Zimbabwe. In the mid-fifteenth century, the center of power of this kingdom shifted northward, and a new capital arose under the leadership of the *monomotapa* (after which the state is named). Monomotapa is a Portuguese corruption of the indigenous title *Mwene Mutapa,* or "lord of the plundered lands." After about 1480, however, a breakaway state was established in the southern portion of what is now Rhodesia under the leadership of Changa. This state and its rulers, focused in the Great Zimbabwe area, was henceforth called *Changamire.* It grew rapidly in strength as the kingdom of Monomotapa declined in the late sixteenth century. It was during this later period that most of the largest and best walls of Zimbabwe were probably built. The Portuguese first allied with Monomotapa, but eventually the Monomotapa state disintegrated and the Portuguese were driven out by Changamire in the 1690s. (It should be noted that Sofala, on the Mozambique coast, was the major outlet for the trade in this region for most of this period and that Arab traders also ventured inland to reach the sources of the trade and thus contributed to the disruption already existing.) For further detail on state formation in this area, see Ranger (1968), especially the article by Alpers.

The processes of state formation in this area extended throughout southeastern Africa, where eventually they were to be affected by the Dutch (Boer) developments in South Africa. Most of these states were to be defeated or dissolved by the mid–eighteenth century from a combination of Boer attacks and the far-reaching invasions of the Ngoni (or Nguni), the group which produced the *Zulu* states, destroyed Changamire, and set in motion many important historical developments in southern Africa. (More information on historical developments in South Africa is found in Modules 31 and 32 and in Mbata, *Essays*, chap. 12.)

3. THE GREAT LAKES REGION

Clans of Bantu-speaking farmers had probably developed small chiefdoms in what is now southern Uganda by the thirteenth century. After 1300, larger kingdoms were established under the leadership of powerful local clans, the most well known of which were the Chwezi who established the large kingdom of *Kitara* (later Bunyoro). Subsequent infiltrations by non-Bantu groups (primarily Nilotic) stimulated further state formation as the migrants established themselves as the predominant ruling group in many areas. The Nilotic-related Bito clan, for example, displaced the Chwezi and became the rulers of *Bunyoro* for eighteen generations after about 1500. Further south, the Nilotic Bahima became the rulers of states such as *Ankole, Rwanda,* and *Burundi,* which became dominated by a system of vassalage, with pastoral Nilotic rulers and subservient Bantu-speaking agriculturalists (e.g., Hima lords and Iru farmers in Ankole, Tutsi lords and Hutu farmers in Rwanda). Processes of fusion and fission, similar to those which occurred south of the equator, also occurred here, but the states were generally more stable. By the end of the seventeenth century the power of the Bunyoro state began to be challenged by the *Buganda* state to the east, which had successfully withstood the attacks of Kitara-Bunyoro and more effectively *absorbed* the Nilotic invaders than was the case in the other states. All were effective in withstanding the violence of the slave raiders (unlike the savanna and Zambezi states). With British penetration, however, the still-powerful Bunyoro resisted and were defeated, while Buganda allied with the British and became by far the dominant kingdom of the Great Lakes region during the colonial period. Even at independence, such states as Buganda (under its ruler, the *kabaka*), Bunyoro, Ankole, Toro, Rwanda, Burundi, and other smaller kingdoms remained as powerful entities. (Important historical studies of this region are found in Oliver and Matthew, 1963; and Ogot, 1967.)

26

Forest States
of West Africa

FROM ABOUT THE SIXTEENTH CENTURY until the present day, a number of state-based civilizations have flourished in or on the fringes of the rainforest zone of West Africa. Among these have been Ashanti in Ghana, the Yoruba states in Nigeria, and the Edo state of Benin, also in Nigeria. All have been characterized by extensive urban social organization, by developing bureaucracies, and distinctive belief systems. Most of the rainforest city-states withstood the Western and Central Sudanic Islamic culture, partly because of ecological factors inhibiting the extension of Sudanic horse culture into the dense rainforest area. One of the best introductory books on these kingdoms is Forde and Kaberry (1967), an edited volume which includes essays on Benin, Ashanti, the Yoruba kingdom of Oyo, the kingdom of Dahomey, the kingdom of Kom in West Cameroon, and the Mende chieftains of Sierra Leone.

1. THE ASHANTI EMPIRE

The Ashanti rose to power about A.D. 1680, and during the period 1700 to 1750 expanded south to the Guinea Coast and north into the savanna zone. During the eighteenth century, West African kingdoms such as Ashanti often expanded at the expense of the small neighboring kingdoms; an almost constant state of warfare existed until 1750. European trading posts along the coast were forced to adapt their policies to this situation. After 1807, when the slave trade was prohibited by Britain and the coast was patrolled by British warships searching for illicit slaving ships, the British began to establish a protectorate in the southern Ashanti areas, with the result that a series of military clashes occurred between the British and Ashanti. Ashanti was finally conquered by the British in 1900 and in 1901 was declared a crown colony. It has continued as a major cultural region in the modern state of Ghana.

From 1750 to 1901, the rulers of Ashanti experimented with the development of a system of government suitable for the administration of the large and complex empire. Basically this was a centralized bureaucracy which existed side-by-side with the old system of traditional chiefs whose authority derived from their local people. At the head of the bureaucracy, and as head of the traditional chiefs, was the *asantehene*, who consulted the opinions of both but was essentially an autonomous decision-maker. After the conquest of Ashanti, the British interpreted the Ashanti political system as being a "confederation" (see

Rattray, 1929), although this now seems to have underestimated the role of the centralizing bureaucracy (see Wilks, 1967).

One of the reasons for the strength of Ashanti was its wealth of natural resources, including large gold deposits. In fact, the Ashanti currency during this period consisted of measures of gold dust. The Akan peoples who composed the Ashanti state were organized into clans, based on family systems in which descent was calculated through the mother's side of the family. Women were often as powerful as men. The queen mother of Ashanti, for example, was extremely influential.

The language of the Ashanti, called Twi, is tonal. That is, the sound of words or syllables goes up and down like tones in music. Consequently, standardized phrases could be reproduced on talking drums, and messages could travel quickly from one village to another. It is also important to note that although the people and rulers of Ashanti were not Muslim they did incorporate some of the technology of the Sudanic belt and, by the beginning of the nineteenth century, Arabic was used in the court of the asantehene. Much of the significance of Ashanti, however, lies in its unique and rich heritage of oral literature and visual and musical art.

2. THE YORUBA CITY-STATES

In the immediate pre-colonial era, Yorubaland consisted of about 50 city-states of varying size, mostly in what is now the western state of Nigeria. The major Yoruba kingdoms included Oyo, Ife, Ijebu, Ilesha, and Ibadan. These city-states shared a common language, common religious belief systems, and common myths of origin.

In the eighteenth century, the main Yoruba center was old Oyo, which, like Ashanti, built up a large empire extending from the savanna to the coast. The power of old Oyo was destroyed by the Fulani of the Sokoto Caliphate during the period 1820 to 1830. As a result, many Yoruba migrated into the towns to the south, and even founded city-states such as new Oyo and Ibadan. The old Oyo dynasty resettled in new Oyo, but by the second half of the nineteenth century much of the economic power in the old Yoruba empire had passed to the newly formed town of Ibadan, which grew into the largest urban center in Black Africa (with over one million people today, rivaled in size only by the more recent growth of Lagos and Kinshasa).

Each of the Yoruba city-states had a ruler (*oba*) with a distinctive title. Although succession to obaship was inherited, the day-to-day power in the kingdom was in the hands of "chiefs" who frequently were nonhereditary. In fact, the oba was not directly involved in the political decision-making but performed ritual and ceremonial types of functions. (Ibadan, as a military garrison town, had no oba.)

The significance of Yorubaland at present is perhaps in its heavily urbanized culture, the richness of its art, and its religious civilization. In addition, partly because of the warfare between the city-states. many of the Yoruba peoples were sold into slavery and became prominent among those groups who settled in the New World. Even today, in Latin America and the Caribbean area there are Afro-American groups with distinctive Yoruba language, religion, and cultural identities (see Module 29).

There are several works on Yorubaland which may be consulted for further details, especially the works by Lloyd, Mabogunje, and Awe (1967), and Ojo (1966).

3. THE KINGDOM OF BENIN

The Edo-speaking people who make up the kingdom of Benin (in present-day mid-west Nigeria) trace their dynastic organization to Yoruba contacts in the fourteenth century. It was during the reign of their fifteenth oba (king) that European visitors first came to Benin City (about A.D. 1485). This initial interaction between the Portuguese and Benin monarchs is recorded in some of the now-famous Benin bronzes, in which Benin craftsmen incorporated European figures into the scenes of Benin court life.

By the late fifteenth century, Benin was a large and powerful state with an army capable of conducting campaigns at considerable distance from Benin City. By the late sixteenth century, its frontier is reputed to have extended westward to coastal areas near Lagos and eastward to the Niger River. By the seventeenth century, the French, Dutch, Portuguese, and English were all trading in Benin. After a period of reduced contacts, a British military expedition in 1897 conquered and burned Benin City.

The city of Benin itself was encircled by an elaborate honeycomb complex of earth walls and dry moats, of which about 100 miles have so far been traced. Within the city, the area was divided into two sections: the royal palace area, and the remainder. In addition to the oba, royalty included seven *uzama*, who were hereditary nobles and kingmakers. The oba himself was the head of the religious and administrative aspects of the kingdom. The palace of the oba of Benin may be visited today, and the Benin Museum contains artifacts from earlier periods.

4. CONCLUSIONS

The kingdoms of Ashanti, Yoruba, and Benin, which flourished as independent states from the fifteenth to the end of the nineteenth centuries (i.e., until the colonial period), had several things in common. First, a system of inherited kingship, as with the asantehene or oba, symbolized the religious and political power of the state. Second, in all cases there were large urban centers which formed the center of the kingdoms (Kumasi, Oyo, and Benin City, respectively) and had similarly high degrees of urban culture. Third, all three of the kingdoms were engaged in interstate warfare and international trade.

The African
Slave Trade

27

Early Western Contact

THE HISTORY OF "WESTERN" CONTACTS with Africa can only be understood if placed within a global perspective. It has in large part been Western ethnocentrism which created the "dark continent" whose features and peoples awaited European "discovery." Africa was not nearly as unknown to the Islamic world, which had been in close contact with many parts of Africa for almost a millennium before the major period of Western European contact with Africa.

1. ANCIENT CONTACTS

Mediterranean Africa, Asia, and Europe have had some contact with Africa south of the Sahara for at least 2,500 years. Most of the early contacts were peripheral and coastal, but much deeper penetration and more intensive interaction developed periodically in ancient times, originating particularly from Egypt and the Nile Valley. (Some of these contacts have already been mentioned in Module 20.) Although records remain fragmentary, there is some evidence that Egyptian seafarers had sailed along the East African coast, perhaps as far as Sofala (in Mozambique) hundreds of years before the time of Christ. Herodotus, writing in 448 B.C., claims that Phoenicians under King Necho may have already circumnavigated the continent (a feat usually attributed to Bartolomeu Dias in A.D. 1487). By the sixth century B.C., the Carthaginians (Carthage is in present-day Tunisia) and others were trading along the northwest (Atlantic) coast of Africa, and some feel that they may even have been in contact with what is now southern Nigeria. Overland contacts also have deep historical roots in the ancient interaction patterns between the Sudanic belt and both the Nile Valley and the northern coast. The full nature of these contacts is still being explored, particularly with respect to developments in the Sahara and the role of Berber middlemen. It is clear, however, that, by the first century B.C., Arab, Indian, Indonesian, and Chinese mariners knew more about tropical Africa than their counterparts in Europe.

2. FROM THE TIME OF CHRIST TO A.D. 1400

European contacts with Africa during the second half of the 1,400-year period after Christ were extremely meager. During this later period, states in the Sudanic belt began to forge close contacts with the North African Islamic world, which acted as a buffer zone between Africa and Europe. Yet the trans-Saharan caravan routes and the East African coastal trade each were linked up to a vast network extending from the Atlantic coast of Africa through the Middle East and across Asia to China and the Orient. Africa admittedly was not central to this trading system, but nevertheless was a full participant, with African gold and ivory being in great demand.

3. THE FIRST WAVE OF WESTERN EUROPEAN EXPANSION

With its new-found autonomy from Castilian Spain and its strategic location facing the open Atlantic, Portugal was the first European country to begin exploring the "uncharted" coastline of Africa. Partly because of the legends of African gold, and partly in an attempt to circumvent Ottoman control over the routes to India and the Orient, Portuguese sailors, particularly under Prince Henry the Navigator, searched for an alternative route around the African continent. Dias passed the Cape of Good Hope in 1487 and ushered in a major period of Portuguese contact with Africa.

The nature of Portuguese influence varied greatly, but six major areas of impact can be identified

1. The capturing of Ceuta and other important Maghrib ports by the Portuguese and Spanish in the early fifteenth century reversed the flow of conquest which had permitted North African dominance in the Iberian Peninsula for about 700 years.

2. The Portuguese established contacts along the West African coast after the 1440s, thereby entering the trans-Saharan trade from the "back door." The Portuguese allied themselves with several of the forest states which were by that time beginning to compete for trade with the older and larger Sudanic states to the north. Welcoming Portuguese support at first, these states permitted the Portuguese to establish several trading footholds (for slaves, gold, and ivory) along the coast: with the Diola and Wolof in the area between mouths of the Senegal

and Gambia Rivers; with the Akan peoples along the "Gold Coast," where the Portuguese fort of Elmina was built in 1482; and with the people of Benin, near the Niger delta. These early footholds were to become the bases for the rapidly expanding Atlantic slave trade, and the Portuguese were soon joined by other European powers.

3. The Portuguese penetrated the Congo Basin, beginning in the 1480s. The first major foothold was with the kingdom of Kongo (centered in northern Angola). Trade was established, ambassadors were exchanged between Lisbon and the Kongo capital, and Christian missions were permitted entry. With Portuguese help, the Kongo became an important base for slave raiding, disrupting and depopulating much of the surrounding area (including the important kingdom Ndongo whose king, the *ngola*, gave its name to the present Portuguese colony). Eventually, the disruptions generated by slaving destroyed not only the surrounding areas but the kingdom of Kongo as well, with the Portuguese remaining in what is now Angola (with only brief interruption) to the present day.

4. To a lesser extent, they penetrated into the Zambezi Basin, and contributed to similar disruption in the surrounding areas. The most important state to be affected was the kingdom of Monomotapa, whose previously prosperous trade in gold and silver was ruined and which became virtually a Portuguese puppet state in 1628 (see Module 25). The colony of Mozambique ("Portuguese East Africa" or *Monomotapa*, as it is increasingly called by the nationalist groups seeking independence) is the remnant of Portuguese contacts in this area and along the east coast. The Portuguese, however, were unable to fulfill their dream of connecting Angola across southern Africa to Mozambique, in large part because of the strength of other interior kingdoms in resisting their intrusion.

5. The Portuguese interlude in East Africa is discussed in Module 23.

6. Christian Ethiopia was also the site of Portuguese contacts, initially as part of the search for the legendary Prester John (presumed to have been a powerful Christian king seeking support from Christian Europe). The major impact of these contacts was to re-establish Ethiopian relations with Europe.

4. PRELUDE TO COLONIALISM

The period from 1600 to 1800 saw the entry of other European powers into the growing African coastal trading system. The Spanish had closely followed the Portuguese and were the first to take African slaves to the New World. Early in the seventeenth century, the Dutch began to effectively challenge Portuguese power in the Atlantic basin, capturing much of the slave traffic, establishing many forts along the Gold Coast, and conquering not only much of Brazil but nearly all the Portuguese bases along the West African coast. (The Portuguese were later able to recover Brazil and Angola.) During the rest of this period, a number of other European states entered into the growing competition for trade in Africa: the English, Scots, French, Danes, Swedes, and Prussians all established forts and trading centers along the West African coast, which were later to attract larger-scale, government-supported trading companies. More immediately, the major period of the Atlantic slave trade had begun.

28

Origins and Growth
of the Slave Trade

THIS VAST TOPIC WILL BE TREATED under three major headings: domestic slavery in Africa; the East African slave trade; and the Atlantic slave trade. For greater detail, special attention should be given to the works of Cowley and Mannix (1962), Davidson (1961), Curtin (1967 and 1969), and others in the *Bibliography*. See also the sections on the slave trade in Collins (1968).

1. DOMESTIC SLAVERY IN AFRICA

A special supplement of *Trans-Action* edited by Ronald Cohen, 1967, presents a general introduction to the issue of African domestic slavery and case studies of domestic slavery in Ashanti and Zanzibar, and among the Ibo, Kanuri, and Ila. Slavery, in the sense of an institutionalized subordination of one group (or individual) by another, existed—and still exists to some extent—in parts of Africa. Most forms of slavery in Africa, however, differ greatly from the Western image of slavery and the plantation system. Owners and slaves, for example, were usually of similar if not identical cultural backgrounds. Indeed, the status of slaves in some African societies was higher than certain groups of nonslaves (as with the Hausa palace advisers and body guards). In general, the condition of slavery did not prevent slaves from occupying a full range of roles in society. With the exception of the very few places where some form of plantation slavery did exist (such as in Zanzibar), slaves in Africa were members of the larger society sharing the status of their master and, after being freed (second- and even first-generation manumission was common) were often absorbed directly into the kinship system of the family they worked for. The major functions served by indigenous slavery in Africa were: (1) to increase the population and wealth of the dominant group by providing workers and subordinate members for households, (2) to provide a means of absorbing prisoners of war from other ethnic groups, and (3) to work off debt payments (i.e., by members of the same ethnic society).

2. EAST AFRICAN SLAVE TRADE

Trade in slaves existed between East Africa and Asia (and from West Africa across the Sahara to North Africa) long before the coming of the Europeans. But compared to the later Atlantic trade, the annual numbers of slaves involved and the extent of the area affected were much smaller. Prior to the late nineteenth century, East African trade in slaves was much less important than trade in gold and ivory (although the latter, due to difficulties of travel and porterage and competition over resources, often caused just as much destruction and death). Slaves were brought to the coastal ports by African "middlemen" located strategically along the major trade routes into the interior. The nineteenth century, however, saw a rapid increase in the slave trade, initially under the Portuguese in the south (Mozambique), who turned for slaves to the east as well as to the west coast. Davidson states that at this time "Portuguese slave exports from the Mozambique coast were running at the rate of about ten thousand per year, very much higher than in any previous period" (Davidson, 1968, p. 224). See Curtin (1969), however, for a more recent evaluation of this point.

A much larger slave trade developed in the central and northern portions of the coast later in the century, particularly after the transfer of the Omani capital from Muscat (in the Arabian Peninsula) to Zanzibar. Zanzibar Town quickly developed into the greatest slave port in East Africa, and Arab and Swahili traders, for the first time in any large numbers, moved into the interior to compete directly with African groups in slave raiding and trading. During this period—the last quarter of the nineteenth century—the horrors of the slave trade were most pronounced. Plantation slavery (for the production of cloves) developed on the island of Zanzibar, enormous societal disruption took place among the people of the interior, and for a long period no people residing anywhere near the main caravan routes into the interior (extending across the East African countries into present-day Malawi, Zambia, and Congo-Kinshasa) could feel safe. In the wake of this disruption, European contacts increased—first as explorers and missionaries and soon afterwards as colonialists.

It must be stressed that the annual volume of the East African slave trade never approached that of West Africa during the major period of the Atlantic trade. More importantly, despite the prevalent attitude in the literature (see Coupland, 1939), current research suggests that "the East African slave trade as a factor of continuing historical significance traces its roots back no further than the first half of the eighteenth century" (Alpers, 1967, p. 4). Prior to this time—really a final episode in the history of the European-dominated slave trade in Africa—trade in slaves was a very minor factor in East African history.

3. WEST AFRICA AND THE ATLANTIC TRADE

The Atlantic slave trade generated one of the greatest intercontinental migrations in world history. Today, one-third of all people of African descent live outside the continent (a proportion surpassed only by that for Europe— almost 50 per cent), although the difference between voluntary and involuntary migration is clear. By the end of the sixteenth century, the need for labor in the New World had created an enormous demand for slaves. Before this time, the framework of a vast trading system linking West Africa to Europe had already been established, comparable to the already well-developed Indian Ocean trading system. Like the latter, slaves originally formed a relatively minor part of this trade, which involved a form of partnership between European merchants and African middlemen. The Portuguese were importing thousands of slaves a year, but this only supplemented an already existing and very profitable trade in European slaves from Venice and elsewhere in the Mediterranean (feeding a system of domestic labor and indigenous slavery similar to that discussed at the beginning of this module). Indigenous African servitude had increased by this time in the large-scale centralized Islamic states of the Sudanic belt. Laborers were bought and sold throughout the area, and the relatively small external demand could have been met without disruption of traditional patterns. But, as noted in Module 28, these were not slave-based economies—household slaves were members of the community and could aspire to nearly all positions in society.

What changed this situation entirely was the development of plantation agriculture in the Americas. There were not enough white European slaves, and their resistance to tropical diseases was very low. The indigenous Indian populations were decimated by European disease (e.g., smallpox) and were unable to adjust to the plantation system. With the first trickle of African slaves, it was soon found that they were much more skilled in tropical agriculture and mining than the Indians or Europeans, were more disease-resistant, and, moreover, appeared to be in plentiful supply. Already established in West Africa, the slave trade rapidly increased as African rulers cooperated with European merchants in their demand for more slaves. Fed by availability of European weapons and encouraged by the enormous external demand, local African rulers—particularly along the Benin-Congo coast—turned to warfare and capture rather than the sale of existing slaves. (Note: this was less true of Ashanti and Dahomey.) It was during this period (although due only in part to the slave trade) that the whole power structure in West Africa began to be modified as new states emerged along the Guinea Coast, older forest states became more powerful, and the center of West African socioeconomic strength shifted from the Sudanic belt to the coast.

This African-slavery chapter in world history lasted for more than 400 years, until roughly the end of the 1870s. There is still much debate as to precisely how many Africans were taken from their homes to be sold as slaves. Some scholars suggest that 15 million Africans actually reached the New World as a result of the Atlantic trade and that deaths due to slave raiding and warfare, societal disruption, and the notorious Atlantic voyage, might actually increase the estimated number taken as slaves threefold. For an interpretation of African settlement in the New World, and for a further assessment of the impact of European slavers on West Africa, see Hammond (*Essays*, chap. 11).

It should be noted, however, that more recent research, particularly by Philip Curtin (1969), suggests strongly that the volume of the Atlantic slave trade was far less than has often been thought. Rowe (*Essays*, chap. 9) also suggests a lower figure. When more research has been done on the longer lasting trans-Saharan trade, this may turn out to be greater in terms of numbers. This research in no way reduces the horror and destruction associated with the Atlantic trade, but it clearly illustrates the need for more detailed study of this volatile and controversial subject.

29

Abolition and States for Freed Slaves

THE AFRICAN SLAVE TRADE created in the European mind an almost complete contempt for African humanity. This contempt was an integral part of the European rationalization for slavery in the New World (see Curtin, 1964). Feelings of racial superiority grew in this fertile soil, as did the drive to bring the "savage barbarians" of Africa into the "civilized" Christian world. These feelings and attitudes intensified still further as Africa was "discovered" by Europeans in ever-increasing detail during the Age of Exploration. The seventeenth and eighteenth centuries in Africa are what Basil Davidson has called the Age of Transition, a period of successive crises and turmoil associated with trade in arms and slaves, the Muslim reformation and revival in the Sudanic zone, the Portuguese invasions and rise of the Sultanate of Zanzibar in East Africa, the collision between Bantu-speaking peoples and the trekking Afrikaners in the south, and many other historical conflicts. By the beginning of the nineteenth century, Africa was as turbulent a continent as Europe or North America, a situation often interpreted by the Europeans as a reflection on African capability. The missionary zeal to save "savage Africa" was accordingly intensified, although the political (and perhaps psychological) objectives behind this zeal often outweighed the humanitarian goals (see Fabian, *Essays*, chap. 19).

1. THE ANTI-SLAVE-TRADE MOVEMENT

The slave trade was so profitable that it discouraged other kinds of trade between Europe and Africa. When groups of radical Christians began to react on moral grounds to the importation of slaves into England, pressures for the abolition of slavery began to build. The abolitionists were supported by those who saw commercial gain in other forms of trade with Africa, and by administrators, especially in the West Indies, who feared that the New World had reached a saturation point which might lead to widespread slave revolts. When the anti-slave-trade movement met with success in Europe (the trade was made illegal in Denmark in 1804, Great Britain in 1807, the United States in 1808), it then became imperative for the abolitionist forces to abolish the slave trade in Africa itself.

By about 1842, it was illegal in nearly every European and American country, at least technically, to carry slaves across the Atlantic. Despite the activities of the British naval patrol and British diplomatic pressure, however, this did not mean the cessation of the trade. Only after the U.S. Civil War and the abolition of slavery in Cuba and Brazil in the 1880s had cut down the demand from the Americas was the trade finally extinguished in Africa. The surge of European humanitarian and religious interests in Africa and the period of European exploration which accompanied these developments are more appropriately discussed as preliminaries to the "scramble for Africa." We now look back to examine other after-effects of the African slave trade.

2. STATES FOR FREED SLAVES

Some "liberated" Africans in the Americas decided, or were encouraged, to return to Africa. They settled in several areas in Africa, including Libreville (in French Gabon), in the Gambia, and at Freretown (near Mombasa, Kenya). By far the most significant of these settlements, however, were in Sierra Leone and Liberia, along what had been called the "Grain Coast" (for "grain of paradise," a kind of pepper). In both cases, humanitarian and commercial objectives were evident: the former with respect to finding a home for freed slaves and a base for anti-slave-trade efforts, and the latter in the desire to establish a base for legitimate trade with Africa. The commercial objectives, for a variety of reasons (see Hargreaves, 1963), were never fully realized. In both Liberia and Sierra Leone, the relationship between the freed slaves and the indigenous peoples proved to be complex. The Americo-Liberians and the Creoles (from the United States and Great Britain respectively), each came to dominate the territories they settled in.

a. Sierra Leone

A small colony had developed around Freetown before the end of the eighteenth century as a private base for anti-slave activities. It was fully taken over by the British in 1808 as their major anti-slave-trade base. As in the other small British colonial enclaves in Gambia and Lagos, European influence in Sierra Leone did not penetrate far inland until around the end of the nineteenth century. In 1827, however, the Fourah Bay Institution (now University) was established in Freetown and became an influential center for African (freed slave) education. British missionary activities spread from Freetown into the hinterland and were extended from the 1840s into Yorubaland and beyond in Nigeria. During this period, long-lasting contacts were established between Sierra Leone and Yorubaland. One of the earliest Fourah Bay students, for example, was Samuel Ajayi Crowther, an outstanding African linguist who later became Bishop of the Niger.

b. Liberia

Liberia was an American-generated equivalent of Sierra Leone. Begun in 1821 as a venture of the American Colonization Society, the first small settlement of freed slaves became an independent republic in 1847 (although it was not recognized by the United States until 1862, with the beginning of the Civil War). Many feel that the primary American objective in Liberia was to rid the U.S. of its rapidly growing population of "Freed Negroes," an unassimilated and potentially troublesome element which had grown in numbers to over 230,000 in 1820. It is noteworthy, however, that of the nearly 12,000 migrants sent to Liberia by 1866, half were not initially freedmen but slaves who were permitted freedom under the promise to migrate. Many historians consider the Liberian experiment to have been basically unsuccessful. The descendants of the first settlers established an essentially colonial society over the indigenous inhabitants—except that the colonists here were black and did not have the resources to build an economic infrastructure. For an excellent comparative study of Liberia and Sierra Leone, see Hargreaves (1964). See also Liebenow (1969) for specific material on Liberia.

3. SLAVERY AND FREEDOM

It is difficult to assess the full impact of the slave trade on African societies and individuals. New estimations as to the numbers of Africans who were taken as slaves are still being made (see Curtin, 1969). Some notion of the feelings and attitudes of the Africans who were enslaved, however, can be found in the autobiographical documents edited by Curtin (1967). This paperback volume contains the first published collection of narratives by West Africans from the era of the slave trade. These personal recollections provide a valuable perspective to the topic of slavery.

It is also possible to study the thought of Afro-Americans who returned to Liberia and Sierra Leone in the nineteenth century. One of the most notable figures was Edward Blyden, who was also a prolific writer (see Lynch, 1966).

30

The African Legacy
in the Americas

THE BLACK DIASPORA, transported from Africa primarily by force and consisting of nearly one-third of the world's black people, has left an imprint of major significance on the cultural heritage of the Americas. African communities in the Americas not only retained many cultural traditions from Africa, but reinterpreted their African experience to meet the realities of the new environment: ethnic identities were modified, syncretisms occurred in religious life, and kinship structures were adapted. Similarly, they introduced important innovations into the dominant cultures in the Americas—English-speaking, Spanish-speaking, and Portuguese-speaking.

As Turner points out (*Essays*, chap. 30), however, only recently has *Africa*—as an image and symbol—been disassociated by Afro-Americans from the experience of slavery. Only recently have researchers begun to ask questions about the African legacy in the Americas which are rooted in a knowledge of West African cultural patterns (see Hammond, *Essays*, chap. 11). The contemporary impact of Africa on the Afro-American community is discussed in Modules 94, 95, and 96. This module will try to summarize three aspects of the African cultural legacy: (1) the social sensitivities which still surround the African legacy; (2) the general pattern of African cultural survivals in the New World; and (3) the specific contributions of particular African ethnic societies—e.g., Yoruba, Ashanti, Dahomey—to the cultures of the New World.

1. USE AND MISUSE OF THE AFRICAN LEGACY

Part of the difficulty in identifying the African cultural legacy in the New World is that it forms a part of the larger question of the history of black people in the Americas. Research and scholarship are providing new information and correcting the "standard" American histories. Such recent and influential research includes the work of Lerone Bennett, Jr., on the early history of the black man in America (1966) and the history of race relations in America (1968); the work of John Hope Franklin on the slave period (1968) and the twentieth century (1967); the work of E. Franklin Frazier on the sociology of the black family in the United States (1948); the careful analysis by Rayford Logan of "the betrayal of the Negro" by American political leaders (1965); the still relevant studies by the pioneer of black sociology, W. E. B. Du Bois (e.g., 1966); and a host of younger Afro-American scholars (see Stuckey, 1969).

For the past four centuries the dominant cultures in the Americas not only have held a distorted view of the role and even humanity of black people but also have been selectively fascinated by African characteristics in the Americas. The voodoo of the West Indies, the Br'er Rabbit stories of the American South, and the stereotypes of the "fatherless Negro family" all relate in the popular white imagination to African cultural patterns. Some of these stereotypes do have a basis in fact, but the overlay of white attitudes toward such "facts," makes it difficult to put African cultural patterns in a proper context. For example, *Sambo* is a legitimate name among the Hausa of West Africa but has become a pejorative name in the United States. Merely identifying Africanisms in the Americas, including vocabulary which has entered the English language (e.g., goober for peanut, gumbo for okra, juke as in jukebox) or even dances (e.g., the samba, rhumba, tango, malagueña, and Charleston) and folk tales (e.g., the Miss Nancy, or spider, stories in Jamaica) is not doing justice to the African contribution to the cultural heritage of the Americas.

In all three major American culture zones—English-speaking, Spanish-speaking, and Portuguese-speaking—what is known of African cultural survivals is a reflection of race relations in general and of research interests in particular. In most of Latin America, the powerful African cultural influences are prompting many local scholars to re-evaluate the contribution of Africa to their cultural heritage. This, of course, is particularly true in Brazil. (The degree of racial prejudice in Brazil is still a controversial question. Most Brazilians claim there is no race discrimination, only class discrimination. Van den Berghe [1967] and Banton [1967], however, take a different view.)

In the United States the acknowledgment of the African legacy has been greatly complicated by the use of African cultural survivals by the predominant white population to create a racial stereotype. This has been a common development in the history of race relations in the West. As van den Berghe notes:

> There is no question that the desire to rationalize exploitation of non-European peoples fostered the elaboration of a complex ideology of paternalism and racism, with its familiar themes of grownup childishness, civilizing mission, atavistic savagery, and arrested evolution (van den Berghe, 1967).

Thus much of the African legacy was selectively interpreted as part of the mythology of white racial superiority. Condescension accompanied the recognition of distinctive Afro-American cultural characteristics while, at the same time, public policy proclaimed the complete erasure of African culture among black Americans and their absorption into the presumed "melting-pot" of Anglo-Saxon/American culture.

Within almost every field of inquiry there are significant African influences on the American heritage in the United States. In linguistics it is only now being realized that English-language patterns in many black populations in the Americas are really English words inserted into African patterns of syntax. In some cases a distinctive language has emerged: the Gullah dialect of coastal South Carolina and Georgia, for example, still contains thousands of words of African origin (see Herskovits, 1966). Such African influences on the language have significantly contributed to the "Americanization" of the English language in North America.

In the field of music, jazz and blues are overwhelmingly African-influenced (see Keil, 1966). African artistic skills played an important role in the industrial development of the American South—in weaving, toolmaking, building construction, and decoration. And African patterns of religious experience have profoundly influenced black (and in some cases white) religious movements in the Americas (see Herskovits, 1966).

2. PATTERNS OF AFRICAN CULTURAL INFLUENCE

Within each of the three major culture zones in the Americas, the factors which have most clearly affected the survival of African culture and/or the absorption of Africanisms by the dominant populations have been (1) the concentration of the African population; (2) the patterns of segregation separating or linking Africans with other peoples; and (3) the relative level of technology of the area. Consequently, probably the most direct and longest-lasting African influences in the New World exist in Brazil (especially the northeast), in Haiti (which remains overwhelmingly black African in its population), and in many other Caribbean islands, such as Jamaica or Martinique, where the population is also primarily of African descent. Here the full range of African cultural influences—in language, folk literature, religion, art, dance, and music—can be identified as prominent elements of contemporary society.

Spanish-speaking America represents a different pattern. Generally much less dependent upon African slaves than was Portuguese-speaking Brazil (where the African slave trade formed one of the central facts of its history), most of Spanish America has probably been much less directly influenced by the African legacy. Where large numbers of Africans were brought in, as in Mexico, they played an important role in cultural and economic development. The slave system tended to be less brutal than in Brazil and the United States, and the Catholic Church tended to act as a tempering influence. Van den Berghe notes that

> Of all the multiracial societies created by the expansion of Europe since the late fifteenth century, those of Spanish America stand out as exhibiting only traces of the racist virus. Indeed, most of these countries constitute such limiting cases that one may more properly speak of ethnic relations (van den Berghe, 1967, p. 7).

A final pattern is characterized by the rigid segregation and racism of the early period in the United States. Here the influence of African culture was much less direct and more sublimated except when it served to reinforce the master-slave relationship. African cultural survivals either became submerged beneath the attempts to create a homogeneous American culture or were utilized as popular stereotypes (generally disparaging) to characterize the minority black population. Nevertheless, the tenacity of the African cultural heritage within the black community in the United States is much greater than generally presumed and in significant ways has influenced the dominant culture (particularly the youth culture) of today. Part of the African influence, of course, has been by way of Europe, where European artists (e.g., Picasso, Klee, Modigliani), theologians (Tempels), philosophers (Camus, Sartre) have been profoundly influenced by the African experience.

The above discussion is intended to underscore the fact that African cultures adapted themselves in varying ways to a variety of different environments in the New World. It is possible to assess the degree to which African cultures did survive in different locations. In Figure 6 an estimation is given by Herskovits as to the different degrees of African cultural survivals in the Americas.

3. CONTRIBUTIONS OF PARTICULAR AFRICAN ETHNIC GROUPS

It is not possible in this section to do more than indicate that portions of many African ethnic societies were "transplanted" into the New World and that a number of good case studies exist to explore this extension of the African experience. Perhaps the three ethnic groups most easily identifiable in the Americas are the Yoruba, the Ashanti, and the peoples of Dahomey. The Yoruba language, for example, is still spoken in northeast Brazil (and in parts of Cuba), along with Fon (from Dahomey) and Kambundu (from Angola). Yoruba religion (particularly the Shango cult) often blended into the Catholic Church, but it still remains clearly identifiable (e.g., in the Macumba cult) in Brazil and many other areas. The collected papers by Herskovits on Afro-American studies (1966) trace in detail the remnants of Yoruba, Ashanti, and Dahomey culture in the New World. There is a clear need for comparative research on West African communities and Afro-American communities throughout the Americas. Figure

7 indicates in general terms some of the directions of African ethnic influence in the Americas. Through a better understanding of the particular ethnic groups involved, it may be possible to assess with more precision the influence of African languages, religions, art forms, conceptual systems, kinship systems, and even political systems on the cultures of the Americas.

FIGURE 6
SCALE OF INTENSITY,
NEW WORLD AFRICAN LEGACY

	Technology	Economic	Social organization	Non-kinship institutions	Religion	Magic	Art	Folklore	Music	Language
Guiana (bush)	b	b	a	a	a	a	b	a	a	b
Guiana (Paramaribo)	c	c	b	c	a	a	e	a	a	c
Haiti (peasant)	c	b	b	c	a	a	d	a	a	c
Haiti (urban)	e	d	c	c	b	b	e	a	a	c
Brazil (Bahia-Recife)	d	d	b	d	a	a	b	a	a	a
Brazil (Porto Alegre)	e	e	c	d	a	a	e	a	a	c
Brazil (Maranhão-rural)	c	c	b	e	c	b	e	b	b	d
Brazil (Maranhão-urban)	e	d	c	e	a	b	e	d	a	b
Cuba	e	d	c	b	a	a	b	b	a	a
Jamaica (Maroons)	c	c	b	b	b	a	e	a	a	c
Jamaica (Morant Bay)	e	c	b	b	a	a	e	a	a	a
Jamaica (general)	e	c	d	d	b	b	a	a	b	c
Honduras (Black Caribs)*	c	c	b	b	b	a	e	b	c	e
Trinidad (Port of Spain)	e	d	c	b	a	a	e	b	a	e
Trinidad (Toco)	e	d	c	c	c	b	e	b	b	d
Mexico (Guerrero)	d	e	b	b	c	b	e	b	?	e
Colombia (Choco)	d	d	c	c	c	b	e	b	e	e
Virgin Islands	e	d	c	d	e	b	e	b	b	d
U.S. (Gullah Islands)	c	c	c	d	c	b	e	a	b	b
U.S. (rural South)	d	e	c	d	c	b	e	b	b	e
U.S. (urban North)	e	e	c	d	c	b	e	d	b	e

a: very African   b: quite African   c: somewhat African   d: a little African   e: trace of African customs, or absent   ?: no report
*Carib Indian influences are strong in this culture.

Source: *The New World Negro: Selected Papers in Afro-American Studies,* by Melville J. Herskovits, reprinted by permission of Indiana University Press, Copyright © 1966 by Indiana University Press.

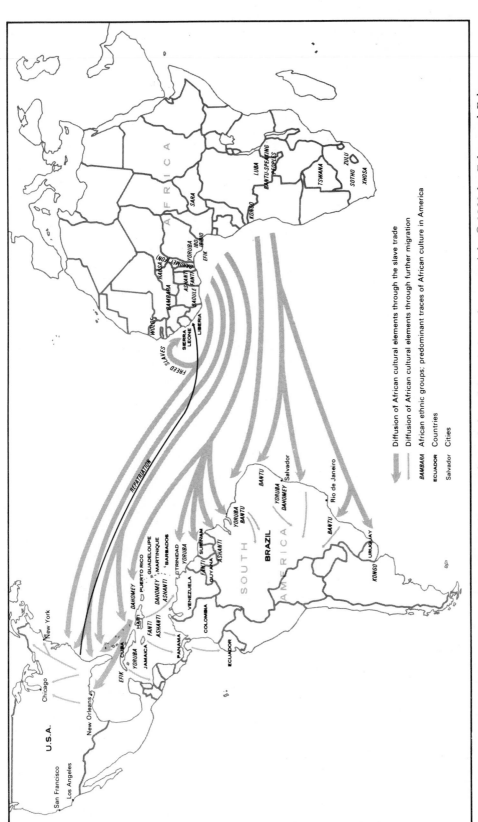

AFRICAN ETHNIC DISTRIBUTION IN THE AMERICAS

Source: Adapted from *Muntu: An Outline of the New African Culture*, by Janheinz Jahn, copyright © 1961 by Faber and Faber. Reprinted by permission of Faber and Faber, Ltd., and Grove Press, Inc.

Race and Resistance in Southern Africa

31

White and Black Migrations in Southern Africa

IN SOUTHERN AFRICA, extensive European and African conflict and competition came earlier and led sooner to some form of colonial hegemony than in other parts of Africa. Given the longer period of direct white rule and the larger numbers of European settlers, particularly in what is now the Republic of South Africa, this section of the continent experienced the impact of European confrontation before the "scramble" of the late nineteenth century fully partitioned the remainder of Africa. In this module the patterns of early contact are discussed. In Module 32 the various forms of African resistance to white minority rule are examined.

1. EXPANSION AND COLLISION BETWEEN BLACK AND WHITE

During the three centuries prior to the first arrival of the Portuguese in 1488, Bantu-speaking African groups had continued to expand southward from the area between the Zambezi and the Limpopo (see Module 25). By the thirteenth or fourteenth century, these peoples were already firmly established in much of what are now the Transvaal, Orange Free State, and Natal Provinces of the Republic of South Africa. Indeed, the Pondo and related groups had reached well into the present Cape Province (beyond their present Transkei region) and were in contact with traders in the Indian Ocean system (see Module 23). In this favorable environment, the Bantu-speaking peoples grew rapidly in numbers and continued to expand into areas occupied by other ethnic groups (including the Bushmen and the Nama, who have generally been called Hottentots).

Beginning in 1652 with the establishment of a refueling station in what is now Capetown, a countervailing, and soon migratory, force of Dutch settlers was established on the southern tip of the continent. Moving inland at the expense of the Bushmen and Nama, the Dutch settlers, subsequently called *Boers* ("farmers") or *Afrikaners*—in much the same process of consolidation which characterized many of the Bantu-speaking migrant groups moving into new territory—developed an integrated ethnic community. The economy of the Boers soon became based on cattle (mainly from the Hottentots), farming, and Coloured slaves (all nonwhites were viewed as destined by God to work for whites). Thus, in this early period of contact, the distinctive color-based class-structure of South Africa had already begun to develop (see Mbata, *Essays*, chap. 12).

These two expansions—Bantu and Boer—collided in the late eighteenth century near the Great Fish River (in eastern Cape Province), and there ensued a series of bitter conflicts—the so-called "Kaffir" wars—which extended into the 1830s. (As mentioned in Module 32, pockets of resistance by some groups such as the Xhosa were not defeated until the 1870s.)

2. THE GREAT TREK AND THE WARS OF WANDERING

By 1830, the Boers found their expansionary thrust into the southeastern sections of South Africa (now Cape and Natal Provinces) frustrated by English settlements established at Port Elizabeth and East London (from 1820 on), while at the same time their initial home base in the western Cape came under the influence of British missionary efforts to end slavery. The government of the Cape had passed to the British after the Anglo-French struggles of 1793–1815 and from even before this time the slave-based economy of the Boers came into conflict with the anti-slavery policies of the British. In an attempt to escape British interference, particularly after the British decision to end slavery in Cape Colony in 1834, the Boers redirected their migration frontier to the interior in what is called the *Great Trek* of 1836. Thousands of families moved across the Orange and Fish Rivers into the interior, alternatively forcing the resident African population to work on their farms, taking their cattle, and pushing them back into their earlier homeland.

During this same period (approximately 1790 to 1830), and possibly related to Boer expansion and the series of "Kaffir" wars, various clans of the Ngoni peoples in Natal began to consolidate themselves into a powerful and aggressive military nation, first under the leadership of Dingiswayo of the Mtetwa clan and later under the military genius of Shaka and the Zulu clan. Under Shaka, the Zulu empire grew at the expense of its African neighbors and generated a widespread and pronounced disruption in the entire region. Several groups of defeated rivals broke off into new territory, destroying the Karanga states in the Zambezi region (see Module 25) and pushing northward into Tanganyika. Some settled in what was to become Southern Rhodesia. Another group established a defensive fortress in the Drakensberg Mountains and formed the nucleus of the Basuto nation (now Lesotho), which (like the Swazi) successfully resisted the Zulu and the Boers. Both Swaziland and Basutoland became British protectorates. This chaotic and disruptive period has been called the *wars of wandering*, or *Mfecane* (in the Zulu language) and *Lifiquane* (in the Sotho language).

The Great Trek eventually brought the Boers into conflict with the Zulu, who were defeated near the appropriately named Blood River in Natal. The Boers, or Afrikaners as they increasingly were called, by then had established themselves firmly on the plateau and had begun to build the administrative structures upon which the contemporary Republic of South Africa is based.

3. TWO MORE TREKS AND THE UNION OF SOUTH AFRICA

On the plateau, the Afrikaners established the Orange Free State Republic and the Republic of South Africa (Transvaal), which were eventually recognized by the British (who now controlled Natal as well as Cape Colony). With the discovery of diamonds at Kimberley (along the Orange River) in 1867, another Trek was begun—this time rooted in economic causes and participated in by fortune seekers from all over the world. Kimberley became the economic capital of South Africa, stimulating the first major phase of railway building. Soon the diamond-bearing region was annexed by the British, although the Afrikaner republics remained independent.

A second and much more important mineral discovery—gold—near what is today the city of Johannesburg (Transvaal) initiated a third Trek in 1884. Another migration of foreign investors and businessmen occurred, and Johannesburg quickly eclipsed all other South African cities in importance (despite Afrikaner resistance to the rapidly expanding role of white foreigners).

Prevented from acquiring citizenship in the Transvaal, the British through a series of misadventures and policy blunders, eventually came into armed conflict with the Afrikaners in 1899 in the Anglo-Boer War. The Boers were militarily defeated, but were granted self government and soon participated in the creation of the Union of South Africa in 1910 (composed of the British colonies in Natal and the Cape and the defeated republics of Orange Free State and Transvaal). The Afrikaners sought and won independent status within the British Commonwealth and steadily increased their influence within the Union. Afrikaner political power and independence reached its ultimate fulfillment in 1961, when South Africa became an independent republic outside the

Commonwealth and with a rigidly imposed policy of strict racial separation and discrimination (see Modules 32 and 89).

African Reactions to European Settlement

"THE BLACK MAN IN SOUTH AFRICA," as noted by Mbata, "has never accepted his subjugation as ultimate and has used every available opportunity to voice his protest" (*Essays*, chap. 12). Because of the continuity of such resistance and reaction, this module—unlike others in Part II—ranges over many centuries and brings its central theme up to the present. It is necessary, therefore, to consider this module as an integral part of a unit on South Africa consisting of Modules 31, 32, 87, 88, and 89, and the essays by Mbata and Carter (*Essays*, chaps. 12 and 28). It is also important to view this unit in a wider perspective, linking it both to the modules on the beginnings of colonialism and African reactions to it (Modules 33 to 35) and to Part V which is concerned with "Africa and the Modern World." The latter group of modules illustrate clearly that South Africa is not an isolated problem-area; its circumstances involve the entire continent of Africa and the rest of the world as well.

1. AFRICAN REACTIONS TO WHITE CONTACT: THE STRUGGLE FOR TERRITORY

The development and maintenance of a master-servant relationship between white and black has been the central thread in South African politics since the establishment of the first Dutch colony in 1652. With the rationale of ensuring the "welfare of the settlement," the white settlers almost immediately began to struggle with the indigenous population for control of resources and territory. The earliest confrontation was with the Hottentots, leading eventually to a virtual expropriation of Hottentot land and cattle. Hottentot resistance was clear and straightforward but insufficient to prevent the actions of the whites. Today, the Hottentot as a distinct group are virtually nonexistent, having been effectively absorbed into the Cape Coloured population.

Confrontation between whites and the Bantu-speaking peoples was longer lasting and more violent. Nine "Kaffir" wars were fought beginning in 1779 and continuing into the nineteenth century. As early as 1736, the Xhosa forcefully resisted the enroachment of white settlers, and it was not until 1877— nearly a century and a half later—that the last pockets of Xhosa resistance fell.

In all these conflicts, the basic pattern was the same: "white provocation, retaliation by the Africans, war, the triumph of superior technology, and peace, with the annexation of more territory by the whites" (Mbata, *Essays*, chap. 12). The end result was a rigid territorial compartmentalization in which the minority white population claimed 86 per cent of the area of South Africa as rightfully theirs.

2. REACTION AND RESISTANCE TO OPPRESSIVE LEGISLATION

The Africans did not submit tamely to discriminatory measures, even after the so-called Kaffir wars had ended. In the Basutoland "Gun War" of 1880, the Basuto (Sotho) peoples, with the support of many other groups, resisted the extension of discriminatory gun laws to their (British-protected) territory. But the Zulu Rebellion of 1906–7 (against the imposition of a poll tax designed to force the African population into the white monetary economy) resulted in hundreds of Africans being killed by government troops (see Omer-Cooper, 1966). By the time of the establishment of the Union of South Africa in 1910, with the major concessions this involved by the British to the local white population, the pattern of African resistance had changed. Attention now clearly focused on discriminatory legislation, particularly the Land Act of 1913 which drastically restricted the rights of African "squatters," and the many discriminatory laws already in existence, such as the pass laws which dated from 1809.

African reaction to discriminatory legislation took a variety of forms. One of the earliest and most powerful was religious. As mentioned in Module 51, South Africa was a major center in the emergence of both the Ethiopian churches (which have broken away from the formal control and European leadership of the orthodox Christian churches, while retaining much of their orientation) and the Zionist churches (which have also broken off from established churches but have evolved distinctive new forms based upon local cultural patterns and beliefs). This independency movement was to affect the entire continent, but South Africa still contains more independent churches than any other area. The independent *African* churches in South Africa were a major source of early drives for African unity and "Africa for the Africans." As such, they provided an important initial thrust toward organized political resistance.

The closely associated themes of resistance to oppressive legislation and the drive for African unity were taken up more directly by the South African Native Congress (subsequently renamed the African National Congress), which was founded in 1912. Although seriously handicapped by restrictions on movement and organization, the ANC and other labor and political organizations (black African, Coloured, Indian, and, in some cases, white) spearheaded sporadic strikes, protests, and passive-resistance movements against the pass system and punitive provisions, and by the early 1950s had successfully established the basis for a large-scale African movement in South Africa. (See Simons and Simons, 1969.)

Also in the 1950s, however, the Afrikaner Nationalist Party government produced new legislation designed to restrict Africans in every sphere of life. In 1953, following the passive-resistance campaign, civil disobedience as a form of protest was made a severely punishable act. In 1956, one year after the joint presentation of a "Freedom Charter" by the ANC, the South African Indian Congress, the South African Coloured Peoples' Organization, and the white Congress of Democrats, 156 people of all races were arrested on treason charges and put on trial over the next five years. In 1960, the period of open and legally organized protest against white domination essentially ended in the aftermath of the tragic incident at Sharpeville, an African township 30 miles south of Johannesburg.

3. SHARPEVILLE AND AFTER

In 1960, the Pan-Africanist Congress (which had broken away from the ANC in 1958) organized a campaign against the hated pass laws. All men were to leave their passes at home and proceed to police stations to submit themselves to arrest. In Sharpeville, some 10,000 men are estimated to have done so, the police panicked, and over 200 unarmed Africans were killed or injured. Demonstrations took place elsewhere in South Africa; the government declared a state of emergency, mass arrests took place, and both the ANC and the PAC were banned. After 1960, a new phase of African resistance and reaction was forcibly born: a phase in which African political organizations have been forced underground or are in exile; in which open criticism or resistance to laws affecting black-white relations, whether by whites or blacks, is severely punished as treasonous (and Communist-inspired); and in which the long-standing African policies of passive and nonviolent resistance have been discarded.

The Impact of Colonialism

The Scramble for Africa

FROM APPROXIMATELY 1885 until the outbreak of World War I in 1914, the continent of Africa was partitioned by European powers into a territorial pattern which has persisted until the present day. This partition, or "scramble for Africa," occurred primarily for reasons connected with European politics and economics (see Robinson and Gallagher, 1961). First, and perhaps most important, there was the military or strategic importance of the coastal areas of Africa, which by now were on the trade routes to the Far East. Secondly, there was the growing importance of commercial outlets in Africa and the need for assurance of raw-material supplies for the industrial expansion of Europe.

1. THE CONGRESS OF BERLIN AND THE "RULES" OF CONQUEST

The "ground rules" for the scramble for Africa were set up, essentially, at a thirteen-week conference in 1884/85 (see Crowe, 1942). Representatives of fourteen European states plus the United States met in Berlin to discuss issues such as freedom of commerce in the Congo area and the criteria for effective occupation of territories in Africa. In essence it was decided that the Congo area should remain a free-trade zone. With regard to criteria for occupation in Africa, several principles were established. First, the European power had to "effectively occupy" the territories under consideration. Second, other states agreed to recognize the authority of the occupying state once it had been established in these territories. The definition of effective occupation became important to the pattern of conquest in Africa. Essentially it required an on-the-spot display of manpower (military or commercial) in the area being claimed in addition to some sort of treaty with the local peoples. This had the effect of encouraging military expeditions in Africa, and, although in certain instances territories were controlled through the signing of nonmilitary treaties, at least two-thirds of the European territories in Africa were gained by military conquest.

2. PATTERNS OF EUROPEAN CONQUEST

Britain, France, and Portugal had long had historic contacts with coastal sections of Africa, but the agreements at Berlin necessitated penetration of the "interior." The partition of Africa into European colonies followed to some extent from the strategic positions of the European powers. These patterns will be described below.

The British were concerned as a primary objective to ensure direct communications and control over the north-south route from South Africa to Egypt. The phrase "Cape to Cairo" indicated the dream of empire builders, such as Cecil Rhodes, who wanted to link up British possessions in the Anglo-Egyptian Sudan with the emerging power base in South Africa. This north-south axis directly confronted the ambitions of three other European powers. The first were the Portuguese, who (in southern Africa) hoped to establish east-west linkages between their possessions in Angola and Mozambique. This ambition was thwarted through the efforts of Cecil Rhodes, who with the establishment of Northern and Southern Rhodesia severed the Portuguese east-west axis.

The second European power to confront the British on their Cape to Cairo dream were the Germans (see Gifford and Louis, 1969). Under the guidance of Bismarck, German foreign policy hoped to establish a German "middle Africa" stretching from Cameroon on the west to Tanganyika on the east and including some links back to South-West Africa. German ambitions in Africa were curtailed after the deposition of Bismarck in 1890 by Kaiser Wilhelm, and German policy became more concerned with strategies in Europe than in Africa. In fact, agreements were made between the Germans and the British regarding spheres of influence in East Africa, whereby the British further extended their hegemony over what is now Uganda in return for cession of the island of Heligoland in the North Sea to Germany.

The major European confrontation in Africa occurred between the British and the French. The French had established control over much of northwestern Africa (the Maghrib), but were also concerned to extend their early contacts in Senegal (on the far western tip of Africa) across the entire Sudanic belt to Somaliland on the eastern Horn (see Roberts, 1963; Kanya-Forstner, 1969). The scramble for Africa was perhaps most dramatic in West Africa. Military expeditions sent out by both the British and the French penetrated the empires of the Western and Central Sudan which had been virtually unknown to Europeans before this time. The major confrontation between the British and the French, which is well documented in textbooks on European as well as African history (e.g., Collins, 1969), was at Fashoda on the Upper Nile in Southern Sudan. There it became clear that the British were able to withstand French military pressure and hence retain their north-south linkages from the Sudan to territories farther south. The French relinquished their hope for a linkage between East and West Africa.

For reasons related to the European balance of power, shortly after the turn of the century Britain and France found themselves in alliance (the *entente*) against rising German power in Europe. The result of this alliance was the establishment of boundary commissions to negotiate demarcations between British and French areas of Africa. Much of this boundary negotiation was conducted in a spirit of good will. One of the most notable boundaries that came out of these negotiations was the line drawn between Northern Nigeria and Niger territory.

3. LAND AND SETTLERS

The consequences of partition in Africa and the establishment of colonial rule during the period 1885 to 1914 differed between the major regions in Africa. In eastern, central, and southern Africa, as well as in the Maghrib, settlers began to emigrate from Europe and establish themselves in Africa on a permanent basis. In Algeria, many of the French settlers were refugees from the Franco-Prussian War of 1870 (particularly from the area of Alsace-Lorraine; See Gorden, 1966). In East Africa the most important settlement area was Kenya, where Lord Delamere actively encouraged British farmers to establish themselves in the desirable highlands (see Low, 1965). In southern Africa the discovery of diamonds and gold in the 1870s and 1880s resulted in a flood of European fortune seekers, with an attendant host of merchants and suppliers of goods and services (see Austin, 1966). In the Belgian Congo, there were fewer settlers initially, but as commerce increased the number of Belgian settlers also increased. The Belgians, however, followed a policy of granting huge tracts of land to commercial companies who were willing to exploit and "develop" these territories (see Austin, 1966; Slade, 1962).

By contrast, in West Africa there were few if any settlers. This was partly for reasons of colonial policy (the British explicitly forbade land alienation in West Africa) but also because health conditions in West Africa were considered to be more difficult for Europeans. The result of these early patterns of settlement have carried over into the present day, and East, Central, and southern Africa have experienced patterns of race relations which differ from those in West Africa.

4. CONCLUSIONS

By the time of World War I, Britain and France had emerged as the dominant colonial powers in Africa, the boundaries of most of the colonial territories had been delineated, and European settlers and companies had become established in certain areas. In most cases, the military conquest of Africa was conducted by a limited number of European officers, equipped with modern machine-guns and armaments, using local African enlisted men (see Haywood and Clark, 1964). In many cases the demonstration of superior firepower was sufficient to forestall widespread resistance. Module 34 considers those types of resistance to European rule that did develop on the part of Africans.

34

African Resistance and Reaction

CROWDER REFERS TO THE PHENOMENON of African resistance and points out that for the most part African resistance to colonial conquest was weak (*Essays,* chap. 13). However, there were a number of significant instances in which local peoples did organize themselves militarily to withstand the incursion of European power. In retrospect, some of these resistance movements are especially important because of their symbolic value to African nationalist movements. (For a detailed analysis of resistance movements throughout Africa, see Mazrui and Rotberg, 1970.)

1. THE RESISTANCE OF SAMORY TOURÉ

The empire of Samory Touré, a Mande-speaking ruler of upper Guinea and lower Mali, was founded in the late 1860s when he gained control over a small chieftaincy in Kankan. In the 1870s he extended this base into a sizable empire. In the mid-1880s, after the Congress of Berlin, French forces in the area began to confront Samory. In 1885, he defeated the French at Nafadie. As a point of honor the French sent a larger expedition against him, which resulted in a temporary truce. In 1887, Samory signed a treaty with the French which ostensibly established a French protectorate in the area; in fact Samory was buying time, and he undertook fresh attacks against the French with varying degrees of success.

The culmination of the confrontation between Samory and the French occurred during the period 1891 to 1898. This so-called "seven-year war" included thirteen major battles with the French. In the end the French defeated Samory at the siege at Sikasso, his major stronghold. (Samory continued to fight sporadically after this, however.)

Crowder (1968) summarizes the significance of Samory's resistance and military genius. He suggests that Samory was particularly successful at logistics (maintaining a supply of arms, ammunition, and horses). Second, he had mastered the art of strategic withdrawal. Third, he was an unusually good organizer of men. And finally, his intelligence system was so good that in most cases he had foreknowledge of French intentions and activities. Perhaps for this reason he was able to withstand major French military efforts for a longer period than African leaders in most other empires in Africa. In later periods, he became a symbol of resistance to colonial rule. It should be noted that the president of Guinea, Sékou Touré, is a collateral descendant of Samory and drew upon memories of this early resistance to fortify his own resistance to the French at the time of independence.

2. THE RESISTANCE OF ASHANTI

Early encounters between the Ashanti and the British occurred in the 1820s when there was a clash over their relationship with the coastal Fanti (whom the Ashanti had earlier conquered) region. However, the British governor, Sir Charles MacCarthy, was defeated and beheaded while fighting against the Ashanti. In 1844 the British government finally took over the administration of the Gold Coast settlement from the Committee of London Merchants. However, Ashanti was still not an acknowledged part of this colonial sphere. In 1874, the British under Sir Garnet Wolseley invaded Ashanti following another Ashanti invasion of the coastal region. But it was not until 1901 that Ashanti itself was formally annexed to the Gold Coast. During this era there was considerable resistance on the part of the Ashanti to British annexation.

In the Ashanti empire during the late 1880s the British precipitated a series of civil wars which affected the trade between the Ashanti and the coastal areas. This provided the British governors with an excuse for action. In 1891 Governor Griffith tried to persuade the Ashanti to join the Gold Coast voluntarily. Instead the asantehene attacked those border states which had submitted to the British. The asantehene declared that the kingdom of Ashanti would never commit itself to the British and would remain independent, although it was the intention of the Ashanti to remain friendly with the Europeans. In 1895 Governor Maxwell sent an ultimatum to the asantehene. The ultimatum was refused and 3,000 troops were sent to Kumasi, which was occupied in 1896. Troops seized the palace, destroyed shrines, and deposed the asantehene, exiling him along with the queen mother to the Seychelles Islands. Resistance nevertheless continued in Ashanti. In 1900 the governor imposed a series of demands which hardened resistance and war was declared. The Ashanti imprisoned the governor in Kumasi along with more than 700 of his troops. Later the governor escaped, and fierce fighting continued until 1901. Larger numbers of British-officered troops returned to defeat the Ashanti, and in 1901/2 Ashanti was formally annexed as a crown colony.

The significance of the resistance of Ashanti is manyfold: it represents a refusal by an independent kingdom with whom the British had been dealing for over 200 years to submit to foreign rule. It also illustrates the protracted period of time that was necessary to establish British rule over Ashanti: roughly from 1820 to 1900, with fluctuations on both sides as to the degree of success or defeat.

3. CONCLUSIONS

The examples of Samory Touré and Ashanti illustrate in both the British and French contexts some of the patterns of resistance in the late nineteenth century. It should be noted that in many other parts of Africa resistance was also to be found. In Nigeria alone this included the Fulani of Northern Nigeria (see Muffett, 1964); the Kanuri of Bornu; the Hausa of Abuja; many of the Ibo, Ibibio, Opobo, and Itsekira of eastern Nigeria; and the Edo of Benin. The Mahdi Rebellion in the Eastern Sudan is well known (see Theobald, 1951; and Holt, 1958), and massive revolts also took place among the Matabele and Mashona in Southern Rhodesia (see Ranger, 1967); the Herero and Nama in South-West Africa (against the Germans); the Ovimbundu kingdoms in Angola; the Nandi in Kenya; several Tanganyikan groups in the Maji Maji war against the Germans (see Iliffe, 1967); and others. As mentioned in Paden (*Essays*, chap. 20), many of these early resistance movements have become incorporated into the nationalist lexicon of symbols and history.

35

The Nature
of Colonial Systems

FROM ABOUT 1900 UNTIL 1960, the European colonial powers in Africa established systems of administrative rule which were characterized by a mixture of principles and patterns. These will be summarized below.

1. THE BRITISH COLONIAL SYSTEM

British rule is notably identified with the policy of *indirect rule* established by Lord Frederick Lugard in Northern Nigeria (see Lugard, 1965). The principles of indirect rule required working through the traditional local authorities in matters of taxation, law, succession to leadership, and community boundaries. Indigenous African communities were allowed to continue under their own leadership as long as that leadership was willing to cooperate with the British. In the Fulani emirates of northern Nigeria, for example, centralized authority systems existed prior to European contact (see Module 24). In other areas, such as among the Ibo of Eastern Nigeria, the effect of the indirect-rule system was to *create* more centralized authority systems. "Chiefs" were appointed to perform the functions of government (see Jones, 1963). (It should be noted that in many of the segmental authority systems, indirect rule was unsuccessful, and a form of direct rule was adopted.)

The most important functions performed by the local authorities (often called *native authorities*) under indirect rule included the following: (1) taxes were often assigned and collected in the traditional way (e.g., in Islamic areas, the system of *zakat* was continued); (2) a police force was continued or developed which was responsible to the local ruler; (3) the local ruler, often with the aid of a council selected from traditional elders, made decisions on a day-to-day basis; (4) the traditional legal systems were continued in most cases, although a defendant might have the choice of being judged by British law.

In formal terms, the British colonial officials were not regarded as having decision-making powers, but rather "advisory" functions. A British *resident* was stationed in a native authority and maintained close contact with the local leaders. (For a discussion of the British residents, see Heussler, 1968.) In a large native authority (e.g., Kano emirate, in Northern Nigeria, with about three million persons in 1959), the resident would be assisted by several British *district officers*, who would circulate throughout the area and ensure that indigenous authorities were performing their duties. (It should be noted that these residents and district officers did have leverage, financial and military, if necessary.)

The effect of the British indirect-rule system, which was in fullest effect during the 1920s and 1930s, was to preserve the cultural unity of the local African communities. This may have led to difficulties at a later period when the African states were trying to bridge such cultural differences. It should also be mentioned that local Africans, in addition to the traditional authorities, were recruited into the colonial administrative structure. However, African civil servants in the English-speaking areas usually retained their cultural heritage, were assigned to their home areas, and usually operated in their vernacular languages.

2. THE FRENCH COLONIAL SYSTEM

French rule has been characterized as *direct* in contrast to British rule (as with the British, there were exceptions to this: e.g., the indirect-rule policy of the French in northern French Cameroon.) Direct rule established administrative units which generally cut across traditional political and/or ethnic boundaries. While traditional leaders were often retained on stipend, they performed mainly ceremonial functions or were regarded as minor clerks. French policy did not recognize the cultural integrity of the local communities in Africa. Administrative districts were organized into "circles" which in turn were subdivided into "cantons." There was a tight, hierarchical structure of colonial authority with relatively little devolution of power. French law (a detailed civil code) was applied, and French administrators collected taxes (see Delavignette, 1950; Deschamps, 1953).

An important distinction developed in the French African colonies between those who were regarded as "citizens" and those who were regarded as "subjects." Subjects were essentially without rights (until the constitutional reforms of 1956—the *Loi-Cadre*). Citizens, however, were accorded the rights of Frenchmen. This small group of Africans essentially represented those who had been assimilated into French culture, that is, those who lived in certain favored coastal areas of Senegal (see Crowder, 1967). A meritocracy developed of those Africans who had received a French education that formed the backbone of the colonial civil service. African administrators were not assigned to their home areas and were required to use French as the language of administration.

Perhaps as a consequence of this elite development, the French-speaking African states have had less subsequent difficulty in terms of ethnic conflict. They have had more difficulty in terms of re-establishing contact between the French-assimilated elite and the common people. Part of the negritude movement in the 1950s was a reaction by French-speaking African intellectuals against the assimilation policy of the French. It was an assertion of the fact that they were African, not French.

3. OTHER COLONIAL SYSTEMS

The pattern of "company rule" was significant in certain parts of Africa. In the Congo, King Leopold of the Belgians had allocated large districts to European mining and agricultural companies, on the condition that these companies administer the areas. Such administrations usually had little regard for local Africans, and some of the cruelest episodes in colonial history came out of these areas. The penalties for noncompliance with regulations were often harsh, including physical mutilation. (See Gide, 1929, for a French writer's account of these atrocities in parts of French Equatorial Africa.) Companies in effect ruled most of the Congo and most of Rhodesia until the 1920s and 1930s, when direct control was recovered by the colonial states.

German rule was also significant in Africa until World War I and was characterized by a very authoritarian system of colonial administration. This system was even more hierarchical in some cases than the French, and German administrators were reputed to be harsh (see Iliffe, 1969; and Austin, 1969). After World War I, the German areas came under the control of the League of Nations and later its successor, the United Nations. These two international bodies entrusted (or "mandated") the administration of the African colonies to the remaining European colonial powers, i.e., Britain, France, and Belgium (for examples from Tanzania, see Chidzero, 1961). A major feature of rule in the Trust Territories was that inspectors from the League and, later, the United Nations required reports on the conditions of local life, and there was less tendency to colonial abuse. (Note that German South-West Africa was mandated to South Africa, which refused to accept United Nations trusteeship. See Module 81.)

4. SUMMARY

Colonial systems in Africa were essentially authoritarian and oriented primarily to administrative matters. The European powers did follow different policies, which seem to have affected social and political patterns in the post-colonial period. Perhaps the most important difference in policy was the British recognition of local traditional authority and culture *vs.* the French effort to break it down. The effects of these colonial policies are still being felt. For a discussion of these matters in West Africa see Crowder (1968). An evaluation of colonialism in all parts of Africa south of the Sahara that is sympathetic to the European contributions is available in Gann and Duignan (1967). An account that is more critical of European rule and that traces African reaction to colonialism is found in Mazrui and Rotberg (1970).

Study Questions

Study Questions: Perspectives on the Past

THE FOLLOWING STUDY QUESTIONS are both analytical and judgmental. While a student should have a clear and documented overview of African history, he should also be encouraged to interpret and even speculate about the issues which are raised in this section.

1. What is meant by continental drift? What are the distinctive physical features, if any, of the African continent? In what types of physical environment have African civilizations flourished?

2. What is the evidence for the assertion that all mankind originated in East Africa? What time period is involved in this claim? At what point, and in what way, did human physical characteristics begin to differ?

3. What is meant by Bantu migration? Why is it an important topic in African history? In what way is it related to the "agricultural revolution"?

4. What is known about the earliest black kingdoms and empires in Africa? What was their relationship to Egypt and the Middle East? To what extent should early Egyptians be regarded as "dark-skinned"? What are the hypotheses relating the peoples of western Africa to those of the Nile Valley?

5. What are the basic elements of Islam? What parts of Africa may be regarded as Islamic? How might Islamic conversion affect the language, culture, religion, law, political system, and economic network of an African ethnic society? In the early period, was Islam spread by the sword or by Muslim trader-scholars

(or both)? How did Muslims regard non-Muslims? Did ethnicity lose all importance in the Muslim empires?

6. Why are Ghana, Mali, and Songhai often considered the high points in black African civilization? Do you think they should be so considered? What did all three empires have in common? What were the differences? What type of political system was used to control the vast areas involved?

7. What are the origins of Swahili culture? Does the term *Swahili* refer to an ethnic group, a civilization, a language, a religion, or all of the above? What was the nature of the contact between Arabs and Africans along the East African coast? Were the trading cities any different from those in Sudanic West Africa?

8. How have the Hausa, Fulani, and Kanuri empires of the Central Sudan continued until the present? In what way do they provide insight into the pattern of city-state evolution in Sudanic Africa? What patterns of urbanism were represented by such cities as Kano or Katsina (e.g., trade-dominant, agriculture-dominant, military-dominant, etc.)?

9. What is the nature of the dispute over the issue of who built Zimbabwe? Why do many white Rhodesians claim that it could not have been built by black Africans? How did the states of eastern and central Africa compare with those of the Sudanic belt? What factors might account for any differences you identify?

10. To what extent were the Ashanti, the Edo of Benin, and the Yoruba involved with the slave trade in West Africa? What was the nature of their social and political organization? To what extent were they urban-based kingdoms? What were the differences between the forest states of West Africa and the states of the Central Sudan?

11. Was slavery, as it is known in the West, indigenous to Africa? What groups were engaged in the capture, transportation, and sale of African slaves? What is the evidence for the magnitude of the slave trade (in duration, in geographical extent of its impact, and in numbers of persons)? What impact did the slave trade seem to have on West African communities?

12. What were the cultural carryovers into the New World by African slaves? How has the cultural legacy of Africa differed in various parts of the New World? What part has Africa played in the growth of American culture? With regard to the African legacy in the United States, which areas do you feel require the greatest amount of further research and/or historical reinterpretation?

13. Who were the first inhabitants of what is now the Republic of South Africa? Is it justifiable to consider the contemporary descendants of the early Dutch settlers as the Afrikaner *nation*? What role did the British play in the historical growth of the policy of racial separatism in South Africa? What

kinds of resistance to white rule have occurred in South Africa? What is the likelihood of increased internal violence in the future?

14. What were the most important reasons for the European "scramble" for Africa? To what extent, if any, was the United States involved with this scramble? What were the means of European conquest? The means of African resistance? What were the major differences between colonial systems (if any)? What do you feel are the differences between slavery and colonialism? To what extent have pre-colonial and colonial legacies persisted in the independence era?

15. What has been the history of contact between Arabs and Africans? Between Europeans and Africans? Between Americans and Africans? What has been the history of African interstate relations prior to Western contact?

16. What are the major features of African civilization in historical perspective? What are the problems of studying African history? To what extent will archaeology aid in the understanding of African history? What are the problems of written sources of historical evidence? What are the problems with oral data?

III

Processes of Change

Modules	Suggested Readings in *Essays*
Modernization and Social Change 37 Concepts of Social Change and Modernization 38 Social Change and Modernization in Africa	14 Major Themes in Social Change *(van den Berghe)*
Personality and Change 39 The Concept of African Personality 40 Characteristics of African Personality 41 Personality and Social Change	15 Personality and Change *(LeVine)*
Education and Elite Formation 42 Educational Systems in Africa 43 Education and Elite Recruitment 44 The New Elites of Africa	16 Education and Elite Recruitment *(Clignet)*
Urbanization and Change 45 The Development of Urban Society 46 The Nature of Urban Life 47 Problems of Urbanization	17 Urbanization and Change *(Mabogunje)*
Communications and Change 48 Spatial Aspects of Transportation and Communications 49 New Modes of Communication	18 Communications and Change *(Soja)*

Modernization and Social Change

Concepts of Social Change and Modernization

SOCIAL CHANGE REFERS TO THE PROCESSES whereby a society is reoriented in its structures, institutions, values, and patterns of behavior. Some scholars prefer the term *social change* to related concepts such as modernization, Westernization, or development, since social change does not imply any particular directionality and hence may be freer from ethnocentric distortion due to the value preferences of the observer.

The term *Westernization* clearly refers to the processes of adaptation to a North American–European technology, value system, and life style. On the other hand, the term *modernization* (which unfortunately is often used as a synonym for Westernization) is directional in the type of social change required, yet is capable of application in non-Western time and space contexts.

In basic terms, modernization involves an "increasing complexity in human affairs" (Apter, 1965, p. 3). This complexity refers to social relationships and to the generation and utilization of technological resources to change the quality of human life. There are several dimensions of modernization which are most commonly discussed in the theoretical literature. These should be seen as reinforcing each other rather than as independent dimensions. Students should be encouraged to decide for themselves which, if any, of the following are essential aspects of modernization.

1. SPECIALIZATION

Occupational specialization leads to a division of labor in which individuals become more interdependent. Specialization also requires the development of institutions to coordinate the endeavors of individuals and to settle disputes which may arise (see Riggs, 1963, p. 122). These institutions also serve to maintain established patterns of socialization and social stratification.

2. SECULARIZATION

The line between what is considered sacred and what is considered profane varies within and between societies. Secularization refers to the desacralization of material and behavioral phenomena previously assigned supernatural or transcendental powers or values. Secularization is usually a precondition to the growth of science and technology, in that fundamental inquiry into cause and effect must be examined with respect to natural rather than to supernatural agents.

3. URBANIZATION

Urbanization refers to the increase in size, number, and importance of urban centers (population concentrations characterized by high density and marked division of labor) in an area (see Module 46). The complexity of urban life as compared with traditional rural patterns is partly a function of the increased number of social relationships which exist in a city (see McElrath, 1968, p. 4).

4. MASS MOBILIZATION

Mass mobilization refers to the involvement or participation of relatively large numbers of persons in the economic and political life of the community (see Huntington, 1966, p. 378; and Nettl, 1967). This greater involvement is perhaps necessary to the performance of specialized roles, but it clearly results in greater social complexity. Mobilization does not require a particular type of authority system, but it does require effective communication within a society.

5. INCREASE IN TECHNOLOGY

The ability to manipulate natural elements and principles to desired results is at the core of modern society. The technology of economic production is perhaps the most visible instance of modernization, but the technology of warfare, medicine, communications, etc., may be directly related to the increase of social scale and complexity (see Ginzberg, 1964). The relationship of technology to nation-building is discussed in Module 75.

6. INCREASE IN SCALE

Increase in social scale refers to the extension and consolidation of the boundaries of political community, to cooperative behavior between states, and to the growth of systems of interlinked and interdependent urban centers. All of these social arrangements extend the potential for division of labor and specialization, and all require an increase in social relations (see Wilson and Wilson, 1965, p. 24).

7. INCREASE IN COMMUNICATIONS

Increase in communications refers to the broad and effective dissemination of messages. Communications may be regarded as part of the general transaction or interaction flow between individuals or groups, and is clearly related to increase in scale. Communications technology, such as printing in post-Reformation Europe or the transistor radio in contemporary Africa, seems to be at the core of the modernization process (Rogers, 1969). As McLuhan (1962) points out, people adapt and react qualitatively to changes in communications media.

8. INCREASE IN ACHIEVEMENT MOTIVATION

Some type of achievement motivation, rather than inherited (ascriptive) status, seems to be necessary to the effective division of labor, i.e., the specialization of occupations based on skill and ability rather than on status or birth. In a system where roles are established by birth, there is probably less effective utilization of manpower resources than in a system where individuals rise or fall according to their merits (McClelland, 1961). This aspect of modernization, however, has been extremely controversial, since it may be argued that individual achievement is a Western life style, and that other types of motivation may be more appropriate in Africa.

9. SUMMARY

Modernization is regarded in the theoretical literature as increase in social complexity, which is closely associated with social differentiation within a society. Differentiation and complexity usually occur through three major processes:

(1) increase in the scale of human systems of interaction (which may be accomplished through increase in technology and communications); (2) increase in division of labor or specialization (which usually requires some degree of urbanization, social mobilization, and increase in individual achievement criteria); (3) increase in control over natural environment (which is based on technological skills and probably requires some degree of secularization).

Modernization is not necessarily a unilinear process which cannot be reversed. Modernization may occur in stages, with thresholds which are the result of cumulative interaction between several dimensions (e.g., urbanization and technology), or it may follow much less regular and predictable patterns. In any case, if modernization is to be useful as a concept, then it should be capable of application in any context (i.e., not only Western). In Module 38 we examine the dimensions of modernization within the African context and over a long period of historical change.

38

Social Change
and Modernization
in Africa

SOCIAL CHANGE AND MODERNIZATION have been occurring in Africa since earliest times. The degree of "complexity" and the "scale" has probably been greater than appearances might suggest, because of the highly developed trade patterns and use of multilingualism to extend communications networks. The eight categories of modernization suggested in Module 37 provide a framework for interpretive assessment of modernization in Africa in a time perspective. The discussion in this module will be illustrative rather than systematic. It is meant to encourage students to see social change and modernization as a continuing process.

1. SPECIALIZATION

One of the key indicators of occupational specialization is the existence of formal bureaucracies in a state. In the kingdoms and empires described in Modules 20 through 26, there were, in varying degrees of sophistication, large and specialized bureaucracies. Such bureaucracies were distinct from the military and political sectors, and were characterized by a large number of "roles" or "offices." In the Islamic states, there was frequently a standard set of offices: a *waziri* who was chief administrative assistant to the head of state, a series of *muftis* (scribes) and *alkalis* (judges) who presided over the administration of justice, a *ma'aji* (treasurer) responsible for finance, and an *imam* responsible for official religious activities in the state (Last, 1967). Within each of these offices there were a large number of minor officials.

In many empires, such as Ashanti, there were offices for "interpreters" and "communicators." It should be stressed that many of these offices were held by merit, not necessarily by heredity (Wilks, 1967). With regard to pre-colonial occupational specialization in the areas of agriculture and light industry, see Mabogunje (*Essays*, chap. 17).

2. SECULARIZATION

Many of the early Islamic empires were theocracies (see Hunwick, in Lewis, 1966), and many of the non-Muslim empires (e.g., the forest kingdoms) were based on the notion of divine kingship (see Lucas, 1948), as had been the case in Europe until about the time of the Reformation (see Pfeffer, 1967). Yet it was not uncommon in African society for a distinction to be made between the sacred and the secular. Secularization of certain concepts of health and disease resulted in rudimentary medical technology and pharmacology. For example, in Hausa society some diseases were regarded as being caused by supernatural intervention (e.g., paralysis) while other diseases came to be regarded as caused by natural forces (e.g., smallpox, for which the Hausa had devised a genuine inoculation). Hausa pharmaceutical practice (based on local herbs), quite apart from faith-healing, has been quite sophisticated, and "medical books" (in Arabic) have been available dating from the fifteenth century. In overview, however, the development of a secular society in Africa has been a recent pattern.

3. URBANIZATION

As pointed out by Mabogunje, urban centers have existed in Africa from earliest known times. Adulis (the port of Axum), the city-state of Kush (based at Napata and Merowe), the trading centers of Kilwa, Sofala, Mombasa, Kano, Katsina, Jenne, Timbuktu, and Gao, and the large forest urban centers of Benin, Kumasi, and Ibadan all bear testimony to the development of a complex pre-colonial urban pattern in Africa. It should be noted, however, that in most cases of pre-colonial urbanization, there was a relatively high degree of division of labor but a low degree of role independency. Thus, an individual may have been a skilled craftsman, but this role was not separated from his social, religious, and political roles. In the nineteenth and twentieth centuries, the cities which grew up as a result of contact with Europe (such as Lagos, Accra, Dakar, Douala, Nairobi, and Dar es Salaam) did not usually have a legacy of traditional society, with its relative "fuzziness" of role boundaries, as did those cities with pre-colonial origins. Furthermore, there was a considerable increase in occupational specialization.

4. MASS MOBILIZATION

Mass mobilization is very difficult to evaluate with reference to pre-colonial Africa. In segmental societies (which were usually small-scale) everyone might participate in economic and political decisions; in large-scale hierarchical societies there was clearly less mass participation. Yet even in centralized kingdoms and empires, there were frequently mechanisms for consulting the local people regarding political decisions, and rural farmers frequently took the initiative with regard to such economic decisions as crop selection and marketing choices. The fact that many African farmers were so quick to take up cocoa, coffee, peanuts, and other cash crops in the twentieth century is a testament to their ability to mobilize, or participate within new systems as they arose.

5. TECHNOLOGY

Technology in Africa has been a subject of major controversy among historians. While the black Africans in the Nile Valley were among the first humans to utilize iron for weapons and tools, there are certain peoples of Africa (such as the Bushmen of the Kalahari) who are still using Stone Age technology. Arab technology, especially in the fields of medicine and architecture, was adopted in the Sudanic zone at an early stage. In the rainforest areas, which were environmentally impermeable to the horse technology that characterized many of the savanna areas, there was probably a lower level of technology. (It is ironic that the coastal forest areas had the earliest contact with Europeans and hence acquired Western technology prior to the interior savanna areas.) The issue of "diffusion of innovations" (which is probably more important in most cases than independent discovery) is clearly related to the factor of geographical isolation or nonisolation.

6. SCALE

The scale, or size, of African communities is a matter on which there is an enormous range. The Songhai empire was much larger than present-day France. On the other hand, most African societies were very small in area and population, and language differences prevented all but minimal communications and relations with other societies. At the present time, one of the most dramatic aspects of modernization in Africa is the way in which small-scale societies are being linked together into larger systems.

7. COMMUNICATIONS

The question of communications has also been a controversial topic in African history. In the Islamic areas, Arabic was frequently used by elites as a written and spoken medium of communication (see Goody, 1969). Thus in northern and Sudanic Africa, an area larger than the United States, there has been an effective communication network for many centuries. Arabic has served in much the same way as Latin in medieval Europe. It is clear, however, that most African societies did not utilize written forms of language, and widespread communication was thus hampered.

8. ACHIEVEMENT MOTIVATION

In some parts of Africa a fluid meritocracy, based on achievement motivation and non-ascriptive criteria, may have been more important in the pre-colonial period than during the colonial period. In the pre-colonial period there was frequently strong competition between individuals for leadership positions in the larger societies or empires. During the colonial era, both the British and the French often ossified the office of "chief" and tried to ensure that succession disputes, which might threaten the general stability of the colonial regime, did not emerge. Patterns of primogeniture were even instituted in some areas where they had not existed previously.

One should not underestimate, however, the degree to which status in traditional Africa was based on ascriptive criteria. Succession to occupational role was most frequently a matter of son following father (as in medieval Europe). With the introduction of Western education a degree of social mobility developed which might be characterized as based on merit, especially in the French-speaking areas. (For a study of achievement motivation in Nigeria, see Robert LeVine, 1966).

9. CONCLUSION

Modernization in Africa has been a continuous process from earliest times. Certain aspects of modernization (such as occupational specialization and urbanization) have been more prevalent than others (such as technology or secularization). In other modules some of the themes of social change and modernization are examined in more detail. However, it must be recognized that the dimensions of modernization and/or social change are closely interrelated. There are several excellent overviews of social change in Africa: Bascom and Herskovits (1962); Herskovits (1962); Lloyd (1967); Southall (1961); van den Berghe (1965); and Wallerstein (1966). There are also a number of excellent case studies of the various dimensions of social change within particular contexts: Brokensha (1966) on Ghana; Wilson and Wilson (1965) on central Africa; Albert (1960) on Rwanda and Burundi; Balandier (1950) on Gabon; Skinner (1960) on Upper Volta; Soja (1968) on Kenya; Riddell (1970) on Sierra Leone; Fallers (1964) on Uganda; and Middleton (1960) on Uganda.

Personality and Change

The Concept
of African Personality

PSYCHOLOGICAL STUDIES IN AFRICA are in the initial stages of development. Most of the existing material on individual behavior, personality, and related themes (e.g., child-rearing, socialization, abnormal behavior, etc.) derives from the work of social anthropologists and psychiatrists, who have often approached the subject without well-defined psychological concepts or instruments. The focus on personality structure and change within the African context, however, is rapidly becoming an issue both in the ideological literature and in the scientific literature. (For a selection of psychological studies, see Wickert, 1967.)

1. AN AFRICAN PERSONALITY?

There has long been a strong tendency for non-Africans to consider Africans as psychologically homogeneous. Instead of deriving from scientific analysis, this notion is based most often on ignorance, intellectual laziness, or racial bigotry. The extremely heterogeneous African environment and the highly variegated mosaic of ethnic societies, in combination with the clear-cut differences of colonial experience are somehow presumed to produce a generalized "African personality," devoid of only the most subtle variations. When one considers, however, the desire to rationalize colonial domination, the felt "civilizing" mission of Western Christianity, and the historically pronounced European ethnocentrism, it is clearer why much of the older literature on Africa, both professional and popular, appears to be little more than "racial

147

stereotypes with scientific window dressing." As LeVine (*Essays,* chap. 15) has noted, these studies have usually been used not only to derogate or dehumanize the African, but also on occasion to defend him. In more recent times, perhaps to bolster pride and identity and to create closer linkages between all the peoples of Africa, some African leaders themselves have asserted a uniform African "personality," "mentality," or "mind," which appears to gloss over the range of distinctive cultural propensities.

These comments on the various proponents of "an African personality" are not intended to suggest that there are not broad consistencies in the behavior of Africans or that studies of African personality must be embroiled in racial stereotypes (either positive or negative). LeVine notes that there are clusters of African social, cultural, and psychological characteristics which, when taken together, indicate certain commonalities in personality in comparison with other major world areas. Although the individual traits are not *uniquely* African, the particular *combination*—the personality "profile"—may turn out to be so.

2. COMPONENTS OF PERSONALITY

Personality refers to consistencies in the behavior of human individuals which are not due to temporary states of the human organism (e.g., disease, fatigue, anxiety) or to temporary conditions of the environment (e.g., social pressure for conformity). Like physical traits (height, skin color), personality traits vary widely among individuals and across societies. As with physical traits, one can compare groups of individuals by their "average" characteristics and the degree to which they vary within groups (in statistical terms, the *mean* and *standard deviation*). Thus one can speak of an African personality if, in fact, there exists a set of traits which, in terms of their statistical tendencies, differ significantly from those of other world groups. Three broad categories of inquiry are relevant here: (1) environmental characteristics (social, cultural, and physical conditions of sufficient permanence and consistency to affect outward behavior), (2) outward behavior, and (3) the impact of early childhood experience and genetic factors on temperament and personality. As in other areas, the genetic factor has been most difficult to analyze, particularly with respect to separating genetic from environmental influences (see Doob, 1966). Due to the absence of data on this subject, only the first two categories will be discussed—environmental influences is considered in this module and outward behavior in Module 40.

3. ENVIRONMENT AND PERSONALITY

Although not limited to Africa nor universal throughout it, the following environmental influences seem to be relevant to understanding African personality patterns (see LeVine, 1961).

a. The Economy

Agriculture is overwhelmingly dominant (with less male involvement than elsewhere in the world); animal husbandry and pastoralism (more closely associated with males than elsewhere) are important and widespread, creating in many areas, as among the Nuer, Masai, and pastoral Fulani, a cultural system revolving around livestock; certain acquisitive values are common, producing status distinctions based on wealth, but these are focused on particular material objects (e.g., the ownership and exchange of livestock in East Africa, trade and marketing in West and central Africa, and probably the support of more than one wife nearly everywhere).

b. Family and Kinship

Africa is the most polygynous major area of the world. Within this context, mother and children occupy separate households more often than elsewhere. Africa also has the greatest incidence of patrilineality, patrilocality, and bride-wealth (the latter usually involving marriage payments to the family of the bride). These characteristics all affect patterns of sexual behavior and child-rearing; furthermore, unilineal descent groups serve political functions in state and state-less societies and are important bases of local organization nearly everywhere.

c. Political Organizations

Partly for reasons of ecology, acephalous societies outnumber centralized states in Africa. But the latter are more numerous than in any other nonliterate area of the world: chiefs, headmen, and royal or aristocratic lineages play important roles in such societies, and individuals tend to display personality characteristics which are clearly associated with status in the lineage or kinship community.

d. Life-Cycle Patterns

Initiation rites (often involving circumcision) are found in nearly every region of Africa, usually occurring at or around puberty, signaling entry into a new status based on age. Also, beliefs and practices relating to ancestors are probably the most prevalent basis for indigenous African religion and seem to be related to the general respect with which elderly persons are regarded. Such clear-cut life-cycle patterns are probably also associated with the processes of apprentice-ship which are necessitated in the economic sphere and with the special respect which longevity commands in an environment with high infant mortality and short life-expectancy.

e. Population Density

Probably related to each of the categories above is the relatively large size and population density of African societies compared to nonliterate societies elsewhere in the world. There are many ethnic groups over one million people in size (e.g., Zulu, Xhosa, Kikuyu, Luo, Luhya, Ganda, Yoruba, Ibo, Hausa, Fulani, Mossi), and densities rise to over 1,000 people per square mile in some areas of contemporary Africa. The effect of such densities appears to include great complexity in the regulation of interpersonal relationships (see Module 37).

40

Characteristics of African Personality

WITH RESERVATIONS AND CAUTIONS, LeVine (*Essays*, chap. 15) tentatively suggests certain uniformities in African behavior which appear to reflect important aspects of the African personality (at least for the primarily agricultural societies in Africa south of the Sahara). It would be most fruitful to examine these personality uniformities together with broader sociocultural similarities outlined in Module 39. It should be noted that these personality traits are not necessarily *uniquely* African.

1. SOCIAL DISTANCE
BETWEEN PERSONS DIFFERING IN AGE AND SEX

Many of the basic divisions within societies are biological phenomena, such as age and sex. In Africa, age and sex differences are institutionalized so that differences in either element are associated with specific rules of behavior. One therefore can tell a great deal about the role or personality of an individual simply by knowing the individual's sex and age (or generation). Differences in age and sex are manifested in many social activities in the form of avoidance behavior (in-law avoidance, generational avoidance), segregation (separate mother-child households, age-villages, distinctive usage of house space), and highly formalized patterns of interaction (required forms of greetings, topics of conversations, etc.). All of these patterns act to maintain a distinct social and emotional distance between individuals as part of the overall structure of society. LeVine also makes the important point that Africans regard this system as "natural" and "normal," while Westerners, with their own distinctive patterns of behavior, might consider the African impersonal, unfeeling, overly restricted, and a "slave to custom." See Cohen (*Essays,* chap. 3) for some idea of how an African might look at Western social relationships.

Status differences based on age and sex are reflected clearly in patterns of deference, respect, and precedence. High status is given to males over females, married men over single men, and men with adult children over others. Thus the senior male within a household usually has position of high status. This is a phenomenon which forms an integral part of African social relations. Western visitors to various parts of Africa are often amazed to find women carrying huge headloads, marching several paces behind their unencumbered husbands. When the suggestion might be made to "shift the burden," so to speak, it is often the women themselves who resist most strongly. The age and sex hierarchy is so intimately interwoven with other aspects of African society that to change it in isolation is extremely difficult.

2. EMPHASIS ON MATERIAL TRANSACTIONS IN INTERPERSONAL RELATIONS

In most African societies, social relationships entail at some point a prescribed exchange or transfer of material goods—food, gifts, financial help, property, babies. The nature of relationships is often gauged primarily by the material goods exchanged, even between husband and wife. Failure to offer food to a visitor, for example, or failure to accept, may be considered a sign of rejection or hostility. (As an aside, it is interesting to examine some of the problems involved in the provision of food and medicine to Biafra by the Nigerian Federal Government during the Nigerian civil war. To accept food is a sign of friendship and even deference between individuals. Conversely, one of the most common ways of dealing with enemies is to poison their food. Still further, food and medicine are often considered to contain certain qualities which the consumer will assume if taken. It is possible that these factors may partially explain why the provision of food to Biafra became such an enormously complicated problem. There are, of course, many other factors involved which do not relate at all to any traditional patterns of behavior.)

3. FUNCTIONAL DIFFUSENESS OF AUTHORITY RELATIONS

As mentioned in other modules (e.g., Module 38), African authority figures tend to wear many hats at the same time—that is, their roles and power are not restricted to a single specific function but extend over a whole range of activities. This functional diffuseness strongly affects relationships between leaders and subordinates, each of which is obligated to perform a variety of functions for the other. School children, for example, often act as domestic servants for their teachers. Similarly, wealthy Africans have a responsibility to take care of their devoted followers. What Westerners might call political patronage or nepotism is often simply a normal and expected fulfillment of responsibilities between leaders and followers.

4. TENDENCY TO BLAME OTHERS WHEN UNDER STRESS

This factor is closely associated with the use of witchcraft and sorcery. Disaster or misfortune usually brings about a search for the "cause" among other individuals in the immediate interpersonal environment. Accusations of witchcraft and sorcery provide the inflicted individual with a legitimate means of reaction.

5. RELATIVE ABSENCE OF SEPARATION ANXIETY

In marked contrast to Western cultures, Africans are usually able to manage physical separation from family and close peers with little apparent anxiety. This is perhaps a reflection of the perception of these relationships in role terms. There are fewer feelings of pity, nostalgia, sentimentality, and self-inflicted guilt than might be found in Western situations of a similar nature. LeVine makes the interesting suggestion that this difference is due in part to the more open and regulated way Africans deal with interpersonal hostility and affect. Hostility in Westerners is more often internalized, creating enormous guilt feelings both consciously and subconsciously that make separation a stressful situation.

6. CONCRETENESS OF EXPRESSION

Africans tend to express themselves more in concrete terms than in abstract terms. This characteristic may be reflected in the emphasis on material transactions or the tendency to blame and fear others when under stress. The rich metaphorical language of African proverbs—the constant attempt to encapsulate generalized or abstract meanings in concrete terms—also reflects this characteristic.

Unfortunately, concreteness of expression is sometimes misinterpreted as inability to think abstractly. It is clear that this not the case. As LeVine notes, generalities and abstract notions may be fully understood but are simply not discussed in general terms.

41

Personality
and Social Change

THE PERSONALITY CHARACTERISTICS dealt with in Modules 39 and 40 are primarily those of traditional ethnic society in Africa. These characteristics and profiles have evolved over centuries of social change and adaptation. In this module, the most recent phase of social change in Africa—that induced by European colonialism, industrialization, and increased urbanization—is examined with respect to its impact on personality.

1. ETHNIC SOCIETY: ADAPTATION OR BREAKDOWN?

The effect of European contact on Africans is a major concern of all social sciences and is dealt with in various ways throughout Part III, "Processes of Social Change." A common problem in handling this topic, however, has been the tendency to oversimplify the impact of European-induced social change and to overlook the enormous diversity of reactions to it. In the writings of both European and African observers, one frequently encounters sweeping generalizations about acculturation in Africa. Urbanization and industrialization, for example, are seen as forces of "detribalization," eroding the traditional kinship-based system of relationships, "Westernizing" the African, or thrusting him into situations in which he cannot cope (thereby creating widespread anxiety and mental disorder). The few reliable psychological studies which have been made, however, portray a much more complex picture. For example, amount of education and degree of attachment to traditional beliefs are closely inter-related among some ethnic groups but not among others. Even within the same ethnic group in the same city, there may be major differences in the degree of traditional orientation. Contrasting results are also found with respect to the extent of personal conflict and anxiety induced by rural-urban migration.

It is probably safest to say that we still know very little about personality and social change in Africa. This is due in part to the lack of detailed information on personality in the pre-European-contact situation and thus the absence of a clearly identifiable baseline from which to measure change. It is evident, however, that traditional African personality and social structures do not simply break down and disappear under the pressures of modern life. There is instead a very complex pattern of adaptation which varies greatly in timing, effectiveness, amount of stress induced, and outcome, not only from individual to individual but from one ethnic group to another.

Based on the small number of studies which are felt to be reliable, LeVine (*Essays,* chap. 15) hypothesizes several aspects of this adaptation process, with special reference to the broad uniformities in African personality patterns discussed in Modules 39 and 40. The remainder of this module focuses on three *additional* topics which are, perhaps, of special importance: the concept of "achievement motivation," the psychological impact of colonialism, and the nature and extent of mental illness in Africa.

2. ACHIEVEMENT MOTIVATION AND SOCIAL CHANGE

Why do some societies experience rapid rates of development while others barely survive? In attempting to explain cultural growth and decline in human history, the psychologist David C. McClelland, in the now-classic study *The Achieving Society* (1961), focused on achievement motivation—an acquired drive for excellence or need to achieve—as a primary factor creating differential levels of economic growth and development among the world's peoples. Drawing from this work, a number of scholars have adapted the notion of achievement motivation to Africa as a hypothesis to explain differential levels and rates of modernization among African ethnic groups.

Certain ethnic groups, such as the Kikuyu in Kenya, the Chagga in Tanzania, the Baganda in Uganda, the Ibo and Yoruba in Nigeria, the Ewe in Ghana, and the Bamiléké in Cameroon, have been widely considered (both by local Africans and by international observers) as exceptionally energetic and enterprising, more easily adaptive to the needs of modern industrial society, and consequently disproportionately prominent in the national economy and political life of their respective countries. Regardless of the accuracy of these stereotypes, there do appear to be great intra-national differences in economic and educational advancement in Africa. In recent years, a growing number of studies have suggested the personality characteristic of "achievement motivation" as an explanation of these variations.

In a pioneering but highly controversial study, LeVine (*Dreams and Deeds,* 1966) examined motivational differences between the three major ethnic groups in Nigeria: Ibo, Hausa, and Yoruba, The study analyzed the written essays and dream reports of schoolboys in an effort to measure their personal orientation to achievement and/or obedience values. Results confirmed the common stereotype of the Ibos as highly motivated toward achievement. This study, although criticized both on methodological grounds (e.g., in the choice of sample subjects, particularly among the Hausa) and conceptual grounds (e.g., the validity of clientship as implying obedience rather than as a means toward cooperative achievement) provides an exciting indication of the potential contributions of psychology to social-science research in Africa.

3. THE PSYCHOLOGY OF COLONIALISM

The topic of colonialism as it has affected both colonizer and colonized extends far beyond the realm of African studies. Yet many of the important studies are coming out of Africa. Frantz Fanon, a West Indian psychiatrist who lived and worked in Algeria, has dealt with the confrontation between black and white races not only in Africa but throughout the world. In *Black Skins and White Masks* (1967), Fanon examines the "psycho-existentialist complex" that emerges from the traditional superior-subordinate relationship between white and black, between colonizer and colonized. In doing so, he both elaborates upon and criticizes the earlier work by Mannoni (*Prospero and Caliban*, 1956) which noted the damaging effects to both superior and subordinate in the colonial relationship. The essays by Albert Memmi (*Dominated Man*, 1969) on the suppression of the black man are also relevant.

Less impressionistic and more academic than the works of Fanon, Mannoni, and Memmi are the detailed studies of African perceptions of Europeans, several of which are briefly reviewed in Doob (1965). Perhaps the best of these studies is by Gustav Jahoda (*White Man*, 1961) who conducted survey research in Ghana (then Gold Coast) from 1952 to 1955. He clearly shows the wide range of perceptions of Europeans held by different groups in Ghanaian society, related to such variables as education, age, political involvement, and degree of traditionalism.

4. THE PSYCHOPATHOLOGY OF SOCIAL CHANGE

It is frequently assumed that tension and related mental disorders will be greater in rapidly changing societies than in more stable ones, particularly for those individuals moving rapidly from traditional to modern ways of life, as compared to those whose life has remained virtually unchanged. In the modern context, the individual is viewed as being faced with an increasing number of alternative behavior choices and new goal choices. But as with so many aspects of the African experience, recent studies have indicated that the relationship between social change and mental disorder is complex and not easily generalizable. Bohannan (1960), for example, illustrates clearly that suicide and homicide are by no means absent in African traditional societies and thus are not necessarily a by-product of societal disruption associated with modernization.

Leighton *et al.*, *Psychiatric Disorder Among the Yoruba* (1963), is perhaps the most illuminating and important of recent studies on psychiatric disorder in Africa. The study was carried out by a team of African and American (Cornell University) psychiatrists, physicians, and anthropologists in Abeokuta, Nigeria. They discovered that the Yoruba of Abeokuta, in comparison with a selected sample in North America, had more psychoneurotic symptoms, but fewer persons seemed to be suffering from certain or probable psychic disorders. With respect to the percentage significantly impaired by psychic disorders, the figures were 15 per cent for Yoruba rural hamlets, 19 per cent in the Abeokuta urban area, and 33 per cent in the North American sample.

What the study seems to suggest is that social change need not dramatically increase individual tension and that some societies, like the Yoruba, may be highly successful in accommodating change without a significant deterioration in mental health. Moreover, the study also indicates that when mental illness does occur, it is often treated quite successfully by traditional means and "native" doctors.

Education and Elite Formation

42

Educational Systems in Africa

EDUCATIONAL SYSTEMS IN AFRICA and their major features — patterns of recruitment, substantive content, relationship of education to modernization, etc. — are examined in this module in three historical phases: the pre-colonial period, the colonial period, and the independence period.

1. PRE-COLONIAL EDUCATION PATTERNS

All African societies have had some institutionalized way of transmitting heritage, culture, and skills to the younger generation. Occupational skills were learned through on-the-job apprenticeship. A son usually followed his father's occupation, although sometimes there was division of labor within families. As discussed by Mabogunje (*Essays,* chap. 17), pre-colonial occupations usually included crafts (e.g., iron-working, weaving, dying), marketing (e.g., long-distance or local trade), healing, farming, and political/legal administration.

Cultural knowledge was transmitted through a variety of agents. Frequently elders would simply relate proverbs and stories of the community and its history to children in the evening (since occupational apprenticeship usually occurred during the day). In other cases, this process of socialization was more formal and complex.

In the Islamic areas of Africa there was an elaborate system of institutionalized education. Children between the ages of five and twelve would attend Koranic schools in the mornings and/or evenings where they would be taught by a specialized teacher. Children would learn Arabic script, certain chapters from the

Koran, and the basic elements of arithmetic. Students who wished to continue could attend Islamic secondary schools where religious history, Islamic law, poetry and grammar, and other subjects were taught. Beyond this point, students might select a particular teacher for work on advanced topics. In the larger Muslim cities of Africa, such specialized learning was frequently conducted at universities. (The universities of Al-Azhar in Egypt and Kairawan in Morocco are among the oldest universities in the world. The University of Sankore in Timbuktu is mentioned in Module 22.)

2. COLONIAL EDUCATION SYSTEMS

In French and British colonial territories in Africa, educational *structures*, were basically parallel, but there were important variations on matters of curriculum, recruitment, and language use. Structurally, the French elementary school was approximately the equivalent of the British primary school (grades one to six). The French lycée was approximately the equivalent of the British secondary school (grades seven to twelve). (In the British system at this same level there were teacher-training colleges, trade schools, and the university-preparatory "colleges" — sometimes called "fifth- and sixth-form schools"). In both British and French systems, universities were reserved for highly specialized training.

The major differences and historical development of the British and French educational systems in Africa are discussed in Clignet (*Essays*, chap. 16). Both were constructed around the need to fill a labor market and both were ambiguous with regard to the categories of persons to be selected for education (although in British areas there was more of a tendency to cater to the "sons of chiefs"). Certain differences, however, did emerge by the end of the colonial period: the preference in French schools for the use of a European language (i.e., French) as the medium of instruction (rather than vernacular languages); the greater centralization of French education as compared to British; and (perhaps consequently) the greater variability in the quality of education in the British areas. It should also be noted that the number of private schools (mainly missionary) in relationship to public schools was much greater in British areas.

In both the French and British areas, stiff examinations mediated entrance into schools at the secondary and university level. These were standardized examinations drawn up in London and Paris. Hence, while there might be variation in the quality of education in particular locations, the successful students could be assumed to have acquired comparable knowledge. It was in the private schools, especially missionary secondary schools in the British areas, that both the quality of education and the substance of the curriculum varied most.

In the Belgian areas of Africa, by contrast, there was a heavy concentration on primary education, but almost nothing in the way of secondary and university education. In the Belgian areas education was frequently in the hands of the Catholic Church. Also, there was a preference for the use of vernacular languages rather than European languages as the media of instruction.

In all three colonial areas (French, British, Belgian), education was used primarily to meet the needs of the administration and the economy. In Belgian areas, however, there was very little training of civil servants, and a greater concentration on technical education. In both British and French areas, in the late colonial period, the university system was used almost exclusively for the production of civil servants. As Clignet suggests, this may have been done partly to offset the rising demands of African nationalism.

3. EDUCATION PATTERNS IN THE INDEPENDENCE ERA

There are four major patterns which seem to characterize African educational systems in the post-colonial period: (1) the sharp increase in school-enrollment figures (with a full range of consequences, including school-leaver unemployment); (2) the reorientation of school location and recruitment policies to reflect new political realities; (3) the growth of African universities; and (4) the Africanization of the curriculum at all levels.

The average elementary school enrollment, as a percentage of total population, in thirty-two sub-Saharan African states in 1965 was still relatively low by international standards: 7 per cent (ranging from 1.1 per cent in Somali to 22.1 per cent in Congo-Brazzaville). Yet the percentage increase within the African states has been most dramatic. The average increase in per-capita enrollment from 1960 to 1965 was 34 per cent, and in five countries increases ranged over 100 per cent (Niger, 163 per cent; Ghana, 126 per cent; Chad, 122 per cent; Mali, 119 per cent; and Ethiopia, 100 per cent).

The same pattern is noticeable at the high-school level. Although the average high-school enrollment, as a percentage of total population, in 1966 was 4.1 per cent (ranging from 21.3 per cent in Ghana to 0.2 per cent in Mali), the per-cent increase in high-school enrollment per capita from 1962 to 1966 was 41 per cent. This latter figure included an enormous range from those countries which have suffered decreases in high-school per-capita enrollment (Burundi, Cameroon, Rwanda, Congo-Kinshasa), either for reasons of political crisis or reasons of population increase, to those countries which have per-capita enrollment increases of over 100 per cent (Mauritania, 1,300 per cent; Congo-Brazzaville, 619 per cent; Guinea, 283 per cent; Ethiopia, 214 per cent; Zambia 174 per cent; Chad, 140 per cent; Lesotho, 120 per cent; Uganda, 111 per cent).

One of the consequences of the increase of both elementary and high-school education has been a growing rate of unemployment of "educated" persons in many African countries. This may be a temporary phenomenon, specific to the transition period in which African economies reorient themselves to internal needs, or it may be a continuing problem—one which has already had consequences for political stability in Africa.

One of the reasons for the increase in elementary and high-school enrollment figures has been the popular demand for schools by local communities. It is clear that African governments are more susceptible to political demands for education than were the colonial regimes. These political demands (which are documented in detail for southern Nigeria by Abernethy, 1969), have led to reorientation of both location of facilities and recruitment policies within the new states. While the patterns are not entirely clear, there appears to be less concentration in the capital-city areas and more opening up of selection channels to all classes within society.

At the university level, there has been an equivalent increase in facilities. Universities have been established in almost all states. While those few universities which dominated the late colonial period are stronger than ever, including the University of Ibadan (Nigeria), University of Ghana at Legon, Makerere University (Uganda), University of Dakar (Senegal), Fourah Bay College (Sierra Leone), and Louvanium University (Congo-Kinshasa), there are now a host of new and beautifully constructed universities in Dar es Salaam (Tanzania), Abidjan (Ivory Coast), Nairobi (Kenya), and several other capital cities. In larger countries such as Nigeria and Congo-Kinshasa a number of new universities have been built. There are, for example, five major universities in Nigeria: Ahmadu Bello University in Zaria, Lagos University, Ife University, University of Nigeria at Nsukka, as well as the University of Ibadan. The University at Nsukka, however, is not in operation due to the civil war. (Note: the university situation in Liberia and Ethiopia is also impressive, but is not included in this discussion because they have not been colonies.)

At all levels in African education, from elementary school to university, there have been significant attempts to revise curriculums to reflect new needs. (For examples of such innovation, see Jolly, 1969.) While there is still some interstate standardization, the European orientation has come to be stressed less than counterpart African history, language, and culture.

43

Education and
Elite Recruitment

SOCIAL CHANGE IN AFRICA is closely related to elite development. As discussed in Clignet (*Essays*, chap. 16), education has been one of the major means of creating an elite and recruiting new members into an elite. According to Lloyd (1966, pp. 2–3), within the African context the term "elite" designates anyone with an annual income of over $700 who is Western-educated. Elite in this sense does not necessarily refer to persons who influence decision-making within institutions of society, but rather to those who may be regarded as having a special potential for influence in the development of national systems by virtue of their education and type of employment.

1. PRIORITIES IN EDUCATIONAL PLANNING

In 1961, at the Conference of African States on Development of Education in Africa (Addis Ababa, Ethiopia), a twenty-year plan for educational development in Africa was designed and approved. There was a follow-up meeting in Paris in 1962 to discuss implementation of the plan. Recommendations regarding priorities in education included (1) development of secondary-school facilities, (2) training of primary and secondary-school teachers, (3) teaching of English and French, and (4) encouragement of research on African languages. Also in 1962, at the Conference on Development of Higher Education in Africa (Tananarive, Malagasy Republic) several additional recommendations were made regarding (1) the need to pool resources for university training; (2) the designation of thirty-two "key" African universities; (3) increase of university enrollments; (4) special needs for increased enrollments in agriculture, fishery, and forestry; and (5) general Africanization of the curriculum. During the 1960s, there has been an impressive implementation of these goals, as mentioned in Module 42.

The educational policy for each African state is determined internally, of course, and there is a wide range of educational strategies and priorities reflected in the national budgets of African states. But the general pattern of priorities is probably reflected in the recommendations of the Addis Ababa and Tananarive conferences.

The implications of these priority recommendations in terms of social change (elite formation in particular) within the African states are open to speculation. The emphasis on secondary education was clearly intended to create a class of middle-level manpower capable of clerical or skilled technical work but also equipped to deal with the multitude of management responsibilities at the middle level in the economic development process. The concentration at the university level of technical expertise (particularly in agriculture) was perhaps intended to replace that class of European technical advisers, upon whom many African governments have had to depend, with an indigenous class of technical experts. The emphasis on language research and training was perhaps intended to generate elites who could communicate with fellow Africans at the international level (in French *and* English) and, through exploration of the possibilities of increased use of vernacular languages in elementary and adult education, perhaps lessen the gap between "modern" and "traditional" social classes. The focus on primary-school teachers was clearly an effort to break the bottleneck through which the vast majority of young people would, hopefully, be drawn into the "modern" sector and perhaps become the "working class" in the new national systems.

2. THE ABSORPTION OF EDUCATED ELITES

In some states the fervor of generating primary-school graduates led to unpredicted consequences. The "school leavers," as they were called, were frequently unable to obtain jobs commensurate with their expectations. This often created an unemployment problem in the urban areas, which, according to Gutkind (1967) has produced an embryonic "class" (i.e., a social stratum which is cohesive by reason of collective socioeconomic status rather than ethnic or individual status) linked by an "energy of despair." There has been an increased recognition by African governments of the need to determine manpower requirements as a preliminary step to turning out persons at particular levels of education (see Taylor, 1962; Curle, 1969).

This problem of unemployment has not yet occurred to the same degree at the high-school level. Most high-school graduates have secured jobs as office workers either in government or in business. High-school graduates with technical skills have generally been absorbed into the economy, and those who attended teacher-training schools were usually assigned jobs for the three-to-five-year period following graduation. There is, however, a growing problem with respect to vocational-school graduates. Given the relatively low division of labor within most African economies, the vocational-school graduate often finds himself *overspecialized* and all too often jobless (or forced to work in a position which takes little advantage of his specialized skills).

In the future, however, if African economic systems do not progress more rapidly, secondary-school graduates may find it increasingly difficult to obtain jobs. This is already beginning to happen in those countries where the educational program is geared primarily to an "arts and humanities" curriculum, with little emphasis on mathematics, natural sciences, or communication skills.

At the university level there has been a continuation of the British and French pattern of selecting only a very few students and expending considerable resources on their training. University graduates have been quickly absorbed into the civil service and into the higher teaching levels, although, in the future, this too will depend on the general level of economic development.

Most of the students who attend universities in Africa are on full government scholarships. One obligation which usually results from acceptance of these scholarships is the commitment of the first three to five years after graduation in an occupation and location assigned by the government. The government may assign a teacher to a backward part of the country when he might prefer to work elsewhere, or a doctor to a small village hospital when he would rather have experience in a larger medical complex. The overall result is probably a more effective utilization of manpower resources than if all decisions were left to individuals, since most graduates prefer the social life and economic opportunities of the capital city. After the initial obligation to work at a specific task is completed, many of the highly educated persons do choose to return to the large cities. As Clignet (*Essays,* chap. 16) describes, some also leave the country altogether and get high-paying jobs in Europe or America. This "brain drain" is becoming a serious problem in many African states (see Dzobo, 1969), especially in the smaller French-speaking countries since there has been a long tradition of black Africans living and working in France (see N'Diaye, 1962). Occasionally these African expatriates do return home, often at a high level of government service. The president of Senegal (Senghor) and the president of Malawi (Banda) had established careers in Paris (teaching) and Scotland (medicine), respectively, before returning to their countries.

3. RECRUITMENT INTO THE EDUCATIONAL SYSTEM

The questions of where to locate schools and what entrance qualifications should be established are at the crux of the recruitment problem. Since education is so clearly related to elite formation, it is possible, through selection-of-students policy, to determine the ethnic and social characteristics of the next generation of elites. Most African governments are acutely aware of this situation. They are caught in the dilemma of choosing between a policy which might result in immediate economic development and a policy which might affect the future fabric of national integration. If educational facilities are increased around the capital-city area, where much of the industrial, commercial, and governmental growth is occurring, then there may be a greater likelihood of immediate payoff in terms of economic development. This means, however, that the educated classes would most likely be from those ethnic groups near the capital city. This might mean increasing the disparity between them and ethnic groups living in the "interior" or "hinterland." National integration may

require that less-advantaged groups gain access to the channels of elite formation. Certain states, such as Tanzania, have consciously decided that all groups
and sections of the country should develop at the same pace (see Resnick, 1968).
Other countries, such as Ivory Coast, are developing rapidly in the coastal cities
but less so in the interior. It should be stressed, however, that policies of ethnic
balance are one thing; actually changing existing situations is another. The
present elites cannot easily exert influence to change the ethnically unbalanced
pattern of elite formation in the future. Furthermore, the costs of "evening
out" educational opportunity are often enormous. (For a discussion of education and nation-building in Africa, see Cowan, O'Connell, and Scanlon, 1965.)

One of the most dramatic instances of low differential selectivity into Western
education resulting in national crisis has been the Nigeria case (see Abernethy,
1969; Ikejiani, 1965; Weiler, 1964). The Ibo peoples of the former Eastern
Region generated disproportionately large numbers of educated persons, who
came to dominate many sectors of national life. The Hausa-speaking peoples,
of Northern Nigeria, who have long resisted Western education (partly because of Islamic apprehensions regarding the missionary-based nature of
Nigerian education) became increasingly concerned about the dominance of
Ibo elites. The results of this tension clearly contributed to the Nigerian civil
war which lasted from 1967 to January, 1970 (see Module 65). Yet the dilemma
remains, for if rapid economic development is not attained (at whatever cost to
equality of educational opportunity), the African states may well succumb to the
explosive pressures of the newly literate urban masses.

44

The New Elites
of Africa

WHILE EDUCATION IS A PRIMARY MEANS of generating elites in Africa, it is not the only means. Labor unions, commerical organizations, and traditional societies have all produced national and international leaders. It should be noted in all cases that the processes of elite formation in Africa have been powerfully dominated by politics. Economic leaders who remain relatively independent of the political elite, for example, are usually viewed by the government with great suspicion. Indeed, much of the leadership which has arisen in business, as well as in trade unions and from traditional organizations, has been selectively generated and to a large extent controlled from the political sector (whether colonial or African).

1. TYPES OF ELITES IN AFRICA

The labor-union movement in Africa was transplanted from Britain and France in the 1930s as a matter of government policy (see Davies, 1966). Most of the African states now have well-established trade unions. Invariably, the leadership of the unions has arisen from within the unions. Yet, since African governments are the major employers, the primary function of the labor elites has come to be the articulation of workers' needs to the appropriate government planning agencies rather than the mobilization of strikes for higher wages. In fact, many of the labor leaders who emerged in the pre-independence period have been absorbed into the dominant political party. Sékou Touré, president of Guinea, was the leader of the major confederation of trade-union organizations in West Africa (Union Générale des Travailleurs d'Afrique Noire). The late Tom Mboya, minister of economic planning and development in Kenya before his assassination in 1969, was head of the Kenya Federation of Labor. (For his autobiography, see Mboya, 1963.) Houphouet-Boigny, president of Ivory Coast, was formerly head of the African agricultural union (Syndicat Agricole Africain).

Indigenous commercial elites in Africa have developed largely as a result of the marketing of agricultural cash crops, which often required middlemen between the small farmer and the government buyers. Although agricultural cash crops were exported to Europe in the pre-independence period through large international companies such as Unilever, there were African middlemen (in British areas called "licensed buying agents") who lent money to the farmers and later purchased the crops from the farmers. Several of these local middlemen became millionaires. Such agents do not necessarily need Western education as much as rapport with the farmers, good trading skills, and a line of credit. It should be recognized, however, that in most African countries, governments, Asian entrepreneurs, or European companies still monopolize the "middleman" role. Other types of African commercial elites include those who engage in textile wholesale activities and those who have gone into real estate in the new cities.

In the field of light industry, many African businessmen have become well established, either by themselves or in conjunction with expatriate firms. In Nigeria, the shoe industry, the match industry, the plastic-goods industry, the rubber-tire industry, and many other types of light industry are partially owned and/or controlled by African businessmen (see Kilby, 1969). Publishing, banking, and the construction industry are becoming ever-important sources of indigenous wealth and leadership.

Traditional society in Africa has also produced many leaders who function in the modern sector as well as in the traditional sector. Chiefs may be "progressive," and although they derive their authority from traditional societies, they frequently carry some influence among the educated elites of Africa (many of whom are the sons of chiefs). In countries with a house-of-chiefs, however, traditional rulers may directly participate in the political decision-making process.

In short, there are many types of elites in contemporary Africa. The educated classes constitute, by definition, an important segment. However, leadership has emerged in all spheres, from labor unions to banking.

2. CHARACTERISTICS OF NATIONAL LEADERS

The original heads-of-government in Africa, that is, those men who led their states to independence and usually remained as the first presidents or prime ministers, form an interesting group. Most were highly educated (to university level or beyond). The former president of Ghana (Kwame Nkrumah), for example, taught in several American universities (see Nkrumah, 1957). As mentioned earlier, the president of Senegal (Léopold Senghor) had been a professor in France (see Markovitz, 1969). Many of the heads of state in Africa were doctors, lawyers, teachers, or journalists (see Figure 8). They were an elite within an elite, and to some extent they were effective because they could deal with European administrators as "equals." It is likely that the second generation of political elites in Africa (excluding military regimes) will be less clearly associated with men from the highest ranks of Western education, since political effectiveness has come increasingly to revolve around internal rather than external forces. (For brief biographical sketches of African political leaders, see Segal, 1961; Reuters News Agency, 1967.)

In examining the characteristics of national leaders in Africa, several variables seem to be of special importance: age, ethnicity, degree of education, ability in

FIGURE 8

CHARACTERISTICS OF FIRST HEADS-OF-STATE
IN 32 SUB-SAHARAN AFRICAN STATES

Country	First head-of-state	Dates in office	Age in 1969	Ethnicity	Education	Original occupation
1. Botswana	Dr. Sir Seretse Khama	1966–	48	Tswana	Fort Hare, University of Witwatersrand, Oxford	Read law
2. Burundi	Andre Muhirua	1962–63		Tutsi		
3. Cameroon	Ahmadou Ahidjo	1961–	45	Fulani	Technical-secondary Yaounde	Radio technician
4. C.A.R.	David Dacko	1960–66	39	Baya	Technical-secondary in Africa (Congo-Brazzaville)	Civil servant
5. Chad	François Tombalbaye	1960–	51	Sara	Primary	Assistant teacher, also trade-unionist
6. Congo-Brazzaville	Fulbert Youlou	1960–63	52	Balari (Kongo)	Seminary in Akono, French Cameroon	Catholic priest
7. Congo-Kinshasa	Patrice Lumumba	6/60–9/5/60	Died 1961, age 36	Batetele	Mission School in Kasai	Tax clerk–postmaster

Country	First head-of-state	Dates in office	Age in 1969	Ethnicity	Education	Original occupation
8. Dahomey	Hubert Maga	1960–63	59	Fon	Technical-secondary in Dahomey	Teacher training and civil servant
9. Ethiopia	Aklilu Habte-Wolde	1961–	57	Amharic	Sorbonne, University of Paris	Civil servant functionary
10. Gabon	Leon M'Ba	1960–67	Died 1967, age 65	Fang	Catholic secondary in Gabon	Civil servant
11. Gambia	Sir Dauda Jawara	1965–	45	Mandingo	Postgraduate veterinarian	Pre-independence organizer
12. Ghana	Kwame Nkrumah	1957–66	60	Nzima	Postgraduate, U.S.	Political party employee, university professor
13. Guinea	Sékou Touré	1958–	47	Malinke	Technical-secondary in Guinea	Clerical, trade-union leader
14. Ivory Coast	Félix Houphouet-Boigny	1960–	64	Baoule (Akan)	University, Dakar	Professional physician
15. Kenya	Jomo Kenyatta	1963–	78	Kikuyu	Postgraduate, England; London School of Economics	Farmer, clerk
16. Lesotho	Chief Leabua Jonathan	1966–	55	Sotho	Mission school (primary)	Miner

17. Liberia	William Tubman	1943–	Americo-Liberian	Cape Seminary	Lawyer
18. Malawi	Dr. Hastings Banda	1964–	Chewa	Postgraduate, Nashville, Tennessee	Doctor, M.D.
19. Mali	Modibo Keita	1960–68	Malinke	University, Dakar	Teacher, civil servant, school inspector
20. Mauritania	Moktar Ould Daddah	1960–	Moor	Postgraduate professor France	Lawyer, interpreter
21. Niger	Hamani Diori	1960–	Djerma (Songhai)	Secondary, Dahomey	Civil servant, teacher
22. Nigeria	Sir Abubakar Balewa	1960–66	Hausa, Gerawa	London School of Economics; Katsina College	Teacher
23. Rwanda	Gregoire Kayibanda	1962–	Hutu	University, Grand Seminary of Nyakibanda	Teacher
24. Senegal	Leopold Senghor	1960–	Serere	University of Paris	Teacher, professor
25. Sierra Leone	Sir Milton Margai	1961–64	Mende	M.D., Durham University	Government doctor
26. Somali	A. A. Shermarke	1960–64, 1967–69	Somali	Ph.D., Rome	Civil servant

(22. Nigeria: Died 1966, age 64)
(25. Sierra Leone: Died 1964, age 69)
(26. Somali: Died 1969, age 50)

Country	First head-of-state	Dates in office	Age in 1969	Ethnicity	Education	Original occupation
27. Sudan	Ismail-Al-Ashari	1956–58, 1964–69	Died 1969, age 71	Arab	American University, Beirut	Teacher
28. Tanzania	Julius Nyerere	1961–	48	Zanaki	Postgraduate, Edinburgh	Civil servant, teacher
29. Togo	Sylvanus Olympio	1960–63	Died 1963, age 67	Ewe	University of London	Business entrepreneur
30. Uganda	Apollo Milton Obote	1962–	44	Lango	Makerere College	Business entrepreneur
31. Upper Volta	Maurice Yaméogo	1960–66	48	Mossi	Secondary	Civil servant
32. Zambia	Kenneth Kaunda	1964–	45	Bemba	Secondary, Zambia, teachers certificate	Farmer, teacher

vernacular languages, religious affiliation, and original occupation. Many of the African leaders have written autobiographies which provide insight into the subjective aspects of their character. (For examples, see Azikiwe, 1961; Awolowo, 1960; Nkrumah, 1957.) Most African leaders have also written extensively on their political thoughts and intentions. (For examples, see *Bibliography:* Sékou Touré, Julius Nyerere, Boubou Hama, Ahmadu Ahidjo, Léopold Senghor, Modibo Keita).

3. SOCIAL MOBILITY, STATUS CRYSTALLIZATION, CLASS FORMATION

The achievement of independence and the rapid socioeconomic changes which have occurred in Africa in the last generation have resulted in a highly mobile social situation. Some rural peasants have become wealthy through commercial acumen. Education, particularly in the French-speaking areas, has resulted in phenomenally high rates of social mobility. At present, this social mobility appears to be slowing down slightly as the sons of the first-generation elite begin to get priority treatment at educational institutions and as the number of better-paying positions in the economy become filled by young men who block the advancement of those under them. In short, those who are now the elite are trying to "crystallize" their status and to ensure that they become secure within the elite structure. To the extent that these elites are beginning to control internally the rewards of the national systems, it is possible to refer to them as a social class. It should be noted, however, that in comparison with Europe, Latin America, or the Middle East, the class structure or elite patterns of Africa are still highly fluid (see Mercier, 1966). Still, one interpretation of the recent *coups d'état* in Africa is that the military is trying to prevent the entrenchment of a privileged socioeconomic/political elite.

Urbanization and Change

The Development
of Urban Society

1. PRE-EUROPEAN URBANIZATION

URBANIZATION IN AFRICA, as Mabogunje clearly points out (*Essays*, chap. 17), was not simply the outgrowth of European contact. Important urban centers, closely associated with trade and the growth of centralized state systems, grew up in the Nile Valley and along the Mediterranean coast (Thebes, Luxor, Carthage); in the Sudanic belt and northern Guinea forest fringe in West Africa (Timbuktu, Gao, Kano, Kumasi); and along the East African coast (Mombasa, Zanzibar, Kilwa). Moreover, many of these cities were in contact with one another within, as well as between, these broad urbanized regions. (Interregional contact involved primarily oceanic trade between the Indian Ocean, the Red Sea, and the Mediterranean and the trans-Saharan caravan trade between northern Africa, the Sudanic belt, and the forest regions to the south).

Equally important, however, is the fact that many of these cities, particularly those in West Africa, were quite different in form, function, and character from the modern industrialized city of the West. (The characteristics of what has come to be called the "pre-industrial city" are described in Sjoberg, 1960.) Many cities, for example, were much more culturally homogeneous than cosmopolitan, acting as the center of economic, political, and sociocultural influence for a particular ethnic group. In others, as in most Yoruba towns in southwestern Nigeria even today, the bulk of the population consisted of farmers. Nevertheless, few if any scholars would deny that the large settled communities which predated European colonial contact were indeed cities in virtually every sense of the word.

173

Interesting source materials for specific cities in pre-colonial Africa include Miner (1953) on Timbuktu; Horvath (1969) on Ethiopia; and Lloyd, Mabogunje, and Awe (1967) on Ibadan. The Ibadan study, in particular, provides an excellent basis for an intensive study of an African city, past and present.

2. THE CITY AND MODERNIZATION

With European expansion into Africa, the city everywhere became an important element in the African cultural landscape. Herskovits writes:

> In some instances, indigenous administrative and trading centers, like Kumasi in Ghana or Segou in Mali, were continued. Elsewhere, towns were created to fulfill these functions, as was the case with Luluabourg, established as the capital of Kasai Province in Congo, or Lusaka, the Northern Rhodesian seat of government. Mining operations were responsible for the founding and rate of growth of other centers. In some, growth was extremely rapid. Enugu, capital of the Eastern Region of Nigeria, was founded in 1909, following the discovery of coal nearby. In 1953, it had almost 63,000 inhabitants, and by 1960, 80,000 (Herskovits, 1962, pp. 263–64).

Africa remains the least urbanized of all the continents, but its *rate* of urban growth is probably the most rapid in the world. The problems generated by this rapid urbanization and associated industrialization are outlined briefly in Mabogunje and discussed in greater detail in Module 47. Below are listed some of the major functions of cities in the modernization process (see Breese, 1966).

a. *Contact with the Outside World*

Diplomatic representatives, tourists, businessmen, and other foreigners tend to concentrate in the major towns, especially the large capital cities. These cities are also focal points for international networks of air travel, postal and telephone communications, radio hookups, etc. Most external information is therefore filtered through the urban areas.

b. *Center of Political and Economic Power*

Because of their focal position with respect to both internal and external communications, cities are usually the headquarters of government and administration, and of industrial, commercial, and other enterprises. National politics in most African countries tend to be heavily concentrated in the urban areas, often just in the capital city. The ease with which a national government is modified after a *coup d'état* is illustrative. A coup, more often than not, involves a small group of people operating in one small portion of the capital city.

c. Center of Origin and Diffusion of Social Change

Cities are major agents of change. Innovative ideas and creative leadership tend to evolve primarily in the cities and, again due to their centrality on the communications network, the cities become the centers from which the effect of these developments spreads to the rest of the country.

d. Magnet for Human and Capital Resources

Cities, particularly the capital cities, have a powerful attraction for rural populations. (For examples from Ghana, see Caldwell, 1969.) Moreover, the cities tend to attract the most-talented or best-educated individuals, the most-skilled laborers, and the wealthiest sources of capital investment. After spending some time in the city, even if not enough jobs are available, few find it easy to return to the rural areas (see Module 47 on problems of social congestion). Similarly, once the economic strength of a city is established, its magnetism for further investment is increased.

3. CONTEMPORARY URBAN PATTERNS

Mabogunje provides statistical and cartographic information on contemporary urban patterns. He distinguishes between four major types of urban centers in modern Africa.

a. The Traditional City

The traditional African city is "a city which in general has failed to integrate effectively into the new spatial economy and transportation network." Miner's work (1953) on Timbuktu provides an excellent case study here.

b. The Rejuvenated Traditional City

The rejuvenated traditional city has successfully linked up to the modern economic infrastructure. As Mabogunje notes, these cities often reflect a complex economic and social "dualism," with "old towns" standing in dramatic juxtaposition to modern commercial and industrial cities (see Lloyd, Mabogunje, and Awe, 1967, on Ibadan).

c. The Colonial City

A colonial city has been well laid out and planned by colonial authorities, yet is populated almost entirely by African migrants. These include most of the prominent port cities of tropical Africa such as Lagos, Abidjan, and Accra. The studies on Freetown (Banton, 1957; and Fyfe and Jones, 1968) make the Sierra Leonean capital an excellent source of case-study materials (even though it was founded prior to the colonial period).

d. The European City

Markedly segregated, with a powerful non-African flavor, these "European cities" are closely associated with large numbers of permanent European (and Asian) settlers. Epitomized by the cities of the Republic of South Africa, they are often characterized by attempts to prevent permanent African residence. Although changing rapidly, many cities in the independent Black African states of eastern Africa (e.g., Nairobi, Lusaka) show strong resemblances to the more clearly European cities of the Republic of South Africa and Rhodesia.

4. FURTHER COMMENTS

Mabogunje (1968) offers some interesting comments on what he calls the functional specialization theory of urbanization, which may provide a fruitful way of pursuing the topic of how and why cities grow — in Africa and elsewhere in the world. The theory rests on the assumption that urbanization is based on the specialization of functions within human communities generated through the division of labor. This specialization will lead to the rise of urban centers, however, only when three additional conditions are met. First, there must be a food surplus to support the class of specialists whose activities are now withdrawn from agriculture. Second, there must be a group with sufficient power to assure that food will be supplied to the specialists by the food producers and that stable and peaceful conditions are maintained between the producing and consuming groups. Third, there must be a class of traders and merchants to facilitate the work of the specialists and to satisfy their needs for raw materials. Mabogunje proceeds to explore these conditions as part of a general theory of urbanization and as a basis for assessing urbanization in Nigeria.

46

The Nature
of Urban Life

IT IS USEFUL TO DISTINGUISH between *urbanization*—a process of urban growth involving population movements and a variety of induced changes and contrasts with pre-existing conditions (e.g., in economic specialization, sociopolitical segmentation, etc.)—and *urbanism*, the way of life in towns. Although there is a strong association between the two, the correlation is not complete. One may increase more or less rapidly than the other. Certain African rural areas, for example, may contain very few towns but nevertheless display many of the characteristics of urbanism. Urbanization must not be considered as identical to Westernization, "detribalization," or even industrialization. This module will concentrate upon urbanization and social change; yet the patterns which emerge are probably the major components of urbanism in Africa.

1. THE URBAN FAMILY

Most scholars consider the family, if it is actually contained within the town (rather than remaining in the rural area), as continuing to be the primary unit of urban social organization. Many changes, however, tend to occur in the traditional patterns of family organization, resulting in what is usually interpreted as a *relative* decline in the importance of the family vis-à-vis other forms of social organization. Allowing for regional variation, the following general trends have been widely observed in Africa: (1) increased importance of the nuclear family vis-à-vis the extended family, although the latter is often reshaped as a type of welfare system for new migrant relatives; (2) increased independence of women in some cities, particularly with their entrance into the cash economy; (3) smaller family size, influenced by a tendency to marry later (especially among the males), the uneven sex ratio in most cities (more men than women), and the decline of polygyny; (4) greater variation and diversity of family life, reflecting the heterogeneity of the urban environment, greater interethnic marriage, etc. (For a criticism and re-evaluation of some of these generalizations, see Clignet and Sween, 1969; and Clignet, 1970.)

There has been a tendency to oversimplify these changes by considering urban family life as inherently unstable and the traditional system as being rapidly destroyed by progressive secularization and other disruptive influences. It is probably more accurate, however, to consider the changes as not necessarily resulting in a breakdown or absolute reduction in importance, but in a restructuring and diversification of family roles and relationships. It is worthwhile here to refer to the discussion on the flexibility and dynamism of "ethnicity" (see Modules 4, 5, 6; and 7). Herskovits' definition of *reinterpretation* is extremely relevant here: A process in which "sanctions and values of a given tradition under contact are applied to new forms, combining and recombining until syncretisms develop that rework them into meaningful, well-functioning convention" (Herskovits, 1962, p. 292).

2. VOLUNTARY ASSOCIATIONS AND ETHNICITY

The distinctive characteristics of the urban milieu are seen perhaps better than anywhere else in the voluntary associations which have developed in Africa over the years. Little, who has studied their history and organization in West Africa, views them as an important "adaptive mechanism" assisting in the adjustment of migrants from the rural areas "by substituting for the extended group of kinsmen a grouping based upon common interest which is capable of serving many of the same needs as the traditional family or lineage." Furthermore, in terms of the urban milieu, the African voluntary associations "provide an outlet for the energies and ambitions of the rising class of young men with a tribal background" and "encourages him [the migrant] to mix with persons outside his own lineage and, sometimes, tribe," thus helping him "to adjust to the more cosmopolitan ethos of the city" (Little, 1965). Little views as particularly important those associations he terms the "traditional-modernized" type, since "their combination of modern and traditional traits constitutes a cultural bridge which conveys, metaphorically speaking, the tribal individual from one kind of sociological universe to another" (quoted in Gutkind, 1962, p. 182; see also, Wallerstein, 1964).

Thus the urban African becomes entwined in a new and complex network of social relations which essentially involves two components: ethnic kinsmen and non-kinsmen (friends, neighbors, workmates, etc.). Within this framework several observations may be made.

a. Ethnicity

Ethnicity remains a powerful force for social organization in the city, although the boundaries of the ethnic group are often redefined much more widely than in the rural milieu. This redefined kinship network provides an element of stability in a highly fluid situation. Ethnicity, as Epstein (1967) points out, serves as a force for social categorization within the city, a guide to behavior, a badge of identity, a marital and social activity source, a friendship network, and a base for forming a variety of associations (mutual aid and burial societies, political pressure groups, etc.). Epstein also comments on the evolution of these ethnic associations: initially dominated by traditional elders; later serving young men seeking positions and status; still later developing into large scale "tribal" unions, which provide the organizational structure for nationalist movements and competitive political parties; or evolving into exclusive social clubs for small groups of immigrants with generally high social status.

b. Nonethnic Voluntary Associations

Voluntary associations which are not ethnic in character serve functions similar to ethnic associations but in addition cut across kinship ties to establish a broader fabric for social, economic, and political organization. Such associations include occupational groups and trade unions, religious associations, political parties, age-groups, various mutual-aid societies, etc. (For one of the best case studies of such associations, see Meillassoux, 1968, on Bamako.) These may be initiated on an ethnic basis and often remain closely associated with ethnic organization, but tend to become more clearly transethnic over time.

3. POLITICAL PROCESSES

It is worthwhile here to summarize briefly some of the general conclusions about the political consequences of urbanization and social change made by Coleman (1963, pp. 536–37). (These observations provide a transition to Module 47 on urban problems.)

1. As centers where the modern elite subsociety is concentrated, the urban areas are the primary if not exclusive locus of national (*vs.* local or regional) politics.

2. Rural-urban links, however, are maintained through the circulation of labor and the retention of traditional contacts by the urban dweller. The cities therefore are major agents for the diffusion of modernity into rural areas.

3. The "magnetism" of the city has frequently attracted more migrants than the urban economy can absorb, resulting in major problems of unemployment and the creation of large dissatisfied elements in the population.

4. Commercialization and industrialization have not always led to social or political integration or the emergence of a large African middle class. One reason for this has been the strong commercial control by alien groups such as the Asians (Indians and Pakistanis) in East Africa and, to a much lesser extent, the "Lebanese" (from all over the Levant) in West Africa.

5. Differential modernization has frequently intensified intergroup tensions. Education and wealth have not been evenly distributed along communal, racial, and ethnic lines, thereby creating a new pattern of "haves" and "have-nots."

6. There has been a general secularization in urban areas, but religious organization remains a powerful political force.

4. OTHER ASPECTS OF URBAN LIFE

Urbanism is also associated with increased social stratification and differentiation and with major changes in economic organization. Key factors in urban social stratification and differentiation include the growth of voluntary associations, progressive economic specialization and industrialization, and the vital role of education. This topic is discussed in Clignet (*Essays,* chap. 16), with a specific emphasis on the formation of elites.

In general, urban centers require an increased division of labor, greater specialization and, hence, greater economic interdependence. See Mabogunje (*Essays,* chap. 17) for a more detailed description of how economic organization changes with urbanization.

47

Problems of Urbanization

SOME OF THE PROBLEMS OF URBANIZATION in Africa have been touched upon in Modules 45 and 46. Many others are problems which are shared by cities all over the world: alienation, congestion, health, impersonality, psychological stress, etc. Some of the distinctive problems of African urbanization are summarized by Herskovits as follows:

> The world-wide movement of peoples to towns and cities, though not peculiar to Africa, was accelerated there. Where these centers did not exist, they were created. Where they developed out of earlier centers, they changed both in form and function. Moreover, urbanization in Africa took on a particular character. Here city dwellers not only had to solve the usual problems of urban life everywhere — questions of housing, of health and hygiene, of recreation, of juvenile delinquency — but the complexity of these problems was compounded by other factors. In the areas of permanent non-African settlement, city life sharpened a sense of differentials based on race, on standard of living, on education, on economic opportunity and the like, since in the city these were experienced at close range, and thereby served to multiply the frictions arising out of continuous propinquity. Even where multi-racial tensions were minimal, the rapidity with which those who migrated to the towns had to adapt themselves to life in the new setting introduced special problems into what is at best a difficult enough process, even in those parts of the world where the city in its later forms had long been known (Herskovits, *The Human Factor in Changing Africa*, 1962, p. 286).

It is also important to emphasize here again that "detribalization" is an inadequate concept in describing social change within the city. Ethnic identity provides, and will no doubt continue to provide for many years to come, a fundamental mechanism for adjustment and absorption into urban life. African urban problems are thus very much like the broader problems of nation-building: to create (via some kind of synthesis between tradition and modernity) stable, cohesive, and developing plural societies from the amalgam of different groups occupying the same area (groups being defined on the basis of ethnic, racial, religious, or other "primary" characteristics).

For references on specific urban social problems and urban integration problems in Africa, see the *Bibliography* (especially UNESCO, 1956). The remainder of this module will focus on problems of social congestion, single-city primacy, and urban-systems growth.

1. SOCIAL CONGESTION

Many African cities have grown so rapidly that population numbers far surpass the availability of jobs and the ability of the city to provide sufficient housing and services. This has been called "overurbanization" and clearly results in social congestion (see Harvey, 1968; Wood, 1968). Kinshasa (formerly Leopoldville), for example, has grown from a city of about 400,000 just before the former Belgian Congo became independent in 1960 to perhaps 1,500,000 in 1969. The results of this phenomenal growth here and elsewhere in Africa include excessive congestion, very high unemployment or underemployment rates, the growth of squalid, slumlike squatter communities (called *bidonvilles* in Kinshasa and other French-speaking areas), enormous pressure on existing sanitary and medical facilities, and many other problems associated with overcrowding. In many cases, although not all, the rural areas have also suffered from the urban drain on its able manpower. Many African governments, reacting to these problems, have begun to promote "back to the land" movements, encouraging a redistribution of population out of the larger cities and into the smaller towns and rural areas. An interesting perspective on this problem with reference to Nigeria is provided by Mabogunje in an article titled "Urbanization—A Constraint to Economic Development" (1965).

2. SINGLE-CITY PRIMACY

Related to the problem of overurbanization is the tendency in many countries for economic and political power and development to be concentrated in a single city, nearly always the capital. It is often contended that these "primate cities" so dominate their countries that they drain investment and manpower from other areas, hinder the development of other urban centers, and consume more than they produce in terms of revenue. On the other hand, it has also been noted that most developing countries can afford only one "great world city" and that primacy can characterize highly developed countries as well (e.g., Stockholm in Sweden). Whether primacy is a problem—assuming that the city can "handle" its larger population—is therefore an open question. Whatever the answer, primacy is a prominent characteristic of many African countries. Soja (1968), for example, points out that Nairobi, with 3 per cent of Kenya's population, has close to 50 per cent or more of the total urban population, postal traffic, radios, television sets, and telephones of the country. About 17 per cent of the entire African labor force in Kenya is employed in Nairobi, and, more important, these laborers earn 28 per cent of all wages paid to Africans in Kenya. Furthermore, one can estimate fairly accurately the level of development of any area in Kenya by knowing the degree to which it interacts with Nairobi—an indication of the powerful role of the primate city in shaping the patterns and diffusion of modernization in a country.

3. THE GROWTH OF URBAN SYSTEMS

The growth of urban systems is closely related to the question of single-city primacy. There has been a tendency in the literature on African urbanization to stress intensive case studies of individual cities (particularly the primate cities), exploring their internal social, psychological, economic, and political character. But often these cities cannot be put into proper perspective without considering the larger urban system in which they are a part. It is important, therefore, to consider the growth and problems of whole systems of cities as part of the more general study of urbanization and social change. (For examples of this in Nigeria and Ghana, see Mabogunje, 1969, and McNulty, 1969.) In addition, a major gap in the literature exists at the "middle level," the medium-sized towns in Africa, which are often few in number but equally often disproportionately important in the overall processes of urbanization and modernization.

African urban systems (which include the individual urban nodes within an area, the linkages between them, and their relationship with surrounding rural areas) have emerged most dramatically from the colonially superimposed structure of transportation, communications, administration, and economic organization. The cities themselves are key points of concentration in what Mabogunje (*Essays*, chap. 17) calls the "spatial economy" of the country and act together to coordinate and control the modern systems of trade, industry, education, and politics. The degree to which traditional urban centers did or did not interact with the superimposed system marks the distinction between "stagnant" and "rejuvenated" traditional cities suggested in Mabogunje. Perhaps the most significant question, however, is to what degree African urban systems have become effectively interactive with traditional society in general. In most of the developed countries, the indigenous populations "grew up" within a modern space-economy; whereas in Africa and elsewhere the modern space-economy has been grafted onto a very different foundation. Moreover, the transplant has "taken" in only a few areas. Viewed in this perspective, therefore, the problems of urbanization are intimately related to the larger problems of political and economic integration, economic development and stagnation, and the nature of social change and modernization.

Communications and Change

Spatial Aspects
of Transportation
and Communications

BROAD DESCRIPTIVE SURVEYS of transport and communications development in Africa are contained in Soja (*Essays,* chap. 18), Hance (1967), and Ewing (1968). In this module, some of this factual and descriptive information will be built upon to illuminate another major factor in the processes of social change and modernization. This factor is primarily spatial, or geographical, although it involves other disciplinary approaches as well. For African case studies using this approach, see Gould (1960 and 1970), Taafe *et al.* (1963), Soja (1968), and Riddell (1970).

1. THE SPATIAL APPROACH TO MODERNIZATION

The themes of modernization and social change have become important foci of interdisciplinary research in the social sciences. In many studies, however, they are viewed as rather abstract processes, divorced from time or place, or as historical developments confined to specific areas or peoples. But it is clear that social, economic, and political change take place in space as well as over time. They have a "geography" in that their impact differs significantly from place to place and, more importantly, they result in major transformations in the way space is organized. Taafe *et al.* and the essay by Soja, for example, illustrate the far-reaching changes which take place with the growth of transport networks—new centers emerge and grow rapidly, others decline, as the relative

185

locational advantages of points in space become altered by the changing patterns of accessibility generated by transport growth. In Module 71, geographically uneven levels of industrial development are referred to as problems in economic planning and in the formation of regional economic organizations.

The important point is that the spatial perspective of geography can provide a framework for the analysis of social change. Throughout Africa, nearly all the industrial-urban and technological developments usually associated with contemporary forms of modernization were not indigenously generated. They evolved as the result of the imposition of a new system of social, economic, and political organization over a mosaic of predominantly small-scale traditional societies. The new system, based on the colonial territories which have emerged as today's independent states, encompassed much larger frameworks of circulation and interdependency (see the discussion of "scale" in Wilson and Wilson, 1965). The superimposed structure (consisting of urban, administrative, and transport subsystems) acted as the channels through which the forces of change were introduced and around which the new patterns of organization and behavior evolved. Following along these lines, we can identify three major dimensions applicable to the spatial analysis of modernization: structure, diffusion, and response.

2. SPATIAL STRUCTURE

The discussion in Soja (*Essays,* chap. 18) of the historical and regional patterns of transport growth outlines perhaps the most important component of spatial structure with respect to modernization: the selection of routes into the interior, of ports from which to start these routes, and of the major centers to be developed along them has had a powerful influence on the patterns of modernization in Africa. Great port cities such as Mombasa, Dar es Salaam, Lagos, Port Harcourt, and Dakar emerged as the major contact points between interior Africa and the rest of the world. Many older centers, less fortunately located with respect to the new routes, often declined to insignificance. In the interior, cities such as Nairobi grew from scratch because of their strategic location along the new railway lines. The development of road and, particularly, railway lines provided the structure through which traditional Africa encountered most directly the forces of change generated from outside the continent. (Note, of course, that much indigenously generated social change had always taken place in Africa. We are discussing here the major changes instigated by colonial contact.)

3. DIFFUSION OF MODERNIZATION

The modern system thus became interwoven with the traditional base in only a few areas, which grew into the major nuclei of modernization and social change for the masses of the population. The African population interacting most closely with such growth points provided the bulk of the indigenous social, economic, and political elite. In a sense, the urban, administrative, and transport systems provided the structure through which modernization diffused and became concentrated. In those areas where major geographical centers of modernization were located within ethnic groups with high propensity to change (high "achievement motivation"? — see Module 44), these groups came to dominate the economy and often the politics of their respective countries (e.g., the Ibo and Yoruba in Nigeria, the Akan and Ewe in Ghana, the Kikuyu in Kenya, the Ganda in Uganda, etc.).

That modernization to date is uneven and concentrated in a few major nuclei is one of the most outstanding features of contemporary African states. In many cases, this situation causes problems. It hinders a wider impact of modernization — industrialization, literacy — on the masses of the population; it cements the dominant position of particular ethnic groups; and it creates ever-widening gaps between the more and less developed areas and peoples. Moreover, in Africa the infrastructure upon which these patterns emerged was more strongly shaped by the objectives and demands of the colonial power than by those of the indigenous population. Whether African states should attempt to "even out" the inequalities of piecemeal modernization is one of the most formidable and perplexing problems they face.

4. RESPONSE: MODERNIZATION AND NATION-BUILDING

Given the framework of structural development and the diffusion of modernization, the dimension of response essentially encompasses the whole range of the modules that are included in Part III, "Processes of Change." It also can provide an introduction to the material covered in Part IV, "Consolidation of Nation-States." With respect to the "geography of modernization," however, there are several sources of maps which may be used quite effectively to illustrate some of the patterns and problems mentioned in this module.. These include Soja (1968) for Kenya, Riddell (1970) for Sierra Leone, Green and Fair (1962) for South Africa, Gould (1970) for Tanzania, and the endpaper map in Weinstein (1966) for Gabon.

49

New Modes of Communication

As NOTED IN SOJA (*Essays,* chap. 18), one of the most striking developments accompanying social change in Africa has been the expansion in breadth, intensity, and impact of communications. This component of social change and modernization has been discussed in Modules 37 and 38 and indeed relates to nearly all the modules in Part III, "Processes of Change." Although the definition of communications used by Soja encompasses the full range of media involved in the exchange of information, thus linking communications growth with the growth of transport networks, urbanization, the money economy, and all factors which expand the "scale" of society, the emphasis in this module will be on the mass media, primarily the press, radio, television, and film.

1. THE STATUS OF MEDIA DEVELOPMENT IN AFRICA

The mass media as we know them in the United States are all present in Africa, and rare is the African who has not heard a radio or seen a newspaper. Given the relationship between communications growth and general economic development, however, it is not surprising that Africa — the least technologically developed of the continents — is also the least developed with respect to the media of mass communication. UNESCO has suggested a number of minimum statistical standards for what it considers "adequate communications." These include the provision for each 100 people of at least the following: ten copies of daily newspapers, five radio receivers, two cinema seats, and two television receivers. The actual figures from Africa in 1965 were, for each 100 persons, about one daily newspaper, about four radio sets (the use of the radio has grown dramatically since independence), one-half a cinema seat, and one-tenth of a television receiver. These figures have increased somewhat since 1965, but it is nevertheless clear that for a continent of over 300 million people and with 42 independent states, the existing mass media (with the possible exception of radio) are grossly inadequate. Moreover, a closer examination of the country-by-country figures would indicate the very high degree to which media facilities are concentrated in just a few countries.

2. THE PRESS IN AFRICA

The earliest newspapers in sub-Saharan Africa were established by the European and Asian immigrant communities and essentially served only their interests. Thus countries in eastern and southern Africa have had daily newspapers since before World War I. Salisbury (Rhodesia), for example, has had a daily paper (the *Rhodesian Herald*) since 1891. During the drive toward independence, there was a proliferation of newspapers, bulletins, pamphlets, and news-sheets, but their number has grown much less rapidly — and may actually have declined — since independence. A selection of the best newspapers in sub-Saharan Africa today would probably include the *East African Standard* (Nairobi), the *Daily Nation* (Nairobi), *Dakar-Matin* (Dakar), *Rand Daily Mail* (Johannesburg), the *Daily Times* (Lagos — probably the paper with the largest circulation in Black Africa), the *New Nigerian* (Kaduna), the *Daily Graphic* (Accra), the *Nationalist* (Dar es Salaam), *Fraternité Matin* (Abidjan), and the *Zambia Mail* (Lusaka). (For a more complete list, see the Panofsky and Koester article in the *Guide to Resources*.) Many of these papers are now government owned and run — an important pattern in post-independence Africa — but nearly all continue to be relatively objective and on several occasions have been highly critical of the government. If possible, students should be encouraged to read copies of at least one African newspaper.

In all, there were about 212 daily newspapers in Africa in 1965, which, along with 18 bulletins, had a total circulation of about 3.2 million, still a remarkably low figure. Furthermore, the bulk of this circulation was in South Africa (nearly 30 per cent), the three Maghrib states (almost 20 per cent) and in the U.A.R. (Egypt — about 15 per cent). Tropical African newspaper circulation, therefore, was only 1.2 million (led by Nigeria, Ghana, and Kenya). Some of the reasons for this low level of circulation include a late start in press development, low literacy levels, the need to import newsprint and equipment, and the lack of rapid low-cost transport. (A detailed examination, with statistical data, of the media situation in Africa, can be found in UNESCO, *World Communications*, 1966.) The situation has begun to improve in recent years, however, with the expansion of the rural press in conjunction with literacy programs. Such newspapers, usually in vernacular languages, are generally weeklies and thus do not appear in the previously mentioned circulation figures. No estimates of their circulation are available. It must also be mentioned that European and American newspapers and magazines are available throughout Africa. In nearly every large city, one can purchase the *Times* (London), the *Observer*, the *Herald Tribune* (international edition), *Time*, and *Newsweek*; or, in the French-speaking areas, *Le Monde*, *France-Soir*, and *Figaro*.

Another significant development, which reflects the importance placed on the media by the new African states, has been the establishment of national news agencies since independence. Prior to 1955, there was only one national agency (the South African Press Association) in Africa. Since that time, over twenty national news agencies have been established, and there are plans for the creation of an African press pool for the exchange of news among African agencies and its distribution throughout the world. The Ghana News Agency already transmits news in English and French daily to its London office, from which it is beamed back to West Africa and is received in an area from Dakar to Lagos. The exchange of news between African countries and from the rest of the world to Africa, however, is still carried out primarily by Agence France-Presse (Paris) and Reuters (London), and to a lesser extent by German (DPA), Russian (Tass) and American (UPI, AP) news agencies.

3. RADIO, TELEVISION, AND THE CINEMA

Radio broadcasting has advanced more rapidly than the press over the past decade, but there are still only about 370 transmitters for the entire continent. There is a similar pattern of heavy concentration of receivers in those countries mentioned in the section on newspapers, but many of the non-English-speaking territories also have relatively high figures (Libya, Somali Republic, Gabon, Senegal). Liberia leads all of Africa in the ratio of receivers to population. Probably the major problem involved in expanding radio broadcasting—a problem which pervades all the communications media—is the very large number of African languages and the political sensitivity of national language broadcasting policies (see Fishman, 1969; and Fishman *et al.*, 1968).

Despite these problems, the radio is probably the most popular communications medium in Africa, a position which has been solidified by the rapid increase in use of transistor radios (which are not dependent on an external power source). The radio is efficient, relatively inexpensive, and can reach the masses of the people, including the isolated and the illiterate. (For a case study of broadcasting in Nigeria, see Mackay, 1969.) Just as it has been suggested that Africa will skip the "railway age" in the growth of modern transport systems, so too has it been said that Africa is likely to skip the "age of newspapers" to enter the "electronic age" of radio, television, and the cinema before widespread newspaper circulation and literacy are established.

Television developed very late in Africa (almost entirely since 1962); experienced a brief burst of expansion—expecially as each independent state set up its own government station, in part as a symbol of status; and has in recent years leveled off in most countries and perhaps even declined. The reasons for this leveling off, which undoubtedly will be temporary, are clear: the high costs of purchase and maintenance, the need for electricity, and the expense and training required in program production. Although there have been major efforts in the more than twenty states which have television transmitting facilities to encourage local programming to suit local needs, nearly all depend primarily on "canned" programs imported from Europe and America. It will be interesting to see the impact of small, transistorized, and portable TV sets in the future, once some of the financial problems are overcome. It should be noted that, despite popular pressure, the South African government has not permitted television service in that country, apparently for political reasons.

Film production in Africa is in its infancy. Feature films are regularly produced in the U.A.R., occasionally in Morocco and Tunisia, and in South Africa
(in Afrikaans), but American, British, French, Indian, and Arabic films dominate the African screen. The number of cinema houses is exceedingly small,
but projection from mobile units is extremely popular throughout Africa. In
Nigeria, for example, these units cover over 80 towns and show to audiences of
over 5,000 at each performance. (UNESCO, 1966, p. 43). The future of the
cinema in Africa is likely to be exciting both in respect to expanding audiences
and to the actual production of feature films by Africans. Dramatic evidence
of the creative potential of African film producers can be seen in the films of
the Senegalese director, Ousmane Sembène. His first film, "Borom Saret,"
produced in 1963, was a view of the problems of a cart driver trying to feed his
family. In 1966 he made "Black Girl," a tragic story of a Dakar domestic servant
pushed to suicide by the degradation of her French employers and her lone-
liness for home. In 1969, "Mandabi," a full-length comedy in color on the theme
of rags-to-riches-to-rags, was the surprise hit of the New York Film Festival and
firmly established Sembène as a director of international consequence. The
film was shot in both French and Wolof; the Wolof version was shown in New
York.

Religion and Change

50

The Impact
of Christianity

THE COPTIC CHURCH OF ETHIOPIA is one of the oldest Christian churches in the world, dating from the fourth century A.D. (see Ullendorff, 1968). It is the official church of Ethiopia and is distinguished by its "monophysite" belief that God and Jesus are one. Until recently, it has been linked to the Orthodox Church in Alexandria (Egypt), but only since 1960 has the Ethiopian church made an impact on Christian communities in other parts of sub-Saharan Africa. The early withdrawal of the Amharic Christian community into the Ethiopian Highlands, where they are centered today, was the result of Muslim confrontation along the Red Sea coast. This African Christian community flourished for centuries in isolation, developing a complex and sophisticated ritual, art, and architecture in their church-centered society.

The Ethiopian Church serves as an introduction to assessing the impact of Christianity in Africa because of the widespread stereotype of Christianity as a European religion. Suffice it to remark that Christianity was flourishing in Black Africa before the fall of the Roman Empire and the emergence of Europe as we know it today.

Nonetheless, this module will focus primarily on the planting of European Christianity in Africa, African responses to such imported religion, the impact of Christianity on social change, and the role of Christianity in contemporary Africa. (For a useful introduction to all of these topics, see Beetham, 1967; and Baeta, 1968.)

1. THE PLANTING OF CHRISTIANITY IN AFRICA

As mentioned in Fabian (*Essays*, chap. 19), Christian priests accompanied the Portuguese navigators to Africa in the late fifteenth century, prior to the splitting of European Christianity into Catholic and Protestant groupings. Portuguese priests made contact in the Kongo and Benin kingdoms, and significant numbers of Africans were converted at that time. Later, this early Christian influence in Africa was to fade almost entirely, as Portuguese international power became diluted, and as African kings reverted to traditional practices.

The renewal of Christian contact in Africa occurred through the freed slaves from the New World, who were returned to Freetown (Sierra Leone) after 1791, and Monrovia (Liberia) after 1820. Most of these ex-slaves were passionate Protestant laymen, and their evangelism made some impact on the indigenous peoples. Many of the Sierra Leonean Christians later migrated to Gambia, the Gold Coast, Dahomey, and Nigeria, where they converted local peoples.

The European Christian-mission movement, as we know it today, began in the nineteenth century and did not gather real momentum until after 1870. Many of the Protestant mission movements were associated with the abolition of the slave trade, and part of the stated intention of the early mission groups was to establish commercial trade in those parts of West Africa which had been formerly dependent on the slave trade for sustenance.

The Roman Catholic Church, meanwhile, through the Holy Ghost Fathers, had established missions in Senegal in 1843 and in Angola and Congo in 1866. In 1878, the White Fathers began work in Tanganyika and Uganda. In 1892, the Society of Jesus began to work in the Belgian Congo. Today, there are more than fifty different Catholic orders in Africa, and certain orders, such as the White Fathers, the Verona Fathers, and the Holy Ghost Fathers, are concerned almost exclusively with Africa. By the end of the nineteenth century, Roman Catholic activities in Africa were centralized and coordinated in Rome. In general, Catholic missions were prohibited from commercial trade, unlike many of the Protestant missions, which were virtually self-sustaining through trade. (For full details of the planting of Christianity in Africa, see the four-volume set by Groves, 1948–58.)

2. MISSION ACTIVITY IN AFRICA

Three essentials of mission activity in Africa were full-time professional missionaries, the existence of mission stations, and affiliational linkage with European "parent" organizations. Among the Protestant missions there was very little coordination of activity, and a disproportionate number of such missions were evangelical as distinct from orthodox. Yet, in general, apart from conversion activities the Christian churches in Africa seemed to undertake work in three major fields of activity: literacy, occupational training, and medicine.

Among the Protestant groups, literacy was seen as the means to reading the Bible. The early classes conducted by the missionary himself quickly developed into primary, and later, secondary, schools and teacher-training institutes. The Bible Association in London commissioned the translation of the Bible into many of the vernacular languages of Africa, which often entailed the writing of dictionaries and the establishment of orthographies as a preliminary to the translations.

Occupational training usually included instruction in farming techniques or utilization of literacy skills in the clerical side of commercial trade. The slogan of the Church Missionary Society (CMS) in the 1850s was "The Bible and the Plough," and, as mentioned above, the intention of the missionaries was to supplant the slave trade with alternative forms of commercial trade. The commercial establishment of the Basle Mission in Ghana, begun in the nineteenth century, was of considerable magnitude by the time of Ghanaian independence.

Although medicine was seen as part of the Christian gospel of healing, it was also necessary for missionary survival in the tropical zones. In West Africa, malaria alone shortened the life expectancy of European missionaries in the nineteenth century to only a few years. But although schools were established almost everywhere the missionaries went, hospitals were much less frequently established, because of the scarcity of missionary resources.

During the colonial era, the Christian missions maintained a variety of relationships to the European authorities with regard to literacy, vocational training, and medicine. In the Congo, the Catholic Church was officially entrusted with much of the primary-school education in the country (see Slade, 1959). In French areas, however, the anti-clericalism of metropolitan France carried over to the colonial office, and in many cases the church was prevented from undertaking educational tasks. (See Debrunner, 1965, for a case study of Togo.) In British Muslim areas, such as Northern Nigeria, missionaries were prohibited from evangelization (including education) by the colonial authorities, who feared that such activities would stir up resistance to European rule. Evangelical groups from the United States, which became increasingly numerous after 1900, were seldom a source of support for the colonial regimes but were often more involved with medical missions than educational missions.

3. CHRISTIANITY AND SOCIAL CHANGE

The Christian missions in Africa were characterized in general by a lack of tolerance for "traditional" cultural practices (especially polygyny). They exerted a powerful influence for social change in the direction of assimilation into rigid, puritanical, European patterns of behavior. It was this rigidity, in retrospect, which seems to account for the rise of independent African churches (see Module 51).

The Nigerian historian Jacob Ajayi, in a recent volume (1965), focuses on one of the major by-products of Christian missions in Africa—the creation of an educated elite. (For further discussion and references, see Modules 43 and 44.) It should be noted that in many cases Africans came to hold leadership and intellectual positions within the local churches (such as Bishop Crowther of Nigeria—a Yoruba), but more often the educational impact of missions was on generations of young African men and women who eventually became secular leaders in secular societies.

A brief note should be made of missionary impact on race relations in Africa. In retrospect, it appears that most missionaries (especially Protestant and/or evangelical) utilized their European racial identities in the subtle balance of power relations with Africans. They became inextricably woven into the European community of colonial administrators, merchants, and settlers, (See Rotberg, 1965, for a case study of Northern Rhodesia.) Also, because the missionaries were often slow to relinquish real control to African pastors, they helped to foster, in many areas, a sense of black racial frustration which took the forms of religious independency movements (discussed in Module 51) and African nationalism (see Shepperson, 1953; and Balandier, 1953). Both phenomena have had considerable impact on social change in Africa. (It should be noted that lack of transfer of authority to indigenous leaders and white racism are two distinctively different things. For example, the Roman Catholic priests in Nigeria, and especially in Biafra, have lived for years on the level of the local people and are widely admired by Africans for their lack of racism; yet according to the official Catholic Directory for Nigeria, 1967, seventeen of the twenty-three bishops in Nigeria were born in Ireland!)

4. CHRISTIANITY IN CONTEMPORARY AFRICA

Although Christianity has increased steadily in Africa, it remains a minority religion in most African countries. There are perhaps 50 million Christians in Black Africa today. Apart from Ethiopia and the Portuguese- and Afrikaner-dominated areas of southern Africa, Christianity is the religion of a majority of the population in only five independent countries: Congo-Kinshasa (40 per cent Catholic, 13 per cent Protestant); Congo-Brazzaville (40 per cent Catholic, 17 per cent Protestant); Burundi (60 per cent Catholic, 1 per cent Protestant); Gabon (50 per cent Catholic, 14 per cent Protestant); and Lesotho (45 per cent Catholic, 38 per cent Protestant). Within West Africa, census claimants of Christianity have increased significantly since 1952. However, even in the coastal areas of West Africa, adherents of Christianity have increased at a slower rate than adherents of Islam. In general, the major centers of Christian affiliation in Africa remain the larger coastal cities rather than the interior areas.

Church-state relations in independent Africa have frequently been strained. To the extent that Christianity was identified with colonialism it has become a target of nationalist sentiment (as in Ghana under Nkrumah, or in Congo-Brazzaville; see Victor DuBois, 1967). Also, the new governments of Africa feel they should have a direct policy voice in the educational and medical facilities of the churches. To some extent this potential conflict is being mitigated by the Africanization of the clergy. It has become clear that if Christianity is to thrive in Africa, it must be under the leadership of Africans (see Idowu, 1965). This was recognized by the Catholic Church implicitly in their appointment of a Tanzanian as a cardinal and explicitly during the Pope's visit to Uganda in the summer of 1969. Most of the orthodox Protestant groups have given their African mission churches full independence from foreign control, and their leadership is now nearly completely Africanized. The pattern with evangelical groups, however, is different, and the Jehovah's Witnesses and even the Sudan Interior Mission have remained self-consciously "white" at the leadership level.

It is important not to exaggerate the conflict between Christianity and the new African nations. Most of the African national leaders were trained in mission schools, and some remain dedicated Christians. Julius Nyerere of Tanzania is a devout Catholic, as is Léopold Senghor of Senegal. Kenneth Kaunda (Zambia) and Dr. Hastings Banda (Malawi) are Protestant laymen with a quasi-fundamentalist orientation. Even Dr. Kwame Nkrumah (Ghana), according to his autobiography, at one time hoped to become a Catholic priest. The educated elite crowd the big churches on Sundays, and university chapels (in contrast to many American colleges) are well patronized. In short, the future of Christianity in Africa is in the hands of Africans. Whether this will lead to a regeneration of Christianity or to increasing decay remains to be seen.

51

Innovation, Synthesis, and Independency

ACCORDING TO BARRETT (1968), there were over 6,000 identifiable independency religious movements in Africa by the end of 1967. It is important to understand these movements as well as to see their impact on social change.

1. THE CONCEPT OF INDEPENDENCY CHURCHES

A major distinction in looking at indigenous innovations within Christianity in Africa is between the "Ethiopian" churches and the "Zionist" churches. Ethiopian churches (which Webster's dictionary refers to as "African Independent Churches") have broken away from the formal control and European leadership of orthodox Christian churches, while retaining much of their orientation. Thus, there may be an African Methodist church and an African Congregational church which are distinguished from the mission-run Methodist and Congregational churches primarily by the fact that they established autonomy and their own leadership.

In contrast, the Zionist, or *aladura* (a Yoruba word meaning "praying man"), or independency, churches in Africa have usually emerged from some established church but have developed new forms of worship (usually involving dancing), a new form of ministry called "prophets," and an emphasis on prayer-healing activities (believed to have great power against witchcraft). In the bibliography by Mitchell and Turner (1966) there are over 1,300 references to Zionist churches (excluding Ethiopian churches) in Africa. The Zionist churches may have varying orientations: they may be prophetic ("a religious awakening founded and led by a charismatic figure or a prophet or prophetess," Barrett, 1968 p. 47); they may be messianic ("a movement centered around a dominant personality who claims for himself special powers beyond the prophetic and involving a form of identification with Christ," *ibid.*); they may be millennial ("a movement which preaches an imminent millennium, Golden Age, or End of the World," *ibid.*); they may be nativistic ("an organized attempt on the part of a society's members to revive or perpetuate selected aspects of its culture," *ibid.*); or a variety of other orientations, such as revivalism or witchcraft eradication.

2. DISTRIBUTION OF INDEPENDENCY MOVEMENTS

Barrett claims that there are about seven million Africans, as of 1968, who were adherents of independency movements. These people are not evenly distributed in Africa, but are concentrated in southern Africa and along the coastal areas of central, East, and West Africa. The study by Sundkler (1961), which lists about 700 distinct churches in South Africa alone, interprets the phenomena as a channel for the release of frustrations through religious means, where economic and political means are not available. H. W. Turner (1967), who has studied these churches in West Africa, argues that they are the product of an African Christian desire to develop an *African* form of Christianity. There is probably no simple answer as to why independency movements develop in particular areas, but the growing literature on these movements would make it possible for a student to examine this question in detail. Some of the better-known movements include the Nigerian Church of the Lord (Aladura), which began in 1930; the Cherubim and Seraphim, founded in Nigeria in 1925; the Christ Apostolic Church (Nigeria, 1931); Harrism, founded by the prophet William Wade Harris, and primarily located in Ivory Coast; the Society of the One Almighty God (Uganda, 1914); Kimbanguism (Église de Jésu-Christ sur la terre par le Prophète Simon Kimbangu), located in Congo-Kinshasa and, with half a million adherents, the largest independency movement on the continent. In South Africa, there are probably several thousand groups, many of which by 1965 had formed into two large federations: the African Independent Churches' Association and the Assembly of Zionist and Apostolic Churches. (For case studies in Kenya, see Ogot and Welbourn, 1966.)

3. INDEPENDENCY MOVEMENTS AND SOCIAL CHANGE

One of the major characteristics of mission Christianity in Africa, as distinct from mission Christianity in other parts of the world, was its insistence on not accommodating local customs and beliefs into church style and ritual. Missionaries in Africa were unusually rigid in forbidding any modification of Christianity as they knew it. This may partially explain why so many of the local African churches broke away from the mission churches and tended toward forms of worship which were more in line with traditional styles. Although many of these churches allow polygyny to their membership, they take a very strong stand against traditional religious worship and magic. The Zionist types provide a functional alternative to traditional magic in their holy water and strong prayers.

Too often the missionaries had answered the African concern for "this-worldly" health with promises of life after death and the establishment of a hospital sometime in the future. A major function of the independency churches in situations of rapid social change is in the area of healing. Disease is a common problem, and faith healing has become very important in such movements as the Aladura (see Peel, 1968).

The influence of independency churches on the nationalistic movements should also be mentioned. In the Belgian Congo, Simon Kimbangu became a symbol of resistance to the Europeans. During the 1960 independence elections (some years after his actual death), many people of the Kongo ethnic group wrote in his name on the ballot, and he became a hero within the Abako party. In East Africa, the relationship between independent church movements and the Mau Mau rebellion remains to be explored, but it appears to have been strong.

Even today, during the period of political independence, the independency churches are occasionally a source of tension for African governments. Many churches have refused to recognize the sovereignty of any authority other than their own spiritual authority. In Zambia, the Lumpa Church of the Prophetess Alice Lenshina came into direct and violent conflict with President Kaunda over a series of minor issues such as saluting the flag.

In summary, the independency churches in Africa are reformation movements which have broken away from the established Christian groups. They are found primarily in the coastal parts of Africa, where contact with mission Christianity was greatest, and also where social and political tensions have been greatest, as in the south. There does not seem to be any diminution of the groups in the post-colonial era, perhaps because the need for security is even greater than before. In the white-dominated parts of southern Africa there has been a great proliferation of religious movements, which seems to be directly related to the intensive heritage of mission activity in the area and the general state of political repression.

52

Islamic Reformation Movements

THE ISLAMIC COMMUNITY IN AFRICA has a full range of orientations—orthodox, unorthodox, evangelical, messianic—comparable in many ways to the schisms in Christianity. The various Muslim groups have reacted in a variety of ways to the general processes of social change. In fact, over the past 1,000 years Islam has been one of the major agents of social change in Africa. The idea of "reform" has many meanings in Islam, but all of them are related to change.

1. TRADITIONAL ISLAMIC REFORM MOVEMENTS

There are two major usages of the word *reform* within the Islamic context: (1) those movements which try to purify Islam by returning to its original form, free from later innovations; and (2) those movements which try to adapt to the modern technological world within an Islamic framework.

Within the first usage of reform, there have been several types of movements in African Islam: (1) the Sufi movements; (2) the Wahabi movements; and (3) the Mahdi movements. *Sufi* refers to *mystical* and designates those denominations which are organized around a primary Muslim saint and which believe in the powers of direct revelation. Sufi brotherhoods (*Tarika*), as they are called, tend to emphasize the powers of direct communication with God (*Allah*) through training of the mind, body, and spirit. This may take the form of hypnotic ecstasy or solitary asceticism. Sufism emphasizes the *essence* of religion and communion with God, and is usually less concerned with the legalism of organized religion.

The *Wahabi* movements have been an austere and puritanical reaction against the excesses of sufism. They espouse a return to the "original" state of Islam, which, they feel, was rational and not highly emotive or superstitious. They rely only on the Koran as a source of revelation, not on "direct revelation" as a supplement to the Koran. The best known Wahabi movement was not in Africa but in Saudi Arabia, where in the nineteenth century a Wahabi state was created which continues to the present day. In West Africa there have been Wahabi movements in many of the large cosmopolitan cities. An observer, however, should be cautioned that "wahabi" has become a pejorative term and in some areas implies "secular."

The *Mahdi* movements are premised on the belief that the Islamic messiah, the Mahdi, has returned, or will return, to earth and that the end of the world is at hand. Most Muslims believe in the concept of the Mahdi, although only a minority believe he has returned to earth. It is generally acknowledged that the Mahdi will return to earth at the end of a Muslim century. The last Muslim century, A.H. 1300, began in A.D. 1882; the year A.H. 1400 will occur in A.D. 1979. (A.H. in the Muslim lunar calendar refers to *anno Higirae*, or "in the year of [Muhammad's] Hegira" from Mecca to Medina in A.D. 622.) The best-known Mahdi movement in Africa occurred in Sudan at the end of the nineteenth century. The Mahdi of Khartoum (of recent cinematic fame) defeated the British forces under Gordon and drew allegiance from many groups across the Eastern, Central, and even Western Sudan (see Theobald, 1965). Those persons in present-day Sudan who believe that the Mahdi did come in the nineteenth century consider the period of time since 1882 an interim period leading to the time when the world comes to an end and those who have accepted the Mahdi will get their reward. They are trying to live exemplary lives, according to the "purest" Muslim standards.

It should be noted that at the end of the nineteenth century in Pakistan, another Muslim leader—Ghulum Ahmad—declared himself to be the Mahdi. His followers are called Ahmadiyya, and in the twentieth century many have come to Africa as Muslim missionaries, setting up modern schools and medical clinics. The Ahmadiyya are particularly strong along coastal West Africa, where there has not been a strong traditional Islamic influence (see Fisher, 1963.)

2. MODERN ISLAMIC REFORM MOVEMENTS

The predominant form of Islam in Africa has been the Sufi brotherhoods. The best known of these in West and North Africa have been the Qadiriyya (based on the saint Abdul Qadir, of Baghdad; see Abun-Nasr, 1965), and the Tijaniyya (based on the saint Ahmed Tijani, of Fez). The Qadiriyya is also strong in East Africa. Within each of these brotherhoods, there have been numerous factions or sub-denominational groups.

In both the Tijaniyya and the Qadiriyya, there have been certain branches which have become identified with modern reforms. One of the most significant groups is the Mouridiyya in Senegal, a branch of the Qadiriyya. The Mourides, under their leader Ahmad Bamba, organized in the 1920s and 1930s some of the most powerful of the peanut cooperatives in Senegal. The movement became involved in modern politics and is identified with a "socialist" orientation (see O'Brien, 1969; Behrman, 1970; Sy, 1969).

Likewise, one of the branches of the Tijaniyya, under the leadership of Ibrahim Niass of Senegal, has organized its followers into modern-sector activities and has been largely responsible for the intensive revival of Arabic literacy which has occurred in Islamic West Africa in the past twenty years (see Paden, 1970; Abner Cohen, 1968).

In short, many of the modern-day Muslims are trying to adapt their beliefs to a world of rapid communications, transportation, and technology. Some of the religious issues which have arisen within these groups have been (1) whether the Koran should be translated from Arabic into vernacular languages; (2) whether the Islamic legal system should be modified, particularly with regard to status of women; and (3) whether the Islamic prohibition against usury prevents capital investment and accumulation through modern banking practices.

3. ISLAM AND SOCIAL CHANGE

The Muslim populations in Africa are not lagging behind other areas in social change. Some states, such as Mali, Guinea, and Tanzania (to say nothing of Algeria, Tunisia, or Egypt), which are largely Muslim have taken the lead in radical reform. Muslim leaders in Africa, such as Sékou Touré (Guinea), Ahmad Ahidjo (Cameroon), or Aminu Kano (Nigeria) are clearly identified with social change.

Because Islam in Africa has not been as rigid as Christianity, especially with regard to traditional African family customs, it seems to provide a transition for many Africans into the modern world. It is a universal religion; it is not identified with colonialism (or, in most areas, with racism); and it is gaining converts at a rapid rate, both in East and West Africa. As mentioned in Abu-Lughod (*Essays,* chap. 27), about one-fourth of the states in Africa have Muslim majorities. In West Africa, approximately one out of two persons is Muslim. Also, four of the major vernacular languages in Africa (Arabic, Hausa, Swahili, and Fulani) are identified with Islamic cultures. The major question facing Islam in Africa is whether it can adapt to the technological modernization of the contemporary period without fundamental reformation in the direction of greater secularization (see Module 37).

Study Questions

53

Study Questions:
Processes of Change

As with the earlier study questions, some are intended to synthesize modules, others are intended to review major points of the modules, and others are judgmental or evaluatory.

1. What are the major elements of social-change theory? What are the major elements of modernization theory? Are these concepts too broad to be of any analytic use? To what extent are the concepts capable of being translated into a pre-Western African context?

2. To what extent are individual personalities a reflection of general cultural values? Within the African context, what are the types of personality traits in which one might find most range and variation? Discuss how display of emotion might be regarded as a personality trait. How might the recognition of mental illness be difficult in a situation where "deviation" or "inability to function in society" is blurred by rapid social change and "normlessness"?

3. What evidence is there to show that social change does not necessarily destroy traditional ethnic society? What aspects of ethnic society are likely to change most with increasing modernization? Where is there the greatest potential for an effective blend between tradition and modernity? Can the degree of achievement motivation in a society change significantly over time? What factors might interfere with an effective measurement of achievement motivation in a society? What impact, if any, has colonialism had on African personality?

4. What have been the major differences, if any, between the French, British,

and American educational systems? What have been the major adaptations made by the new African states since independence in the field of education? What are some of the problems of a low literacy rate? Of a high literacy rate? In what language do you think elementary school children in Africa should be taught?

5. How does the educational system affect the formation of new elites or even the rise of social classes? Can government policy determine this pattern? What educational policies do you think would be most useful to the African states in terms of economic development? In terms of national integration? Given the high cost of education, who should pay for it (central governments, local governments, parents)? What might be some of the reasons why African parents might resist Western education? Do you think the Christian churches should continue to play such a large role in African education?

6. What is meant by the phrase "the new elites of Africa"? To what extent do these elites continue to maintain contacts with their ethnic and traditional communities? Do you think they should or should not break off all traditional links? The present generation of leadership in Africa is highly educated. Do you think that intellectuals make good politicians? Are there any alternative elites which might be more suitable to the tasks of nation-building? Do you think that the new African states are being dominated by any particular set of elites?

7. Trace the development of urban society in Africa. To what extent has it been dependent on trade? To what extent has it been a pre-Western phenomenon? What types of cities emerged during the colonial regime? How do you account for the dramatic increase in rates of urbanization at the present time? Do you think that African governments should control immigration to the cities?

8. What is different about urban life compared to rural life? What specific examples of "division of labor" and "functional differentiation" can you think of, either in an American or an African context? What is likely to be the difference between an ethnically homogeneous African city and an ethnically mixed African city? What conditions to you think should be most important in the selection of a capital city?

9. What are some of the major problems of urbanization? How does it affect family life? Economic life? Political life? To what extent is there an "urban crisis" in Africa at present? What is meant by "return migration"? Do you think that city planners can anticipate some of the social problems of the city? If you were a city planner in Africa or a technical assistant in that field from the United States, what basic demographic information would you need? What priorities would you establish in planning?

10. What is the present pattern of transport and communication in Africa?

Do you think that air transport will do away with the need for larger scale railroad construction in Africa? What is meant by the spatial structure of modernization? How might you map the diffusion of modernization in a country? Why are so many large African cities seaports? To what extent should African states even out the inequalities of modernization which emerged during the colonial period?

11. What has been the impact of the mass media on African society? How has linguistic diversity affected the growth of mass media? Is multilingualism a hindrance or an advantage or both with respect to the development of mass media? Do you think that African states should maintain tight controls over the media at this state in their development?

12. Trace the history of Christian contact in Africa. To what extent have missionaries collaborated with colonial regimes? Is Christianity still identified with European culture, or has it become indigenized? How might Christianity affect the kind of traditional African society and culture discussed in the first segment of this syllabus?

13. How do you account for the dramatic proliferation of syncretist sects in Africa? What, if anything, do these sects have in common? Do you think they provide a legitimate form of religious expression? To what extent do they affect the process of social change? What kinds of conflict might you anticipate between the sects and the new African governments?

14. Discuss the two major types of Islamic reforms. What, if anything, do they have in common? Are there any parallels between traditional reformism in Islam and the nativistic or revivalistic forms of Christian movements? How might modernization reform be conducted in an Islamic state? Is there anything inherent in Islam to prevent or to enhance modernization?

Consolidation of Nation-States

Modules	Suggested Readings in *Essays*
Nationalism and Independence 54 Concepts of Nationalism 55 Patterns of African Nationalism 56 Independence	20 African Concepts of Nationhood *(Paden)*
Nation-Building 57 Interethnic Integration 58 Mass-Elite Integration 59 Territorial Integration and Boundaries 60 The Role of Ideology in Nation-Building	21 Patterns of Nation-Building *(Zolberg)*
Political Systems Development 61 Types of Civilian Regimes 62 Institutions and Bureaucracy 63 Participation and Mobilization 64 Elite Instability and Military Rule 65 The Implications of Nigeria-Biafra	22 Political Systems Development *(Crawford Young)*
Legal Systems Development 66 Legal Systems in Africa 67 The Integration of Legal Systems 68 The Development of Constitutional Law	23 Legal Systems Development *(Roland Young)*

Nationalism and Independence

Concepts of Nationalism

NATIONALISM REFERS TO THE EFFORTS to obtain political autonomy on the part of a group which feels itself to have a high degree of common interest and identity. In the African context, there have been many different types of nationalism. Some have focused on the national states — most important as the locus of sovereignty in the modern world — inherited from the colonial period. Local or ethnic nationalisms have also been important, while still others have focused on groupings of states, that is, the supranational level.

1. NATIONAL-LEVEL NATIONALISM IN AFRICA

The boundaries of present-day African states emerged at the turn of the twentieth century primarily as a result of negotiations between the European colonial powers (see Module 33) and as modified by patterns of African resistance (see Module 34). These boundaries provided the framework for the emergence of administrative structures. Civil services were established, commercial planning took place within these units, and political decision making was usually in the hands of the governor of each territory.

The anticolonial African nationalist movements which emerged after World War II for the most part focused their grievances and claims on the territorial compartments created by the colonial boundaries. (See Paden and C. Young, *Essays*, chaps. 20 and 21, respectively.) Political parties were established which (with important exceptions in the French areas) operated within these contexts. The result was that the "national" context became increasingly important in the day-to-day operation of affairs and as a focus for emerging African identities.

211

Because the nationalist spokesmen often found it difficult to rationalize the acceptance of one of the major symbols of foreign rule—the territorial boundaries of the colonial era—there was less explicit ideological writing about peoples in terms of the colonial units in Africa (Nigerian people, as distinct from Kenyan people or Ivoirien people) and more focus on the "African" level (contrasting Africans with Europeans). Boundaries of the new states were accepted as "temporary" and a prelude to some future consolidation of African peoples, that is, some form of Pan-Africanism.

In the immediate post-colonial period, however, there was an increase in the nationalist literature which did focus on the inherited states as the "natural" bearers of African destiny. Kwame Nkrumah of Ghana, in *I Speak of Freedom* (1957), refers to the process whereby "Ghana is born" and discusses the "building of a new nation" with reference to Ghana. He discusses "Ghana in world affairs," "Ghana and the United Nations," and the constitutional core of "the Republic of Ghana." Nkrumah still remained one of the most articulate of Pan-Africanists, but even he was drawn into the necessity of fostering a distinctive Ghanaian nationalism.

Other African spokesmen experienced the same upsurge of state-level nationalism. Senghor (1964) atttibuted the breakup of the Mali federation to the fact that Senegalese and Malians were more conscious of their territorial differences than anyone had realized. The proposed East African Federation became outweighed by the component nationalisms of Kenya, Uganda, and Tanzania. Kenneth Kaunda (1966) began to write specifically about Zambia, and Sékou Touré (1961) about Guinea.

The backbone of this national-level nationalism was the fact that peoples in a particular country had clear common interests which differed from those at the continental or Pan-African level (e.g., Ivory Coast, Nigeria, and Ghana were strong competitors for the world cocoa market). Citizens of particular countries also began to develop a sense of having worked together to achieve independence and of sharing a common destiny.

2. SUBNATIONAL-LEVEL NATIONALISM

Most of the educated elite which led the nationalist movements prior to 1960 were very definite in their rejection of ethnicity as a basis for modern nationalism. Ethnic nationalism occurred most commonly in situations where national boundaries had cut across major ethnic-group lines and hence had divided communities with a will and a potential capacity to reunite. The Somali looked to their cousins in Kenya and Ethiopia and demanded reunion (see Touval, 1963). The Kongo people, at the mouth of the Congo River and divided among three states (Congo-Brazzaville, Congo-Kinshasa, and Angola), began to demand a separate state (see Young, 1965). The Ewe of Ghana and Togo began to demand reunion (see Welch, 1966).

This particularistic form of nationalism did not generate a large body of literature in support of its claims. Political and sometimes violent action was often undertaken to enforce these felt demands for ethnic autonomy. African statesmen were concerned about the problem of irredentism, but few were able to devise ways of reconciling nationalism at the state and ethnic levels.

It should be mentioned that a number of subnational nationalisms did emerge in the post-colonial period. Katanga nationalism, based partly on the ethnic cohesiveness of the Lunda people and partly on the economic self-interest of the mineral-rich province, demanded secession from Congo-Kinshasa in 1960 (see Young, 1965). The Nilotic people of Southern Sudan demanded independence from their Arab countrymen (see Barbour, 1964). In 1967, the Ibo people of the Eastern Region of Nigeria demanded their own political autonomy in the form of Biafran nationalism (see Module 65). The Baganda, with recognized autonomy since Ugandan independence, attempted unsuccessfully to reassert their subnationalism in 1966 in response to the introduction of a greater centralization. The deposed king (*kabaka*) of Buganda, Mutesa II, went into exile in London where he wrote *The Desecration of My Kingdom* (1967) before his death in late 1969.

The remarkable thing about African states is that relatively few ethnic communities have demanded political autonomy. There are at least 150 ethnic groups divided by international boundaries, to say nothing of the large-scale kingdoms (such as those of the Ashanti or Yoruba) within particular countries which have had a strong potential for nationalism (see Widstrand, 1969, for a general overview of boundary problems in Africa).

3. SUPRANATIONAL-LEVEL NATIONALISM

In the period prior to African independence, as mentioned above, much of the ideological attention of the nationalists was focused on the supranational level. Nationalists frequently identified themselves as "Africans," which was natural in light of the fact that many of them had lived in Europe or the United States where they had been ascribed this identity. Furthermore, the anticolonial struggle was directed, in contrast, against "Europeans."

There were important variations, discussed in Paden (*Essays*, chap. 20), on the theme of "African nationalism." Some nationalists favored a Eur-Africanism, which legitimated the rights of Africans, but recognized the close relationship of Africa with Europe. Others espoused a form of Marxism-socialism, which was localized in the form of "African socialism" (see Module 60). Others focused on the "blackness" of Africa, and elaborated concepts of "negritude" (which was widely interpreted as excluding North Africa from the mainstream of African nationalism). Others were emphatic in wanting to include North Africa into a continent-wide form of Pan-Africanism. Still others saw

Africa as a major component in a coalition between all of the colored peoples of the world—a bloc which came to be known as the "Third World." Finally, there were many African nationalists who thought in terms of regional federations of African states. Some espoused an amalgamation of French-speaking states, others of English-speaking East African states, and still others of English-speaking West African states.

These variations in supranational-level nationalism were most noticeable in the pre-independence period. However, it is likely that some of them will regain importance in the future (see Module 77).

55

Patterns of African Nationalism

IN 1945 IN LONDON a handful of African expatriates met and demanded that colonialism in Africa be abolished. There were probably few at that time who thought they would see an independent Africa within their lifetime. Fifteen years later, by 1960, most of Africa had achieved independence. The achievement of independence was not without struggle, but for the most part it was peaceful. It required enormous energies and discipline to establish political organizations which were capable of both enforcing their demands and at the same time accepting the increasing burden of responsibilities in the administration of new states.

1. EARLY PATTERNS OF AFRICAN NATIONALISM

In the 1920s, there developed in British West Africa organizations which might be termed the first genuine nationalist movements (see Kilson, 1963). To some extent in the 1930s, there emerged new, usually urban-based organizations which were also focused on the inequities of colonialism. It was not really until during and after World War II, however, that the demand for independence began to take organized form. During World War II it became apparent to the Africans, both on mass and elite levels, that the European powers were vulnerable, and also that Africans were helping the Allies fight a cause for human freedom and justice which should rightly include themselves. On several occasions during the war, President Roosevelt declared the opposition of the United States to the idea of colonialism. When the French-speaking African leaders met with General de Gaulle in Brazzaville in 1944, there was a frank discussion about the reforms which were needed in Africa after the war. French-speaking Africans were invited to participate in the constitutional reforms of France which led to the establishment of the Fourth French Republic in 1946 (see Schachter Morgenthau, 1964).

In Britain, a postwar Labour government decided to grant independence to India (split to include Pakistan) in 1947. The impact of this event was not lost on African students studying in London during this period. In almost all the British territories in Africa, constitutions began to be introduced by Great Britain which gave an increasing control of government to local Africans. Nationalist political parties began to form in almost every African state.

2. VIOLENCE AND NONVIOLENCE

In only two countries did widespread anticolonial violence develop: Algeria and Kenya. Unlike most of Africa, these two areas contained large numbers of European settlers. Algeria had been governed as part of France since 1830, and more than a million *colons* had settled there. They included persons from all walks of life. In Kenya, British farmers had been encouraged to migrate to the fertile highlands area since the early 1900s, while after World War I many British soldiers were attracted to Kenya by low land prices and other features. There was still another surge of immigration after World War II, stimulated largely by unfavorable postwar conditions within Great Britain.

In 1954 there was a coordinated uprising in Algeria in seventy different localities, led mainly by a few hundred young men with limited weapons. Within eighteen months, these young men had organized themselves into the Front of National Liberation (FLN) and eventually the French were forced to place 500,000 troops in Algeria. By 1960, the toll on both sides was high. At least 250,000 Algerians had been killed, and another 250,000 were refugees outside the country. The French were suffering such heavy losses, with no apparent sign of victory, that in 1958 the French Fourth Republic collapsed, General de Gaulle was called to power, and the Fifth Republic was formed, dedicated to executive stability and the bringing of a swift end to the war. On July 5, 1962, Algeria became an independent republic as a result of political negotiations. (For further details on Algeria, see Clarck, 1960; Gorden, 1966.)

In Kenya, the history of Mau Mau as a nationalist movement is still controversial, although the recent volume by Rosberg and Nottingham (1967) is a major contribution to our understanding of this movement. (Compare their findings with the *Corfield Report* of 1960, which presented a strongly pro-British evaluation.) Rosberg and Nottingham view what came to be called Mau Mau as part of an ongoing process of African political development, begun in the 1920s, which received little positive response from the colonial government.

Outbreaks of violence eventually took place, leading to the declaration of an "Emergency" in October, 1952 (lasting eight years). During the Emergency, with large numbers of British troops stationed in Kenya and with the many severe reprisals taken by the colonial government against what they perceived as a primitive and virtually psychotic uprising, many lives were lost and the movement splintered in various directions. To a great degree, Mau Mau became an internal civil war among the Kikuyu (largely between the landless and those loyal to the colonial government). In all, only about 30 Europeans were killed (and a slightly larger number of Asians) against about 1,700 Kikuyu and other "loyalists" and 10,000 "Mau Mau" (probably mostly Kikuyu). Nearly 90,000 were detained until the "rebellion" came to an end. The uprising, however, also remained a political movement which eventually succeeded in attaining independence for Kenya in December, 1963, under the leadership of the one individual the British erroneously held largely responsible for stimulating Mau Mau, Jomo Kenyatta. Although Kenya received its independence later than most other African states, many view Mau Mau as one of the key turning-points in colonial history, a violent indication of the desire for greater African political control. (For an autobiographical account by one of the Mau Mau leaders, see Itote, 1967. An account of a Mau Mau detainee is contained in Kariuki, 1963.)

By contrast, in most of the rest of Africa, the philosophy of nonviolence became an integral part of the nationalist movements. Spokesmen such as Nkrumah of Ghana and Nyerere of Tanzania drew explicitly on the experience of Gandhi. This philosophy of nonviolence was most articulate in English-speaking Africa. In French-speaking Africa, especially after the administrative reforms of 1956, there was in general a residual of good will between French politicians and African leaders, perhaps dating back to the war years. In 1958, only one French-speaking state (Guinea) voted to discontinue its relationship with France.

3. NATIONALIST POLITICAL PARTIES

In French-speaking Africa, the political parties which developed after World War II were usually linked with political parties in France. Thus, for example, there existed African branches of the French Socialist and Communist Parties. These parties were organized in French-speaking Africa as "interterritorial" parties, i.e., as transnational parties, but with national branches. In most cases, the parties ultimately broke with their French counterparts. The most notable of the transterritorial parties were the Rassemblement Démocratique Africain (RDA), founded in 1946; the Indépendents d'Outre-Mer (IOM), founded in 1948; the Mouvement Socialiste Africain (MSA), founded in 1957; and the Parti du Regroupement Africain (PRA), founded in 1958. (For details on parties, see Schachter Morgenthau, 1964.)

In English-speaking Africa, nationalist parties were limited in scope and concern to the particular countries. As discussed in Module 61, at the initial stages there were usually several parties in each of the countries. Yet in almost all countries (with the exception of Nigeria and possibly Uganda), by the time of independence a consolidated nationalist party had been achieved. For example, in Ghana there was the Convention People's Party (CPP), and in Tanzania, the Tanganyika African National Union (TANU). In Nigeria, the strong regionalism and federal structure encouraged single parties dominating each of the three regions: in the East, the National Council for Nigeria and the Cameroons (NCNC); in the West, the Action Group (AG); and in the North, the Northern People's Congress (NPC).

In all cases, political parties during the nationalist period were concerned to pressure European colonial powers into a transfer of government. The primary technique in this process was to campaign in elections on the basis of an independence platform and to demonstrate that they were able to assume the responsibility of government as it devolved upon them.

56

Independence

DURING THE FIFTEEN-YEAR PERIOD from 1950 to 1965, most of the African states achieved independence. In this module, we will discuss the timing of independence, the process of constitutional reform, and the meaning of independence.

1. THE TIMING OF INDEPENDENCE

Figure 9 provides a summary of the sequence and timing of independence. It will be noted that Ghana in 1957 was the first state wholly in Black Africa to achieve independence (see Apter, 1962; Bourret, 1960).

2. THE PROCESS OF CONSTITUTIONAL REFORMS

In English-speaking Africa there had been a relatively long period of involvement of African spokesmen in the affairs of government. In many territories, Africans were electing representatives to urban city councils by the 1920s. (For the example of Nigeria during 1923–47, see Tamuno, 1966.) In West Africa,

FIGURE 9

NEW STATES OF AFRICA, 1950–68

| Name | | Date of | Former name or names |
Short form	Long form	Independence	
1. Libya	Kingdom of Libya	December 24, 1951	Libya
2. Sudan	Republic of the Sudan	January 1, 1956	Anglo-Egyptian Sudan
3. Morocco	Kingdom of Morocco	March 2, 1956	French Morocco (also Spanish Morocco, Tangier Zone, Zona Sur del Protectorado de Marruecos)
4. Tunisia	Republic of Tunisia	March 20, 1956	Tunisia
5. Ghana	Republic of Ghana	March 6, 1957	Gold Coast (also Ashanti, Northern Territories, Trust Territory of Togoland)
6. Guinea	Republic of Guinea	October 2, 1958	French Guinea
7. Cameroon	Federal Republic of Cameroon	January 1, 1960	Cameroun (or French Cameroons) and Southern Cameroons
8. Togo	Republic of Togo	April 27, 1960	French Togoland
9. Madagascar	Malagasy Republic	June 27, 1960	Madagascar and Dependencies
10. Congo-Kinshasa	Democratic Republic of the Congo	June 30, 1960	Belgian Congo
11. Somalia (Somali)	Somali Republic	July 1, 1960	Somalia and British Somaliland
12. Dahomey	Republic of Dahomey	August 1, 1960	Dahomey
13. Niger	Republic of Niger	August 3, 1960	Niger
14. Upper Volta	Republic of Upper Volta	August 5, 1960	Upper Volta (also Volta)
15. Ivory Coast	Republic of Ivory Coast	August 7, 1960	Ivory Coast
16. Chad	Republic of Chad	August 11, 1960	Chad
17. C.A.R.	Central African Republic	August 13, 1960	Central African Republic (also Ubangi-Shari)
18. Congo-Brazzaville	Republic of Congo	August 15, 1960	Middle Congo

19. Gabon	Gabon Republic	August 17, 1960	Gabon
20. Senegal	Republic of Senegal	August 20, 1960	Senegal (also part of the Federation of Mali)
21. Mali	Republic of Mali	September 22, 1960	Soudan (also part of the Federation of Mali)
22. Nigeria	Federal Republic of Nigeria	October 1, 1960	Nigeria (also Northern Cameroons)
23. Mauritania	Islamic Republic of Mauritania	November 28, 1960	Mauritania
24. Sierra Leone	—	April 27, 1961	Sierra Leone (colony and protectorate)
25. Tanzania[a]	United Republic of Tanzania	December 9, 1961	Tanganyika and Zanzibar
26. Burundi	Kingdom of Burundi[b]	July 1, 1962	Urundi (in Ruanda-Urundi)
27. Rwanda	Republic of Rwanda	July 1, 1962	Ruanda (in Ruanda-Urundi)
28. Algeria	Democratic and Popular Republic of Algeria	July 3, 1962	Algeria
29. Uganda	Republic of Uganda	October 9, 1962	Uganda
30. Kenya	Republic of Kenya	December 12, 1963	Kenya (colony and protectorate)
31. Malawi	Republic of Malawi	July 6, 1964	Nyasaland
32. Zambia	Republic of Zambia	October 24, 1964	Northern Rhodesia
33. Gambia, The	—	February 18, 1965	The Gambia (colony and protectorate)
34. Botswana	Republic of Botswana	September 30, 1966	Bechuanaland
35. Lesotho	Kingdom of Lesotho	October 4, 1966	Basutoland
36. Mauritius	—	March 12, 1968	Mauritius
37. Swaziland	Kingdom of Swaziland	September 6, 1968	Swaziland
38. Equatorial Guinea	—	October 12, 1968	Rio Muni and Fernando Po

[a] Tanganyika became independent in 1961 and joined with independent Zanibar in 1964 to form Tanzania.
[b] This became Republic of Burundi in 1966.

Note: Ethiopia and Liberia were not formal colonies; Egypt and South Africa were independent throughout most of the 20th century. Rhodesia declared itself independent in 1965.

councils of chiefs were established in most territories by the 1930s. In the post-war period, written constitutions were enacted in most territories, establishing procedures for elections, and for African involvement in local and national government. The most important vehicle for involvement on the national level was the legislative council, which was composed of representatives from different districts throughout the country, and, in East and central Africa, from the major non-African ethnic and racial communities as well. Elections at first were often held indirectly or by stages, as in Nigeria in 1951. By 1951 there was (moderately qualified) universal adult suffrage in Ghana. Africans were elected to the legislature, and an African-dominated cabinet was appointed from the legislature. *Self-government,* which refers to the complete control of the cabinet and legislature by Africans, usually preceded formal independence by a year or two, so that British withdrawal was "phased" to this extent (see Apter, 1962).

In French-speaking Africa, there had always been a distinction between the African *citizen* and the African *subject.* The African citizen was a full participant in French political life. He could vote in French elections and could be elected to French national office. (Houphouet-Boigny was a cabinet member in France in the mid-1950s.) He could also vote and hold office in his own state. French-speaking Africans had hoped that the Fourth Republic constitution of 1946 would extend citizenship to greater numbers of Africans. They were disappointed, however, with the 1946 constitution, which eventually emerged as a compromise between factions in France to the neglect of the Africans. But in 1956, with the passage of the *Loi-Cadre,* citizenship was extended to a vastly increased number of Africans and local political authority was greatly increased. In 1958, after de Gaulle had assumed power in France, the Fifth Republic constitution extended almost complete autonomy to the African states, which were at the same time to form a "community" of associated states with France (see Crowder, 1965; Neres, 1962). In the referendum on the Fifth Republic constitution (September, 1958) only Guinea voted against continued affiliation with France. By 1960, however, most of the French-speaking states had decided to declare their complete independence from France, although several, like Senegal, continued within the French Community, and all maintained close bilateral ties (see Lusignan, 1969).

It should be noted that the pattern of political transfer in the Belgian areas was different from that in the British and French areas. Until 1958 the Belgians made no preparations for the establishment of political institutions in the Congo, except some at the local level. In that year there were violent riots in Leopold-ville, and King Baudouin of the Belgians announced constitutional reforms. Essentially, the reforms allowed for the establishment of political parties, which immediately proliferated. A Round Table Conference was held in Brussels in January, 1960, which was attended by the party delegates, and elections were held in May. Because of the large number of political parties, it was necessary to form a coalition government (that is, a "national" government) after the elections, with Patrice Lumumba as prime minister, and Joseph Kasavubu as head of state. Immediately upon independence in June, 1960, there was a series of national crises in Congo which prevented the development of civilian government (see Young, 1965).

3. THE MEANING OF INDEPENDENCE

The transfer of powers to African states has sometimes been interpreted as a mere façade for the continued influence of European power in Africa. It is argued, for example by Nkrumah (1965), that Britain, France, and Belgium have continued to exert political and economic influence in their former colonies. This assertion is examined more closely in Module 82. It should be mentioned, however, that much of the political activity and orientation in independent Africa has maintained a strong neutralist stance vis-à-vis Europe. There can be no question that political independence was a turning point in African history. Political decision making was now firmly in the hands of African statesmen. If they were subject to pressures from home and abroad, this did not distinguish them from politicians in other states, both new and old.

Nation-Building

57

Interethnic Integration

DURING THE COLONIAL PERIOD, the problem of interethnic relations was largely solved by the fact that the colonial administration most often dealt directly and separately with each of the ethnic groups. This is the classical definition of a plural society: one in which two or more communal groups exist within a context, but have only economic, not political or social, relationships with each other (see Furnivall, 1948; Kuper and Smith, 1969). One of the major problems of the independence era was to build new kinds of linkages between different ethnic groups. This was particularly complicated when ethnic groups had different status levels within the new states (see Shibutani and Kwan, 1965).

1. INTERETHNIC CONFLICT

In a number of important cases, ethnic groups in the post-colonial era felt that they had genuine grievances. In Nigeria from 1961 to 1965, for example, the Tiv, who numbered over one million, were in a state of active guerrilla rebellion against the government. Since the Tiv were a segmental people with no real political hierarchy, it was extremely difficult to deal with this situation. The Tiv were protesting the imposed governmental authority, and, in particular, the fact that Hausa-Fulani elites dominated them at the regional level. (For the white paper on the Tiv rebellion, see Northern Nigeria, 1965.)

In another case from Nigeria, that of the Hausa and the Ibo, there was a tenuous political coalition for the first few years of independence, which finally broke up and took the form of interethnic violence in many of the northern cities where Ibo migrants had settled. During the summer and early fall of 1966,

223

the Ibos emigrated back to the Eastern Region, and in May, 1967, declared their independence as "Biafra." While the British had been in Nigeria, ethnic migration could occur without political consequence. With the removal of the British, ethnic groups in competition for scarce goods had to confront each other. (A discussion of the Nigeria-Biafra conflict is found in Module 65.)

This same pattern had been first noticeable in the former Belgian areas. In the Congo, Luba peoples had migrated during the colonial period into the urban areas of the Lunda people of Katanga. Apart from the international aspects of the Congolese civil war, much of the conflict had an ethnic dimension (see Libois, 1966). In Burundi and Rwanda, the ruling-class Tutsi people were confronted with violence when the masses of the population, who were Bantu-speaking Hutu, demanded a greater voice in government. (Lemarchand, 1968, compares interethnic violence in Rwanda and Zanzibar.) And the secessionist tendencies of the Barotse (Lozi) people in Zambia is of increasing concern (see Caplan, 1968).

In many parts of Africa interethnic violence was averted, but political tensions have remained high. In Ghana, the Ashanti people confronted the coastal Ga, Fanti, and Nzima. In Guinea, the inland Fulani have been balanced off against the coastal Malinke. In Kenya, the Kikuyu have jealously guarded their favored position against other groups such as the Luo, Luhya, and Kamba. In Mauritania, there has been a delicate situation between the Moorish populations and the black African populations. In Cameroon the northern Fulani have been able to balance off such southern groups as the Bamiléké, the Basa, and the Fang. In Gabon, the Fang have dominated the political scene vis-à-vis an array of minority groups. In short, there are few countries in Africa which do not have potentially active problems of interethnic competition or conflict. Lesotho, Botswana, and the Somali Republic remain the only sub-Saharan countries essentially based on a single ethnic group.

2. THE PROCESSES OF INTERETHNIC INTEGRATION

In the theoretical literature on integration there are usually five processes, or types of linkage, which are regarded as significant in the overall phenomenon of integration.

The first is simply *cooperative interaction* between groups. This may be based on marginal benefit to each group and it does not entail their loss of identity. Trade relations are a good example of this type of linkage.

The second type of linkage is *economic interdependence*. This is a stronger linkage than mere cooperative interaction, and although it is based on a division of labor (and hence trade), the economics of the situation link groups together in a vital way: i.e., groups become dependent on each other and (in some cases) could not survive without each other. Thus, if one group can raise cattle (or other protein foods) and another group raises staple agricultural goods, some exchange is necessary for each to maintain a given level of subsistence.

The third and fourth types of linkage are *value congruence* and *identity congruence*. Value congruence refers to the fact that groups share the same values, and hence may be able to interact in broad areas of social and political life. Identity congruence means that the two groups are willing to think of themselves as members of an identifiable system. This does not necessarily mean that they forego their own ethnic identities, but merely that they be able to utilize an additional identity, usually that of the national state.

The fifth type of linkage between groups is the establishment of a *common authority* which is respected by each side or, alternatively, which has the coercive potential to enforce its claims.

These five types of linkage — cooperative interaction, economic interdependence, value congruence, identity congruence, and existence of central authority — lead not only to integration but to political order, since violence and confrontation can usually be averted in an integrated system through various mechanisms of conflict resolution.

As an addendum, it should be noted that there are three dominant patterns of ethnic relations in integrated systems (see Gordon, 1964). The first is a pattern of *assimilation*, where the subordinate groups take on the values and identity of the dominant group; the second is a pattern of *amalgamation*, where the blending of two groups produces a new group; the third is a pattern of *cultural pluralism*, where each group retains its own identity but is willing to interact and become interdependent on other groups. (Compare this with the discussion in Module 6.)

3. INTERETHNIC INTEGRATION IN AFRICA

The pattern of assimilation in Africa has been common for centuries (see Cohen and Middleton, 1969). The Hausa have assimilated many of the surrounding minority peoples; the Ashanti have assimilated many of their neighbors; the Fang have been very inclusive in their social boundaries; and in East Africa the category of Swahili has come to include a growing number of peoples.

The pattern of amalgamation is likewise well represented in traditional Africa. The blending of the Hutu and the Tutsi in Rwanda has resulted, to some degree, in the creation of a new group, called the Rwanda (see Maquet, 1961).

The pattern of cultural pluralism is perhaps the most widely distributed pattern. Groups live in close proximity to each other and maintain full relations but retain their identities. This pattern is most common in the urban areas, such as Accra (with Ga, Ashanti, and Fanti quarters), or Freetown (with its Creole, Mende, Temne, and Limba populations). However, it is also found in rural areas, as in the zone between Bornu and Hausaland.

In the modern, nation-state context, these same patterns appear. In Liberia, the policy of assimilation (into Americo-Liberian culture) has been long established. Some states, such as Ghana under Nkrumah, seemed to be working toward an amalgamated identity which might be called "Ghanaian." In countries such as Ivory Coast there is a recognition of the diversity of peoples, yet a sense of national integration seems to exist. It remains to be seen, however, which policy of interethnic integration will be most productive in nation-building.

58

Mass-Elite Integration

A SECOND PROBLEM OF NATIONAL INTEGRATION in the post-colonial period has been the so-called "mass-elite gap." The idea of elites is referred to in Modules 43 and 44. In essence, the process of Western education has created a stratum of men and women who operate in the modern sector and who have de-emphasized their linguistic, ethnic, and cultural heritage. This has been problematic to the extent that these people must continue to deal with the traditional sector in the state and must generate widespread support for the building of political and economic structures. In one sense, this is the social form of the economic dualism discussed in Modules 70 and 72.

1. PROBLEMS OF MASS-ELITE CONFLICT

Much of the literature on political development in Latin America stresses the way in which the masses of people become frustrated with their standard of living or with their political leaders, and apply pressure, often through violence, which results in the rapid turnover of political leadership.

In the African context, this pattern has not yet emerged to the same extent. In Nigeria, however, it appears that the first *coup d'état* against the civilian regime (January, 1966) was well received by most elements in the country. There had been an increasing frustration with the political elite, who were regarded as corrupt, self-seeking, and short-sighted. The General Strike in 1964, which was supported by labor unions throughout the country, was largely a protest against the Nigerian national leaders rather than simply a demand for higher wages (see Sklar, 1967). The civilian takeover of government in Sudan in 1964 was directed against the military junta and was perhaps motivated by these same factors.

The symbol of political elitism in Africa was frequently the Mercedes-Benz automobile, which seemed to be a favorite with politicians (who are often called *Wa-Benzi* in Swahili). There was a strong reaction by the masses in Upper Volta, when it appeared that some of the highest-level politicians were spending more time in Paris, in grand style, than at home.

In other countries, by contrast, leaders have been very conscious of the need to appear to maintain close connections at the grass-roots level. President Nyerere of Tanzania has walked many miles on foot to demonstrate that a big car is not necessary to economic development and to symbolize the closeness between political leaders and the masses. President Touré of Guinea has not forgotten his trade-union origins. The late Tom Mboya of Kenya held regular office-hours each week, which were open to ordinary people from the streets who wanted to bring their problems directly to persons in political power.

2. TYPES OF MASS-ELITE LINKAGE

Perhaps the most important structural linkage between political leaders and the people have been the political parties. Scholars such as Thomas Hodgkin and Ruth Schachter Morgenthau, writing as early as 1960, began to distinguish dominant political parties into those which were "patron" and those which were "mass" parties. Patron parties were essentially oligarchies, consisting of local notables and not involving large memberships. The NPC of Nigeria was considered an "elite" party, while the CPP of Ghana and the PDG of Guinea were considered mass parties (see Hodgkin, 1961; Schachter Morgenthau, 1964).

In time, however, these distinctions have tended to diminish insofar as most ruling parties have broadened into mass parties with the dramatic rise of the single-party state. (Although note Crawford Young's discussion of "oligarchic party states," *Essays,* chap. 22). Yet a wide variety of party structures exist. Of particular relevance to the linkage between mass and elite is the party structure at the grass-roots or local level. Some parties give considerable latitude to local branches, even to the extent, as in Tanzania, of choosing their candidates for national elections. In other party structures, such as in Mauritania or Niger, most decisions are made at a central level.

Vertical structures within political parties may be used for communications from top-to-bottom, from bottom-to-top, or in both directions—what Nyerere describes as a "two-way, all-weather road." In Ghana under Nkrumah there was an elaborate party structure at the local level, but its major function was to transmit information and decisions which had been made by the CPP central committee (see Apter, in Coleman and Rosberg, 1964). In Ivory Coast, by contrast, the local branches of the ruling PDCI seem to transmit demands and information up to the national level, where pragmatic negotiations are then conducted between representatives from various local groups (see Zolberg, 1964 and 1967). In Liberia, the True Whig Party of William Tubman has probably represented a two-way flow of communications, but the local-level group was largely restricted to the Americo-Liberian community which constitutes only 2 per cent of the Liberian population (see Liebenow, 1969).

3. THE REPRESENTATIVE FUNCTION OF ELITES

One of the most problematic aspects of nation-building in Africa has been the way in which interethnic and mass-elite relationships intersect. Even though Western-educated elites may be cut off from their ethnic heritage, the relatives of those elites and the broader ethnic communities may continue to regard the elites as representative of their particular ethnic interests. "Ethnic arithmetic" at the political-elite level has continued to be an important factor in satisfying the various ethnic groups in a country that they *are* represented. A forthcoming study, (Morison *et al.*, 1970) demonstrates that in thirty-two sub-Saharan African states, there was less communal violence in those states in which the cabinet was representative of the ethnic pluralism of the country as a whole. On the other hand, it was also shown that when the cabinets were representative much of the conflict in the country was focused at the cabinet level itself. Some balance, thus, seems necessary between the demands of elite stability and communal stability. One frequent solution has been to have political elites from the very small minority groups, which cannot threaten any of the larger groups. President Nyerere of Tanzania, former President Nkrumah of Ghana, or General Gowon of Nigeria seem to be examples of this pattern.

Finally, it should be noted that "ethnic arithmetic" in the broad sense includes any type of communal pluralism within the state. In some areas this will be religious, racial, or regional pluralism rather than ethnic pluralism in the narrow sense. Some type of representational factor seems necessary for local people to feel that they have a stake in the new nation.

59

Territorial Integration
and Boundaries

A THIRD PROBLEM OF NATIONAL INTEGRATION in the post-colonial period has been that of territorial boundaries, both external and internal. A good introduction to African boundary problems is found in Widstrand (1969).

External boundaries had been established in the early colonial period and were arbitrary to the extent that they often cut across ethnic communities. Of equal importance was the fact that in some cases, mainly between territories of the same colonial power, boundaries were left vague and undemarcated, since it was not anticipated that boundary disputes would arise. In still other cases, lands which had belonged to traditional kingdoms in the pre-colonial period, but which had later been allocated to other territories, again came into dispute in the independence era.

Internal boundaries between provinces or regions were also subject to dispute. For example, Bunyoro (Uganda) demanded that the so-called "lost counties" be returned to it from Buganda control. Regionalism within countries, as between "northerners" and "southerners" in most of West Africa, has also been a source of tension. Some type of territorial linkage was clearly necessary within countries if centrifugal forces, or demands for regional autonomy, were not to threaten the national state.

1. PROBLEMS OF EXTERNAL BOUNDARY CONFLICT

In the post-colonial era, the Moroccan government has tried to enforce its claim to much of Mauritania, which it considers as traditionally part of the domain of the king of Morocco. Nation-building in Morocco was felt to require the re-establishment of the old empire. Throughout the early 1960s the Morocco-Mauritania border was closed and there was sporadic fighting (see Reyner, 1963; Zartman, 1965).

The boundary between southern Algeria and Mali was an example of an undemarcated zone. Since both were French territories, it was not felt necessary to do more than put a line of broken dots on the maps. With independence, the exact territorial limits of each state became a matter of national concern and border tensions ensued (see Reyner, 1964; Prescott, 1963).

The problem of international boundaries cutting across ethnic lines, usually resulting in a minority portion of the community in another country, has led to a variety of types of "irredentism," or demand for reunion. The Ewe in the old Transvolta region of Ghana, which was a trust territory under British administration, demanded reunion with their fellow Ewe in Togo in the years immediately prior to and following Ghanaian independence (*ca.* 1956–1960). Both sides engaged in significant fortifications, and sporadic shooting occurred. The president of Togo, Sylvanus Olympio, who was assassinated in 1963, periodically announced that President Nkrumah was plotting to overthrow him as a means of dampening the hopes of Ewe irredentists. (For further details, see Welch, 1966; Austin, 1963.)

The Republic of Somali has engaged in armed raids into both Kenya and Ethiopia to reinforce its demands for lands which the Somali pastoralists have been using for centuries (see Touval, 1966; Castagno, 1964). It is written into the constitution of the Republic of Somali that one of the goals of nation-building must be to unite all Somali peoples, including those in other countries (see *Africa Report,* February, 1969). At present, the border fighting seems to have abated, but the potential for further conflict still remains. (For further discussion of these and other boundary problems, see Widstrand, 1969; Kapil, 1966.)

2. PROBLEMS OF INTERNAL REGIONAL CONFLICT

In almost every country in West Africa there has been a recurrent pattern of political tension between the southern coastal areas and the northern savanna areas. Historically, these two zones consisted of kingdoms and empires which seldom overlapped the ecological boundary (Old Oyo, in Nigeria, was a major exception, but was destroyed in the nineteenth century). The colonial administration often reinforced this difference by dealing with "northern" and "southern" peoples as two distinct categories. Even when these regions were formally amalgamated, as were Northern and Southern Nigeria in 1914, it was frequently decades before any administrative linkages were established. (In Nigeria, the first direct political contact between northern and southern leaders occurred in 1951).

In other parts of Africa, there has been an amalgamation of territories during or after independence, which has necessitated the creation of new national linkages. The two best examples of this have been Cameroon and Tanzania, which are the only two federations left in Africa (excluding Nigeria, at present, because of its "constitutionless" status). In 1961, as a result of United Nations–sponsored plebiscites, English-speaking Northern Cameroon became part of Nigeria, and English-speaking Southern Cameroon united with the French-speaking portions of Cameroon. Western Cameroon remains English-speaking while Eastern Cameroon is French-speaking. The government of Cameroon is trying to establish policies of bilingualism which will unite the country (similar perhaps, but in reverse ratio, to the problem in Canada).

The Federation of Tanzania consists of Tanganyika and the island of Zanzibar. After the revolution in Zanzibar in early 1964, the new government in Zanzibar petitioned for merger with Tanganyika. Policies are being initiated, especially with regard to the balance of leadership between the two regions, which may eventually link the units together into a centralized state although Zanzibar still remains virtually autonomous within the very loose federation.

Many examples could be cited of instances where redefinition of external boundaries has created a problem of internal territorial integration. One interesting case has been the merger of Eritrea into Ethiopia, which in the mid-1950s took a federal form, but later shifted to a unitary form.

3. TYPES OF TERRITORIAL LINKAGE

With regard to international boundaries, the Organization of African Unity (OAU) has established a Mediation Commission to assist in arbitration. This commission was of considerable use in the Morocco-Algeria border dispute. According to a 1964 OAU resolution, the existing external boundaries in Africa were to be respected and the existing territorial states were to be the basis of future Pan-Africanism (see Modules 78 and 79).

Internally, many of the processes of linkage cited with regard to interethnic integration are also appropriate to territorial integration, for it is frequently difficult to separate ethnic from regional bases of identity (see Module 7). The establishment of an administrative, economic, transportation, and communications infrastructure linking the component regions of a state seems to be especially important (i.e., for "cooperative interaction" and "functional interdependence"). The existence of an acceptable "national" government also seems important (even when that form of government is federal).

The issue of value congruence and identity congruence is of major concern to leaders in the process of territorial integration. One of the major means of influencing the growth of common values and identities has been the conscious policy of developing a "national ideology." This is the subject of Module 60.

60

The Role of Ideology in Nation-Building

IDEOLOGY REFERS TO THOSE VALUES and beliefs which are held about society as a whole, which provide legitimacy to present policies, and which serve as an imperative to future action. Ideology may be used to explain poverty or social deprivation, or it may be used to explain and justify social domination. It may be used to break up a colonial empire, or to weld together a new state. Ideology may either be explicit, normally taking the form of writings or speeches by spokesmen, or it may be latent, the unarticulated feelings of the masses. Most societies, whether traditional or modern, have some organizing principles which may be regarded as a dominant ideology. Ideological conflict occurs when competing or incompatible values and beliefs are juxtaposed within a context. (For a useful discussion of the concept of ideology, see Apter, 1964.)

1. IDEOLOGICAL CONFLICT IN AFRICA

The major ideological conflict in twentieth-century Africa has been between modern and traditional values and beliefs. Traditional values may espouse the restricting of community membership to those with common language, culture, or kinship. Modern values may espouse the extension of community membership to national, continental, or even universal boundaries. Traditional beliefs may be prescientific, while modern beliefs may be scientific.

This ideological dualism which exists in most states should not obscure the fact that many aspects of traditional society may not be in conflict with modern values. In Tanzania, the political authority structure of most traditional societies is egalitarian. It is less difficult for the leaders of Tanzania to adopt an egalitarian ideology at the national level because this is already part of the political culture of most people. Likewise the hierarchical structure of traditional society in northern Nigeria may carry over into modern politics and may or may not be incompatible with modernization. (Centralization of authority, for example, is frequently a necessary prerequisite to increase in scale.)

A type of ideological conflict which is perhaps more noticeable to the world outside of Africa is the so-called capitalist-socialist dispute as to the purposes of the state and the means of organizing economic life. States such as Ivory Coast and Kenya have become associated with a "capitalist" approach, and states such as Guinea or Tanzania have become associated with a "socialist" approach. (It should be noted that in no country in Black Africa is there a flourishing communist ideology.) To a large extent, the capitalist-socialist debate in Africa is artificial. Due to colonialism, few Africans became major capitalist entrepreneurs or "captains of industry." By default, the governments of the independent African states have become heavily involved in all aspects of economic life. On the other hand, there are few large-scale African societies which are not characterized by a class of traders (sometimes women, as in Ghana and Yorubaland) who are among the most astute merchants in the pre-industrial world. The capitalist-socialist debate is largely for external consumption, although increasingly "African socialism" is a rallying ideology in the process of nation-building (see Friedland and Rosberg, 1965).

2. THE SOURCES OF AFRICAN IDEOLOGY

The three major sources of contemporary African ideology have been traditional precepts and values, Islamic jurisprudence and ideology, and Western political thought (primarily British and French).

In a recent book, W. E. Abraham (1962) explores his own Ashanti cultural heritage as a source of modern ideas. By contrast, Islamic ideology, especially of the advice-to-rulers variety, has been existent in written form in West Africa since the fifteenth century (see, for the Nigerian example, Hiskett and Bivar, 1962). Islamic ideology has strongly affected at least a dozen states in Africa, and in a few states, such as Mauritania, Morocco, and the Republic of Somali, it is the official state ideology. (Likewise, Coptic Christianity is the official ideology of Ethiopia.)

The influence of Western thought in Africa is more apparent to Western observers. There are clear echoes of Rousseau in the writings of those who espouse totalitarian democracy. References to John Locke are frequent in the writings of the liberal democrats. The influence of Karl Marx, particularly his early writings on alienation, is noticeable in most of the ideological writings which emerged during the struggle against colonialism. (For a discussion of these themes in Africa, see Mazrui, 1967; Skurnik, 1968; Legum, 1965.)

The influence of twentieth-century Europeans on African ideological writing is acknowledged by many of the African writers. Senghor (1962) drew heavily on the liberal Catholic ideas of Pierre Teilhard de Chardin; Nkrumah (1965) drew explicitly from a Leninist tradition; and Kenyatta (1964) has drawn on many of the values and ideas of the prominent anthropologist Bronislav Malinowski. The acknowledgment of this influence does not detract from the genius of many of the African writers. The writings of Mamadou Dia of Senegal, Nnamdi Azikiwe of Nigeria, or Julius Nyerere of Tanzania will take their place among some of the world's greatest political literature. The prolific insights of Kwame Nkrumah may be granted a new respect by future generations of Africans. (His latest volume—*Handbook of Revolutionary Warfare*, 1969—may be more controversial than most.) One of the consequences of the fact that most heads of state in Africa are well-educated intellectuals (see Module 91) has been that in every state volumes of political writings have emerged in both the nationalist and the nation-building stages.

3. TYPES OF "MODERN" AFRICAN IDEOLOGY

There are many references in the *Bibliography* which indicate the wide range of ideological writings in Africa. At this point it seems appropriate to list only major identifiable categories of ideology. Many of these categories of ideology are re-examined in other modules.

The first ideology is *negritude*, best known through the writings of Senghor (see Markovitz, 1969). Basically, negritude was a reaction to the assimilationist policy of France which tried to make black Frenchmen out of Africans. Negritude as an ideology asserted that "black is beautiful" and that the African cultural heritage is impossible of assimilation by Western culture (see Berrian and Long, 1967). This ideology was especially relevant in the struggle for independence, but has had less political relevance in Africa since independence.

A second ideology has been called *consciencism*, after a volume of that title written by Nkrumah (1964). Consciencism asserted that the emergent African ideology should be a synthesis of Euro-Christian, African traditional, and Islamic heritages. It was an ideological plea for a type of Pan-Africanism based on continent-wide "value congruence."

A final category might be termed *African socialism*, although both Nkrumah and Senghor would claim to fit that description. African socialism asserts the values of egalitarian society, and the importance of justice in the distribution of economic wealth. This ideology was espoused as a rallying symbol by many leaders in the early period after independence. The term has come to take on a variety of meanings, depending on its context. (Compare, for example, its meaning and implication in Kenya and Guinea as illustrated in the writings of Tom Mboya and Sékou Touré.)

Political Systems Development

Types of Civilian Regimes

MOST OF THE INHERITED POLITICAL SYSTEMS in Africa, as is mentioned in Module 56, were based either on the British Westminster model or the French Fifth-Republic model. Crawford Young (*Essays,* chap. 22) also distinguishes between the characteristics of regimes at the time of independence and those in the later "post-independence" phase, i.e., after major adjustments had been made. In this module the focus will be primarily on political parties in Africa as they emerged in the post-independence period.

1. THE ROLE OF POLITICAL PARTIES IN AFRICA

Political parties may be regarded as functioning as *inputs* to the political decision-making system (articulating and aggregating demands by the people), as *converters* of political demands into decisions, and as *outputs* from the system, insofar as the government party may be responsible for the enforcement and execution of the law (see Wiseman, 1966).

In Africa, these functions have each assumed a different importance in different time periods. Prior to independence, political parties functioned to rally (or aggregate) the people around nationalist demands which were then presented to the colonial government (Hodgkin, 1961). In the independence period, the dominant party served as the government itself. To some extent, there was a tendency for the various coalition components of the nationalist party to fragment after the major goal (independence) was won. However, this tendency was resisted by various means, and the parties took on the new goals of unifying the country and promoting economic development (see Zolberg, 1966).

235

In the study of political parties in Africa, there are certain widely accepted categories of analysis (see Coleman and Rosberg, 1964). The first category is usually party structure and organization. Most parties have an annual convention, or congress, made up of delegates from throughout the country. These delegates select a central working committee to represent them during the year, and this committee in turn selects a national executive committee which handles the executive functions of the party. The chairman of the party is usually the most powerful figure in the party, and if the party is governing the country the party chairman usually becomes the prime minister.

A second category is membership requirements. The organization of parties at the lower levels will vary. Some extend membership to anyone who is willing to join; others try to limit party membership to those with an active interest in politics. Some local districts elect representatives to the national convention directly, while others do so indirectly.

A third category is the nature of party ancillary elements. These may include a women's branch of the party, a youth branch of the party, and frequently a labor-union or farmers' branch of the party. These ancillary branches are usually directly represented on the national working committee and may retain some autonomy in their own affairs.

A final category may be the nature of party goals and purposes. While the dominant parties receive most attention in Africa, there are frequently many smaller parties, often splinter groups, which act more like third parties or even "interest groups" in the United States. Such parties may exist in both a one-party system and a two-party system. To use examples from Nigeria, they may be regionally based, (e.g., the Bornu Youth Movement), ethnically based (e.g., the Tiv party), religiously based (e.g., some of the revisionist Muslim parties), locationally based (e.g., Kano Peoples Party), personality based (e.g., the Zikist youth parties, after Azikiwe), special-interest based (e.g., the Socialist Workers and Farmers Party), occupationally based (e.g., the Labour Party). In practice, such parties act as interest groups in the articulation and protection of members' interests. (For further case studies, see Coleman and Rosberg, 1964.)

2. SINGLE-PARTY SYSTEMS IN AFRICA

In most cases, the nationalist party that led the drive for independence continued in the post-colonial period as the government party. Those members of parties excluded from government had the choice of acting as the "loyal opposition" or joining the dominant party. In many cases, because of the scarcity of quality leadership, key leaders from an opposition party could be co-opted (through the attractions of prestige, power, or wealth) into the ruling party. In some cases, opposition parties were banned as detrimental to the unity of the country. The result was a single-party state (see Emerson, in Weiner, 1966).

Political scientists working in Africa, such as Coleman and Rosberg (1964), have found it necessary to distinguish two major types of single-party systems: the pragmatic-pluralistic type and the revolutionary-centralizing type. These types are distinguished on the criteria of ideological concern, degree of popular participation, and certain organizational aspects. *Pragmatic-pluralistic states,* such as Senegal, Ivory Coast, Sierra Leone, and Cameroon, are interpreted as national coalitions of various interest groups within the country. *Revolutionary-centralizing states,* such as Guinea, Mali, and Ghana, are seen as ideological one-party systems with a high degree of centralization. (Note that the examples refer to the early 1960s, although in most cases they still pertain.)

In single-party systems of whatever variety, dissent and opposition usually do not disappear but are contained within the party itself. Most frequently, the locus of decision making changes from the legislature (which consists of persons from the dominant party) to the central committee of the party (see Wallerstein, in Weiner, 1966).

3. OTHER PARTY SYSTEMS IN AFRICA

There are perhaps three other types of party systems in Africa: no-party (or embryonic party) systems, two-party systems, and multi-party systems. No-party systems, such as that of Ethiopia, are usually historic oligarchies. Ethiopia was one of the two African states (along with Liberia) which was not a colony and hence did not have an anticolonial nationalist movement. It appears that Ethiopia has been trying to set up a single-party system and will probably have one in the future (see Donald LeVine, 1965; Hess and Loewenberg, 1966).

Two-party systems in Africa have been relatively rare, although modified varieties have existed in Zambia and Uganda. In Ghana until 1960, the United Party stood in opposition but was then made illegal (see Austin, 1968). In Kenya, the activities of Oginga Odinga and the Kenya Peoples Union (KPU) have represented less a two-party system than a minority party within a one-party system. (Indeed, the KPU was banned and Odinga arrested in October, 1969.) In Nigeria in the 1964 election, there were two national coalitions: (1) the Nigerian National Alliance (NNA), consisting of the dominant northern party (NPC) and the governing western party (NNDP); and (2) the United Party Grand Alliance (UPGA), consisting of the western opposition party (AG), the eastern dominant party (NCNC), and the northern opposition party (NEPU). This two-party coalition system was ill-fated and in 1966 the military took over (see Module 65; Sklar and Whitaker, in Carter, 1966; Dudley, 1968).

Multi-party systems have been more common than two-party systems but seem to be highly unstable. Congo-Kinshasa and several of the French-speaking areas have had multi-party systems (partly the result of "list" voting procedures), but many of these parties were minority parties and acted primarily as interest groups (see Crawford Young, 1965; Weiss, 1968).

In short, the dominant form of party system in Africa has been the single-party system. Further aspects of these systems are considered in Modules 62, 63, and 64.

62

Institutions and Bureaucracy

LEGISLATIVE, JUDICIAL, AND EXECUTIVE INSTITUTIONS in the new African states will be examined in this module. In considering executive institutions, special emphasis will be placed on the structure of the civil-service bureaucracy. Note that in many states with military regimes, the civil service virtually runs the country.

1. LEGISLATIVE STRUCTURES

As mentioned earlier with regard to political parties, decision-making in a one-party state may reside in the central committee of the party rather than in the legislature. All civilian regimes in Africa, however, have continued some type of legislature. In most states it is unicameral. In a few sub-Saharan states, it is bicameral: Botswana, Ethiopia, Lesotho, Liberia, Morocco (although still under suspension), pre-coup Nigeria, and Swaziland.

Where there is an upper house, a variety of means have emerged for selecting membership (although in many cases the "traditional" leaders form the upper house). In Liberia and Morocco, it is elected by the citizens but with regional representation; in Ethiopia, Lesotho, Botswana, and Nigeria, the upper house has been appointed by the chief executive and consists mainly of specified traditional leaders. (For a discussion of the role of the house of chiefs in Botswana, see Proctor, 1968.)

Terms of office in the lower house also vary. Most states (both French-speaking and English-speaking) have a five-year maximum term; a few have four-year terms (Ethiopia, Liberia, Senegal).

Most national legislatures meet twice a year, once for a separate budget session. Certain other legislatures, particularly those in English-speaking Africa, meet only once a year.

Although the role of a national legislature in a single-party system is less important than in a system where an opposition party may ultimately secure power, it should be stressed that debate does continue within the national legislature of a one-party state. Frequently such debate is an important indication of the subtleties of feelings within a country. In most African states, a verbatim record is kept of such debates, comparable to the American *Congressional Record* or the British *Hansard*. Verbatim records, however, are less readily available from the legislative "committees" which play such a vital role.

2. JUDICIAL STRUCTURE

There is a complex judicial structure in every African state. The most important questions regarding such structure are that of its relationship to the political decision-making process and that of the autonomy of the judiciary. In a few countries, the head of state is empowered to remove supreme-court judges (Sierra Leone, Ghana under Nkrumah); in other states the head of state must also have the approval of the national legislative body (Liberia, Nigeria, Rwanda); in still other states the head of state may appoint a special tribunal to investigate and dismiss judges (Kenya, Malawi, Tanzania, Uganda, Zambia). Certain states make it explicitly impossible to remove supreme-court judges (Chad, Congo-Brazzaville, Dahomey, Senegal, Somali, and Togo), and the remainder of the states in Tropical Africa have no constitutional provision for removing judges (Cameroon, Central African Republic, Congo-Kinshasa, Ethiopia, Gabon, Guinea, Ivory Coast, Mauritania, Mali, Niger, Sudan, Upper Volta).

More detailed aspects of judicial structure are discussed in Module 68.

3. EXECUTIVE STRUCTURE

The chief executive in a country is usually the prime minister. (In a few systems, the president is chief executive.) Certain countries have retained traditional rulers as heads of state (as distinct from heads of government): in Burundi, prior to the coup, the office of chief executive was hereditary; in Ethiopia, the emperor is head of state; in many former British territories, the British Queen, Elizabeth II, continues as titular head of state.

In most African countries, the chief executive is the head of the dominant political party and is elected by universal adult suffrage (including women). In a few states, however, he has been elected by the legislature: for example, at one time or another, Botswana, Congo-Brazzaville, Mauritania, Nigeria, and Uganda.

The most important power of the chief executive is his prerogative to select a cabinet of ministers, who serve as heads of executive departments (or ministries) as well as links to the political party and legislature. The number of ministers that may be appointed is usually left to the discretion of the chief executive, but the normal range is between ten and twenty. (For a complete listing of each cabinet, see Legum and Drysdale, 1969.) These ministers have the responsibility of translating government policy into action. Most African states have ministers of foreign affairs, economic development, education, communications, local government, internal affairs, finance, public health, transportation, and agriculture.

The structure of a ministry, or department, is usually divided into three main categories: the leadership level, which consists of political appointees; the professional level, which consists of "tenured" civil servants who are appointed and promoted on the basis of merit or examination; and the clerical level. Each minister usually has a parliamentary secretary, who is also a political appointee, to assist him. These men work with the permanent secretary and deputy (or assistant) permanent secretary, who are the top civil servants. Under the permanent secretaries there are usually a number of functional divisions, each with a chief of division. (For example, a ministry of agriculture might have divisions of research, training, fisheries, veterinary medicine, forestry, development, game and wildlife, and so on.) These divisions may have separate field stations or offices at the local-government level. (For further details, see Adu, 1965.)

With the increase in the number of military regimes in Africa has come an increased importance of permanent secretaries. These men often come to make the day-to-day decisions which are the backbone of executive administration. These men are usually well-educated and highly professional.

At the time of independence, the primary concern was to Africanize the highest levels of the civil service. (The political level had, of course, been almost entirely Africanized.) In most African states these high-level civil-service posts are now held by Africans, although in a number of the French-speaking countries (plus the English-speaking states of southern Africa, such as Malawi, Lesotho, and Botswana), European technical experts are heavily involved in the executive administration.

Two main structural problems seem to have emerged regarding the civil service in Africa: the relationship of the civil service to the political party structure, and the relationship of the national civil service to local government. Thus, in Ghana during Nkrumah's later years, there was an exact parallel of offices within the government party and the civil service (see Apter, in Coleman and Rosberg 1964) and questions as to rights of jurisdiction created tension which clearly contributed to Nkrumah's overthrow. With regard to local government, the problem centers on the disparity between the well-educated professional civil servants at the national level and the relatively untrained administrators at the local level. The bottleneck in administration is most frequently at the local level (see Dryden, 1968; Adedeji, 1969). Most African states have set up institutes of administration on a "crash-course" basis to train large numbers of persons for local-level government.

63

Participation and Mobilization

THE CONCEPTS OF SOCIAL MOBILIZATION and participation are defined in Module 37 as part of a process of increasing complexity. The idea of participation is also mentioned in Module 58 as a central type of linkage in the process of national integration. In this module, special attention will be paid to the electoral process as a means of popular participation in the processes of government. Other mechanisms of participation, such as party structure, interest groups, and mass media, will also be mentioned.

1. EARLY ELECTORAL EXPERIENCE IN AFRICA

Although the four *communes* in Senegal had elected representatives to the National Assembly in Paris since the nineteenth century, most of the French-speaking areas of Africa first held such elections immediately after World War II (see Schachter Morgenthau, 1964). In the period from 1945 to 1960, there were elections at all levels (regional, territorial, federal — in the federations of French West and Equatorial Africa — and to the National Assembly in Paris), an average of about six elections per country. English-speaking West African states had a relatively brief but intensive history of pre-independence electoral experience (see MacKenzie and Robinson, 1960). In English-speaking central and eastern Africa, however, experience with both local and national elections began at a slightly later date (generally the mid-1950s), except for those elections restricted to the resident European community (see Bennett, 1963; and Mulford, 1964).

In reviewing the literature of these pre-independence elections, it is important to note the common restrictions on suffrage. Thus, in Northern Nigeria there were a series of stages whereby a qualified popular vote selected certain candidates from whom the final representatives were chosen by a college of electors. This system of indirect election prevailed until the 1959 federal election when, for the first time in Nigerian history, there were direct elections based on universal suffrage (excluding women—who still do not vote—in the north). For details on the Nigerian election, see Post, 1963; Dudley, 1963; Whitaker, 1970. In eastern and central Africa, various experiments with such procedures as multiple voting and dual rolls (one for whites and one for Africans) were undertaken as a means of securing a racial balance in the legislative council (see Bennett and Rosberg, 1961; and Mair, 1962). Also, there were usually educational, occupational, or property qualifications. In French-speaking Africa prior to 1956, voting was restricted to "citizens," i.e., resident French and Africans who used the civil code (see Robinson, 1960). It is not surprising that one of the common slogans during the independence drive was "One man, one vote."

Still, a large number of Africans did have the experience of participating in elections prior to independence, and, furthermore, elections did become more or less accepted as a legitimate means of selecting national leaders.

In every country, the pre-independence election of crucial importance was the "independence" election, i.e., the election that demonstrated that the African government had national support to lead the state through independence and, in most cases, its first four or five years. It is important to stress that the African states thus came to independence with elected governments. In all cases, however, these elections were held in the colonial period, usually a year prior to independence. In reviewing the case studies on independence elections, data are frequently available on the number of persons registered, the number of registered persons who voted, and the percentage of votes cast for the dominant party. One measure of the popular acceptability or legitimacy of a regime is probably a high voting turnout and a high percentage of votes cast for the dominant party.

2. POST-INDEPENDENCE ELECTIONS

Because of the time period permitted by law between elections (usually four or five years), most African states did not have to confront the issue of elections during the early years of their independence. By 1963/64, however, there were pressures for elections. In some cases elections had already been held, as in Ghana, the first all-black African state to achieve independence from the colonial powers. Electoral commissions were usually set up, consisting of high-level civil servants and frequently high-level political figures as well.

The results of these post-independence elections were mixed (see Crawford Young, *Essays*, chap. 22). In most cases, the dominant party was returned with an overwhelming majority. (The Westminster model of "winner-take-all," in particular, led to massive government victories.) In other cases, as in Sierra Leone or Nigeria, some national crisis was provoked by the elections, resulting in military intervention. Only in the Somali Republic was a dominant party replaced (through electoral means) by an opposition party. Yet despite the tendencies for elections to reinforce the position of incumbent government, elections became a symbol of mass participation in national politics.

Since the pattern of military takeovers is discussed in Module 64, it might be useful to focus here on some of the innovations which emerged in the post-independence elections. One innovation, explicitly based on the American concept of the "primary" election for selecting from several candidates within a party, was undertaken in Tanzania during the 1965 election. Although Tanzania was a one-party state, President Nyerere was concerned it remain a *democratic* one-party state. Consequently local constituencies were allowed to nominate their own candidates, and anyone within the party could be nominated. An interesting result was that much of the cabinet-level leadership of the government party (TANU) was not re-elected, and a new infusion of local-based leadership was absorbed within the party (see Kimambo and Temu, 1969; Liebenow, 1970; and Cliffe, 1967). In late 1969, Kenya experimented with the Tanzania election model and achieved essentially similar results — widespread defeat of party (KANU) incumbents and the infusion of young, locally based leaders into the National Assembly. Both these examples illustrate clearly the wide scope for representative and democratic elections in essentially one-party states.

3. OTHER MODES OF PARTICIPATION

Three major means of participation in the political process within the African states have been as follows: working within the party structure at the local level; working through interest groups which have direct contact with government; and utilizing the mass media for the dissemination of messages.

In many African states, the party is open to all who wish to participate at the local level (see Module 61). There may even be women's leagues (see Brooks, 1968), or youth branches to encourage the participation of particular groups. In Ghana under Nkrumah, there was an effort to involve as many people as possible in party activities. A Young Pioneers club, based on the Soviet model, was established for children, and even the churches were encouraged to engage in party activities (Apter, 1964).

The growth of organized interest groups in Africa has been a remarkable feature of the past twenty years. Most of these groups are located in the rapidly growing urban centers. They are organized around occupational groups (e.g., the butchers' union, or transporters' association); around religious groups (various Muslim and Christian leagues, and improvement societies); or around social groups (radio clubs, funeral societies, hobby groups). (Ethnic interest groups are mentioned in Module 47.) Most interest groups have been able to establish direct access into the political process, both local and national, and to exert influence on behalf of their members.

Finally, many Africans are availing themselves of the development of the mass media. Although many newspapers in Africa are under close government supervision, they do provide, to some extent, a two-way vehicle of communication (see Module 49). As the number and distribution of newspapers increases, so does the number of "letters to the editor." A number of private printing companies have also sprung up, printing a wide range of literature including political tracts. Radio clubs have been organized in which young people not only correspond with each other but with the radio stations. Mass participation in national life has come to be accepted as a basic right by many Africans.

64

Elite Instability and Military Rule

BETWEEN 1958 AND DECEMBER, 1969, there were twenty-eight successful *coups d'état* in seventeen different African countries. There have been at least seventeen unsuccessful coups. (In addition, Nasser came to power in Egypt through a coup in 1952.) In most coups, the military assumed control from a civilian regime. In a few cases portions of the military took over from an existing military regime (e.g., Nigeria in July, 1966, or Dahomey in 1967). In one case (Sudan, 1964), civilian forces took over control from the military, although in May, 1969, the military returned to power. Increasing evidence of "elite instability" and the important role of the military in Africa must be carefully interpreted. African patterns appear to differ from those in Latin America, where there has been a long period of independence, and a deeply entrenched social elite that provides most of the military officers. In Africa, military institutions are a more recent phenomena, and military officers have been recruited from all strata in society. The high frequency of African military takeovers is probably a reflection of transition problems (including political instability) in the second-stage post-independence period. See Welch (1970) for an up-to-date analysis of the role of the military in Africa.

1. THE MILITARY IN AFRICA

At the time of independence, the military forces in most sub-Saharan African states were very small. A number of states had no military at all. Most had forces ranging from 1,000 to 6,000 men. Only a few had over 10,000 men, and the largest armies (those in Congo-Kinshasa and Ethiopia) numbered only 35,000 (see Kitchen, 1964; Welch, 1970, includes a table listing the size of armed forces and defense budgets for all African states). In most cases (excluding Ethiopia) these armies at independence had European officers at the highest levels. In Congo-Kinshasa, the July, 1960, mutiny by the Congolese officers and enlisted men was directed against the entrenched Belgian officers. One of the first tasks in most countries at independence was to Africanize the officer corps. Large numbers of Africans went to the military academies in Britain (Sandhurst) and France (St. Cyr). Some countries, such as Ghana, also began to accept training aid from the Soviet Union. Officers who returned from European training were usually imbued with the professionalism, discipline, technical skills, and austerity of their European counterparts (see Afrifa, 1966). By the mid-1960s, most armies in Africa were officered by Africans of this professional quality.

The functions of African armies have been varied. Ghanaian, Ethiopian, and Nigerian troops were among the finest of the United Nations contingent in the Congo. In those states which had irredentist movements or border disputes (e.g., Kenya, Ethiopia) the military was often involved in border patrol. Internally, military force was occasionally used to quell disturbances within a state, (as during the Nigerian General Strike of 1964 or the current rebellions in Sudan and Chad). In other cases, the military was used internally to engage in engineering and developmental tasks. (For example, Israeli advisers in Ivory Coast helped establish a *corps civique,* in which military recruits were located in villages along the Ivoirien border and taught to engage in agricultural improvement and educational services.) To some extent the military as an institution came to symbolize both modernization and national integration (since most armies were relatively integrated, some even having ethnic quotas). It is against this background that the military coups must be viewed.

2. MILITARY *COUPS D'ÉTAT* IN AFRICA

There have been several different patterns of coups in Africa. In some cases, as in Dahomey, the military took over just prior to elections and then returned control to an elected civilian regime (see Le Marchand, 1968; Welch 1970). In other cases, as in Burundi or Nigeria, the military reflected the basic social unrest within the country. The question as to why coups have occurred in some countries and not in others has been a matter of much speculation (see Zolberg, 1968; Welch, 1967.) Coups seem to occur in both large and small states, in both French- and English-speaking states, and in most of the major geographical regions. Figure 10 summarizes these patterns.

FIGURE 10

COURS IN SUB-SAHARAN AFRICA, 1958–69

Country	Time	Comment
1. Sudan	November 18, 1958	Lt. Gen. Abboud takes over with apparent approval of Prime Minister Khalil.
2. Congo-Kinshasa	September 14, 1960	Col. Joseph Mobutu "neutralizes" all politicians.
3. Togo	January 13, 1963	Army mutiny—President Olympio killed by dissident elements in army. Civilian succession: Grunitsky.
4. Congo-Brazzaville	August 15, 1963	Civilian/military group forces President Youlou to resign.
5. Dahomey	October 27, 1963	Col. Soglo deposes President Maga.
6. Gabon	February 18–20, 1964	Coup by junior officers temporarily ousts M'Ba. French troops put down revolt and restore M'Ba.
7. Sudan	October 30–November 15, 1964	Civilian counter-coup overthrows Abboud.
8. Algeria	June 19, 1965	Minister of Defense Boumedienne replaces President ben Bella in army takeover.
9. Congo-Kinshasa	November 25, 1965	Gen. Mobutu assumes power from President Kasavubu to resolve constitutional crisis.
10. Dahomey	November 29, 1965	Gen. Soglo removes civilian regime.
11. Dahomey	December 22, 1965	Provisional President Congacau ousted by Gen. Soglo, who takes over office of president.
12. C.A.R.	January 1, 1966	Col. Bokassa, Chief of Staff, overthrows government of President Dacko.

13.	Upper Volta	January 3, 1966	Col. Lamizana, Chief of Staff, overthrows President Yaméogo.
14.	Nigeria	January 15, 1966	Junior Ibo officers overthrow Balewa/Azikiwe government and install General Aguiyi-Ironsi.
15.	Uganda	February 22, 1966	President Obote assumes all powers and suspends constitution.
16.	Ghana	February 24, 1966	Military overthrow of President Nkrumah. General Ankrah heads junta.
17.	Burundi	July 8, 1966	Prince Charles deposes King Mwambutsa VI.
18.	Nigeria	July 29, 1966	Military counter-coup. Aguiyi-Ironsi killed. Col. Gowan heads government.
19.	Burundi	November 28, 1966	Prince Charles (who had proclaimed himself King Mwami Ntare V) overthrown by Col. Micombero.
20.	Togo	January 13, 1967	Army Chief of Staff Lt. Col. Eyadema leads coup against Grunitsky.
21.	Sierra Leone	March 21, 1967	General Lanzana seizes power from newly elected Stevens.
22.	Dahomey	December 17, 1967	Gen. Soglo ousted in bloodless coup by army.
23.	Sierra Leone	April 18, 1968	Counter-coup by noncommissioned officers. Stevens returned.
24.	Congo-Brazzaville	August 3, 1968	Army seizes power after extended disturbances.
25.	Mali	November 19, 1968	Military committee ousts Keita.
26.	Sudan	May 25, 1969	Pro-Arab military dismisses civilian government.
27.	Libya	September 1, 1969	King Idris is deposed in military takeover.
28.	Somali Republic	October 15, 1969	President Shermarke is assassinated and several days later the army takes over to restore order.

3. MILITARY REGIMES IN AFRICA

As is evident from the above figure, coups have occurred in a variety of patterns. In several cases (e.g., Dahomey) the military did not form a regime. In cases where the military did form a regime, however, the first task has usually been to form a "national council" (consisting of military officers, although civilians are sometimes included). The council usually seeks to do several things immediately: secure international recognition, legitimize its position within the country (usually by focusing attention on the corruption of the former administration), secure its physical survival by precautions against the return of former elite elements, encourage the civil service to continue with the administration of the country, and announce "constitutional reforms" to be forthcoming (see Ankrah, 1966).

In some cases, such as Congo-Kinshasa, Sudan, and Nigeria, military regimes were also faced with impending or actual civil war. In the case of Nigeria, the size of the army was approximately 10,000 at the time of the first coup but was increased to approximately 100,000 within two years because of the secession of Biafra. The impact of a military regime engaged in civil war is likely to be much greater than in a situation where the military regards itself as a "caretaker government" until the politicians can agree on workable rules of political process.

In several of the French-speaking countries (e.g., Dahomey, Togo, Congo-Kinshasa), the military has returned control voluntarily to civilian regimes. In English-speaking Africa, Ghana in August, 1969, held elections and turned control of government over to the successful party (the Progress Party of Kofi Busia); and the counter-coup in Sierra Leone returned control to the civilian government of Siaka Stevens. It is difficult to predict the future role of the military in African political development, except to note that many African armies seem to regard themselves as the "watchdogs" of effective civilian government. (For further discussion of the role of the military in Africa, see Lee, 1969; Welch, 1970; Gutteridge, 1967; and Morison *et al.*, 1970.)

65
———

The Implications
of Nigeria-Biafra

THE GENERAL PATTERN in this syllabus has been to focus on broad conceptual themes rather than individual case-studies (references to case-studies are included in the *Bibliography*). The civil-war situation in Nigeria-Biafra, however, which occurred between May, 1967, and mid-January, 1970, has such far-reaching consequences in its implications for nation-building in Africa that it clearly constitutes more than a case-study and hence is discussed in detail in this module.

Even in retrospect, students should be encouraged to distinguish between the humanitarian and the political implications of the Nigerian civil war. This module will try to remain neutral on the actual causes of the conflict, but it will present "facts" (clearly open to alternative interpretations) on the background to conflict, the period of military rule and the beginnings of civil war, and the course of the war. In conclusion, an attempt will be made to speculate on the implications of the conflict.

Even before the end of the civil war, Nigeria remained the largest and probably the most important Black African state. With the end of the war, attention has shifted to reconstruction, yet the broader issues of Pan-Africanism, economic development, nation-building, and neocolonialism may be determined to some extent by the success or failure of Nigerian national integration in the decade of the 1970s. The struggle for self-determination by the predominantly Ibo Biafran people has become a chapter in African history which will not easily be forgotten. Estimates as to the number of persons who have died from hunger, disease, and battle casualties range between one and two million. The moral issues continue to be ambiguous: blame and praise seem strongly out of place in what has clearly been both a human and an African tragedy.

1. BACKGROUND TO CONFLICT

Approximately one out of four black Africans in independent Africa (i.e., excluding southern Africa) is a Nigerian. It is not surprising then that Nigeria should have come to mirror the full range of problems of nation-building on the continent. There is a high degree of ethnolinguistic pluralism in Nigeria (see Module 11); there are large-scale ethnic societies (the Hausa, Yoruba, and Ibo are all groups of over 8 million); and the major ethnic groups represent very different cultural values (e.g., the hierarchically organized Hausa as compared to the segmentally organized Ibo). Because of its size and resources, Nigeria had begun to develop economically on an impressive scale. Relatively large numbers of persons were settling in cities—there are more cities with populations of over 20,000 in Nigeria than in the rest of sub-Saharan Black Africa combined—yet urban unemployment was high; the "mass-elite gap" seemed to be rapidly widening; those with power can control wealth and those without power are left in poverty.

The territorial components of Nigeria have been historically separate. The amalgamation of Northern and Southern Nigeria in 1914 was essentially an administrative device for the convenience of the colonial government. It was not until 1951 that Northern Nigerians and Southern Nigerians came together in a common political arena. At that time, the ecological, economic, and cultural differences between the regions (the north being savanna, cattle raising, peanut growing, and Islamic in culture, the south being primarily rainforest, cocoa and oil palm growing, increasingly industrial, and to some extent Christian) were quickly translated into mistrust and suspicion.

Not surprisingly, Nigerian independence in 1960 heightened the problems of interethnic, mass-elite, and territorial integration. The political formula imposed by the colonial regime for dealing with such pluralism was a federal system (based at first on three regions—Northern, Eastern, and Western—and later to include also the Mid-West), with a Westminster model of political decision-making—although later the office of "president" was added (see Awa, 1964; Sklar, 1963). This political formula was inherently unstable in that the Northern Region was larger (in voting population) than the rest of Nigeria combined, and hence certain southern groups perceived themselves as being permanently excluded from national political life.

The actual political patterns of the period 1960 to 1966 (i.e., the period of the post-independence civilian government) are well described by a number of scholars (e.g., MacKintosh, 1966; Sklar and Whitaker, in Carter, 1966; Schwarz, 1965). In brief, the elections of 1959 resulted in a plurality for the Northern party (the Northern Peoples' Congress, or NPC) which then formed a coalition government with the Eastern party (the National Council of Nigerian Citizens, or NCNC), while the Western party (the Action Group, or AG) formed the opposition. The period prior to the December, 1964, national elections was crisis-filled: the leaders of the opposition party (AG) were jailed for treason in September, 1963 (for discussion of the Awolowo trial, see Sklar, 1966); the national census of 1962 was discarded and redone in 1963 because of apparent political tampering with the results; the Mid-West Region was carved out of the Western Region (1963/64); and the General Strike of June, 1964, brought the economy to a halt over the issue of wage differentials between the political class and the working class. In 1964, however, there emerged for the first time a two-party system in Nigeria: one, a coalition of "progressive" elements called United Party Grand Alliance (UPGA)—consisting of the NCNC, the AG, and the Northern opposition party, the Northern Elements Progressive Union (NEPU)—and the other a coalition of moderate and conservative elements called the Nigerian

National Alliance (NNA)—consisting of the NPC and the ruling party of the Western Region, the Nigerian National Democratic Party (NNDP). The NNA won the federal elections, but in an atmosphere of crisis and mistrust. The resultant government of Nigeria, formed in January, 1965, was a *coalition* of ministers from both the NNA and the UPGA.

This compromise, however, did not satisfy many of the Yoruba people of the Western Region, who continued to feel under-represented, and disruptions intensified in that region. The federal government was apparently on the verge of using the army to quell these disturbances when on January 15, 1966, the army took over control of the country and suspended the constitution.

2. MILITARY RULE AND THE BEGINNINGS OF CIVIL WAR

Perhaps by chance many of the young officers who led the *coup d'état* were Ibo. Perhaps also by chance the two regional premiers who were Ibo remained alive while the two premiers who were non-Ibo were killed. Furthermore, the resultant military regime of General Aguiyi-Ironsi (an Ibo) was heavily dominated by Ibo advisers. Whatever the intentions of the leaders of the coup and of the Aguiyi-Ironsi regime, the coup and its aftermath were widely regarded in the north, and to a lesser extent in the west, as an Ibo attempt to dominate Nigeria. Partly in reaction to these fears, Northern city dwellers rioted against Ibo residents in May, 1966 (see Paden, in Melson and Wolpe, 1970), and Northern elements of the army staged a successful counter-coup in July, 1966. The new government of Colonel Gowon (who was a member of one of the minority groups in the "Middle Belt" area of Northern Nigeria and a Christian) stressed a return to some sort of decentralized federal formula. The second coup, however, provoked fear among the Ibo who lived in the North (many of whom began to return to the Eastern Region) and in the army itself (which began to divide up according to region of origin). In September and October, 1966, further Northern attacks on resident Ibo occurred. Biafrans estimate that 30,000 persons were killed (from May through October), while the Nigerian official figure is closer to 5,000. The actual figures are of less importance than the fact that approximately two million Ibos in the North began to return to the Eastern Region. It was clear that while constitutional discussions were being held in Lagos and Aburi (in Ghana), the civil war had, in fact, begun.

In May, 1967, the start of the civil war was formalized by the official secession of the Eastern Region, which called itself *Biafra*. The issue to Colonel Ojukwu, leader of Biafra, was clearly "self-determination." It was argued that the Biafran people could no longer live in safety within Nigeria and hence must form their own state (see Ojukwu, 1969). The Nigerians, on the other hand, argued that some political formula could be reached through negotiation which would allow Biafra to remain within a federal framework, and that to allow Biafra to secede would be to encourage dozens of other secession movements within Nigeria by groups which had grievances (see the Enahoro statement at the Addis Ababa meeting of the OAU, in Legum and Drysdale, 1969).

3. THE COURSE OF THE CIVIL WAR

In the summer of 1967 the Biafran army made a "pre-emptive strike" through the Mid-West and came very close to Lagos, capital of Nigeria and a city of about one million people and appeared to be threatening other large cities, such as Ibadan. The effect of this attack was to mobilize the Yoruba people of the Western Region to join in coalition with the Hausa-speaking peoples of the North in an effort to defeat Biafra. Over the next year federal troops surrounded Biafra on all sides (including a naval blockade) and successfully occupied those portions of the Eastern Region (Biafra) which were "non-Ibo" (i.e., occupied by minority groups, such as the Ijaw, Kalabari, and Ibibio). Also, federal forces, after much effort, came to occupy most of the major urban centers of the Ibo portions of Biafra. By the fall of 1968 it was clear that the Biafrans were militarily surrounded, but also that the Biafrans had become adept at guerrilla fighting. The heavy rainforest and the village-centered structure of Ibo society were ready-made for long-term guerrilla resistance. The war was a "civilian's war" to the Biafrans, since most felt they were fighting for their survival. Charges of "genocide" prompted the delegation of a team of U.N. observers who reported that this was not the case (i.e., that Ibos were not being maltreated in "liberated areas" nor in other parts of Nigeria, such as Lagos). However, widespread starvation was occurring and, due to intransigence on both sides, humanitarian efforts to alleviate civilian suffering were restricted. This continued to be the situation as of fall, 1969. In early January, 1970, the Uli airstrip, which had been the life-line for Biafran "relief" was taken, and within two days Ojukwu fled and the remaining Biafrans surrendered. The surrender was formalized on January 15, 1970.

4. IMPLICATIONS OF THE NIGERIA-BIAFRA CONFLICT

The international implications of the Nigeria-Biafra conflict are of considerable importance: the Soviet Union (see Klinghoffer, 1968) and Great Britain have supported Nigeria with military supplies; France (and apparently Portugal) supported Biafra with medical and military supplies. The United States, while continuing some economic aid to Nigeria, and providing cargo planes for relief in Biafra, did not supply arms to either side. (Perhaps U.S. policymakers were aware of growing public opinion against U.S. military intervention in non-

Western countries.) Only four African states broke OAU unanimity and recognized Biafra: Ivory Coast, Gabon, Zambia, and Tanzania (see Nyerere, 1968). In all, Nigeria was not so much a "cold war" issue as an issue which involved big power maneuvering for some desired position in Africa. (For a view which stresses the importance of international involvement, see Sklar, 1969.) It is also clear in retrospect that international "relief efforts" were partly responsible for the prolongation of the war since, when relief was finally cut, Biafra fell.

The international involvements in the Nigeria-Biafra conflict, however, are perhaps less important to the course of the war than the range of local factors which have resulted in the conflict. Two important changes have occurred in the political structure of Nigeria which might influence national integration after the war: (1) the four-region structure of the original federation has been replaced by a twelve-state structure which more nearly accommodates local feelings of identity and interest (with the exception of the three "eastern states," i.e., Biafra); and (2) the civilian leadership of Nigeria, consisting primarily of "progressives" from the old UPGA alliance (e.g., Obafemi Awolowo, Anthony Enaharo, Aminu Kano, Joseph Tarka) are actively undertaking social reforms within their respective states. In short, the civilian leadership of Nigeria consists of progressive men who "suffered" under the original civilian regime (1960–66) and who cannot be held responsible for the policies of that regime.

An additional factor in both the international and internal aspects of the conflict has been the huge petroleum resources of Nigeria, now believed to be among the largest in the world and strategically located in close proximity to major European and American markets (in comparison with Middle East sites). Most of Nigeria's petroleum resources are concentrated in the Rivers and Mid-West states, and secondarily in the adjacent South-East and East-Central (primarily Ibo) states. Although it is difficult to evaluate the role petroleum played in the patterns of international involvement in the civil war, there is no trouble in assessing the potential role of petroleum in Nigeria's future, assuming that some equitable method of distribution for the growing oil income is devised. Faced with perhaps the greatest challenge of nation-building in any African state, contemporary Nigeria has also been endowed with one of the greatest sources of wealth on the continent to aid in implementating its programs for national construction.

Yet very deep social cleavages and frustrations have resulted from almost three years of fighting. Biafran identity and interests may have become consolidated during this period, and it is clear that some remnants of Biafran resistance will continue in exile. The strategy of nation-building, which is now clearly the core concern in Nigeria, remains contingent on dozens of factors. Reconstruction may provide, however, an opportunity to realistically assess the problems of the past as well as create solutions for the future. All of the African states are likely to be affected by the precedents which have emerged from the Nigeria-

Biafra conflict: (1) on the manner of resolving the conflict; (2) on the issue of reconstruction; and (3) on the basic matter of ethnic self-determination *vs.* national integrity. It should also be mentioned in conclusion that there is as yet no single scholarly volume available on the Nigeria-Biafra conflict. The literature which does exist tends to be partisan and in scattered form.

Legal Systems Development

66

Legal Systems in Africa

LEGAL SYSTEMS ARE THE CODES OF CONDUCT which societies enforce upon their own members for the resolution of conflict and the maintenance of justice. Such systems may be written or unwritten. Legal codes may range from those where broad general principles form the framework of law to those in which specific precedents form the corpus of law. In the African context, there has been an overlay of legal systems: colonial legal systems were often superimposed over the existing traditional systems. These traditional systems were either of the Islamic variety (called *shari'a* law) or were peculiar to each ethnic society. The term customary law is normally applied to the latter types, although it is occasionally used to include Islamic law as well.

1. THE ROLE OF CUSTOMARY LAW

Customary law in ethnic societies was usually unwritten. Each society had its own way of resolving conflict. Some scholars (Allott, 1966, p. 433) note that in less complex segmental societies, such as the Kikuyu of Kenya or the Ibo of Nigeria, there was frequently an informal judicial structure with emphasis on the role of third-party arbitration. Also, there was somewhat more emphasis on civil wrongs than on criminal wrongs, although no special effort was made to distinguish them. This is in contrast to those societies like the centralized Hausa-Fulani emirates, some of which had well-developed judicial systems and a full elaboration of types of criminal offenses and punishments.

Customary law has been modified everywhere, but it probably retains most force in those areas of British colonization where rule was indirect (e.g., Nigeria,

Uganda) rather than direct (e.g., Kenya). In most cases, criminal law was fundamentally modified even though civil law might be relatively unchanged. In the French and Portuguese-controlled areas customary criminal law was replaced by a criminal code. The trend everywhere is to encourage the development of criminal law in the form of legislation specifically describing the nature of the crime. Customary social law is particularly important in the area of family law and property law, for throughout Africa (in both British and French areas) the customary ways of dividing inheritance, regulating marriage and divorce, and allocating land, have continued into the post-colonial period. One of the major tasks of the independent African governments is deciding the place of customary law in an integrated legal system. (For further discussions of customary law, see Elias, 1956; Nekam, 1966; Gluckman, 1969; Allott, 1960.)

2. ISLAMIC LAW

As mentioned in Module 21, most Islamic law in Black Africa follows the Maliki school. This school is based on the writings (called the *Muwatta*) of a scholar named Malik Ibn Anas who lived in Arabia shortly after the time of the Prophet Muhammad. Two major works have subsequently been added to the category of primary sources: the *Risala* of Ibn Abi Zayd al-Qayrawani (translated into French by Bercher, 1945) and the *Mukhtasar* of Sidi Khalil (translated by Ruxton, 1916). These works cite precedents which are felt to be applicable to judicial decisions.

The major source of Islamic law, however, is the Koran itself. Certain things are recommended or prohibited in the Koran and these have the force of law. Another source of Islamic law in Africa is the *hadith,* or reports about the decisions and statements of the Prophet Muhammad and how he adjudicated particular situations.

Islamic law, in essence, divides all human behavior into five categories: prohibited, discouraged, neutral, recommended, and required. It has been applied in many parts of Sudanic West Africa in a very legalistic manner. Thus, drinking of alcohol, eating of pork, or collection of interest (usury) are strictly forbidden (there are also other dietary restrictions); the number of wives is limited to four; and exact prescriptions are laid down for matters of divorce, inheritance, sale of goods, criminal offenses, and so forth.

Of equal importance to the substance of Islamic law in Black Africa are the procedural requirements and the judicial structure. Thus, for example, procedure requires that the evidence of a Muslim witness be weighed more heavily than the evidence of a non-Muslim, and that of a man more than that of a woman. Elaborate judicial structures, often based on dynastic succession within learned families, were established in the larger Islamic state systems. Even in the small forest towns, a learned man was usually available to arbitrate cases.

Anderson (1954) has described the variations within Islamic law in Africa and particularly its relationship to the colonial system and social change. One of the important problems within contemporary Islamic law is how to interpret new types of behavior and action. Some conservative Muslims maintain that all innovation is bad, while the reformist Muslims argue that the consequences of decisions should be considered.

3. EUROPEAN LAW IN AFRICA

Three major European legal systems have been introduced into Africa: common law, civil law, and Roman-Dutch law. Common law is found in most of the English-speaking areas and refers to principles of jurisprudence and doctrines of equity which have developed over the centuries in England. Precedents for new cases are found by examining the rulings on prior cases.

The civil-law areas included the French-speaking areas, plus those areas colonized by Belgium, Portugal, and Spain. Such law was based on the codification which emerged in Europe during the time of Napoleon. It is usually regarded as more legalistic and detailed than common law, and the code is the principal referent in deciding cases.

The Roman-Dutch areas include the Republic of South Africa, Rhodesia, Lesotho, Botswana, and Swaziland. The law is based on the Dutch modification of Roman law and may also be described as codified law.

European law in Africa was established during the colonial period and has served as the base for legislative codes in the post-colonial era. Roland Young (*Essays*, chap. 23) documents some of the areas of European law, or "received law," which have conflicted with customary or Islamic law (e.g., land law, criminal law). However, many aspects of European law deal with modern-sector behavior and hence do not usually come into direct conflict with customary or Islamic law. One of the major problems in the post-colonial period has been to consolidate or integrate the various legal systems which exist within a country into a single system. In many African states Islamic law and customary law have been retained in certain situations, such as family disputes, and European law, for instance corporate law, has been applied in other situations. Module 67 deals more specifically with problems of legal integration and conflict-of-law in Africa.

67

The Integration
of Legal Systems

THE SUPREMACY OF NATIONAL LEGISLATION is a prerequisite of a sovereign unitary state. In a federal system, local law may have equal status, but it is essential that the relationship between national and local legal jurisdictions be well demarcated. If, in some areas of action, "law is the command of the sovereign" (i.e., positive law), then law will play an important role in the transformation of African societies and in the consolidation of nation-states. In this process, there has been a major effort to consolidate and integrate the various legal systems, customary and received, into a single national legal system.

1. THE PROCESS OF LEGAL INTEGRATION

The three main aspects of legal integration deal with structure, values, and personnel. In many African states prior to independence, there coexisted two or three different legal structures within the state. In states such as Guinea, Kenya, Mauritania, Nigeria, Senegal, Somali, and Sudan there existed a separate Islamic legal structure, which in fact, carried over into the post-colonial period. In Ethiopia, there was a separate religious legal structure based on Coptic (Christian) law (see Lowenstein, 1965). Problems arise when a plaintiff could use one legal structure and a defendant another. Thus, in a situation where the consolidation of nation-states leads to interethnic and interreligious contact, there is a greater need for a unified judicial structure for conflict resolution and for rules on conflicts-of-law (see Kuper and Kuper, 1965).

The two major ways in which structural integration may occur are (1) the creation of a single set of courts or (2) the linkage at the appeals level of the various legal systems. In both cases, courts of appeal would be able to decide issues of appropriate jurisdiction, procedure, and substance.

States may be reluctant to abolish existing legal structures (either customary or Islamic), even if it were politically possible, as long as the legal systems are meeting the needs of the people and the people fully support these systems. In many instances, and particularly where the state does try to abolish such traditional structures, arbitration may occur outside the formal legal system. That is, people will go to learned men for arbitration of local disputes. This "informal law" is an interesting social phenomenon in contemporary Africa.

With regard to the integration of legal values, or concepts of jurisprudence, a more difficult problem exists. People are usually socialized slowly over time into new value systems. Beliefs and values regarding family life are particularly slow to change. Thus a new state such as Ivory Coast may outlaw plural marriage, but it is difficult to enforce this set of values in the face of widespread acceptance of the idea of plural marriage. As a means of dealing with such a problem, the government of Ivory Coast has said that the law does not apply *ex post facto* to existing plural marriages but will apply to future marriages. Since marriage laws affect inheritance settlements (e.g., if legal heirs include only the children of a legal marriage, the children of second and third wives would be cut off without any inheritance) it may take considerable time before the full impact of these marriage laws is felt.

2. THE INTEGRATION OF LEGAL PERSONNEL

The two major professional roles in any modern legal system are those of judge and counsel. One key to legal integration in the new states is to train personnel to become familiar with both European law and with traditional law. African states increasingly have come to establish their own law schools, although many law students continue to receive their specialized training in Europe and the United States. Because of the rapid changes in African national law, however, there is a tendency for African states to require a short training period at the local law schools after a student has returned from abroad.

In cases where the Islamic legal structure is regarded as legitimate in the national context, there is an effort to train young Islamic scholars in the more modern versions of Islamic law. In London, there are advanced courses in Islamic law, and many students also attend universities in Arabic-speaking countries such as the U.A.R. (Egypt).

A major obstacle in the process of legal integration is the lack of trained personnel. Although in countries such as Nigeria and Ghana there are third- and fourth-generation African lawyers, in many other countries there are almost no lawyers at all. By 1965, according to Peaslee (1965), the states with the most lawyers (in absolute, not per-capita, terms) in sub-Saharan Africa included Ethiopia (1,967) and Nigeria (1,600), with a major gap then to the country with the third-largest number, Ghana (400). Kenya, Liberia, Sudan, and Tanzania all had over 100 practicing lawyers, but a number of states, such as Rwanda, Dahomey, Mali, Togo, Gabon, Guinea, and Upper Volta each had less than 10 lawyers. While these figures have increased substantially in the past five years, they are still indicative of the shortage of trained legal personnel.

A number of American universities, such as Syracuse, Columbia, Yale, and Northwestern, have initiated programs whereby young American lawyers can work in Africa on a one- or two-year basis to help meet the needs for legal personnel. The African Legal Center in New York City does most of the recruiting. (For an overview of the African "challenge to the legal profession," see Gower, 1968.)

3. VARIATIONS ON LEGAL INTEGRATION: THE NORTHERN NIGERIAN EXAMPLE

Northern Nigeria was ruled indirectly by the British from 1900 until 1960. During most of this period the British permitted the Islamic legal structure to service the needs of most of the north. In non-Islamic areas, as well, customary legal structures were elaborated into "native courts." In cases where a plaintiff or defendant wanted to subject himself to English law, the British "resident" served as magistrate. Only in 1959 did a panel of jurists examine the situation in Northern Nigeria and recommend a unified legal system. Thus, Islamic law, with the exception of family law, became a matter of civil legislation (based largely on the Sudan legal code). The Islamic legal structure was retained in matters of family law, with a separate *shari'a* court of appeals. A defendant could "opt out" of an Islamic legal structure into the Northern Region legal structure. A number of problems arose from this dualism including that of the status of non-Northern Nigerians within the Northern legal system.

Those problems were not resolved when the military took over the government in January, 1966, and again (a counter-coup) in July, 1966. Since that time the military government has divided the north into six states and has put all legal personnel (including Islamic legal experts) on a civil-service basis. The exact status of legal systems within the particular states of Nigeria will remain undecided until a new national constitution is adopted.

4. CONCLUSIONS

There are many specific case studies of legal integration in Africa which illuminate the problems involved and also many of the creative approaches to solving these problems. Senegal (see Farnsworth, 1964) and Tanzania (see Cotran, 1963) have both been particularly innovative in this area.

68

The Development
of Constitutional Law

THE HISTORY OF CONSTITUTIONAL DEVELOPMENT in Africa is mentioned in
Modules 35 and 56 on colonialism and independence. Briefly, in the French-
speaking areas there were three distinct relevant constitutional documents
prior to independence: the Fourth French Republic Constitution of 1946, the
Loi-Cadre reforms of 1956, and the Fifth French Republic Constitution of
October 4, 1958. (Only Guinea, which rejected this latter constitution, became
technically independent. The other states remained part of the Franco-African
Community until 1960.)

In the British areas, the situation varied for each state. In West Africa there
were two or three different constitutions in each state prior to independence.
In East Africa, there were early provisions for legislative councils, but only one
formal "independence" constitution. In all British cases, the constitutional
debates took place in London, and included Colonial Office officials and representatives of major political groups within the particular African state. (Note:
the debates over the Central African Federation in 1953 were not fully representative.) Since independence, there have been a number of modifications in
African constitutions (e.g., the Nkrumah Constitution) including the current
pattern of constitutional review which is occurring under most military regimes.

1. CHARACTERISTICS OF INDEPENDENCE CONSTITUTIONS

a. French-Speaking States

The states of French-speaking Africa had almost identical constitutions (see
Lavoff and Persir, 1961, for comments and texts; see also Blondel, 1961;
Robinson, 1958). In almost every case they described themselves as democratic
and secular. All had an initial section on human rights. Most of the regimes
followed a presidential model, as discussed in Module 62. Constitutions were
divided into sections, with a series of articles in each section. These sections
may be summarized below in prototype form:

Section One: Matters of state sovereignty, such as the symbols of sovereignty
(national emblem and anthem), official language(s), the designation of a capital
city, and the guarantee of universal suffrage.

Section Two: Description of the duties of the President of the Republic.

Section Three: Discussion of the National Assembly.

Section Four: Details of the relationship between the government and the
Assembly.

Section Five: Aspects of international treaties.

Section Six: Scope of the Supreme Court.

Section Seven: Spheres of judicial authority.

Section Eight: Powers of the High Court of Justice (consisting, in most cases, of deputies from the assembly who have the power to judge members of government for dereliction of duty).

Section Nine: Nature of the Economic and Social Council.

Section Ten: Role of subnational collectivities.

Section Eleven: Relations with other sovereign states.

Section Twelve: Procedures for revision of the constitution (usually as follows: "at the initiative of the President or the members of the National Assembly . . . an amendment may be presented to three-quarters of the members of the assembly and must be approved by a majority; it is then submitted to the country in the form of a referendum . . .").

Section Thirteen: General matters.

In most cases, the independence constitutions of the French-speaking areas were short—about ten pages in length.

b. British-Area States

By contrast, the British-area constitutions of independence were usually long and complex. The Nigerian Constitution of 1960 is over 150 pages, although this includes each of the regional constitutions which were included as part of the national constitution. The Constitution of the Federal State of Nigeria was divided into chapters, which in turn were divided into sections. These chapters are summarized below in general terms.

Chapter One: The federation and its territories.

Chapter Two: Eligibility for citizenship.

Chapter Three: "Fundamental rights" of citizens.

Chapter Four: Duties of the governor-general (later, when Nigeria became a republic, the office of the president).

Chapter Five: Role of Parliament (composition, procedure, legislative powers).

Chapter Six: Executive powers.

Chapter Seven: Role of police.

Chapter Eight: Role of courts.

Chapter Nine: Finances.

Chapter Ten: Role of civil service.

Chapter Eleven: Miscellaneous powers.

The procedures for amendment were difficult and complex, including the requirement that a majority of the regional legislatures consent. (For a discussion of constitutional development in Nigeria, see Ezera, 1964.)

Part of the initial constitutional complexity of Nigeria and other British areas (especially Kenya and Uganda), was that the internal relations between regions and/or ethnic groups was a matter of more explicit constitutional concern than in the French-speaking areas. Hence a fuller set of civil liberties were elaborated and a more detailed delineation of local government prerogatives was established.

2. CONSTITUTIONAL CONFLICT AND CRISIS

The military coups, as described in Module 64, usually reflected some constitutional crisis. Military coups, however, had one of three different types of effects on constitutional development: (1) they perpetuated the basic constitutional patterns but replaced the incumbent leaders (as in many of the smaller French-speaking states); (2) they fundamentally changed the nature of the constitutional regime (as in Ghana); (3) they established constitution-review commissions which left open the question as to which type of government would be recommended (as in Nigeria).

Constitutional crises or abuses are always a matter of perception and interpretation. In the case of Nigeria, a major crisis developed in December, 1964, after the federal elections, as to whether the president (Azikiwe) or the prime minister (Balewa) had certain decision-making powers. In Uganda a similar dispute occurred which resulted in the prime minister (Obote) suspending the constitution in 1966 and deposing the kabaka of Buganda (then president).

In Ghana, President Nkrumah proposed, and had ratified, an entirely new constitution which essentially gave the CPP leadership complete powers over all aspects of the state (see Rubin and Murray, 1961). In Kenya, greater centralization was imposed by amendment. By 1965, most of the French-speaking states had modified their 1960 constitutions in a number of important ways (see Module 62).

It is of considerable importance in considering constitutional crises to inquire about the role of the supreme courts. It will be noted that there is no reference to "judicial review" in the United States Constitution, yet by precedent this has become the guiding doctrine granting the court powers to review the enactments and orders of the legislative and the executive branches. In Africa, the issues which divided states internally were so fundamental that the supreme courts became very cautious about asserting themselves as arbitrators. Both in Nkrumah's Ghana and more recently (summer, 1969) in Zambia, unpopular judicial decisions have led to dismissal of judges.

3. CONSTITUTIONAL REVIEW UNDER MILITARY REGIMES

In most states under military rule, the main corpus of laws on the statute books and, where applicable, the common law based on precedents continued to be enforced by the civilian courts. In a few areas, martial law was declared, but in general the military left the day-to-day legal issues to the courts.

What is of concern to the military regimes are the fundamental processes by which laws would be enacted, i.e., the nature of the decision-making process. In both Nigeria and Ghana constitutional review commissions were established by the military. Under General Aguiyi-Ironsi in Nigeria, a unitary form of government was proposed. It was in partial reaction to this plan for centralized control that the counter-coup occurred, with its stress on a return to federalism. Volumes of literature, both legalistic and political, have come out of the subsequent period. Chief Obafemi Awolowo combines both in his two books, *The People's Republic* (1969) and *Thoughts on the Nigerian Constitution* (1966), in which he proposes a particular type of federalism—one based on linguistic groups.

In Ghana, a new constitution was drafted and elections were held in August, 1969. A number of political parties were formed to contest the election, but two major parties emerged. The success of the Progress Party, under Dr. Kofi Busia, has resulted in the military (i.e., the National Liberation Council) turning over its power to this newly elected civilian regime, but with a three-year extension of certain reserved powers for the military. It is quite possible that in the future other African states will explicitly incorporate the role of the military into constitutional law.

In conclusion, the growth of constitutional law in Africa has reflected the full range of economic, political, and social problems discussed earlier. The extent to which integrated legal systems will emerge is clearly dependent on the resolution of fundamental issues of constitutional law.

Economic and Technical Systems Development

An Assessment
of Resources

THE PHYSICAL RESOURCES OF AFRICA will be discussed in this module as a background to discussions of economic problems of nation-building. More detailed analysis by country or by resource can be found in most of the general geography texts listed in the *Bibliography* and in the Oxford *Regional Economic Atlas of Africa* (P. H. Ady, 1965).

1. ENERGY RESOURCES

Africa has the greatest water-power potential in the world (about as much as Europe, North America, South America, and Australia combined). Huge hydroelectric stations—one as big as any in Europe—were in operation in Katanga by 1950 (the Congo Basin contains a very large proportion of Africa's hydroelectric potential). Other important projects either in operation or approaching completion are located at Owens Falls (opened in 1956 in Uganda on the Nile and serving much of East Africa); Kariba (the highly strategic installation serving Zambia and Rhodesia); Aswan in Egypt; the Volta River Project in Ghana; Edea in Cameroon; Kainji in Nigeria; and Konkouré in Guinea. Other large hydroelectric schemes exist in Mozambique (one of the largest projects in the world, financed largely by South Africa, is now in progress at Cabora Bassa); Ethiopia; Angola; Sudan; in the Maghrib states; and throughout the Congo Basin (which, near its outlet, was to have the world's largest hydroelectric project—at the Inga Rapids—until the project was postponed as

265

a result of the political troubles of 1960). But only a small proportion of Africa's water-power potential has been developed and much hope for future industrial development is understandably placed on this rich resource.

With regard to other future sources of energy development, Africa has the world's largest known reserves of *uranium* ore (Republic of South Africa, Gabon). This could prove another major asset for industrial development. Finally, from an oil-poor continent, Africa has emerged in the past twenty years as an increasingly important *petroleum* producer. The largest known deposits are in Libya, Algeria, Egypt, Gabon, and Nigeria, the latter having experienced a spectacular growth in petroleum production since 1960. Other significant deposits are being worked in Angola (especially the tiny enclave of Cabinda), Congo-Brazzaville, and Morocco.

The potential role of water power and other energy resources is emphasized still further by the lack of good quality *coal* in Africa. The absence of abundant coal resources has hindered both the development of transportation facilities and the growth of industry.

2. OTHER MINERAL RESOURCES

There is a vast wealth of mineral resources in Africa, and the rate of discovery of new mineral deposits has been rapid. It should be noted, however, that minerals at present are mined almost entirely for export in raw form and do not contribute as much as they could to increased employment and local industry. Also important is the concentration of minerals in only a few outstandingly rich areas, the most notable of which are the Witwatersrand (or Rand) area of South Africa, which produces most of the world's gold (providing one of South Africa's greatest diplomatic strengths on the international scene), and the Katanga-Copperbelt of Congo-Kinshasa and Zambia. It has been estimated that not more than ten countries in Tropical Africa exceed the world average in mineral output per capita (highest, in approximate order, are South-West Africa, Zambia, South Africa, Congo-Kinshasa, Swaziland, Rhodesia, Ghana, and Morocco).

In addition to *copper* and *gold*, Africa is also fairly rich in *iron ore* (South Africa, Rhodesia, the three Maghrib states, Sierra Leone, Liberia, Mauritania, and Guinea—the latter containing the world's largest-known deposit of lateritic iron ore). But in Tropical Africa, iron-ore deposits are not found near high-grade coal, thus hindering the growth of an iron and steel industry at present levels of technology. Other important minerals include *diamonds* (the vast majority of the world's industrial as well as gem diamonds come primarily from Congo-Kinshasa, South Africa, Ghana, and Sierra Leone); *bauxite* (from Guinea and Ghana, where it is playing a major role in stimulating local hydroelectric and industrial development, although neither is yet a major world producer); *cobalt* (over 50 per cent of the world's total comes from Congo-Kinshasa, while Zambia and Morocco also are among the largest producers); *manganese* (South Africa, Ghana, Morocco, and Congo-Kinshasa are among the top ten producers); *vanadium* (South-West Africa and South Africa rank behind only the United States in the production of this important element used to toughen steel); *chrome ore* (South Africa and Rhodesia rank among the top four in the world); *tin* (Congo-Kinshasa and Nigeria together account for 10 per cent of world production); *antimony* (Algeria and Morocco); and *asbestos* (Rhodesia, Swaziland, and South Africa are among the six largest producers). In short, most mineral resources necessary for economic development are available, although these are not equally distributed among the African states. At the same time, however, much of Africa has not yet had extensive mineral surveys. When these do take place, it is quite possible that major new mineral deposits will be identified. See DeKun (1965) for a detailed survey of existing mineral resources in Africa.

3. AGRICULTURAL RESOURCES

Africa's soil, although rich in minerals, is generally thin and not very fertile. Most of the rainforest and savanna soils are heavily leached latosols, markedly deficient in many soil nutrients and, especially when cleared of vegetation, very low in organic matter. Throughout much of Africa, the traditional response to this low fertility has been a pattern of shifting cultivation, in which patches of ground are cleared, cultivated for a limited number of years, and then left fallow to regain fertility. This system, although probably highly adaptable to the tropical environment (given low levels of technology), can rapidly exhaust soils and lead to extensive soil erosion, especially when population density is increased. In addition to improved farming techniques, the two most frequently mentioned aids to Africa's soil problems have been the use of chemical fertilizers and the wider introduction of mixed farming. Both have enormous potential, but face major problems—because of the intrinsic difficulties in the use of fertilizers in a tropical environment (e.g., washing away), their high costs, and the enormous barrier to mixed farming arising from the prevalence of the tsetse fly and other insect pests. The latter situation is indicative of how closely intertwined are many of Africa's problems: soil fertility can be improved with the application of animal manure, but the tsetse fly must be eradicated for animals to survive. See Phillips (1959) for a good discussion of ecological factors in African agriculture.

Many consider the climate of Africa to be the greatest factor retarding economic growth. About 60 per cent of Africa is steppe or desert, with low and unreliable rainfall. At least another third (i.e., most of Tropical Africa), is savanna, with its distinctive dry season and, more important, its unreliability and inconsistency of rainfall. Excessively wet years often follow years in which drought prevailed. One can understand the importance placed on water-control schemes in Africa, both large-scale (Gezira-Managil in Sudan, Office du Niger in Mali) and small-scale (small dams, wells, and reservoirs). Hance (1967) concludes that only 12 to 15 per cent of Tropical Africa has a climate which, under present techniques, is suitable for agriculture—although this amounts to about one-third the area of the United States.

4. PHYSICAL IMPEDIMENTS TO DEVELOPMENT

The resource situation is such that, although certain favorably endowed areas exist, Africa as a whole is beset by many physical problems. They include the following: (1) lack of energy and mineral resources in many areas (especially East Africa); (2) the large areas of poor soils (the best usually consist of areas of volcanic and alluvial soils, which are relatively limited); (3) widespread climatic handicaps, particularly inadequate and unreliable rainfall; (4) poor accessibility from the coast to the interior, due to the huge size of Africa, the frequency of rapids and waterfalls on rivers near the coast, and the small number of good natural harbors and inlets; (5) the prevalence of pests and disease-bearing organisms affecting both animals and man.

All of these impediments, however, do not form impenetrable barriers to development. Modern science and technology—disease control, irrigation and hydroelectric schemes, improved fertilizers, better transport, more detailed resource surveys—have already produced promising results. Given the rapidly increasing mineral inventory, the enormous scope for improving the generally low yields of agricultural crops, the potentials for mixed farming and the expansion of cultivated land, many, if not most, of these problems can be reduced significantly in the future—providing that social, economic, and political developments keep pace with technological progress, and economic growth keeps in advance of the growth of population (see Kamarck, 1967).

70

Agricultural Reorganization

ONE OF THE MOST POWERFUL FORCES of social change in Africa has been the introduction and extension of a monetary economy, particularly with respect to cash-crop agriculture. Agricultural reorganization has become a major agency for change in the rural areas and, through the encouragement of rural mobility, in the urban areas as well.

1. THE IMPORTANCE OF AGRICULTURE IN AFRICA

Even today, at least 75 per cent of all Africans are farmers, and farm products dominate the export economies of all African states except South Africa, Congo-Kinshasa, Zambia, Sierra Leone, and Mauritania (which are primarily mineral producers). But for a number of reasons, some technological and some environmental, African farmers are only one-third as productive as the world average. The majority still produce primarily for their own subsistence. Although there have been very few major food shortages in Africa, the rapid rate of population growth and the increasing demands for rural labor by urban industry and commerce are likely to place great strains on the agricultural sector in the future.

At the same time, there is scope for increased yields and the extension of cultivated land through social and economic reorganization and especially technological improvement. This will require, however, great efforts and expenditures in both the private and public sectors of most African countries.

2. AGRICULTURAL CHANGE

Herskovits (1962) outlined three major phases of agricultural development in colonial Africa: the early period of conquest and concessions, during which the money economy was extended on a large scale and European establishments and settlement were introduced; an intermediate period of agricultural development schemes, conceived of on a large scale, generally remote from the masses and resulting in little cultural change; and lastly, a period when new agricultural methods were introduced and greater emphasis placed on land reform. The end result at the time of independence was, for most African countries, a pronounced *dual economy*, one segment composed of relatively advanced commercial farmers (such as cocoa farmers in Ghana) highly specialized in the production of cash crops for export; the other consisting of the majority of the population who remained basically subsistence farmers with perhaps a small surplus for sale. One of the major problems facing African agriculture today arises from the difficulties in effectively accommodating traditional agricultural systems geared to producing food crops for local consumption to modern systems of cash-crop production for local and overseas markets (see Abercrombie, 1967). The two sectors remain poorly connected, and developments within the modern sector often remain isolated and without major impact on the larger population.

3. A "FALSE START"?

A stimulating but controversial statement on the problems of agricultural development in Africa can be found in René Dumont's *False Start in Africa* (1966) and his more objective U.N. Report, *African Agricultural Development* (1966). These volumes provide a fruitful basis for discussion as well as excellent lecture material. (Dumont is a French agronomist of radical political persuasion and clear pro-African orientation. Yet the volumes are critical of the new African governments for their failure to effectively use foreign aid and their propensity to exploit the peasant farmer.) Dumont makes specific suggestions as to how the African countries can create conditions to make foreign aid more effective. These include the following: (1) increased government efficiency (many of his comments here—on austerity and participation in manual work—are mirrored in the policies of Tanzania's Julius Nyerere, particularly in the *Arusha Declaration*); (2) improved training of personnel, particularly those in supervisory and advisory positions; (3) closer attention to related developments which encourage change, such as land reform, increased availability of popular consumer goods, and community development projects; (4) closer integration of all aspects of the agricultural system, especially with respect to soil conservation and fertilization, more mixed farming, better marketing and credit facilities, and the development of various forms of cooperatives; and (5) a speeding up of industrialization, particularly with labor-intensive rather than capital-intensive priorities, to overcome the severe problems of underemployment. (Dumont notes that these steps may require larger economic federations of existing states, a subject which will be considered in Module 78.)

4. CASE STUDIES

Numerous case studies of development schemes are available in the literature. From the colonial period, two extremes can be found in the disastrous Tanganyika Groundnut Scheme and the relatively successful Gezira Scheme in Sudan (Hance, 1967). See also the volume on the Zande Scheme (Reining, 1966). Freitag (1963) provides an excellent survey of schemes originating before 1963.

Despite the many problems of agricultural development, some genuine success stories exist. These include the growth of cotton cooperatives in northern

Tanzania, the Kilimanjaro coffee industry, the Ghana cocoa industry, the previously mentioned Gezira scheme, land reform and tea and coffee production in Kenya, agricultural diversification and productivity in Ivory Coast and Gabon, and many others. Some excellent works have recently been published which provide good case-study material: deWilde, *et al.* (1967), and Wharton (1969).

71

The Industrialization Process

INDUSTRY IS STILL in its initial stages in Africa. The net value of total industrial output from the continent (excluding South Africa) is about $5 billion, which is roughly equivalent to that of Sweden. In sub-Saharan Africa, only Rhodesia, Kenya, Congo-Kinshasa, and, of course, South Africa, have as much as 10 per cent of their gross national product derived from industry. Although the rate of growth of industrial output has been relatively high over the past four decades, the industrial output per capita in the industrial countries as a group is twenty-five times greater than that in Africa (excluding South Africa). For agriculture, the comparable figure is only twice as large (United Nations, 1963). An excellent survey of the problems and prospects of industrial development in Africa, including several good case studies, can be found in United Nations (1967).

1. PATTERNS OF INDUSTRIAL DEVELOPMENT

Four categories of development may be identified with respect to industrialization among the states in Africa (see Ewing, 1968). The first includes South Africa, the only state in Africa which has gone beyond the early stages of industrialization. With about 7 per cent of Africa's population, South Africa accounts for about 40 per cent of the continent's industrial output. It produces 43 per cent by value of African minerals (including 80 per cent of its coal), generates twice as much electric power as the rest of the continent combined, has the only large iron and steel industry, and is beginning to move into wider industrialization by producing capital goods and equipment for its own industries.

A second category includes those countries that have begun to change the structure of their economies and approach more advanced stages of industrial production. This group includes only Tunisia and the U.A.R. The third category is much larger. It includes those countries with a fairly wide range of industries and relatively large population size (thus providing large markets) that have not yet significantly changed in economic structure: Algeria, Cameroon, Congo-Kinshasa, Ethiopia, Ghana, Ivory Coast, Kenya, Morocco, Nigeria, Rhodesia, and Senegal. The fourth category includes countries where industrialization has barely begun, that is, the remaining African countries. Of this group, the most promising are Congo-Brazzaville, Guinea, Gabon, Mali, Tanzania, and Uganda.

Although industry is poorly developed in Africa, it has played a major role in the growth of the more modern, urbanized sectors of African economies. Furthermore, total industrial output has increased 400 per cent since the start of World War II (albeit from a small base). But the important structural transformations in the economies of African states, such as the shift in proportions of agricultural *vs.* industrial employment, have hardly begun.

2. TYPES OF INDUSTRIES

The major share of African industry (excluding South Africa) still consists of small-scale light industries, led by the food, drink, and tobacco industries, closely followed by textiles and the production of building materials such as cement and bricks. In contrast, heavy industry is very poorly developed. Small iron and steel mills exist in Kenya, Uganda, and Rhodesia, and plans are in progress for development of an iron and steel industry in Nigeria. It is unlikely, however, that heavy industry will grow rapidly in Africa in the near future.

For some time to come, the expansion of industrial production will consist largely of processing local agricultural and mineral raw materials and producing locally many commodities which have previously been imported (i.e., import substitution). Industrial growth will most likely involve a "nibbling away" at the manufacturing process from both ends: increasing the amount of local processing of raw materials (e.g., exporting partially refined or processed materials rather than crude ores or agricultural commodities) and finishing off or assembling imported manufactured goods (e.g., automobile assembly).

3. STRATEGIES FOR INDUSTRIAL DEVELOPMENT

A number of strategies have been suggested to guide industrial development in Africa. Each of the following has been frequently discussed, although universal agreement as to their potential benefits or modes of implementation does not exist.

a. Import Substitution and Export-Oriented Industry

Africa, even more than other parts of the developing world, is dependent upon trade. In general, raw materials (processed and unprocessed) are exported, while manufactured goods are imported. This situation has tended to be disadvantageous because prices fluctuate more widely for raw materials than for manufactured goods. As a means of enlarging industrial production and reducing the proportion of total income derived from exports of raw materials, many economists suggest policies aimed at import substitution.

> If all the items imported at present were to be produced domestically, the manufacturing output could increase three to four times. . . . The present heavy import dependence in Africa is thus a double-edged advantage. It indicates a large potential for import substitution and at the same time furnishes in the form of foreign exchange the very resources for carrying it out. . . . Far-sighted management of the import structure is thus of crucial importance (U.N., *Industrial Growth in Africa*, 1963, pp. 14–15.

Import substitution, however, often requires larger imports of machinery, equipment, raw materials, and other inputs which must be paid for in exports. It is necessary, therefore, to achieve a harmonious balance between import substitution and export-oriented industries (especially through increased local processing of raw materials). In this way, not only can an unfavorable balance of trade be reduced but consumption and production can be more evenly balanced as well.

b. Industrialization through Protection

Most African countries have erected substantial tariff barriers and other protective devices in order to promote local industry, particularly with respect to import substitution (which is unlikely to be successful without them, given the tendency for many imported goods to be cheaper than locally produced ones at the initial stages of local industrial growth). Although there is great scope for growth through these policies in Africa, some economists have criticized these policies for diverting investment away from the key growth industries producing capital and intermediate goods (basically machinery and the products of heavy industry). Here we have a clear example of the unfortunately frequent conflict between short-run and long-run strategies—a conflict which can only be resolved by some kind of compromise and balance (the nature of which is still an open question).

c. Regional Coordination

Perhaps the greatest barrier to industrial growth in Africa is the small size of local markets, due both to generally low income levels and purchasing power and to the inadequate infrastructure of transport and communications. Many economists feel that rapid industrialization will require the creation of larger markets within regional economic groupings of states (see Ewing, 1968; Green and Seidman, 1968). Many industries simply cannot exist if they are to be based on the small market areas of contemporary African countries. Twenty-three states in Africa have populations of 4 million or less; some, such as Gabon and Gambia, have less than a half a million people. African countries have an average size of 271,000 square miles and a population of 6 million. The comparable figures for Asia and South America are 448,000 and 43 million, and 528,000 and 11 million. Many industries require "economies of scale," called by one economist "the main engine of growth." However, relatively little progress toward economic union in Africa has occurred thus far (see Module 78), due in large part to the overwhelming practical and political problems involved.

d. Concentration vs. Dispersal of Industry

There has been a great deal of emphasis in the economics literature on the concept of "growth poles," that is, the notion that countries should select those locations where the potentials for growth appear most promising and concentrate effort on these areas in the hope of stimulating a rapid transformation and development of the entire economy (for a review of the growth-pole literature, see Derwent, 1968). The major problem arising from this policy, however, is that the impact of industrialization in the developing countries is often restricted by such factors as poor transport, low personal incomes, low education levels, etc. Growth tends to become polarized without effectively "multiplying," or "trickling down" through other sectors of the economy. (See Hirschmann, 1958; Myrdal, 1957, calls the same two countervailing phenomena "backwash" and "spread" effects.) This results in an increasing gap between the more and less favored areas (sections within a state or states within an economic union) which is likely to increase the possibilities for internal social and political turmoil. At the same time, however, it is also difficult to encourage foreign investors to help spread economic development by investing in hitherto neglected areas. The problem of locational planning and decision making with respect to industry has therefore become increasingly important in Africa.

4. THE PROSPECTS FOR INDUSTRIAL DEVELOPMENT

The problems of industrial development are immense, and no clear paths have been universally agreed upon. Economic development contains a powerful political component, particularly with respect to the need for greater economic cooperation between African states. Indeed, the problems involved require a coordination of all branches of knowledge and experience. Africa is just setting out to do what took Europe and America hundreds of years to accomplish. Whether significant shortcuts can be found is not yet known. For further investigation, there are several excellent textbooks on the problems and processes of economic and industrial development, including Myint (1964), Hagen (1962), and Lewis (1966).

72

Planning for Development

DEVELOPMENT PLANNING IS A CRITICAL ISSUE in contemporary Africa, where the absolute standard of living is low and where an increasing rate of economic improvement is probably necessary if states are to survive in the modern world. As Rivkin (*Essays*, chap. 24) suggests, there is controversy between experts as to the best types of development plans given the great diversity of circumstances. Yet he notes that "there can be little question that the formulation of a correlated and realistic series of development goals, priorities, policies, and approaches is urgently required."

1. THE NATURE OF DEVELOPMENT PLANS

A development plan is a comprehensive blueprint outlining public policy and coordinating private and public allocation of investment over a given time period so as to achieve specific socioeconomic objectives, such as income growth and the provision of more educational and health facilities. Most development plans are national, but subnational regional plans also exist. At one extreme, a perspective plan sketches goals to be pursued over a 15- to 20-year period. In contrast, a short-term plan usually assumes the form of a capital budget of expenditures on roads, buildings, and public utilities for perhaps one year. In between are medium-term plans, usually 3 to 5 years, which indicate planned policy more specifically than perspective plans but do not necessarily commit expenditure. According to the Princeton economist W. A. Lewis (1966), a West Indian who has worked extensively in Africa, an idealized plan generally includes the following types of information: (1) a survey of current economic conditions (e.g., national income, productivity, foreign trade, and trends in each major sector); (2) a survey of the current social situation (population changes, education, health, housing, and social security); (3) an evaluation of progress under the preceding plan; (4) a statement of the general objectives of social and economic policy; (5) estimates of targets for each sector during the plan period; (6) suggested measures for increasing the rate of economic growth (e.g., measures to stimulate saving and investment, to increase productivity, and to improve the institutional framework of economic activity—such as land reform or reorganization of the labor market); and (7) a program of government expenditures (capital and recurrent).

Development plans can vary widely in the nature of their objectives. Some countries may elect to consume more now and allocate less to capital formation. Others may choose short-run sacrifices to gain future benefits. Plans also differ in that they reflect different resource endowments and earnings of foreign exchange. Another difference involves the relative importance of the public, as distinct from the private, sector in each country, although this may in itself be a result of planning. One good source on planning (in Nigeria) is Stolper (1966).

2. FORMULATION, IMPLEMENTATION, AND REVISION

One of the major problems in formulating plans is the inadequacy of statistical data upon which to base projected targets. Data collection has been given high priority in most African countries, and the amounts of data available are increasing rapidly each year. Before a plan is formulated, the various separate ministries collect and submit base data and request specific considerations in the plan. At implementation, the support of the leading decision makers and ministries is required. In addition, the planning ministry must have authority over the other ministries to ensure that the crucial decisions, usually regarding budget outlays, are taken.

Plans usually are not completely on target, since it is virtually impossible to forecast precisely the reactions of the various sectors to the autonomous and induced changes initiated in the plan. One obvious reason is that negative rather than positive control is most often exerted over the private sector. For example, the plan can state where the private sector is not to invest (very clear outlines of this are given by the Tanzanian government), but can at best only encourage investment in areas the planners consider favorable. Often the plan may appear unrealistic—sometimes deliberately to prevent internal tension or to attract greater foreign investment. The value (symbolic and real) of plans will clearly decline unless they are systematically revised and made more realistic. Revision is customarily done on an annual basis.

3. CENTRAL ISSUES IN DEVELOPMENT PLANNING

a. *Agriculture* vs. *Industry*

Development experts often emphasize the central importance of industrialization and of supranational economic cooperation between groups of developing countries. The terms of trade are turning against primary producers and primary production involves greater market instability. These problems are made still more acute if, as is the case with most African countries, there is a dependence on only one or a few commodity exports. How then should the balance between agricultural and industrial development be handled?

There appears to be an increasing concentration on agriculture in the more recent African development plans, partly as a result of unsuccessful industrialization schemes. At the same time, however, the plans reveal continuing efforts at diversification and the importance of large industrial schemes such as the Volta project in Ghana. It is clear, however, that agriculture and industry cannot be treated separately. Indeed, one of the most important prerequisites for industrial growth in Africa is increased agricultural production, especially on a per-capita basis, so that more of the labor force can become involved in non-agricultural pursuits. (It is interesting to note that African urban migrants, unlike those in Europe during the early stages of the Industrial Revolution, are not primarily agricultural laborers but actual landowners with major social and economic stakes in the rural areas.)

b. "Permissive" vs. Direct Investment

Planners recognize the need to consider social as well as private benefits from investment — investments in what is called social and economic overhead (education, health, welfare, infrastructure) which does not produce direct or quick economic benefits. Transportation is considered by others one of the key factors in promoting development; it and other infrastructural investment remains the largest sector for investment in most development plans. This issue as well as others (e.g., the mobilization of domestic resources) are discussed further in Rivkin (*Essays*, chap. 24).

c. Other Problems of Choice and Balanced Growth

Several problems of choice and balance (e.g., between import substitution and export-oriented industries) have already been mentioned here and in Module 71. In addition, planners must contend with such problems as the balance between labor-intensive and capital-intensive industries (another question with long-run *vs.* short-run implications), resource-oriented and market-oriented industries, light and heavy industries, and the degree of emphasis on local, national, and regional development. (See United Nations, 1967.) In all of these areas, the questions are not of the either-or type but focus on the attainment of a harmonious balance which can maximize the opportunities for significant transformations in the entire economic system. The search for this balance and its adjustment to and implementation in particular and varying local contexts is the essential challenge facing development planners.

4. CONCLUSIONS

Most of the major issues in development planning do not have purely technical answers, since social values and a host of unpredictable factors are involved. The nature of African planning may well be described as experimental and formative. It is necessarily so because of peculiarly local conditions and the limited transferability of conventional monetary and fiscal techniques to dual economies with low monetization. Planning lacks the precision it has attained in Europe and is further complicated by the paucity of hard data as well as by the political aspects of nation-building.

Development of Economic Systems

THE ENORMOUS CHALLENGES AND PROBLEMS involved in African economic development are illustrated in Modules 69 through 72 and in Modules 47 through 49. In this module an attempt will be made to examine certain historical aspects of African economic development and to assess the relationship of economic development to nation-building. A discussion of social and demographic constraints in economic-systems development is found in Module 74, technological developments in Module 75, and the prospects for regional economic union, a key factor in the future of African development, in Module 78.

1. THE COLONIAL INHERITANCE

Given the problems involved in restructuring the colonial economy and the short time that has elapsed, it is not surprising that independence did not bring about markedly increased rates of development for most African countries. Working with the generally low levels of productivity which characterized traditional economic systems in Africa, the colonial powers constructed new systems geared primarily to European needs. One must also remember that European colonization came later to Africa than it did to Asia and Latin America. Although some efforts were made in health, education, transport development, and the introduction of monetary economy, the major goal was to make each colony self-supporting and to protect and encourage metropolitan investment in the colonies. Thus colonial economies became geared to the export of primary commodities (agricultural and mineral) and consequently subject to the vagaries of world (or metropolitan) market prices for these goods when not protected by preferential price supports by the colonial power.

Little interterritorial trade developed and the entire infrastructure (i.e., the underlying foundation of education, transport, administrative organization, etc., providing services to the entire economy) evolved as a means of maintaining internal peace and serving the external orientation of the economy. Most of the major transport routes, for example, were corridors to the coast and siphons for export commodities. There was very little local processing of produce or minerals, and many situations developed in which a product such as sisal would be exported only to be imported at higher prices in the form of rope or sacking.

The general result of colonial economic policy was the creation of *dual economies*, in which small islands of modern technology and organization (e.g., mining and plantation agriculture) existed in a sea of traditional subsistence agriculture. Development in the post-colonial period has been powerfully shaped by this legacy of dualism and directed toward introducing changes which could bring about more widespread modernization.

2. CONTENDING WITH ECONOMIC DUALISM AND REGIONAL INEQUALITIES

In some African economies, there has been "growth without development," or an increase in national income without a sharing of this increase by most of the people and with little concomitant change in the underlying political, social, and institutional framework. An example is the case of Liberia (see Clower *et al.*, 1966), where rubber and iron-ore production have increased rapidly in recent years, as has the gross domestic product, but the impact of this growth has been restricted to a small fraction of the area and population of the country and has not brought about major changes in the economic system. In essence, this represents a continuation, perhaps intensification, of the dual economy.

In those economies where significant development has occurred, the economic system has become more specialized, functionally differentiated, and interdependent. Concurrently there has been an increasing shift from subsistence to market-oriented activity, with secondary processing and import substitution playing important roles. But even in these cases, the dual structure of the economy and regional inequalities of income have often become further intensified.

There has been a general tendency, therefore, for economic inequalities (within developing countries as well as between the developing and developed world) to increase. Some economists feel that the reasons for this lie primarily in the dynamics of spatial interaction between "mature" and "immature" regions. The former generally consist of major urban centers and their immediate hinterlands. Given an initial surge of development, the "mature" regions attract flows of labor, capital, and commodities from other areas, which, consequently, suffer from what Myrdal calls "backwash" effects. This initiates a cycle of cumulative causation, in Myrdal's terms, which worsens the situation by further widening the inequalities or "gap." At the same time, however, expansionary momentum from the growth of the city (or region) may produce "spread" effects on nearby areas favoring development. Should this outweigh the backwash effects, the cycle may be reversed (see Myrdal, 1957).

In Africa, the major existing centers of wealth (e.g., the large "primate" cities) are generally growing in income more rapidly than the rural areas, thus making the urban-rural dualism more pronounced. This is viewed with concern by most African leaders because of their commitment to the political and economic integration of the *entire* nation-state and their desire to involve the whole population in the processes of development. Attempts have been made in several countries (e.g., Kenya, Nigeria) to encourage people to move back to the farming areas from the big cities. Special tax benefits and other privileges are offered private investors if they choose to locate a factory in a small town rather than in the capital city. Large-scale projects, such as the creation of cooperative village schemes in Tanzania and the extensive resettlement projects in the former "White Highlands" of Kenya (the former European farming area now being settled by African smallholders), are aimed directly at reducing many of the structural and regional inequalities generated during the colonial period. In practice, however, it has been found very difficult to reverse the cycle of cumulative causation — to counteract the backwash effects — once the cycle has started. Complicating the problem still further is the fact that policies aimed at reducing regional inequalities are costly, often involving much social and economic overhead investment in education and infrastructure. Equalizing development within a country may actually slow down the rate of national development in the short run; conversely, working with the existing structure may produce more rapid immediate gains in national income, but at the cost of greater income inequalities between regions and between ethnic groups.

3. ACHIEVEMENT AND PROSPECTS

Gross domestic product is not really a satisfactory measure of the growth of economic systems, since it may represent "growth without development" and does not indicate internal regional variance. Yet it is a useful indicator of the actual level of production within a country, and Rivkin (*Essays*, chap. 23) suggests that comparisons between the African states may be usefully based on this criterion.

In 1960, the only Tropical African countries which had a gross national product per capita of over $200 were Senegal, Ghana, Gabon, and Southern Rhodesia. Since 1960, only Gabon has continued to grow rapidly and uninterruptedly. By 1965 (see Rivkin), the list of all African states with $200 GNP per capita came to include also Zambia and Ivory Coast (as well as South Africa, Algeria, Tunisia, and Libya). Liberia and Swaziland were added by 1966, with significant growth also taking place in Angola, Cameroon, Ethiopia, the Malagasy Republic, Mauritania, Mozambique, Nigeria (before the civil war), Sudan,

Kenya, and Uganda. Although $200 GNP per capita is not a large figure, the growing list of countries in this category suggests that progress has been made. It should be emphasized again, however, that it is probably much too early to evaluate effectively the growth of the economic systems in African countries since independence.

74

Population Pressure
and Social Factors
in Development

DEVELOPMENT THROUGHOUT THE WORLD has been a process in which economic, political, and social factors have been closely intertwined. Indeed, Adelman and Morris (1967) associate national modernization with "the progressive differentiation of the social, economic, and political spheres from each other and the development of specialized institutions and attitudes within each sphere." One of the key characteristics of underdevelopment in Africa, therefore, is the degree to which the economic sphere is *not* differentiated from the matrix of social and political organization, both traditional and modern. Political aspects of economic development, and vice versa, are mentioned indirectly in the modules on national integration (Modules 57, 58, and 59), and considerable attention is given to the subject by Rivkin (*Essays*, chap. 24). In this module, we focus on two additional factors of national development: demographic patterns and socio-cultural change.

1. IS AFRICA OVERPOPULATED?

This question is discussed briefly in Soja and Paden (*Essays*, chap. 2), with the general conclusion that although overall densities tend to be fairly low for most of Africa, there are many pockets of extremely high density and large areas where population numbers appear too great for local resources and technology. Hence, population pressure of some kind exists in roughly 47 per cent of the area of Africa and for about 45 per cent of its population (see Hance, 1968). One must add to this the fact that the African population is growing at one of the highest rates in the world (again varying from area to area). Simple arithmetic would illustrate that economic growth must keep pace with this high rate of population growth just to maintain the same level of per capita income. Unfortunately, arithmetical growth is not relevant, since economists estimate that countries whose populations are growing at 2 per cent per year will need a rate of economic growth appreciably greater than 2 per cent (perhaps over two or three times that figure in some cases). This puts the question of "population explosion" in a different light with regard to its potential impact on national development. High rates of economic growth may have little impact on individual citizens if population growth is also very high. The answer to this problem does not lie simply with curbing the growth of population (in some African countries this is not only unnecessary but possibly could hinder development). What it does require is close attention to demographic characteristics in economic planning. They must be considered intrinsic parts of all development plans.

2. SOCIOCULTURAL ELEMENTS IN THE DEVELOPMENT PROCESS

From Karl Marx to Talcott Parsons, social scientists have long recognized the importance of changes in social organization and values in economic growth. Only recently, however, have non-economic factors received prominent attention by theorists and planners in development economics. Many of these factors are included in the quantitative analysis of Adelman and Morris (1967). The remainder of this module will examine some of the variables used in that study and will assess the relevance of such variables in the growth of economic systems in Africa.

a. Character of Basic Social Organization

Economic development has usually been associated with changes in family structure growing out of increased urbanization in particular, and increased differentiation and specialization within society in general. One example of this is the greater emphasis on the nuclear family and/or the individual as the basic unit of social organization in modern society. When family ties and obligations extend more widely, as they do in much of Africa, the economically successful individual is often obliged to distribute his wealth to a large number of family members, thus discouraging capital formation and encouraging consumption. The emergence of the nuclear family is thought to aid development by more closely linking individual effort and rewards, encouraging achievement motivation, placing more emphasis on merit rather than traditional status in the allocation of roles in society, and perhaps even facilitating family planning. It should be noted, however, that the cross-cultural bases of these generalizations have not yet been fully explored. What has been established is that modernization reduces the individual's dependence on wider family and ethnic relationships.

b. Extent of Social Mobility

Like many social variables, the key aspect here is attitudinal. Individual attainment, innovation, and entrepreneurship may be promoted if increase in social status is commensurate with increase in economic status. Also mobilization for economic development will occur in more depth if opportunities to obtain skills and education are open to all classes. A somewhat related variable is the opportunity for adult literacy and general availability of education. Africa, in general, has not had the major problems arising from rigidly structured traditional hierarchies of status (epitomized perhaps in the caste system of India). Educational and economic achievement have tended to be more clearly recognized and rewarded than in many other developing areas. Because of low levels of educational development, however, most African countries still rank low in social mobility.

c. Degree of Cultural and Ethnic Homogeneity

The early stages of development nearly always tend to accentuate cultural and ethnic differences. Old orders are disrupted without the implantation of alternative, tightly integrated forms of social, economic, and political organization. Thus it is reasonable to assume that cultural and ethnic heterogeneity on the national level is likely to hinder development. Many African countries are among the most heterogeneous in the world (e.g., Nigeria, Kenya, Cameroon). Others, however, are relatively homogeneous (Libya, Tunisia, U.A.R., the Somali Republic). While homogeneity does not ensure development (and in several cases is only symptomatic of small-scale organization), it clearly facilitates social cooperation.

d. Degree of Social Tension

Change is almost by definition disruptive. It is still not clear, however, whether the strains and conflicts of change slow down development or actually become important mechanisms for more rapid transformation. (This view has already been mentioned in the introduction to the *Essays* with respect to political instability.) Although more study is needed, it is likely that a certain amount of social tension and instability is functional to the growth of economic systems in the early stages of development.

e. Modernization of Outlook

We have already mentioned the importance of attitudes and values in the development process. This variable refers more specifically to the degree to which attitudes and values favorable to innovation and change exist within both the mass and the elite, and in both cases to the sense of participation in the on-going process of development. This participatory dimension is associated by Daniel Lerner (1958) with a kind of "psychic mobility," a feeling of identity with and importance in the major changes taking place. The difficulty in measuring such attitudes, however, is representative of the problem of obtaining statistical or "concrete" indicators of development as well as the interdisciplinary nature of problems involved in the study of economic development and nation-building.

3. CONCLUSIONS

This brief examination of demographic and sociocultural factors in the growth of economic systems is in many ways an extension of earlier discussions on the "Processes of Change." Yet the problems of national and/or regional economic development also telescope into the broader question of Africa's role in the modern world. The problems of African economic development, whatever their magnitude, cannot be ignored by the developed countries, for the international linkages of all national economies are such that problems in one area may affect all parts of the world. The international dimension of economic systems development is discussed in more detail in Part V, "Africa and the Modern World."

75

Technology and Nation-Building

THE PROBLEMS OF NATION-BUILDING in Africa have been discussed in Modules 54 through 74 in terms of the social, economic, and political institutions and organizations which have been developing to deal with these problems. In this module, we look specifically at how science and technology can contribute to the solution of some of the problems.

Technology has been defined in Module 37 as "the ability to manipulate natural elements and principles to desired results." In Africa, and in all the developing countries, technology occupies a central role in the strategy of development and nation-building. A gigantic leap is needed, and science and technology are viewed as providing the key propulsive forces—for improved agriculture, industrial expansion, better health and sanitation, innovative methods of education, and, indeed, for the creation of stable and productive communities. Advanced technology can be adopted without necessarily following the preliminary steps which have characterized the development of the now technologically advanced countries. Africa may never go through a "railway era," for example, but will move straight into the age of air transport. There may never be a "newspaper age." Instead, the electronic age of radio and television will be reached before there is a widespread increase in newspaper circulation and literacy. Hopefully, the increasing availability of military technology will not preclude an "age of political systems development" in which the values and goals of African nations will be determined by nonmilitary means.

1. THE TECHNOLOGY OF ECONOMIC DEVELOPMENT

The technological needs for economic development in Africa can be summarized under five main headings:

1. *Improved techniques (particularly in agriculture):* The great majority of Africans are still occupied in agriculture, which probably requires much greater adaptation to the specific African context than does industry. Particularly needed are improved methods of water technology (e.g., flood control, irrigation, hydroelectric development); detailed studies of mechanization appropriate to the African environment; and the development of better techniques of crop selection, artificial fertilization of soils, and cultivation (e.g., crop rotation, mixed cropping, green manuring, etc.). Another important area involves improvements in transportation and communications technology (see Kliphardt, *Essays,* chap. 25; and Module 49).

2. *Disease control for plants and animals:* Much more extensive research is required in the area of pest control and insect-borne diseases which affect African agriculture and animal husbandry. Of particular importance is trypanosomiasis, carried by the tsetse fly, which, because of its fatal effect on animals and man, has prevented huge areas of Africa from developing to their full potential.

3. *Scientific and technical education:* Many more institutes and training centers are needed in veterinary medicine, soil science, bioclimatology, geology, engineering, etc. There is a particularly acute shortage of trained agricultural personnel.

4. *Exploration and surveys (soils, plants, minerals):* Large areas of Africa have never had an adequate geological survey, and, given the importance of recent mineral discoveries (petroleum in the Sahara and in Nigeria), it seems likely that a vast mineral potential still remains untapped.

5. *Conservation of natural resources:* Deforestation, soil erosion, and decreasing water supplies have all become major problems in much of Africa. Overgrazing and overcultivation, caused in part by rapid population growth, have ruined many areas for agriculture and cattle keeping, particularly in the drier parts of the continent. In addition, it is not too early to plan for preservation of the natural beauty of Africa and to avoid the environmental catastrophes which have beset the United States and other developed countries. Of special importance perhaps is the conservation of game and wildlife and the use of certain

game animals as a source of food (some successful attempts have been made, for example, to domesticate the eland, largest of all antelopes).

2. THE TECHNOLOGY OF SOCIAL WELFARE

Here we can identify five major categories of needs:

1. *Housing:* Africa has a great need for low-cost housing, but very little study has been made of this subject. Particularly needed are studies which focus on the use of light-weight and low-cost local materials to avoid the widespread problems of unsuitability to the African environment and the production of "low-cost housing" which only the wealthy can afford.

2. *Medicine and Health:* A good deal of work is now proceeding in this field, particularly with respect to communicable diseases (insect-borne diseases such as malaria, virus diseases such as smallpox and yellow fever, parasitic diseases such as bilharzia and "river blindness," and bacterial diseases such as meningitis). Some advances have also been made in the field of preventive medicine (e.g., a recent major vaccination campaign against measles), but the field is still in its infancy in Africa. Much of Africa suffers from a high incidence of disease and high mortality rates. In part, this is responsible for low levels of economic development in certain areas, and in part it is caused by underdevelopment. Whatever the direction of the relationship, it is clear that disease prevention and improved health is central to both social welfare and economic growth. Special mention should be made of the potential pharmacological uses of African herbs and plants, which Baffour (in Bown and Crowder, 1964) states "might change the entire world systems of curative and preventive medicine."

3. *Nutrition:* Closely related to the problems of medicine and health are the nutritional deficiencies which affect much of the African population. Of particular importance is the shortage of protein in the diet, which has been shown to cause the widespread disease kwashiorkor and significantly reduce working efficiency and mental alertness in many areas. The production of fish protein and control of the tsetse fly will probably be of great importance here.

4. *Family planning:* As mentioned in Module 74, certain parts of Africa are overpopulated. Moreover, rapid population growth absorbs large portions of any increases in national income, often hindering economic development. Methods of controlling the rate of population growth are likely to become increasingly important in the future of many African states.

5. *Education:* There is considerable experimentation at present in techniques of education which maximize technological resources. The innovative use, for example, of closed-circuit television (especially in science), inexpensive duplicating procedures, and prefabricated classrooms may help offset the lack of teachers, teaching materials, and schools which are central to educational development.

3. THE ROLE OF TECHNOLOGY IN MODERN AFRICA

When one speaks of Africa as "underdeveloped," one means primarily the lack of modern technology; it is in the realm of economic development, as conventionally measured, that this technological gap is perhaps most manifest. Western technology has, to some extent, failed to contend with the specific problems and conditions of Africa: the character of its tropical soils and climate, its major plant and animal diseases, its unique mix of resources. A major portion of modern technology was developed in and *for* the middle latitudes and has too often proved untransferable to alternative environments. In addition, it is likely that too little attention has been given to indigenous technologies in Africa, technologies which have evolved in specific African contexts to meet specific African needs. Africa thus faces a multiple challenge with respect to technology: the application of existing nonindigenous technology when it suits the African context; the adaptation of such technology where it is needed but not yet suited to African problems; the creation of new technologies when required; and the development of existing African technologies to determine their applicability to contemporary situations.

But there remains a major question with respect to technology in Africa: To what extent is Western technology separable from Western values and social institutions? Can Africa borrow one and not the other? The "hardware" of technology clearly requires the "software" of social organization but whether such emergent social systems will assume a Japanese model, a Chinese model, an Israeli model, a Russian model, or an American model—if any—remains to be seen. It is perhaps appropriate to end this module with a statement from President Julius Nyerere of Tanzania (as paraphrased in Hunter) that is indicative not only of the problems of technology but also of the much broader issue of the character of emergent social systems of Africa:

> We need clean drinking water for our people, and that means we must have analysts and doctors. Doctors mean universities to train them, and hospitals and scientific equipment, and administrators. Thus we are forced to create your institutions; and because they must be paid for we must enter the world of economic competition; we must make our people want these things so that they will work for what they want. Yet we do not desire either the extreme individualism of your society or the extreme collectivism of Russia (Hunter, 1962, p. 319).

Study Questions

76

Study Questions: Consolidation of Nation-States

As IN THE OTHER STUDY-QUESTION MODULES, some questions will be specific, others of a general or synthesizing nature, and still others judgmental.

1. When and where did African nationalist movements begin? Did they originate in Africa or were they begun by African expatriates in Europe and America? What are the early forms of nationalism in Africa? To what extent did African nationalism take on racial overtones? What was the reaction of the respective colonial powers to African nationalism? How was the timing of independence determined? Why did West Africa achieve independence earlier than East or central Africa?

2. What is meant by *nation-building*? Do you think the major problems of national integration in Africa are interethnic, mass-elite, or territorial? What types of ideologies do you think have been most successful in building national integration? Do you think African states are more concerned with national integration or Pan-Africanism? Do you think that French and English should be used as the languages of national integration in Africa, or should some vernacular language(s) be selected?

3. What accounts for the existence of irredentism in Africa? Why do you think there has been so little violent irredentism? Do you think that the "mass-elite gap" was caused by the colonial powers or by a particular type of education? What can be done to close this gap, or do you regard its continuation as inevitable? Who should arbitrate in African state boundary disputes? How should interstate conflict be resolved?

4. Why is the one-party state so common in Africa? Do you feel this is an infringement on individual liberties? How is opposition expressed in a one-party state, both of the pragmatic-pluralistic variety and the revolutionary-centralizing variety?

5. What types of political systems were inherited from the colonial powers? What were the weaknesses of these systems within the African context? What changes have been attempted and with what success? What role does the civil service play in African nation-building? What function do you think elections play in a one-party state? Why have elections been associated with political crises in Africa?

6. What indicators do you feel best represent electoral "legitimacy" in the African context? What are the major indications of political instability in Africa? Has such instability been generally violent or nonviolent? In interpreting these events, do you feel that military rule is a relatively permanent form of government in Africa or a transition back to a new form of civilian rule? Do you think that deposed leaders such as Nkrumah will continue to play an important role in African nation-building? What types of political systems in Africa seem to be most stable?

7. What elements in customary law, Islamic law, and European law in Africa seem to be most similar and/or dissimilar? Do you think that customary law and Islamic law should be discarded by the new states? Do you think that the diverse legal systems should be integrated? How would you persuade people to change radically their marriage and family law? What can be done, if anything, to ensure some comparability of legal framework between the various African states, on the assumption that at some future point they might want to work more closely with each other?

8. How does constitutional law affect the integration of legal systems? What have been the developments in constitutional law since World War II? How would you change African constitutions, if at all, to reflect the political realities of changing societies? Do you feel that the military, rather than the supreme court, should "guarantee" the constitution? What are the major problems of legal personnel development? What would you recommend be taught in an African law school?

9. What are the major resources of Africa? What will be necessary for the effective utilization of these resources? Do you think that African states should concentrate on agriculture or should they move into industrialization? What kind of planning is necessary in Africa? Does planning at present seem to be effective? How could it be improved? What is meant by "infrastructure"? To what extent has an infrastructure been built in Africa?

10. What are the major unsolved problems of African economic systems de-

velopment? How do population pressures and social factors bear on these problems? What are the best measures of economic development (e.g., GDP per capita, diversification of the economy, strength of export sector, amount of investment)? What is meant by "growth without development"? What political or ideological factors seem to impinge most clearly on economic development? What are "backwash" and "spread" effects, and how do they influence development?

11. What is the role of science and technology in contemporary Africa? Why is it difficult to apply modern technology directly to the African context? Do you think the adaptation of modern technology can take place in Africa without "strings" (i.e., without the necessity of accepting the values or institutions of the more technologically advanced countries)?

V

Africa and
the Modern World

Modules	Suggested Readings in *Essays*
Regionalism and Pan-Africanism 77 Concepts of Supranationalism 78 Emergent Patterns of Regionalism 79 Pan-Africanism and Continental Unity 80 International Organizations in Africa	20 African Concepts of Nationhood *(Paden)* 26 African International Relations *(Mazrui)*
Africa and the Major Powers 81 Africa at the United Nations 82 Africa and the Former Metropoles 83 Africa and the United States 84 Africa and the Communist Bloc	26 African International Relations *(Mazrui)*
Africa and the Third World 85 Africa and the Third World 86 Africa and the Middle East	26 African International Relations *(Mazrui)* 27 Africa and the Islamic world (Abu-Lughod)
The Problem of Southern Africa 87 The Remnants of Colonialism 88 Race Relations in Southern Africa 89 Politics and Race in South Africa	28 Confrontation in Southern Africa *(Carter)*

Regionalism and Pan-Africanism

77

Concepts of Supranationalism

CERTAIN PRE-INDEPENDENCE CONCEPTS of nationalism encompassed units which were larger than the national-state boundaries deriving from the colonial period (see Module 54 and Paden, *Essays*, chap. 20). They included concepts of Eur-Africanism, Marxism-socialism, negritude, Pan-Africanism, Third-Worldism, and African regionalism. Modules 77 through 80 deal with these questions of broader African contexts in relation to issues of nation-building and provide background to the discussions of African international relations in the other modules of Part V, "Africa and the Modern World."

1. THE RISE OF NATIONAL SELF-INTEREST

As many of those who worked hardest to create supranational communities in Africa had feared, independence ushered in a period of parochial nationalism, a period in which the territorial boundaries inherited from the colonial era became even more formidable barriers to interterritorial cooperation. The problems of nation-building proved so formidable that little impetus existed for building interstate linkages. Perhaps the most important single illustration of this development was the failure of attempts to federate East Africa (Kenya, Uganda, Tanganyika/Tanzania). Contiguous and under one colonial power since World War I, the East African countries had enjoyed the benefits of territorial cooperation throughout much of the colonial period and by 1960 had already progressed far toward economic union. In 1961, the old East Africa High Commission (established in 1948) was replaced by the East African Common Services Organization, an even more powerful and independent coordinator of interterritorial activities in transportation, communications, trade, and banking. In 1962, however, Uganda began to doubt the wisdom of larger federation. This was followed by other difficulties, and by 1966 many of the earlier interterritorial linkages had dissolved. (In recent years, there has been a revival of interest in federation and an East African Economic Community has been created. But even this has not yet led to significant increases in actual interterritorial cooperation. See Module 78.)

The year 1963 marked an important turning point for supranational concepts in Africa. Pan-Africanism was revived but was significantly reoriented with the establishment in 1963 of the Organization of African Unity. The OAU continued to foster the dream of continental unity, but with the clear recognition that the basic units were to be the existing states. Moreover, from 1963, it became increasingly evident that economic unions were much more likely to be successful than political federations, a realization which has come to characterize subsequent interstate relations.

2. EUR-AFRICANISM AND NEOCOLONIALISM

Eur-Africanism (see Paden *Essays*, chap. 20) died a formal death with the independence of former French West and Equatorial Africa and the rapid disintegration of the French Community. Ideas of Eur-Africanism, however, continue to be a rationale for close links with France for several countries (Ivory Coast and Gabon are perhaps the prime examples), and in some ways the nonideological associateship of former French territories with the European Common Market (see Module 82) is another continuation of this concept. A similar pattern has emerged for many of the former British territories—a decline in the importance of the Commonwealth as a political community accompanied by the retention of close economic ties with Britain.

Many view these continued forms of Eur-African relations as a form of *neocolonialism,* a term which was not widely used until after 1960. Eur-Africanism has been also plunged further into disrepute in many African countries due to Portuguese support for this concept (i.e., the notion that Angola, Mozambique, and Portuguese Guinea are integral parts of Portugal and not colonies). Even South Africa has begun to speak of a similar concept as characterizing its relationships with independent Black Africa.

3. AFRICANIZATION OF SOCIALIST IDEOLOGY

Marxism-socialism as a political ideology in Africa (see Paden) has likewise suffered a decline. Most of the regimes materially supporting socialist ideas in Africa, such as Nkrumah's Ghana and Keïta's Mali, are now gone; nearly all the military regimes which replaced these and other civilian governments have tended to be nonideological (except perhaps that of the Central African Republic under Bokassa). The Simba rebellion in Congo-Kinshasa was socialist oriented and aimed at setting up a "peoples republic" centered in Stanleyville (now Kisangani), but it was unsuccessful.

Marxism-socialism has not disappeared, but it has been significantly transformed and made more distinctly African under the banner of *African socialism.* In one form or another—and there have evolved a great variety of forms— African socialism has become official government ideology in many African countries (see Friedland and Rosberg, 1964). In some countries (such as Kenya), it refers primarily to the importance of economic planning and the recognition of traditional cultural values, without negating the importance of free enterprise, dependence on foreign aid and investment, and the establishment of various institutions necessary to capitalist economic systems (such as a stock exchange). (See Republic of Kenya, 1965.) In other countries, such as Tanzania under Julius Nyerere, African socialism has evolved as a creative, innovative, and distinctly African philosophy of government. In addition to reducing dependence on foreign aid, Nyerere has stressed egalitarianism, the importance of hard work for everyone (including the elite), the enormous importance of agriculture as the basis for development, the social security derived from traditional ethnic patterns, and, symbolizing all these values, the concept of *Ujamaa*— Swahili for *familihood,* a powerful sense of cooperativeness. More than any other leader in Africa, Nyerere has attempted to implement his policies of African socialism, particularly through the now-well-known *Arusha Declaration* of 1967 (see Tanzania African National Union, 1967). Detailed attention to the declaration would provide a fruitful classroom exercise. (See also Nyerere, 1967 and 1969.)

The concept of Third-Worldism (see Paden) has also declined rapidly in Africa since 1963 (see Module 85). Just as national introspection diluted the impulse toward Pan-Africanism, so the problems of nation-building and the establishment of the OAU weakened interest in uniting "all peoples of color, all peoples of poverty." (See Mazrui, *On Heroes and Uhuru Worship,* 1967, chap. 13.) There appears, however, to be an increased ideological interest throughout Africa in the example of Communist China, and the works of Mao Tse Tung are now widely available in European and vernacular languages. (For example, since 1966, Hausa versions have been readily available in all large cities throughout northern Nigeria—reputed to be ideologically conservative—and Radio Peking broadcasts regularly in Hausa.)

4. NEGRITUDE

The concept of *negritude,* like Eur-Africanism, withered after independence when assimilation into French civilization was no longer a major political issue in Africa. Negritude remains an important literary and cultural movement, but even Léopold Senghor, one of the major proponents of the concept, has increasingly moved away from the stress on *blackness* to a more general emphasis on African culture and its contributions to world culture.

There is the possibility, however, that cultural differentiation reflected in color can complicate black African relations with Arab Africa. There have been indications of this primarily in the extremely bloody rebellion in Sudan—the three southern black provinces, mostly Christian or pagan, fighting the predominantly Arab and Muslim north. Refugees and guerrilla fighters appear to have crossed into neighboring black African states (Uganda, Central African Republic, Chad), and tensions are increasing in those areas. Similar internal cultural and color cleavages also exist within countries such as Chad, Central African Republic, and Mauritania. In Chad, the split between Muslim/Arabs and non-Muslim/black Africans had reached violent proportions at the time of this writing, and President Tumbulbaye felt forced to call in the French Foreign Legion. In Mauritania, the introduction of Arabic language as a requirement in schools and administration caused African-Arab riots in early 1966.

It may be interesting to compare the rise of black nationalism, and particularly black separatism, in the United States with the earlier forms of negritude in Africa. In this light, it is not surprising to find that many Afro-Americans react emotionally against African leaders who do not support, without qualification, the global solidarity of blacks; witness the reaction to the speech by the late Tom Mboya in New York's Harlem in March, 1969.

5. CONCLUSIONS

The trend toward national (as distinct from supranational) bases of political and economic cooperation in Africa has become pronounced in the post-colonial period. The reasons for this are complex, but certainly include the enormous resources required to maintain and consolidate the inherited national systems and the erosion of some of the original rationale for such concepts as Eur-Africanism, Marxist-socialism, and negritude.

78

Emergent Patterns of Regionalism

EFFORTS AT POLITICAL FEDERATION in post-independence Africa generally have not been successful (see Module 77). The Mali Federation disintegrated, the East African Federation was never fully established, and the Federation of Nigeria became embroiled in a lengthy civil war. At the same time, however, there have been some promising developments with respect to economic unions, the primary concern of this module.

1. THE COLONIAL LEGACY OF REGIONALISM

The broad regional patterns which developed during the colonial period are described briefly in Soja and Paden (*Essays*, chap. 2), and numerous case studies of colonial groupings of states (economic and political) are included in the *Bibliography* (see especially Hazlewood, 1967). It is sufficient here simply to note again that many of the interterritorial linkages which developed during the colonial period—particularly with respect to shared colonial power and language—have continued to shape inter-African state relations in the post-colonial era.

2. THE RISE AND FALL OF POLITICAL REGIONALISM

All that remains of both pre- and post-colonial attempts at formal political regrouping in Africa are Ethiopia (with Eritrea now formally incorporated), the Somali Republic (consisting of former British and Italian Somalilands), Morocco (incorporating Spanish and French Morocco and other small pieces of Spanish territory), Tanzania (loosely uniting Tanganyika and Zanzibar), and the ongoing federation of Cameroon (the southern portion of former British Cameroons and former French Cameroon). Unwilling to surrender their new-found authority and sovereignty and challenged by overpowering internal problems, most new states of Africa appear to have set aside temporarily the task of political federation and accepted, like Western Europe, the notion that economic union must precede political federation as a goal. This, however, does not mean that political considerations are disregarded, for the task of economic union has also become a political problem. As Hazlewood (1967) notes: " 'Seek ye first the Political Kingdom' may as a slogan have lost some of its popularity, but it is as well to remember that it is a precept which will continue to guide the actions of the politicians." It should also be noted that economic integration always requires some political channels of conflict resolution.

3. THE CONCEPT OF ECONOMIC UNION

There are various types of economic integration. Customs unions generally involve a defined trading area with common import tariffs and free or preferential internal access, plus common institutions for economic coordination and planning. This form represents a critical step toward full economic integration. More limited are attempts at cooperative export marketing, joint development schemes, and the joint operation and development of particular services such as transport, power, and research. Somewhere in between is cooperative planning for industrial development, usually involving a joint market and a variety of mutual agreements (e.g., to avoid duplication).

There are five major (but overlapping) arguments for such economic linkages: (1) They permit countries with small internal markets to benefit from economies of scale accruing to industries which require large markets. (2) They promote greater specialization based upon the comparative advantages of each unit for particular resources or industries. (3) They reduce vulnerability to external factors such as price fluctuations because of greater diversification. (4) They produce a larger unit potentially more powerful as a bargaining agent. (5) They attract more industries than would normally locate in the smaller units.

According to conventional economic theory, an economic union would be beneficial only if it created new trade, not simply diverted that trade which already existed. This, however, requires well-developed domestic trade and a complementarity in the economies of the potential partners—situations not commonly found in Africa. The key arguments for African economic integration revolve around the idea of larger markets and stimulus to new ventures, particularly industry. Some economists feel that large-scale industrialization will be impossible without regional economic integration. Thus, contrary to conventional theory, African economic integration is usually forced to involve a diversion of trade from external sources to higher cost intra-union ones. Moreover, "infant industries" generally must be protected even when external sources are cheaper. This built-in short-run inefficiency is one of the major barriers to economic integration.

In addition to the above problems (and the whole range of political problems directly involved in integration efforts) other difficulties include the lack of well-developed interstate transport and communications networks and the vast array of operational questions involved in creating a union: What is the optimum size of the unit? What is the best time for integration—should it wait until the benefits of national economies are reaped, such as attracting competitive foreign capital or increasing import substitution? How can existing economic inequalities between African partners be overcome? (This has perhaps been the most vexing of all operational problems.) Should the poorer partners receive fiscal compensation? Should special protective barriers be constructed within the union to give preference to one of its units? Should the poorer units be made more attractive to industry?

These questions almost inevitably become political ones. It is interesting to note that one of the major reasons for the recent resurrection of the idea of economic union in East Africa has been the agreement to establish the East African Development Bank, into which Kenya deposits a greater proportion of funds than either Uganda and Tanzania and is permitted to withdraw proportionately less. It is evident that this kind of "sacrifice" is essential for the prospects of any African economic union combining states that differ in economic strength.

4. ECONOMIC UNIONS IN AFRICA

The major economic unions which have begun to emerge in Africa (full economic integration exists nowhere as yet) include the following.

a. Afro-Malagasy Joint Organization (OCAM)

This includes Senegal, Ivory Coast, Upper Volta, Togo, Dahomey, Niger, Cameroon, Gabon, Congo-Brazzaville, Chad, Central African Republic, Congo-Kinshasa, Rwanda, and Malagasy Republic. It was established in 1965 (formerly OAMCE, and even earlier UAM) when Mauritania withdrew from the already existing OAMCE. It is primarily a union of French-speaking states devoted in large part to cooperative relations with the European Common Market. Senegal and Cameroon have tended to assume leadership.

b. West African Economic and Customs Union (UDEAO)

This includes Togo and all of former French West Africa except for Guinea (established in 1959, a new treaty was drawn in 1966). Economically dominated by Ivory Coast, which is not one of its greatest supporters, it is essentially unstable and relatively ineffective.

c. Entente Council

This includes Ivory Coast, Upper Volta, Togo, Dahomey, and Niger. (It was formed in 1959 with just Ivory Coast and Upper Volta.) It is a fairly well-developed union, dominated and promoted strongly by Ivory Coast (which also maintains independently a poorly developed free-trade area with Guinea, Liberia, and Sierra Leone).

d. Central African Economic and Customs Union (UDEAC)

UDEAC was formed in 1966 with the addition of Cameroon to the Equatorial Customs Union, which consisted of the states of former French Equatorial Africa. It became basically defunct after Chad and Central African Republic joined the UEAC, although the recent re-entry of C.A.R. may signal an increased importance in the future.

e. Union of Central African States (UEAC)

This included Congo-Kinshasa, Chad, and Central African Republic at its formation in 1968. Its establishment appeared to reflect the growing importance of Congo-Kinshasa in central African affairs. The withdrawal of the Central African Republic, however, has severely hindered its growth.

f. East African Community (EAC)

This includes Kenya, Uganda, and Tanzania, and was formally established in 1967, although it is based on much older patterns of cooperation. There is a great interest in a wider union expressed by many surrounding countries, with Zambia, Ethiopia, the Somali Republic, and Burundi having formally applied for admission by mid-1969. Other proposed members include Rwanda, Malawi, Botswana, Lesotho, Swaziland, and the Malagasy Republic.

One might also add the *Maghrib Union* (Algeria, Tunisia, Morocco, and Libya), which shows signs of increasing integration. In addition, there are a number of more specialized economic unions: (1) the *West African Monetary Union* (UMOA), consisting of the same members as UDEAO except for Mali; (2) the *Central African Monetary Union* (UMEAC), consisting of the same members as the old UDEAC; (3) the *Organization of Senegal River States* (OERS), consisting of Mauritania, Senegal, Mali, and Guinea; (4) the *Niger River Commission,* consisting of Mali, Guinea, Upper Volta, Ivory Coast, Niger, Nigeria, Chad, and Cameroon; and (5) the *Lake Chad Commission,* consisting of Nigeria, Niger, Chad, and Cameroon.

A West African Economic Community has been proposed, to include all of West Africa from Senegal to Nigeria. This has not yet progressed much beyond a provisional treaty for a West African Iron and Steel Community, but it must be considered an important focus for the future (see Plessz, 1968). Continent-wide organizations are discussed in Module 79.

79
___

Pan-Africanism and Continental Unity

PATTERNS OF ECONOMIC AND POLITICAL integration were examined in Module 78 for regional groups of states. In this module we take a continental view and examine the growth of wider interstate relations involving larger groups of African countries. (See Wallerstein, 1967, for a more detailed account of what he calls the "Politics of Unity.")

1. THE PERIOD OF UNIVERSALITY, 1957–1960

During this period, there was a strong attempt, influenced largely by President Nkrumah (Ghana), to create and maintain a broadly based union of African states. The period basically begins with the founding by President Nasser (Egypt) of the Afro-Asian Peoples' Solidarity Organization, in 1957. Its primary aim was to bring together the more radical African nationalists and to provide a basis for closer interaction between communist powers (China and the Soviet Union were members) and the Third World.

In 1958, Nkrumah took the initiative in an attempt to establish an explicitly political organization designed to bring together *all* African states regardless of ideology. He convened the first Conference of Independent African States (CIAS). The CIAS had two sessions: one in Accra and another, two years later, in Addis Ababa. The continent-wide scope of CIAS was reflected in the fact that initially even South Africa was invited. At the first meeting, informal agreements were reached on the needs for cooperation in foreign policy matters and in the continuing drive against colonialism. But Ghana and Guinea, disappointed by the slow pace and the weakness of these early agreements, undertook a more forceful effort for African unity at the All African Peoples' Conference (AAPC) in December, 1958, at Accra. This weakened CIAS, which eventually disintegrated after it was unable to absorb effectively the newly independent French African states (including Algeria) and their diversity of views. An additional outgrowth of these developments was the establishment of the Pan-African Freedom Movement of East and Central Africa (PAFMECA) in 1958. Centered in Dar es Salaam, PAFMECA aimed to bring together the different nationalist movements in East and Central Africa, to discuss and exchange ideas, and to act as a channel of mediation when necessary. Unlike CIAS, it lasted until 1964 (expanding to include black Southern Africa as PAFMECSA), by which time its functions had been assumed by the OAU.

2. THE PERIOD OF PARTICULARISM, 1960–1963

By 1960, the period of universality had ended, owing in part to divergent African views over the Congo crisis and the growing mistrust of Ghana and Nkrumah. The new francophone states began their process of regrouping starting with the Union Africaine et Malgache (UAM) in 1961 (the predecessor to OAMCE and OCAM). In the same year, crosscutting language lines, a clear ideological division emerged with the formation of the "Casablanca" (radical) and later "Monrovia" (conservative) blocs. UAM was itself ideologically based, as evidenced by the exclusion of French-speaking Guinea and Mali. Even PAFMECA was basically a regional rather than a Pan-African organization. There were several attempts to bring these diverging groups together, especially after the Congo crisis began to subside temporarily. Eventually this led, in May, 1963, to the formation of the Organization of African Unity (OAU), an important milestone in the post-colonial history of Africa.

3. INTRA-AFRICAN ORGANIZATION SINCE 1963

The OAU represented a compromise between radical and conservative ideologies in Africa. There was general agreement on certain issues: membership should be open to all independent states; the functions of all other African groupings (except purely functional regional organizations such as UAM, which re-emerged as OCAM), should be assumed by the OAU; and machinery for conflict resolution should be created. The major compromises arose between the "conservative" demands for noninterference in internal affairs (including respect for sovereignty and existing territorial boundaries, and condemnation of subversion—essentially a powerful support for a status quo regarding internal African affairs) and the "radical" demands for international nonalignment and continued struggle against colonialism (especially with respect to southern Africa). In essence, both views were accepted. These agreements set the tone for interstate activity in Africa for the years which followed.

Six major features have characterized intra-African organization since 1957 and particularly since the formation of the OAU (see Hoskyns, 1967). These include the following.

1. The abandonment of any organizational approach to continental federation or political union (reinforced further with the deposition of Nkrumah) has been accompanied by a greater acceptance of functional cooperation for specific objectives, especially economic ones; attempts at political union—as between Tanganyika and Zanzibar—are to be left to the individual states.

2. A reorientation away from attempts to achieve a single voice in international affairs has been accompanied by a stronger concern for regulating relations between member states.

3. Support for regional economic cooperation has been growing. It is interesting to note that Nkrumah opposed regional groupings—he was bitterly hostile to the projected East African Federation—contending that regionalism would hinder continental unification in much the same way that national introspection had hintered the growth of regional unity, i.e., by reinforcing existing cleavages.

4. A greater emphasis has been placed on the "linkage" role of governments and heads-of-state as distinct from political parties or pressure groups (the notion that extra-governmental organizations, including trade unions, could act as foundations of wider unification has been virtually abandoned).

5. The principle that no single state should dominate the continent has been supported. (Nigeria, the only state with the size, population and wealth to become a continental leader, has been beset with internal problems—indeed, there are some who feel that disunity in Nigeria has been encouraged by other African states and by certain European powers such as France and Portugal). Those states which have developed leadership qualities in Africa have done so primarily on the consistency of their ideologies and stability of their governments; these include pre-coup Ghana, Ivory Coast, Tanzania, Kenya, and Ethiopia, and more recently, Cameroon, Gabon, and Zambia.

6. Finally, and related to many of the other trends, there has been widespread agreement that the territorial boundaries inherited at independence outline the basic building blocks of continental unity and are no longer simply the artificial "scars" of colonial history. (For a formal discussion of the OAU, see Cervenka, 1969.)

In summary it is clear that political integration in Africa is occurring primarily at the national-state level, although the continental linkages which are beginning to emerge (e.g., the OAU and the economic unions) suggest that something like a United States of Africa may some day be accomplished.

80

International Organizations in Africa

THE ACTIVITIES OF INTERNATIONAL ORGANIZATIONS in Africa as a further aspect of interstate linkage will be examined in this module. Again, the stress is on suprastate regionalism and Pan-Africanism.

1. ACTIVITIES OF THE OAU

Various specialized agencies of the Organization of African Unity (see Module 79) have played an important part in African interstate relations since 1963. There is a Commission on the Problem of Refugees, and other commissions concerned with economic and social affairs, education, health and nutrition, defense, research, law, and transportation and communication. We will discuss briefly here the activities of two additional agencies, the African Liberation Committee and the Commission of Mediation, Conciliation, and Arbitration.

a. Liberation

The Liberation Committee has had relatively little impact. More pressure was probably brought to bear on colonialism before 1963. The committee has tried to encourage unified liberation movements and has attempted to organize boycotts and sanctions against the remnants of colonialism. The most notable successes have been scored by anti-Portuguese liberation forces, especially in Guinea-Bassa (as Portuguese Guinea is now called by some African nationalists) and parts of Angola, and—until the assassination of Eduardo Mondlane in February, 1969—by FRELIMO, the Mozambique Liberation Front (see Mondlane, 1969). The most prominent failure has been with regard to Rhodesia (see Wallerstein, 1967), but this has been due in part to the disunity of black Rhodesian nationalist movements as well as to an inability to persuade Britain to use force to curb the white minority regime. All OAU member states, except Malawi, have broken relations with the Republic of South Africa and Portugal, but this has had very little economic or policy impact.

b. Settlement of Disputes

Despite a number of important setbacks, the OAU has emerged as the major vehicle for the resolution of conflicts between African states. Even before the establishment of the special commission in 1964, the OAU had successfully mediated the boundary conflict between Algeria and Morocco and had provided a useful channel for contact in the Ethiopia-Somali border dispute. That the

North African countries chose to go to the OAU rather than to the Arab League (whose offer to mediate was rejected) proved a valuable stimulus to the early growth of the OAU. In 1964, with Morocco dissenting and the Somali Republic absent, the OAU formally pledged "to respect the frontiers existing on [the] achievement of national independence"—a major step in solidifying the territorial integrity of the former colonial boundaries. Relatively little success was achieved, however, in fully resolving the Somali-Ethiopia-Kenya dispute over the Somali Republic's claims to all land occupied by the Somali people. Although the OAU was useful in bringing the disputants together, temporary settlement of the problem was based mainly on bilateral negotiations, the mediational skills of President Kaunda of Zambia in 1967, and the conciliatory policies of the Somali prime minister, Egal. Likewise with regard to the Congo rebellion of 1964 to 1965 and the Nigeria-Biafra conflict of 1967 to 1970, the OAU has failed to achieve its goals, although both these major conflicts were (and, with respect to Nigeria-Biafra, are) complicated greatly by influences from outside Africa. Both also represented major challenges to OAU policy, the Congo crisis involving competitive interference by several African states in the internal affairs of another (forcing a new pledge against subversion of this type in 1965) and Nigeria-Biafra generating a deviation from the principle of territorial integrity in the recognition of Biafra by four African states (Tanzania, Zambia, Gabon, Ivory Coast).

2. THE AFRICAN DEVELOPMENT BANK

The formation of the African Development Bank in 1964 (after several years of proposals and negotiations) marked an important step in the creation of a continental agency for development finance. Totally African (governmental) in ownership, officers, and executive personnel, the ADB is aimed at facilitating intra-African investment and trade—acting as a channel and focus for foreign aid and investment—and at actively promoting development projects which are multinational or regional in scope (e.g., the Tanzam Railway between Tanzania and Zambia). Although the United States has supported the objectives of the ADB and has agreed to channel much of its aid through it (and thus assist multinational development), the bank still has extremely limited capital ($250–350 million) and has not been particularly successful with respect to other sources of foreign capital (most notably French). Despite these problems, the ADB is likely to become increasingly important in future African economic development, particularly with the growth of regional economic unions. It has already accomplished one major feat: an agreement on a voting formula among member states taking into account differences in population size, national product, income per capita, and international trade. These factors were used to determine a subscription quota in which each state has a base of 625 votes plus one for every share ($10,000) subscribed. In 1968, vote allocations ranged from 3,625 for the U.A.R., 3,075 for Algeria, and 3,035 for Nigeria, to 725 for Togo and 715 for Dahomey.

3. THE UNITED NATIONS ECONOMIC COMMISSION FOR AFRICA

Since 1961, the Economic Commission for Africa (ECA) has become a major pressure group promoting and providing technical advice to projects and proposals for economic integration. Green and Krishna (1967) identify five major elements in the "ECA position." These are as follows: (1) an emphasis on large subregional groupings, which include East Africa (Ethiopia through "Zimbabwe"—the proposed name for an independent black Rhodesia), West Africa (Mauritania to Nigeria), North Africa (Maghrib to Sudan), and Central Africa (the old UDEAC, mentioned in Module 78, plus Congo-Kinshasa); (2) an insistence on industrialization, including export processing, as central to economic development strategy and economic integration; (3) a stress on the need for coordination in transport, communications, finance, and trade (the latter based primarily on industry and secondarily on agricultural specialization); (4) creation of appropriate channels to present coordinated African positions to international bodies such as the United Nations Conference on Trade and Development (UNCTAD) regarding trade, commodity agreements, and international aid and finance; (5) opposition to European Economic Community (EEC—"Common Market") Associateship arrangements in Africa, which are viewed as hindering regional trade and industrial planning and development. (For more on the EEC, see Module 82.)

4. SOME GENERAL CONCLUSIONS

Pan-Africanist activity today centers primarily on the promotion of closer relations and the settlement of disputes between states. The earlier desires for continental political unity (see Module 54) as well as the strong emphasis on liberation and anti-colonialism have been de-emphasized (temporarily?) for practical and political reasons. Due largely to the enormous challenges of nation-building, Africa has become much more nationally introspective. There has been as yet no major shift of power from the individual states to any of the existing suprastate bodies, including the OAU.

The colonial legacy of regionalism and territorial boundaries continue to be perhaps the most powerful force shaping interstate political development in Africa. The division between French- and English-speaking Africa is particularly important in this respect and has hindered efforts at comprehensive unification.

The colonial legacy has also permitted outside powers, through political and economic pressure, to try to divide the African states. Nevertheless, some degree of interstate cooperation has been achieved, especially in the OAU, which may encourage greater interstate cooperation and a more solid common front with respect to Africa and the outside world in the future.

Africa and the Major Powers

Africa at the United Nations

IN 1950 THERE WERE 4 African states in the United Nations. By 1969 there were 41 African states (including Malagasy) out of a total United Nations membership of 124. Thus, at present, almost one out of three member states in the United Nations is African. The dramatic increase in African participation at the U.N. has come to symbolize the new African role in world affairs.

There are three major topics which will be discussed in this module: the general impact of Africa on the United Nations, the issues at the United Nations of most concern to the African states, and the relationship of the African states to the specialized agencies.

1. THE TRUSTEESHIP SYSTEM AND AFRICAN INDEPENDENCE

The involvement of the African states with the United Nations began prior to the independence of most African states. A number of African territories were supervised by the United Nations as "trusts" (deriving from the mandate system of the League of Nations, which covered the former German territories after World War I). After World War II, the United Nations Trusteeship Council was charged with ensuring that the particular trust territories were being advanced to independence by the respective European powers (Britain, France, Belgium). Inspection teams made on-the-spot observations and recommendations. The trust territories of Africa included Tanganyika (British), British Cameroon, French Cameroon, British Togo, French Togo, Ruandi-Urundi (Belgian), and former Italian Somaliland and Libya (the Italian territories, however, had not been mandates).

311

Although South-West Africa was also a mandate under the League of Nations, the Union of South Africa refused to relinquish its supervisory powers and initiated a conflict with the United Nations which has lasted for over two decades. In 1966, the General Assembly of the United Nations voted to revoke the South African mandate over South-West Africa on the grounds that the original conditions of the mandate to develop the country had not been met. In complete opposition to world opinion and the World Court decision that it could not change the international status of South-West Africa unilaterally, South Africa had by 1968 completed blueprints for full incorporation of South-West Africa as its fifth province, including the extension of apartheid principles and the creation of South-West African Bantustans (the first of which is proposed to be "Ovamboland"). Also in 1968, the United Nations voted to change the name of South-West Africa to Namibia and resolved to take effective measures to force South Africa to relinquish its control over the territory (see the summary of these events in Legum and Drysdale, 1969), although these efforts have thus far not been successful. For studies of South-West Africa and the United Nations before the developments in 1968, see First (1963) and Segal and First (1967).

The European states involved, in conjunction with the United Nations, began to prepare early in the 1950s for the self-government and independence of the trust territories. In the case of (former Italian) Somaliland, a specific ten-year deadline for independence was established. Many African statesmen came to New York to present evidence before the Trusteeship Council, and hence gained familiarity with the workings of the international body.

2. AFRICAN MEMBERSHIP AND INVOLVEMENT IN THE U.N.

The major impact of independent African states on the United Nations has been the result of the great increase in U.N. membership which occurred with inclusion of the African states. By October, 1968, when the small state of Equatorial Guinea (formerly a Spanish territory) became a member, it was clear that any state in Africa, of whatever size, could make its voice heard in the international forum—especially in the General Assembly, where the Third World states collectively held the balance of power. It was also clear that African resources for staffing this increased involvement in the U.N. were limited: as late as 1967, thirteen of the thirty-eight African states appointed ambassadors to the U.N. (i.e., heads of permanent missions) who were also ambassadors to the United States. Yet, as a symbol of African participation in world affairs, the United Nations has been paramount—a fact recently confirmed (in September, 1969) by the election of Miss Angie Brooks from Liberia as president of the United Nations General Assembly.

In retrospect, one effect of African involvement in the U.N. was the pressure for enlargement of the major U.N. organs, such as the Security Council and the

Economic and Social Council. Another effect was to help increase the importance of the General Assembly as the debating forum of the world.

In 1960, however, at the time of independence (and U.N. membership) for most African states, two critical issues dramatized the impact of the African states on the U.N. The first was the general tension of the Cold War, which made it possible for African states to hold the balance of votes in the General Assembly on most East-West issues. The second (and related) issue was the Congo crisis, which began in the summer of 1960. Although this module will not elaborate on the Congo crisis, it is necessary to mention the role of the United Nations in the Congo and the African impact on that role.

With the mutiny of the Congolese army against their Belgian officers in July, 1960, a crisis developed in the Congo. Belgium announced that its nationals would be protected, and Katanga threatened secession (see Module 59). Although the Republic of Congo was not yet a member of the United Nations, the Security Council met at the request of the secretary-general, Dag Hammarskjöld, to consider the alleged "aggression" of Belgium. On July 14th, a U.N. peace force was created by resolution (in which troops of the permanent members of the Security Council were not included). A United Nations Operations in the Congo mission was established, but there was considerable controversy as to its purposes and powers. The details of the U.N. involvement in the Congo are available in Young (1965) and Hoskyns (1964). It should be noted here, however, that African troops were the backbone of the U.N. contingent against the Katanga secession, that the whole Congo episode became a Cold War issue, that the African states themselves were deeply divided over the issue, and that the Congolese situation shook the U.N. to its foundations, forcing a major reappraisal of its objectives and activities.

3. ISSUES OF CONCERN TO AFRICAN STATES IN THE U.N.

The experience of the U.N. in the Congo produced a sharp reassessment by African states of their role in world affairs. They consciously came to take a "neutral" stance on Cold War issues (African states have abstained on more than half of all "Cold War" votes), and began to build their own machine—through the Organization of African Unity (see Modules 79 and 80)—for the resolution of conflict within Africa. They increasingly came to focus on problems of colonialism in southern Africa as an issue on which there was widespread African agreement (see Weigert and Riggs, 1969).

It is clear from the record which issues did concern the African states. Judging from the number of speeches given by African spokesmen in both the plenary and main committee meetings (there have been an average of about 1,000 speeches by Africans each year), the issue of South Africa and decolonization in southern Africa made up the overwhelming bulk of African concern.

These topics were four times more common than the second major topic, which was economic development and aid. Other topics, such as admission of China, problems of refugees, the nature of international law, and disarmament, were raised, but in statistically insignificant proportions (see Kay, 1969).

As early as 1962, the African states were successful in steering through both the Security Council and the General Assembly a resolution calling for an arms embargo and voluntary economic sanctions against South Africa. This issue illustrates, however, the relative inability of the African states to actually influence the international behavior of the three most powerful Western states (Britain, France, and the United States). None of the major powers has refrained from trading with South Africa, and the French have even continued to sell arms. (It should be noted that the United States had established an *arms* embargo prior to the U.N. resolution.)

Many Assembly resolutions condemning South Africa have in fact been passed since the earliest days of the U.N. The Security Council in April, 1960, ten days after the shooting at Sharpeville (see Module 32), censured the South African government for its actions in that tragic episode.

After 1965, African and U.N. attention became focused on Southern Rhodesia, whose white minority had unilaterally and unconstitutionally declared Rhodesian independence without acceding to the British demand to guarantee progress toward majority role (see Module 87). Voluntary sanctions were voted by the General Assembly (on British request), and in 1968 mandatory sanctions were voted. Although some international business concerns have circumvented the sanctions, and South Africa and Portugal have openly aided Rhodesia, the sanctions have been supported by the major powers. Nonetheless, the white-controlled government has not changed its discriminatory policies (see Modules 87 and 88 and Carter, *Essays,* chap. 28).

Increasingly, the Portuguese position in Mozambique, Angola, and Guinea is also coming under attack from the African states at the United Nations, (for details, see Modules 87 and 88). These resolutions range from general condemnation of Portuguese colonialism in Africa to specific grievances by African member states (e.g., in July, 1969, Zambia complained that a Portuguese plane — engaged in anti-guerrilla activities — flew over and crashed on Zambian soil).

In short, African activity at the United Nations has kept alive the issue of decolonization and racism in southern Africa and has served to unite the African states around a common issue and goal. In the long run, it may be this unifying function which will be of most importance.

4. AFRICA AND THE SPECIALIZED AGENCIES

The United Nations specialized agencies are concerned with problems of health, welfare, international cooperation, and economic development. These are matters of deep concern to African states, and in an undramatic day-to-day manner Africans have become increasingly involved in the specialized agencies. And the agencies have become increasingly involved in Africa.

The International Labor Organization (ILO) has an African regional office in Lagos, Nigeria; the Food and Agricultural Organization (FAO) has an African regional office in Accra, Ghana; and the World Health Organization (WHO) has an African regional office in Brazzaville. An Economic Commission for Africa (ECA) was established, with headquarters in Addis Ababa, Ethiopia (see Module 80).

The United Nations High Commissioner for Refugees, which is responsible directly to the General Assembly, has assumed ever-increasing responsibilities in relation to the vast numbers of refugees in Africa, now numbering nearly a million. These refugees are mainly from white-dominated southern Africa and Portuguese Guinea, the southern Sudan, and Rwanda. Working with host governments and voluntary organizations, the UNHCR has provided legal status and has stimulated rural settlements for refugees in asylum countries, notably Tanzania, Senegal, Uganda, Burundi, Congo-Kinshasa, and the Central African Republic.

The budgets of all U.N. specialized agencies have increased severalfold in the past ten years. The specialized agencies also have published a wealth of survey material on development problems in Africa. Some of these are on an individual state basis and others are arranged thematically (e.g., role of women, structure of civil services, problems of demographic survey, etc.). These materials are publicly available from the United Nations at a nominal cost.

82

Africa and
the Former Metropoles

DURING THE TWENTIETH CENTURY, Britain, France, Belgium, and Portugal have become increasingly involved in African affairs. The colonial system was decisive in linking African and European economic systems. It also created European language zones in Africa, and has resulted, in most cases, in continuing European political influence on the continent. The term *metropole* refers to the European states which formed the focus of large colonial empires and reflects the fact that London, Paris, Brussels, and Lisbon were the centers of decision making regarding Africa for most of the colonial period. While countries such as West Germany, Italy, the United States, Japan, and the Soviet Union are becoming involved in African economic development, the major influence continues to be the former metropoles. This influence may be economic, political, or cultural. It has sometimes been called "neocolonialism." This module will focus primarily on British and French relations with Black Africa since independence. In general, France (under de Gaulle) has exerted a far greater influence on its former colonies than has Britain on its.

1. METROPOLE-AFRICAN ECONOMIC RELATIONS

Monetary zones in Africa have continued to be either French-based (the franc zone) or British-based (the sterling zone). Some time after independence, a few African states (Ghana, Guinea, Mali) refused to have the value of their money linked to European monetary systems and tried to establish their own local currency. In most cases this has not been successful because of conversion problems; such "soft" currency is not readily accepted by other countries engaged in international trade. Ghana remains part of the sterling zone (although the cedi is not easily convertible), Mali has recently returned to international monetary standards, and Guinea is considering a similar move. One drawback to these changes, of course, is that a devaluation in the European currency (e.g., the 1969 devaluation of the French franc) usually results in the necessity for devaluation in Africa. (This did occur in the French-speaking states in 1969, but not in most of English-speaking Africa, including Nigeria and East Africa, after the 1967 devaluation of the British pound.)

Investment in independent Black Africa has also continued to be dominated by commercial and industrial concerns from the former metropole. Although American investment is increasing, it has been heavily concentrated in a few

Black African countries and remains only a fraction of the total European investment.

Trade patterns also continue to be heavily dominated by the former metropoles, although more so in the case of many of the former French colonies. In many African states, well over half of all exports go to the former metropole (e.g., in 1962, Rwanda, 85 per cent; Dahomey, 80 per cent; Sierra Leone, 80 per cent; Cameroon, 70 per cent; Senegal, 70 percent; Chad, 60 per cent; Gabon, 59 per cent; Somali, 52 per cent; Togo, 52 per cent; Ivory Coast, 50 per cent). Conversely, many African states are still dependent on their former metropole for more than half of all imports (e.g., in 1962, Dahomey 75 per cent, Mauritania 73 per cent, Cameroon 70 per cent, Congo-Brazzaville 67 per cent, Ivory Coast 66 per cent, Gabon 62 per cent, Senegal 60 per cent).

Most foreign aid to formerly colonial Black Africa still comes from Britain and France or from combined resources through the European Economic Community (EEC). In the case of France, this latter pattern is particularly important as a multilateral source of economic aid to Africa. Shortly after the Treaty of Rome was signed in 1957 establishing the European Common Market (the "Six"), the French-speaking African states (excluding Guinea but including the Belgian areas and also the Somali Republic) became "associated" with the EEC, and these "eighteen" states were eligible for both trade and aid advantages (see Okigbo, 1967). (Note: Algeria, Morocco, Tunisia, and the three East African countries have developed "special relations" with the EEC, although Nigeria announced in late 1969 that it no longer desires associate membership in the EEC.) In several of the French-speaking states, French aid is given for recurrent budget items as well as for development projects (as Britain continues to do for Malawi).

Most of the larger African states have tried to diversify their international economic relations. Thus, Nigeria has come to trade with Japan, Germany, Italy, the United States, and the Soviet Union. Ghana (under Nkrumah) explicitly tried to redress the imbalance of its economic (and political) relations by establishing contact with the Soviet bloc countries (see Thompson, 1969).

2. METROPOLE-AFRICAN POLITICAL AND MILITARY RELATIONS

Political independence does not mean the end of political association. The French Community, although formally dissolved, continues as a reality in Africa through OCAM (see Module 78) and through bilateral ties with France. Representatives of the British Commonwealth countries (including the Black African English-speaking states, except Sudan) meet regularly to discuss issues of mutual concern. Most recently these discussions have focused on the problem of Rhodesia (Zimbabwe). It should be noted, however, that political influence is a two-way process; when Tanzania broke off diplomatic relations with Britain

over the Rhodesia issue, there was pressure within Britain to intensify its resistance to the Rhodesian Unilateral Declaration of Independence (UDI).

The symbols of political sovereignty, however, have been carefully preserved
by African states. One such negative symbol in English-speaking Africa came
to be "mutual defense" agreements with the former metropole. Nigeria abro-
gated its defense agreements with Britain under considerable internal political
pressure (see Phillips, 1964). Most French-speaking states (exceptions include
Mali, Guinea, and Upper Volta) do allow French troops to be based within their
territory (see Crocker, 1968). The actual influence of French and, briefly, of
British armed forces is clearly apparent in the background of African politics.
Gabon called in French troops to put down an attempted coup, and Tanzania
and Kenya called in British troops in early 1964 to put down an army mutiny.
In November, 1969, more than 2,000 white troops of the French Foreign Legion
were called into Chad (which had invoked its defense treaty with France) to
help put down Muslim "rebels."

Britain and France continue to train most African officers, and most of the
African states are heavily dependent on their former metropole for military
aid (e.g., Burundi, 100 per cent; Cameroon, 80 per cent; Congo-Brazzaville,
80 per cent; Dahomey, 80 per cent; Sierra Leone, 80 per cent; Upper Volta,
80 per cent; Zambia, 80 per cent). French military bases exist at Dakar, Fort
Lamy, Tananarive, Diego Suarez, and Djibouti. In addition, France has a peace-
corps-type program wherein members of the French army are given civilian
status and may fulfill their military obligation by working on development
projects. (They also have a regular civilian peace-corps program.) By contrast,
the British peace-corps program—called "Voluntary Service Organisation"
(VSO)—is detached from political or military implications and is administered
by nongovernmental agencies.

3. THE IDEA OF NEOCOLONIALISM

African statesmen such as Nkrumah (1965) were concerned about what they
called neocolonialism, that is, the continuation of colonial patterns in the independence period (see Module 77). They were concerned about economic dependence (e.g., trade, investment, monetary zones, and control of development
priorities); political dependence (e.g., the pressures which could be brought to
bear to influence the internal and external policies of African states); the "bal-
kanization" of Africa; the use of French, Belgian, or British troops plus the
direct intervention of European states in African politics, as in the Congo crisis;
and cultural dependence (the predominance of the French and English languages, the influence of Western styles of dress, etc.). Throughout his career
Nkrumah has called for the emergence of a Pan-African economic system
which was not dependent on Europe, a Pan-African union of African states

which would strengthen the voice of Africa in the world, and the emergence of an "African personality" which would be an authentic representation of the people of the African continent.

Other African statesmen, however, such as Houphouet-Boigny of Ivory Coast, have argued consistently that linkage to Europe was necessary for African development and that the real danger was European disengagement from Africa. He considered "neocolonialism" to be a myth to the extent that decisions about dealing with European influences were being made by Africans themselves on the basis of "national interest." Dr. Hastings Banda of Malawi has developed a similar policy of "pragmatism" which even includes economic co-operation with South Africa.

The idea of neocolonialism has often been extended to include United States and Soviet influence in Africa, since, it is argued, alien rule is the essence of colonialism and in present-day Africa, many African states are being manipulated by the international powers.

It is not the purpose of this module to argue for or against the concept of neocolonialism. It is sufficient to point out how the concept is being used and to try to delineate the actual economic and political links which do characterize African relations with the former metropoles.

83

Africa and the United States

THE UNITED STATES HAS HAD a relatively short history of relations with Black Africa (excluding the earlier slave trade and return of freed slaves to Liberia). Until the African-controlled states became independent, formal United States relations with Africa were handled through the appropriate European power. In fact, there was no African Bureau in the U.S. State Department until 1961. Instead, the African colonies were regarded as appendages to the relevant European desks.

Since 1958, the increase of United States interest in Africa has been dramatic (see Emerson, 1967). Even so, it has usually been acknowledged that official U.S. policy in Africa is largely dependent on U.S. policy toward the NATO countries in Europe. Thus, the United States has essentially supported the European powers—especially France and Britain—in their relations with Africa. The U.S. has not directly supported Portugal, but NATO arms are apparently being used by Portugal against the nationalist insurrections and rebellions in their colonies.

At the same time, however, three factors have made it necessary for the United

States to follow an independent foreign policy in Africa: (1) At least one-tenth of the population of the United States is Afro-American, and hence Africa forms a significant part of the cultural heritage of the United States. (2) The opportunities for investment and economic development in Africa are considerable, and American business is often in direct competition with European business for raw materials and markets. (3) The stability and peaceful development of African states is in the national interest of the United States, since major disruption in Africa (such as in the Congo) is likely to involve the United States and the Soviet Union in some type of confrontation. (For a useful overview of U.S. policy and attitudes toward Africa, see G. Mennen Williams, 1969.)

1. ECONOMIC RELATIONS

United States private investment in Africa increased significantly during the period 1960 to 1965. By 1965, there were major U.S. investments in Libya, U.A.R., Ethiopia, Ghana, Guinea, Kenya, Liberia, Nigeria, and Zambia. The U.S. foreign-aid program extended insurance to cover political risks (e.g., expropriation) at a nominal cost. It should be mentioned that U.S. private investment in South Africa has also increased during this period largely through reinvestment. (For an overview of U.S. relations with southern Africa, see Hance, 1968.) Projecting current rates of new investment, however, the economic interests of the United States are probably more clearly tied to Black Africa than to the white South African regime. Interestingly, one of the major U.S. private investments in Africa during the 1960–65 period was Kaiser (Aluminum) finance for portions of the Volta River Project in Ghana (during the Nkrumah regime); this has apparently been extremely profitable to Kaiser (which gets Volta power at low rates for the smelter at Tema), and the project has been the backbone of Ghanaian development plans. It is estimated that for the whole of Africa since 1959, U.S. aid has totaled $3.6 billion (as compared to about $7 billion from France, $1.5 billion from Britain, $1 billion from the Soviet Union, and $300 million from China).

U.S.–African trade has also increased. Much of American economic aid has been tied to the purchase of American heavy equipment, so that companies such as Caterpillar, Ford, and General Motors have become involved in modern African markets. In return, African states have exported agricultural and mineral products to the United States. U.S. foreign aid has concentrated heavily on two categories of the African countries: those which are felt to have the greatest economic potential (e.g., Ghana, Nigeria, Kenya, and Congo-Kinshasa), and those which for various historical reasons did not have traditional access to European aid (e.g., Liberia and Ethiopia), although this pattern is changing. In recent years, greater emphasis has been placed on the principle of concentrating aid on multilateral and regional projects, although the impact of this policy has not yet been felt.

It is important to note that the relationship of U.S. aid to the "Containment of Communism" has continued to be an important criterion for Congress in the allocation of U.S. aid. In 1965, the two largest aid recipients in Africa, per capita, were Guinea and Egypt, both of which were also getting extensive aid from the Soviet bloc. (For an account by the former U.S. ambassador to Guinea, see Morrow, 1968.)

Perhaps the most innovative U.S. program in Africa, with respect to socio-economic development, has been the U.S. Peace Corps program. At the request of African states, Peace Corps volunteers have been primarily engaged in teaching, although agricultural and community development projects have also been common. The "do-it-yourself" approach of the Peace Corps in Africa seems to have been useful and a catalyst to local initiative, although there are both European and African critics who question the relative lack of "technical expertise" in the Peace Corps compared to other types of technical-assistance programs.

In summary, American economic relations with Africa in the areas of investment, trade, aid, and technical assistance have been relatively small, but are increasing.

2. POLITICAL RELATIONS

Perhaps the most important political fact about Africa for U.S. official policy is that it is not located on the periphery of the Communist world, and hence does not fall within the "containment" policy area. African states, furthermore, have emphatically stressed that they do not want to become involved in the Cold War (see Mazrui, *Essays,* chap. 26). Instead of an east-west division of world interests, they have begun to stress a north-south axis. Africans are concerned with the completion of decolonization in southern Africa, with the problems of racism, and with the disadvantageous nature of the terms of trade between northern/rich/white countries (including the U.S., Europe, and the Soviet Union) and the southern/poor/colored countries (e.g., Latin America, Africa, Asia). It is within this context that the revolution in black-white relations in the United States may have an impact on United States–African relations, mainly in the direction of causing U.S. policy makers to take more note of the political sensitivities of African states on matters of race relations.

There have been several crises of confidence between the African states and the United States on issues which have racial and/or colonial overtones. The first such issue was the Congo-secession crisis of 1960–63, in which official U.S. policy (which supported the United Nations troops in suppressing the secession of Katanga) was apparently being counterbalanced by international (including U.S.) private business interests which seemed to be supporting Tshombe, the political leader of the secessionist province.

A second crisis of confidence also occurred in the Congo when the United States sent airplanes with Belgian paratroopers into Stanleyville on November 24, 1964, to airlift American and European citizens who had been caught in the middle of the "Simba Rebellion." It was alleged by several African states that the U.S. was both intervening in African politics and was concerned only with the saving of white people.

A third crisis of confidence has occurred as a result of the white takeover in Rhodesia (discussed further in Modules 87 and 88). In this situation the United States supported Britain, but did not urge the use of force which many African states felt was appropriate. This stand tended to confirm the impression that the United States tacitly supports the South African white regime as well.

3. THE AFRICAN IMPACT ON RACE RELATIONS IN THE UNITED STATES

The African states have had a major impact on race relations and civil rights in the United States. By demanding and achieving independence during the period 1955 to 1965, they served as a catalyst to much of the civil-rights movement. African students were actively involved, in some cases, in the U.S. civil-rights movement. On the other hand, most African states have tried to avoid taking a racist position themselves on the issue of white-black relations. Even in states such as Kenya or Algeria, with histories of anticolonial violence, there is evidence that the African governments are working to create multiracial societies rather than monoracial societies. The African impact on Afro-American identity and social change are discussed in more detail in Modules 94 and 95.

84

Africa and the Communist Countries

THERE ARE A VARIETY OF MEANS of contact between the Communist countries and Africa: in some cases, there are communist parties in the African states, although most of these are illegal and very small; in other cases, the contact is through international organizations such as the World Federation of Trade Unions; in still other cases, the contact is diplomatic and/or economic through normal bilateral channels.

1. INTERNAL COMMUNIST PARTIES AND INFLUENCE

One of the earliest and largest of the transnational political parties in West Africa, the Rassemblement Démocratique Africain (RDA), was officially allied with the Communist Party in France. This alliance was broken in 1950, and the RDA (and its territorial organizations) began to follow independent African policies.

The actual existence of communist parties in Africa in the 1950s and 1960s has largely been limited to the northern and southern rim of the continent. Within sub-Saharan Africa the colonial powers prevented, in most cases, the growth of internal communist parties. There have been small communist parties in Algeria and South Africa. There is a small (approximately 1,500 persons) Madagascar Communist Party. Several political parties have had the active support of the Chinese or Soviet government (e.g., the Union des Populations du Cameroun, and certain groups in Congo-Brazzaville). In Nigeria, a Communist Party was formed in 1961 with an estimated 500 members, but this party has played no role in Nigerian political life.

In many African states, the Communist Party is outlawed. This is true of South Africa, where the remnants of the Communist Party work underground in active cooperation with banned African nationalist movements. The South African Communist Party publishes a regular journal in London called *The African Communist,* which gives news from around the continent. Most South African communists are white, and many are now in exile.

The Communist Party is also outlawed in Tunisia, Sudan, Morocco, and U.A.R. In Ghana (under Nkrumah), Mali (under Keïta), and in Guinea the dominant African nationalist parties have not been hostile to communist parties in other countries, but, being official one-party states, do not allow internal party formation by groups other than the ruling party.

2. INTERNATIONAL COMMUNIST ORGANIZATIONS

McKay (1963, p. 216) estimates that in 1961 there were about 40 Communist-inspired "friendship associations" operating in Africa, including both a Soviet Association for Friendship with the Peoples of Africa (set up in April, 1959), and a Chinese African Peoples' Friendship Association (set up in 1960).

Of more significance, however, have been the international Communist organizations, such as the World Federation of Democratic Youth (WFDY) or the World Federation of Trade Unions (WFTU). The WFTU was formed after World War II in cooperation with other Western trade unions, but by 1949 the Cold War had divided the unions, and the non-Communist trade unions broke off to form their own International Confederation of Free Trade Unions (ICFTU). The WFTU continued under Communist leadership, and one of its major member organizations has been the French Communist union, the Confédération Générale des Travailleurs (CGT). Many of the unions in French-speaking Africa were affiliated with the CGT, and hence with the WFTU. In 1956, Sékou Touré of Guinea broke with the CGT and formed CGT-Africaine. Within the next two years, Touré had led most of the African unions out of both the CGT and the WFTU with his formation of the Union Générale des Travailleurs d'Afrique Noire (UGTAN). Although UGTAN maintained cordial relations with WFTU, it followed an independent line and eventually led to the formation of an All African Trade Union Federation (AATUF).

3. COMMUNIST-BLOC RELATIONS WITH AFRICA

In 1958, the Soviet Union created an African desk within the Foreign Ministry and began to establish diplomatic and consular representatives in Africa. McKay (1963, p. 229) estimates that in 1961 eighty-five or more "Soviet-bloc" trade delegations came to Africa, most of which were able to negotiate trade agreements. Also by 1961, there were 1,250 Soviet technicians in Africa, about 450 of whom were in U.A.R.

The sub-Saharan African states which developed most trade with the "Soviet-block" countries have been Ghana, Guinea, Mali, Sudan, and, more recently, Nigeria. Major Soviet-aid recipients in Africa have included U.A.R., Guinea, Ghana, Congo-Kinshasa, Sudan, the Somali Republic, and Tunisia (see Stokke, 1967). One of the major Soviet projects in Africa has been the Aswan Dam in U.A.R.

On the diplomatic side, most of the Eastern European countries, plus the Soviet Union and China, have been actively engaged in establishing contacts in Africa. A summary of the initial programs of each bloc country is contained in Brzezinski (1963).

There have been many cultural exchanges between the Communist countries and Africa, ranging from scientific delegations to programs including the arts, drama, sports, and broadcasting. African students also have received scholarships for study in Communist universities. The People's Friendship University (later called Patrice Lumumba University) was established in Moscow in 1960 for students from the Third World. In 1961, the estimated number of African students studying in Communist countries was about 1,200, most of these in the Soviet Union, East Germany, and Czechoslovakia. (For an autobiographical account of a Ghanaian student in China, see Hevi, 1967.) The major African countries sending students were Guinea, Algeria, Sudan, and the Somali Republic.

Just as there has often been tension and competition between the United States and France (under de Gaulle) in Africa, so there has been competition between the Russians and the Chinese in Africa. The Chinese had established diplomatic relations with Egypt, Sudan, Guinea, and Ghana by 1960, but in 1961 they became involved in a major way in the Somali Republic. This was partly in response to Russian support for the Ethiopians in the Somali-Ethiopia border skirmishes. Sino-Soviet competition has also occurred in Congo-Kinshasa, in Guinea, and in Burundi. During the 1965 tour of Africa by Chou En-lai, there was an apparent attempt by the Chinese to encourage African support for China (*vs.* the Soviet Union) on the basis of racial criteria. (The speeches of Chou En-lai in Africa have been published, 1965.) It is extremely important that Sékou Touré of Guinea, perhaps reflecting his Muslim heritage and his preference for ideological rather than racial alignments, rejected the Chinese overtures.

One of Peking's major investments has been in the projected railway linking Guinea and Mali. The Chinese have also become involved in the large railway project to link Tanzania and Zambia, but both these African governments are maintaining a careful balance of aid donors, which include the Soviet Union, the United States, Canada, Great Britain, and others.

In short, the Chinese have become involved in only a few countries. The Soviets have set up contacts in a much broader range of countries. Most recently, the Soviets aided the Nigerian federal government in their prosecution of the Nigeria-Biafra civil war (see Klinghoffer, 1968) and as a result have apparently secured a stable relationship with Africa's largest state. (Certain Nigerian officials claimed that the Chinese supported the Biafrans, but there is little to support this claim.) Finally, it should be noted that with the overthrow of President Nkrumah in Ghana, Soviet and Chinese technicians left Ghana (a few Russians have now returned).

In the future, it is likely that Soviet and Eastern European relations with most African states will be "regularized" if it becomes apparent that the political elites of Africa (most of whom are middle-class nationalists) are not threatened by the relationship (see Legvold, 1969). In contrast, Chinese activities in Africa, which seem to be primarily focused on support for radical opposition groups (or groups in exile) within most African states, will probably continue to be strained (or nonexistent) at the official level except where Chinese aid is actively sought, as in Tanzania. (For a recent overview of Soviet activities in Africa, see Morison, 1969.)

Africa and
the Third World

Africa and the Third World

THE MOMENTUM FOR INDEPENDENCE in Africa gathered speed with the independence of India in 1947, which the British Labour Party, then in power, encouraged. Indians had long been in contact with Africa, and Gandhi had in fact lived at the beginning of the century in South Africa, where he developed and practiced the notion of *satyagraha* (i.e., passive resistance to create change).

The independent state of India carried the demand for decolonization throughout the colonial areas including Africa. By the mid-1950s, it was clear that many of the colonies would become independent, and an important bond began to develop between the peoples of the world with experience under colonialism (see Mazrui, *Essays*, chap. 26). This bloc came to be known as the *Third World* because it was not a part of the West nor of the Soviet bloc. (Communist China is a marginal exception, since it had not been a formal colony but had suffered from European/Russian imperialism.) These countries had several things in common: they were "people of color," they had for the most part experienced colonialism, and they did not want to become involved in Soviet-American disputes (see Paden, *Essays*, chap. 20). This latter feeling resulted in a policy of "neutralism" (excluding China) which in the 1950s was not acceptable to either the West or the East. Except for the earlier ties between Egypt and the Soviet Union, it was not until the Moscow Conference of November, 1960, that the principle of *coexistence* between the Soviets and the Third World was widely accepted. About the same time (with the retirement of U.S. Secretary of State John Foster Dulles) the United States also accepted the idea of *neutralism*. During the 1960s, however, the Third World countries have begun to pursue policies determined by their individual national interests. These policies have brought Third World states into conflict over international markets and investments and have precipitated boundary disputes. In short, an age of national foreign policy has arrived (see Module 77).

1. THE ORIGINS OF THIRD WORLD SOLIDARITY

The first major conference where African and Asian statesmen met together was held at Bandung (the Conference of Asian-African States) in April, 1955 (for selected documents, see Legum, 1962). In attendance were Chinese premier Chou En-lai, Egyptian president Gamal Abdel Nasser, and Indian prime minister Jawaharlal Nehru. (Kojo Botsio and other prominent Ghanaians were at Bandung as "observers.") The major theme of the conference was "anti-imperialism," and as a direct result of the conference, several of the Asian states established diplomatic representation in those few African states which were independent. In particular, Egypt politically recognized Communist China and Egyptian-Chinese trade and cultural relations were firmly established.

One of the later outcomes of the conference was the decision to set up an "Afro-Asian Solidarity Committee," which held its first conference in Cairo from December, 1957, to January, 1958. The second conference was held in Conakry, Guinea, in 1960. Increasingly, however, the organization became identified with a pro-Soviet foreign policy, and Chinese-Soviet disputes were largely responsible for the decline of AASC. Also, with the burst of independence in Africa in 1960, the AASC was superseded by various Pan-African efforts (see Module 79).

In the 1960s, the African states have continued to maintain relations with the Asian states (although many did not have formal relations with China). But the initial impetus to Third World unity seemed to fade as the decolonization process reached fruition and as the harsh realities of nation-building preoccupied national attention.

Since independence, Africa has had minimal relations with Communist China. The Chinese have extended assistence to Guinea, Tanzania, the Somali Republic, Mali, Algeria, and Congo-Brazzaville and to southern African liberation movements, but have been restricted in most other African countries.

Increasingly, Japan has developed trade relations with Africa. Inexpensive transistor radios and textiles as well as quality items have been easily accessible to the African market to the extent that Nigeria (under the civilian regime) had to restrict trade with Japan because of the impact on Nigeria's balance-of-payments reserves. Japan is increasingly becoming an importer of African raw materials as well. It should be mentioned that Hong Kong, through its Commonwealth connections, has also been a major supplier of textiles, clothing, and plastic goods to Africa.

2. AFRICAN RELATIONS WITH INDIA AND PAKISTAN

India, more than other Asian countries, has had a long and intimate involvement on the African continent (see Mangat, 1969; Ghai, 1965; Dotson and Lillian, 1969). In 1960, just prior to independence in East and central Africa, there were approximately 1,000,000 Indians living as semipermanent residents in Africa. Most of these Indians were living in South Africa (477,414, mostly in Natal province), because of the labor migrations beginning in the 1860s; in East Africa (329,134), because of early coastal settlement and British efforts in 1896 to attract railway workers; and in central Africa (19,081).

Indians in South Africa had long been involved in the struggle against white discrimination and domination. Gandhi founded the Natal Indian Congress in 1894 and led a passive resistence movement in South Africa from 1906 to 1914. When British African countries demanded their independence in the 1950s, the example of Gandhi's success in India was very much part of their thinking. After Indian independence in 1947, Nehru led the major efforts in the United Nations to demand independence for the African states. In Kenya and Tanganyika, Indians were fully involved in the independence movements.

In the post-colonial period, however, there have often been tensions between the Indians and the Africans in certain African countries. *Asians* (a general term to cover Indians and Pakistanis) in Kenya and elsewhere in East Africa were given the choice of becoming British (Britain had unrestricted "Commonwealth" citizenship) or local citizens. Many in Kenya took British citizenship rather than become Kenyan citizens, and those who left East Africa chose primarily to go to England rather than to India or Pakistan, probably for economic reasons. One of the major factors in this early Asian exodus was the feeling that "Africanization" in several of the East African states would restrict future job opportunities. In December, 1967, however, a crisis was provoked when the British government began to restrict Indian entry despite their nominal British citizenship. Rumors of this policy change and its actual implementation resulted in a rapidly increased migration out of East Africa. This emigration is still continuing from Uganda and Tanzania as well as Kenya and, through the denial of work permits, has come to involve citizens and noncitizens alike (although much less so in Tanzania).

The Indian government has continued to maintain a strong interest in Africa, particularly in the area of cultural relations. Also, since there is a clear difference among East African Indians between those who are highly educated and professional and those who are minor traders or clerks, the Indian government has tried to attract those with technical and professional skills back to India. In short, the East African Asians verge on being "persons without a country," a situation with potential for serious social conflict.

As mentioned above, the term *Asians* includes Pakistanis as well. The government of Pakistan has become increasingly interested in Africa, especially in those areas which are predominantly Islamic.

3. AFRICAN RELATIONS WITH CARIBBEAN AND LATIN AMERICA COUNTRIES

The two major sources of African linkage with the Caribbean and Latin American areas have been, first, the common colonial experience with metropolitan France or England (primarily in the Caribbean), and second, the African cultural ties which persisted after slave settlement in the New World.

The British and French colonial holdings in the Caribbean area meant that West Indians had close educational and cultural contact with Africans in London and Paris. Thus, Aimé Césaire and Frantz Fanon became active participants in French-speaking African development, while George Padmore and Arthur Lewis have played major roles in English-speaking African development (see *Bibliography*). Several English-speaking West Indians have interacted with Africa after migrating to the United States, e.g., men such as Edward Wilmot Blyden, Marcus Garvey, and, more recently, Stokely Carmichael (see *Bibliography*). In addition, several scholars on Africa, teaching in the U.S. — such as M. G. Smith, Hollis Lynch, St. Claire Drake, and Wilfred Cartey — are West Indian (see *Bibliography*).

The cultural linkage between Afro-American communities and Africa is discussed in Modules 30, 94, and 95. Suffice it to remark here that most of the Latin American and/or African states have not yet begun to develop fully their potential for interaction. Brazilian/African relations seem to be increasing and, because of the Portuguese position in Africa, are likely to be of major political significance in the future.

86

Africa and the Middle East

THE ISLAMIC WORLD consists of approximately 500 million persons distributed along a belt stretching from Morocco east to Indonesia and China. This Islamic zone represents all major races of the world. As mentioned in Module 21, Muslims share a common belief-system, cultural heritage, and an acceptance of Mecca (in Saudi Arabia) as the spiritual center of the Islamic world.

The Arab world, by contrast, consists of those persons who speak the Arabic language as their mother tongue and who regard themselves as Arab. While most Arabs are Muslim, many of the Lebanese and Palestinian Arabs are Christian, and in historical fact the Christian Arabs have been among the most ardent supports of pan-Arab movements. About 70 per cent of the Arabs in the world live in Africa (primarily North Africa, especially Egypt). Other Arabs live on the Arabian peninsula (Saudi Arabia, Yemen, the coastal sheikdoms) and in the fertile-crescent area (Lebanon, Syria, Jordan, and Iraq) surrounded by Turkish peoples to the north, and Persian (Iranian) peoples to the east.

The relationship between Africa, Arabs, and Islam presents a complicated and interwoven picture. In light of the growing importance of Middle Eastern political problems, especially between Arabs and Israelis, it is important to explore those relationships which have most relevance to Africa. Although the history of relations between Pakistan and Africa have been extremely interesting and important (e.g., the Ahmadiyya, Ahmadi, and Ismaili movements discussed in Abu-Lughod, *Essays,* chap. 27), this topic will not be dealt with in this module.

1. AFRICA, ARABS, AND ISLAM

The Ottoman (Turkish) Empire, centered in Constantinople (Istanbul), regarded itself as being the seat of the Islamic Caliphate and had nominal control over most of North Africa, the Sudan, and southwest Asia until approximately the time of World War I. At that time, Arab nationalism began to reject Turkish dominance and, in collaboration with the British and the French, set up the Arab state system more or less as it appears today.

Historically, relations between Black Africa and Mediterranean Africa (and the non-African Arab world) have ranged the full spectrum from cooperation to conflict. Arab slave raiding in Africa, which persisted until the early twentieth century (see Module 28), has clearly had a major negative impact, but Islamic ties remain strong. As Arab states began to emerge in the twentieth century, however, they sought to develop their own national identity (e.g., as Egyptians, Moroccans, or Iraqi), worked to develop closer links with other Arab states (as evidenced by the creation of the Arab League in 1945), and attempted to increase their relations with Black Africa. President Nasser of Egypt, for example, symbolized the desire to link these multiple identities (national, Arab, African) in his volume *The Philosophy of the Revolution* (English edition, 1959).

With African independence, many of the states along the Sudanic belt found themselves with mixtures of Arab and non-Arab black populations, but with an Islamic legacy and Arabic as a lingua franca. Such states as Mauritania, Niger, Chad, and Sudan came to symbolize the historical interaction of Arab and Black Africa (Important Arab minorities also exist in Kenya and Tanzania.)

Black African Muslims found it increasingly easy to make the pilgrimage to Mecca (and to visit other holy areas in the Arabian peninsula) where they came into direct contact with the major centers of Arab/Islamic civilization. An air route had been established between Kano, Nigeria, and Khartoum, Sudan, as early as 1935. In the post-colonial period, there have been flights twice weekly from Kano to Cairo, and each year, during the month of pilgrimage, a large number of chartered flights are available to Saudi Arabia. In addition, Arabs along the east coast have continued to maintain close ties with Arabs in the Middle East, particularly in the Arabian peninsula.

Also, in the early twentieth century a significant number of Syrian and Lebanese Arabs (from "Greater Syria") became established in many of the urban centers of West Africa (see Winder, in Fallers, 1967). In 1960, they were estimated to number about 15,000. They have engaged in trade and light industry and are in many respects comparable to the Asians in East, Central, and South Africa. However, most of these Lebanese (as they are generally called) are Christian rather than Muslim. There has developed a complex set of relationships between the Lebanese and West Africans which seems to result in mixed feelings of economic frustration and dependence on the part of many Africans. Like the Asians in East Africa, the Lebanese were given the choice of taking out local citizenship at the time of independence, but most did not.

2. POLITICAL LINKAGE BETWEEN NORTH AND SUB-SAHARAN AFRICA

In 1960, the Congo crisis produced an ideological division in Africa (described in Module 81). The Casablanca group, which emerged from this division, was particularly important in terms of relations between North and West Africa, since it included states such as Egypt, Morocco, and Algeria, along with states such as Ghana, Guinea, and Mali. Although this linkage was officially abandoned in 1963, the impact was not lost.

When the Organization of African Unity was established in 1963, several of the North African delegations, especially that of the U.A.R., wanted to link the political interests of North and sub-Saharan Africa even more closely by introducing the Arab-Israeli conflict as an agenda item. It is extremely significant that the African states voted not to consider this conflict, on the grounds that it was not the proper concern of the OAU.

Since 1963, the Arab-Israeli conflict has been a policy matter for African states individually rather than collectively. Thus, during the June, 1967, Arab-Israeli war, Mauritania and Sudan both broke diplomatic relations with the United States because of its alleged support for Israel. Likewise, some states (or even regions within federal states, such as Northern Nigeria under the late sardauna, Ahmadu Bello) refused to accept Israeli technical assistance. However, the bulk of the African states have regarded themselves collectively as a potential mediator or buffer in the Middle East dispute. To this extent, Israeli foreign policy in sub-Saharan Africa (which has tried to keep Africa "neutral") has been successful.

3. ISRAELI AND EGYPTIAN POLICIES IN SUB-SAHARAN AFRICA

In addition to an active political and economic program in Africa, the Egyptians have also tried to promote cultural (mainly Islamic) solidarity between North, West, and East Africa (see Abu-Lughod, 1964; Ismael, 1968). Radio Cairo has been broadcasting in Hausa and Swahili since the 1950s, and a large number of scholarships are available for African students to study at Al-Azhar University and other educational institutions in Cairo. Part of the difficulty in achieving Islamic solidarity has been the diversity of sects within African Islam, the powerful nationalisms based on the state system, and the historic links between West African Islam and groups in Morocco, Tunisia, and Sudan that are often bitterly opposed to Egyptian leadership in religious matters.

The Israelis, likewise, have regarded Africa as a major field of their foreign policy. Diplomatic relations were established with Ghana in early 1957, and a number of important Ghanaian (and later Nigerian) commercial ventures were financed by Israelis. Israeli technical advisers have been active in many countries of Africa, and African labor leaders have visited the labor unions and *kibbutzim* of Israel. A full description of these programs is contained in Kreinin (1964).

The extent to which the Arab-Israeli conflict will involve non-Arab African states remains to be seen. Israel has been relatively successful in projecting an image of economic development through "cooperative" approaches which is attractive to many African states. On the other hand, there are indications that the Islamic zones in Black Africa are increasingly being linked to Arab Africa and that commerical ties between Israel and Black Africa have not reached the levels initially anticipated by Israel. Furthermore, the 1969 coups in Libya, Sudan, and Somalia solidified the tier of radical military leadership in North Africa, which now stretches across the continent from Algeria to the Somali Republic. Perhaps never before has there been greater unity among the Islamic states of northern Africa with respect to the Israeli problem.

The Problem
of Southern Africa

87

The Remnants
of Colonialism

THE THREE MAJOR ZONES of colonialism (defined as external alien rule) in Africa today are the Portuguese territories, Rhodesia, and the few remaining Spanish and French areas. The Republic of South Africa's control over South-West Africa (Namibia), which has been declared illegal by the United Nations (see Module 81), will not be considered in this module (see Wellington, 1967). White minority rule in the Republic of South Africa — essentially a form of "domestic" colonialism — is discussed in greater detail in Module 89.

1. THE PORTUGUESE TERRITORIES

There are five Portuguese territories in Africa (population estimates are for 1965): Angola (5,200,000 population, including 173,000 whites and 53,000 mulattoes); Mozambique (6,850,000 Africans, 100,000 Europeans, 40,000 mulattoes and "integrated" Africans, 20,000 Asians); Portuguese Guinea (530,000 Africans, 7,000 Europeans and mulattoes); Cape Verde Islands (165,000 Africans, 3,200 Europeans); and the islands of São Tomé and Principe (62,000 Africans, 1,200 Europeans).

The five are regarded as Overseas Provinces of Greater Portugal. In all five, Portuguese contacts date back some 400 years (see Modules 25 and 27). Portugal has come to be economically dependent on the two largest of these territories, Angola and Mozambique, which contibute approximately 25 per cent of the Portuguese annual budget. (For further details on Portuguese Africa, see Duffy, 1959; Abshire and Samuels, 1969.)

335

Portugal does not consider these territories to be "colonies" but integral parts of Portugal. Portugal has an official policy of "assimilation" (unlike South Africa) whereby a relatively small proportion (probably less than 1 per cent) of Africans have become citizens by learning Portuguese, becoming Catholic, and being occupationally self-sufficient (see Module 88 for further qualifications). The Portuguese government feels itself to have a "Christian civilizing mission" and is proud of its official nonracial history. (Portugal has encouraged inter-racial marriage, and a significant number of persons in Portuguese Africa and Portugal are mulatto.)

For the vast majority of Africans who do not assimilate, however, there has been a system of forced labor and a lack of individual rights which approaches certain forms of slavery. A highly efficient intelligence service, a pass-card system, and widespread use of physical punishments keep close control over the African population.

For the past several years, there have been increasing numbers of guerrilla liberation movements in Mozambique, Angola, and Portuguese Guinea (see Module 88). There are nationalist "governments-in-exile" in Tanzania, Congo-Kinshasa, and Guinea, respectively. The Portuguese government has responded by drafting Portuguese young men to fight these movements (with, it is widely claimed, NATO planes). Large portions of the African population have been forced into fortified towns guarded by Portuguese troops. Villages which are suspected of sympathy for the nationalists are bombed in air strikes. The most effective nationalist movement is probably that in Portuguese Guinea (now called Guinea-Bissau or Guine by the nationalists), which by 1969 controlled most of the country. The main nationalist group is PAIGC (Partido Africano da Inde-pendencia de Guine e Cabo Verde), led by Amilcar Cabral, who comes from Cape Verde. The major liberation movement in Mozambique is FRELIMO (Frente de Liberação de Moçambique), which holds most of Niassa and parts of Cabo Delgado and Tete Provinces. Until his assassination in Dar es Salaam in 1969 (see Marcum, 1969), FRELIMO was led by Eduardo Mondlane, a North-western University Ph.D. and former professor of anthropology at Syracuse University. (See Mondlane, 1969, for his description of the liberation move-ment in his native Mozambique.) A second small liberation movement is COREMO (Comité Revolucionário de Moçambique), based in Lusaka, Zambia. In Angola there are three major liberation movements: the GRAE (Governo Revolucionário de Angola no Exilio), which is based in Congo-Kinshasa and is supported by the thousands of Kongo refugees who have fled into that country; the MPLA (Movimento Popular de Liberação de Angola), which is working very effectively in eastern and southeastern Angola; and UNITA (União Na-cional para a Independencia Total de Angola), operating mainly in the east and south. (For further details on Angolan liberation, see Wheeler and Pelis-sier, 1970; and Institute of Race Relations, 1962.) There has been virtually no coordination of efforts between these three groups. (Background to the anti-

Portuguese nationalist movements can be found in *Africa Report,* November, 1967; more recent developments are detailed in Legum and Drysdale, 1969.)

Although Dr. Antonio Salazar, the prime architect of contemporary Portuguese policy in Africa, officially retired as head-of-state in 1968 (having served since 1930), there is no indication of a change in Portuguese policy under his successor, Marcello Caetano. The liberation movements are growing in their determination to free their countries from Portuguese control. Their military activities have become increasingly successful in recent years and it is clear that major political changes are likely to occur in the near future in these Portuguese territories.

2. THE ISSUE OF SOUTHERN RHODESIA

From 1890, to 1923, Southern Rhodesia was administered under royal charter by the British South Africa Company. Since 1923 it has been a "self-governing colony," dominated by the local white-settler group (see Leys, 1959). A small number of Africans had the vote on a restrictive (but color-blind) franchise, although there were no Africans in the legislature until 1962. At that time, voting rolls were divided on an economic basis which allocated only a small number of seats to the low-income group. Under this arrangement, Britain gave up its "reserve powers," but did not extend independence to Rhodesia. From 1953 to 1963 Southern Rhodesia was part of the Central African Federation, in association with Northern Rhodesia (Zambia) and Nyasaland (Malawi)—a federation always opposed by African spokesmen who resented the domination of white settlers in Southern Rhodesia (see Chitepo, 1964.)

In 1964, a year after the federation was dissolved, Zambia and Malawi became independent, and white Southern Rhodesians demanded the same status. Britain refused on the grounds that the Rhodesian government was not supported by the majority of the population. Ian Smith was elected prime minister and, in November, 1965, unilaterally and unconstitutionally declared Rhodesia to be sovereign and independent. The phrase UDI (Unilateral Declaration of Independence) became a rallying call for European settlers in Rhodesia and a symbol of repression and racism for Africans.

The irony of the Rhodesian situation is that African states have demanded that Britain fulfill its "legal colonial right" to suppress the "rebellion." It was clear to African leaders of all persuasions by 1965 that Britain was anxious to ensure, ultimately, an African majority government in Rhodesia. Still, the rebellion of Ian Smith created a new type of colonialism in the minds of African spokesmen, for local white minority rule now appeared comparable to the repressive South African situation. Despite the imposition of economic sanctions against Rhodesia on British request, and in accord with resolutions passed in the United Nations, the government of Ian Smith has survived, largely due to the support of the South African and Portuguese governments.

Prior to UDI, there were two African nationalist movements in Rhodesia (or *Zimbabwe* as the nationalists call it): the Zimbabwe African Peoples' Union (ZAPU), led by Joshua Nkomo; and the Zimbabwe African National Union (ZANU), led by the Reverend Ndabaningi Sithole. Both leaders (and many supporters) are now in prison, but both parties have continued to work in exile, although separately, for the independence of Zimbabwe (see Rake, 1968). ZAPU is supported militarily by the African National Congress, a South African nationalist group which is also in exile. As the guerrilla thrusts into Rhodesia have increased, the white South African government has supplied arms and some troops to support the white Rhodesians.

The population of Rhodesia (Zimbabwe) in 1968 was approximately 4,700,000, of whom only 237,000 were Europeans. The issue of the freedom of the over four million Africans has become a matter of high priority for both the individual adjacent African states and the Organization of African Unity. (For further details, see Clements, 1969.)

3. SPANISH AND FRENCH ENCLAVES

Spain, bound by an adherence to a policy of self-determination in support of her claims to British Gibraltar, has in recent years begun to relinquish control over many of its remaining African territories. The territory of Equatorial Guinea (consisting of the mainland area of Rio Muni, the island of Fernando Po, and several smaller islands) became independent in the fall of 1968. At about the same time, final preparations were made towards ceding Ifni to Morocco. All that remains of Spanish Africa are Spanish Sahara (also called Rio de Oro) and the resort towns of Ceuta and Melilla. Spanish Sahara is actively claimed by Morocco (and, more recently, by Mauritania and Algeria), but there do not appear to be any local movements to end Spanish control of the area. Spain appeared ready to cede Spanish Sahara to Morocco at the time of its independence in 1956 (when Morocco absorbed other Spanish areas), but Morocco refused to accept the Spanish condition of recognizing Spain's control of Ceuta and Melilla, a demand which Spain has continued to make despite its policies of "decolonization." The discovery of rich phosphate deposits in Spanish Sahara has been a primary factor behind Mauritanian and Algerian claims to the area. Spanish Sahara, Ceuta, and Melilla are garrisoned with Spanish troops.

As mentioned in other modules, most French colonies in Africa gained their independence between 1958 and 1960. The French Territory of the Afars and Issas (F.T.A.I.), however, remains as France's last overseas African territory. Formerly called French Somaliland or the "French Somali Coast," the territory was renamed in large part to dampen hopes of annexation by the Somali Republic by encouraging the local identities of the two major ethnic groups.

Ethiopia has also made strong claims to the territory, which includes the port of Djibouti, outlet for Ethiopia's major exports. A referendum was held in 1967 offering the choice of remaining under France with limited autonomy (oui) or becoming independent without further financial assistance from France (non). The majority chose continued French control, but there were several factors complicating the issue. Although the Issas are a clan of the Somali (who as a whole number about 58,000 compared to 48,000 Afars), most non-Issa Somali were considered "foreigners" and not permitted to vote. In the referendum, 22,000 Afar were registered against less than 15,000 Somali (mainly Issas), roughly the proportion of oui *vs.* non votes. There have been several assassination attempts since 1967, but recent developments suggest an increasingly unified progression toward total independence from France. It is difficult to foresee, however, what Ethiopia and the Somali Republic will do should independence for F.T.A.I. be obtained. (See Legum and Drysdale, 1969, for further detail.)

4. CONCLUSIONS

The remnants of colonialism in Africa are primarily concentrated in the southern portion of the continent. European settlers, as in Kenya and Algeria prior to independence, are prepared to use power and force to maintain their positions. The result has been a potential for violence which will clearly have major international repercussions, parallel perhaps to the continuing Middle East crisis. The Republic of South Africa is the key to the future of white domination in southern Africa. Many African nationalists, however, have increasingly concentrated on the "buffer-zone" states, since, if isolated from each other, the remnants of colonialism are more vulnerable.

88
—

Race Relations
in Southern Africa

AFRICA'S MOST SERIOUS INTERNATIONAL PROBLEM lies within its own borders. The continent is split—ideologically, politically, and strategically—between the independent African-controlled states and the last major remnants of colonialism and white control in Africa (the Republic of South Africa, Rhodesia, and the Portuguese territories). At the roots of this division are basic political and moral conflicts over the nature of government, the importance of majority rule, the use of force, and, overlapping all the others, the role of race in human relations. Race relations in southern Africa is an international problem not just because African states want it to be. It has global significance because of its increasing role in shaping the relations within and between all nations and, perhaps most important, because of its relevance to the essence of humanity: man's relationship to man. In this module, race relations throughout southern Africa will be discussed. In Module 89, the situation in the Republic of South Africa is examined in greater detail.

1. THE REGIONAL STRUCTURE OF WHITE CONTROL

The political, economic, and ideological heartland of white domination in southern Africa lies in the Republic of South Africa, more particularly in the urban and rural areas stretching from the Transvaal (and parts of Natal) through Orange Free State and into Cape Province. Fringing this heartland is a complicated set of buffer regions separating it from Black Africa to the north. This buffer zone consists of five major components.

1. *The Portuguese Colonies of Angola and Mozambique:* About 350 thousand whites retain control over more than 11 million blacks in these two territories. Particularly important to South Africa is southern Mozambique, where the port of Lourenço Marques serves as a major outlet for the highly industrialized Witwatersrand area of Transvaal.

2. *Rhodesia (Zimbabwe):* A key link in the buffer zone since the Unilateral Declaration of Independence (UDI) in 1965, Rhodesia has moved steadily closer to South Africa economically and ideologically.

3. *Former High Commission Territories (Swaziland, Lesotho, and Botswana):* These states are constitutionally independent enclaves within the South African economic sphere of influence (to which they are tightly tied). Although each is strategically located with respect to the heartland and each is a potential base for anti–South African activity, all three are so dependent economically upon

South Africa that they must struggle to avoid becoming *de facto* Bantustans.

4. *Bantustans and other "Bantu Areas" (within the Boundaries of South Africa):* The first Bantustan to be established was the Transkei, in 1963. Although it has some degree of legal autonomy, the Transkei and other "Bantu areas" scheduled to be advanced to full Bantustan status are essentially internal colonies of South Africa. (See Carter *et al.,* 1967.)

5. *South-West Africa (Namibia):* This former German colony and League of Nations Mandate remains under South African control despite the 1966 U.N. statement recognizing it as a U.N. Trust Territory. South Africa treats this area as an integral part of the state, and it extends its apartheid policies into South-West Africa.

Swaziland, Lesotho, Botswana, the internal Bantu areas, and South-West Africa essentially form the major inner portion of the buffer zone, with Angola, Mozambique, and Rhodesia forming the outer flank. It might also be added that Malawi (under Dr. Hastings Banda) retains close relations with South Africa and has become increasingly dependent upon South African aid.

2. RACE RELATIONS IN THE PORTUGUESE TERRITORIES

Duffy (1962) notes the following:

> Until 1930 native policy was only incidental to the administration and exploitation of Angola and Moçambique. The African majority was ignored, enslaved, or "pacified," depending upon the necessities of the age, and Portuguese actions and attitudes were based on little more than expediency.

Beginning in 1930, a policy was instituted permitting Africans to enter a privileged class of assimilated persons—*assimilados*—and thereby become Portuguese citizens. To do so, the African had to be eighteen years of age, prove his ability to speak Portuguese, submit a birth certificate, a certificate of residence, a certificate of good health, a declaration of loyalty, two testimonies of his good character, and pay various fees equivalent to sixty dollars. In return, he can travel around his own country without securing permission, he does not have to pay the head tax, he is exempt from contract (forced) labor, he can receive (theoretically) the same pay as a European doing the same job, he can vote and become certified as "Europeanized." In 1950, Angola had about 30 thousand *assimilados* (out of nearly 4 million Africans), but Mozambique had less than 5 thousand (out of 5.7 million Africans). Since that time, there has probably been no significant increase in these figures.

Before some minor reforms in the early 1960s, the population of Portuguese Africa was divided into two legal categories: the *indigenas* (non-assimilated Africans) and the *não-indigenas* (whites and the assimilated Africans or mulattoes). In reality, the *assimilados* formed a third category although they were legally considered "non-indigenous." Race relations were guided by these three divisions, which became progressively more restrictive as population pressure in Portugal generated a stream of unskilled and often poorly educated migrants to the colonies. Thus, although theoretically aimed at assimilation, Portuguese colonial policy has been essentially based on cultural racism and inequality.

3. RACE RELATIONS IN SOUTHERN RHODESIA

There has been a "color line" since the establishment of Southern Rhodesia in the 1890s. It has been reinforced by the rigid partitioning of land between black and white and the favorable government policies toward European immigration (e.g., the maintenance of artificially high salaries, even for relatively unskilled labor, in order to attract larger numbers of migrants). Nonetheless, until about the time of UDI in 1965, there was a slow but perceptible lessening of the social and economic gap between the African and European populations through improved education, economic development, and urbanization. Whereas the Portuguese professed a policy of assimilation, the professed goal of the British settlers in Southern Rhodesia was, for a time, a "partnership" between the races in which, after some unspecified time, Africans would eventually attain a position of political equality. Racial restrictions and segregation were, therefore, not generally written into the law, and there were some indications of increasing fluidity and interaction in the racial situation.

The election of Ian Smith followed by UDI, however, reversed this slow process of change and Rhodesia today shows every sign of increasing restrictions and adapting the South African "model" of racial relations.

89
Politics and Race in South Africa

ALTHOUGH INTERNAL RACIAL POLICY in South Africa still reflects concepts of *baaskap* ("bossdom," a master-servant relationship), the official racial policy of the South African government is based on the somewhat less restrictive concept of *apartheid*, or "separate development." While in white areas this policy involves rigid discriminatory controls, separate development also includes territorial apartheid, or the development of separate areas under African control. Territorial apartheid is presented as South Africa's official "solution" to the challenge of cultural and racial pluralism—an approach which perhaps is without parallel anywhere in the world. Asserting that integration and racial mixing leads to cultural and moral decay as well as to biological/genetic degradation, the South African government has presented a blueprint for separate living in which each major ethnic or racial segment of the population would develop at its own pace, leading eventually to the political independence of each group but the retention of close economic interdependence. Each "Bantu" (black African) ethnic group would have its "homeland" where its distinctive culture could be developed under the leadership of its own people. This theory of separate development has thus far borne little relationship, however, to the realities of economic and racial relations in the Republic of South Africa, a subject which will be examined in greater detail in this module (see also Carter and Mbata, *Essays*, chaps. 28 and 12).

1. RACIAL DISTRIBUTION IN SOUTH AFRICA

The Republic of South Africa (R.S.A.) has a population of about 18.5 million and is divided into four provinces: Transvaal, Orange Free State, Natal, and Cape Province. Of this population, about 68 per cent is African (or "Bantu" as they are called in R.S.A.), consisting mainly of two groups, the Nguni (including the Xhosa, Zulu, and Swazi) and the Sotho (north and south Sotho groups and the Tswana). Europeans represent about 19 per cent of the total and are divided into two major groups: the *Afrikaners* (descendants of the early Dutch, German, and French Huguenot settlers, who speak Afrikaans as their home language) and the *English*. The Afrikaner/English proportions are roughly 60/40. The *Coloureds* are a mixed racial group (Hottentot, white, black African, Southeast Asian) forming about 10 per cent of the population. Almost all live in Cape Province and most speak Afrikaans. The remaining 3 per cent are *Asiatics* (mainly Indian), who are regionally concentrated in Natal

Province, especially in the city of Durban, and in the areas outside Johannes-burg (Transvaal). The white population is heavily urbanized but does not form the majority in any major city in R.S.A. In Johannesburg, the nearly 370,000 whites are outnumbered almost two to one by Africans.

2. THE ORIGINS OF APARTHEID

As is emphatically asserted in Mbata, for more than three centuries South African whites have attempted to maintain and intensify white power and domi-nance in South Africa despite frequent and forceful African resistance (see also Modules 31 and 32). In 1910, the Union of South Africa became an inde-pendent member of the British Commonwealth of Nations under a constitution that permitted only whites to be elected to the national legislature but retained an electoral compromise under which male Africans and Coloureds in Cape Province who could meet economic and literacy tests were permitted to vote for the same representatives as did whites. These provisions were changed in 1936 when Africans were placed on a separate roll to vote for three whites (supposedly to represent them) in a legislature of 156 members.

When the Afrikaner Nationalist Party succeeded to political power in 1948, it embarked on systematic and drastic policies of discrimination based on color and embodied in legislation rather than custom. These laws instituted new barriers in personal and social relations and in living areas. They also steadily reduced still further the minimal political participation of Africans and Coloureds in national life. Thus at a time when the European colonial powers were extending political rights to Africans in territories under their control, the South African government systematically reversed the world-wide trend and imposed new restrictions on South African Africans, Asians, and Coloureds. (For further details, see Carter, 1952; Ballinger, 1969.)

Sources of support for the practices of apartheid are often sought in the Old Testament and are embodied in the elitist philosophy of historic Calvinism embraced by the conservative wing of the Dutch Reformed Churches. More subtle support for the preservation of rigid controls comes from simple expe-diency (as perceived by the white minority): the fear that relaxation of controls might lead to violence. Unwillingness to impair the privileged position of whites has led English-speaking whites in the main to accept Afrikaner Nationalist policies and the formidable police state apparatus that maintains them. Alan Paton, the leading white South African writer, has called apartheid "the finest blend of idealism and cruelty ever devised by man."

3. WHAT APARTHEID MEANS TO THE BLACK AFRICAN

Africans cannot vote (except in the Transkeian elections), have no national political standing or influence, and no recognized rights to protest against anything in the 86 per cent of South African territory which is considered the white "homeland" (with its overwhelming non-white majority). Passes or permits are required to travel outside a "reserve" territory, to change address, to seek work, to reside in a town, to be out after dark. It is a criminal offense not to have a pass in one's possession or to sit on a park bench, ride a bus, enter a hotel or restaurant, or use a toilet which is for "whites only." An African who was born in a town and who may have lived there for fifty years cannot by right (i.e., without permission) reside somewhere else and then return to his birthplace for more than three days. Until an African has lived in a town and worked for the same employer for a specified number of years, neither his wife nor his dependent daughter is entitled to live with him for more than three days. Any policeman is entitled, generally without warrant, to enter and search at any time any premises in a town where he believes an 18-year-old boy might be committing the criminal offense of living with his father.

Controls are maintained by separating African living centers from the white urban areas by broad belts easily dominated by machine-guns and helicopters. An intricate network of African informers pervades every township. The prison population and the incidence of capital punishment are among the highest in the world. Those (white or black) who openly criticize government policy affecting black-white relations are almost always subject to penalties, including house arrest, banning of publications, or, as with Alan Paton, removal of their passports.

On a more general level, territorial apartheid means the creation of poor, semi-autonomous Bantustans in scattered areas adjoining the developed "white" sections of South Africa. These Bantustans, on the model of the Transkei (the only area to achieve full Bantustan status as yet), would remain economically dependent on white South Africa, as to a large extent do independent Lesotho, Botswana, and Swaziland (see Carter *et al.*, 1967). Today, the potential Bantustan area (essentially the area encompassing the Bantu reserves and the Transkei, including certain areas which would help to consolidate the highly fragmented reserves into contiguous groupings) contains not more than 43 per cent of the African population in at most 13 per cent of the land area of R.S.A. Some of this land is fertile and well-watered (large parts are dry steppe) but nearly all is overcrowded and badly affected by soil erosion. It could not, without enormous financial aid, support viable African economies even with its present population. The majority of the African population lives outside these areas and many have probably never seen their supposed "homelands." The South African government has invested small amounts in the Transkei and other Bantu areas but until recently has prevented private white businessmen from investing in these areas even when they might wish to do so. Indeed, there has even been criticism of government investment policies on the grounds that they are discriminatory (against whites) and that investment would be more productive if it remained almost entirely concentrated in the white areas.

4. CONCLUSION

Territorial apartheid if extended to its logical conclusion—full racial separation—would be economically disastrous. The prosperous South African economy was built and still rests on the interdependent contributions of all races. Blacks outnumber whites in the "white" areas almost two to one. If territorial apartheid were fully implemented, the white area would be virtually deprived of its labor force in farming (about 80 per cent) and mining (90 per cent), and nearly half its labor force in manufacturing.

Most South African whites appear to believe that rigid discriminatory controls based on color are required in the white areas to guarantee peace, prosperity, and a continued European presence in South Africa. But on a purely practical level, questions can be raised as to whether the current and increasing degree of economic integration can be combined with a large-scale move toward territorial separation. If not, even the official white South African attempts at justification for the inhuman effects of apartheid would be irrelevant. And, if current white political developments are any indication, few white South Africans believe in the attainability of territorial separate development. Unfortunately, the alternative some whites suggest is an official return to *baaskap*. (For a further evaluation of the future of South Africa and its territorial buffer zone, see Carter, *Essays*, chap 28; for an overview of African opposition in South Africa, see Mbata, *Essays*, chap. 12; Feit, 1967.)

Creativity in
Contemporary Africa

Contemporary
African Literature

A THEMATIC AND INTERPRETATIVE APPROACH is taken to African literature in the Cartey essay (*Essays*, chap. 29). Students should be encouraged to read the actual African authors and develop their own interpretations. In this process it is important to realize that much of the literature written in French has not yet been translated into English; hence, students should be cautious about generalizing about Africa and African literature from the English sources alone. In Africa, writers are using English, French, and vernacular languages. In the long run it may be the vernacular literature which will come to be regarded as the truly "African literature." For purposes of this discussion, however, attention will be focused on the English- and French-speaking authors, and their contribution to world literature. (A special list of Swahili and Hausa published literature appears in the *Guide to Resources*.)

1. CONTEMPORARY AFRICAN AUTHORS

As Cartey stresses, African literature should be considered with respect to its social context. Since there is a wide diversity of social contexts in Africa, it may be useful to review some of the biographical characteristics of the major African authors and to try to relate these details to the social context in which the author is working. Chinua Achebe, for example, was "minister of information" for Biafra, and Wole Soyinka was jailed for about two years for alleged subversive activities against the Nigerian federal government. (Soyinka was released in

FIGURE 11
SELECTED AFRICAN AUTHORS: BIOGRAPHICAL NOTES

Name	Country	Ethnicity	Birth date	Education	Major Literary Works
1. Chinua Achebe	Nigeria (Biafra)	Ibo	1930	Ibadan University	*Things Fall Apart* (1959) *No Longer at Ease* (1960) *Arrow of God* (1964) *Man of the People* (1966)
2. Cyprian Ekwensi	Nigeria (Biafra)	Ibo	1921	London University (Pharmacology)	*People of the City* (1954) *Jagua Nana* (1961) *Burning Grass* (1962) *Beautiful Feathers* (1963)
3. Amos Tutuola	Nigeria	Yoruba	1920	primary school	*The Palm-Wine Drinkard* (1952) *My Life in the Bush of Ghosts* (1954) *Simbi and the Satyr of the Dark Jungle* (1956) *The Brave African Huntress* (1958) *Feather Woman of the Jungle* (1962)
4. Wole Soyinka	Nigeria	Yoruba	1935	Ibadan University and Leeds	*A Dance of the Forests* (1963) *The Lion and the Jewel* (1963) *Three Plays* (1963) *The Interpreters* (1965) *Kongi's Harvest* (1967) *The Forest of a Thousand Daemons* (1968)
5. Ayi Kwei Armah	Ghana	Ashanti	1941	Harvard University	*The Beautiful Ones Are Not Yet Born* (1968)
6. Mongo Beti	Cameroon	Beti	1932	Sorbonne	*Mission Accomplished* (1958) *King Lazarus* (1961)
7. Ferdinand Oyono	Cameroon	Bulu	1929	Paris (law)	*Houseboy* (1966)

8. Camara Laye	Guinea	Malinke	1924	Paris (engineering)	*The Radiance of the King (1956) *The African Child (1959)
9. Léopold Sédar Senghor	Senegal	Serere	1906	Paris	*Selected Poems (1964)
10. Cheikh Hamidou Kane	Senegal	Fulani	1928	Paris (law and philosophy)	*Ambiguous Adventure (1963)
11. James Ngugi	Kenya	Kikuyu	1938	Makerere, Leeds	Weep Not Child (1964) The River Between (1965) The Black Hermit (1968)
12. Peter Abrahams	South Africa	African (father = Ethiopian; mother = Cape Coloured)	1919	little formal education	Dark Testament (1942) Song of the City (1945) Mine Boy (1946) The Path of Thunder (1948) Wild Conquest (1950) Return to Goli (1953) Tell Freedom (1954) A Wreath for Udomo (1956) A Night of Their Own (1965)
13. Ezekiel Mphahlele	South Africa	African (Zulu)	1919	external degree	Man Must Live, and Other Stories (1947) Down Second Avenue (1959) The Living Dead, and Other Stories (1961)
14. Alex Laguma	South Africa	African (Zulu)	1925	—	A Walk in the Night (1962) And a Threefold Cord (1964)

*Translation from French

October, 1969.) In both cases, the civil war in Nigeria has clearly affected their recent writing.

In broadest terms, African authors may be grouped into four categories: (1) English-speaking West African; (2) French-speaking West African (including Cameroon); (3) English-speaking East African; and (4) southern African. Within these major cultural contexts, it would also be important to know the national and ethnic identities of the authors, so that background reading on cultural influences could be undertaken, if desired, by students. An author's educational history may also be important, as well as some notion of the range of literary forms which he uses (e.g., poetry, drama, novel, short story). This information is not always available from the literature itself. An attempt to bring together some of this material is summarized in Figure 11.

2. THEMES IN AFRICAN LITERATURE

There are a number of ways in which African literature can be categorized or analyzed (see Wauthier, 1964; Moore, 1966; Zell, 1970). In Cartey, six categories are selected to represent the range of thematic concerns of the contemporary African writers (mainly novelists). Some of these themes, such as confrontation of black and white, have a geographical (e.g., South Africa) or time (e.g., colonial period) context. Others, such as "the nature of man," are not bounded by time and place.

1. Autobiography: Examples are given of Peter Abrahams, Camara Laye, and others, who have used the stories of their own lives to illuminate the rich mixture of feelings, thought, and behavior which are distinctively African. The work by Laye, in particular, is not a historical autobiography, but an interior monologue of the sort found in James Joyce's early writings.

2. Confrontation of Black and White: Writers such as Achebe, Oyono, and Beti deal with the impact of colonialism on traditional societies. Ngugi of Kenya focuses more directly on white settler–African relations, and all the South African writers find that their universe is defined by patterns of black-white relationships.

3. Alienation: This refers, in particular, to the discontinuity of feelings and relationships of the younger, educated, urban Africans from those of their older, traditional, rural families. The "generation gap" is probably large in Africa, and the urbanization rate, as mentioned elsewhere, is probably the highest in the world. It is against this setting that African authors have sought to define new identities and to reassess old ones.

4. Search for the Political Kingdom: Nigerian writers in particular have been caught in the cross-tides of political crisis and have used their pens to draw in fine detail the corruption and chaos of the civilian regimes, often to the frustration of their military successors (see Achebe, 1966). Some authors imply that in terms of political leadership, "The Beautyful Ones Are Not Yet Born" (see Armah, 1969).

5. Negritude: This theme was important primarily in French-speaking Africa, especially in the 1950s and early 1960s. It became less important after independence when assimilation into the French culture and the consequent dilution of the local African cultural heritage was no longer so important an issue.

6. The Nature of Man: In many ways this theme encompasses all of the others and goes beyond them in its search for the universal in mankind, for the depth and breadth of human emotions and behavior which only incidentally are acted out within an African context. Some of the stories by Amos Tutuola, although particularistic in their reliance on Yoruba proverbs and legends, are truly universal in their representation of quest for moral and spiritual truth.

3. THE READERSHIP OF AFRICAN LITERATURE

It is important to identify the audience for whom African literature is intended and the actual patterns of readership. Most African authors find themselves caught between several worlds: the Western (often university) world of their academic colleagues, the traditional world of their childhood, and the emerging world of contemporary African life. Furthermore, some of the writers from South Africa or Portuguese territories are in exile (e.g. Mphahlele, Abrahams) and their works are prohibited in these areas.

As a result, many African authors have claimed to be writing for *themselves.* They are their own critics and audience. Historically, many of the African writers were read more widely in Europe than in Africa. This is changing dramatically, however, as secondary schools and colleges in Africa have begun to offer courses on African literature, and as inexpensive editions or anthologies are available both in the original language and in translation throughout the continent. It is clear that African authors are increasingly writing for an African audience (see Irele, 1969).

91
___

Contemporary Social Thought

SOCIAL THOUGHT MAY BE DEFINED as writing which assesses contemporary events and processes from within an intellectual tradition that attempts to relate or explore human experience. Social thought is distinct from literature in its concern for nonfiction and in its mode of presentation (usually essay or expository, rather than poetic or novelistic). Some social critics are also men of letters: e.g., James Baldwin or Léopold Senghor. Social thought may be distinguished from ideology in that it need not be comprehensive and it need not be an imperative to action. Certain writers of social thought may, however, *be* ideologues; e.g., Kwame Nkrumah or Jomo Kenyatta.

Those who formulate social thought are referred to as *intellectuals*, although this term has had a variety of other meanings in Western history. In a recent volume, *On Intellectuals* (Rieff, 1969), J. P. Nettl distinguishes between two groups of intellectuals according to types of ideas: the first group generates ideas which extend the scope of inquiry or discussion; the second focuses on the quality of understanding within a defined scope.

Within the African context the ideas of Léopold Senghor, Cheikh Anta Diop, and Kwame Nkrumah have clearly expanded the scope of intellectual discussion. Such writers have interpreted the new synthesis of values and identities which is emerging in Africa. To the extent that the ideas (as distinct from the imperatives) of negritude and consciencism (see Module 60) are *comprehensive* in their interpretations of human history, they represent the broadest possible scope of ideas.

By contrast, the work of W. E. Abraham (*The Mind of Africa*, 1962) takes one corner of reality—the social fabric and values of Akan society—and plumbs the depths of meaning and experience to be found within that context. In so doing, Abraham transforms what might be an anthropological case study into a profoundly universal exploration of experience.

Social thought may try to persuade with a minimum of hard facts (using facts to illustrate rather than to exhaust a subject). The concerns of social thought may or may not be amenable to social-scientific investigation, although a number of the best social thinkers in Africa are also social scientists. The themes of African social thought elaborate and relate the basic concerns of intellectual history: the nature of man (and in particular, the nature of African man), the processes of history and social change, and the alternative futures of African individuals, societies, and states.

The purpose of this module will be to indicate themes in contemporary African social thought, to identify contemporary African social philosophers, and to comment on the media of expression. The time period under consideration will be somewhat arbitrary: from the end of World War II to the present. The module will suggest that there have been three distinct generations of intellectuals during this period. Students may wish to compare the thought and characteristics of these three groups.

1. FIRST-GENERATION INTELLECTUALS

The first generation of postwar African intellectuals attended universities outside Africa, primarily in France and Britain. A few—notably Azikiwe and Nkrumah—studied in the United States, but the locus of the intellectual milieu was London or Paris. For the most part, they mastered the intellectual traditions of Europe and were highly interactive with European intellectuals, such as Harold Laski and Jean-Paul Sartre. It should not be surprising that in the immediate postwar period, when the issues of nationalism, identity, and racial justice were of urgent concern, African intellectuals articulated concepts and engaged in dialogues (among themselves and with the European colonial powers) which focused on the transition to a new order. The question as to the nature of that new order became central to the intellectual community. In 1947, under the directorship of Alioune Diop (Senegal), the journal *Présence Africaine* was begun in Paris. The journal attracted literary review articles, essays on current topics, short thought-pieces on questions such as African personality and philosophy, tributes to African intellectuals, and sometimes special interpretive articles about a particular country. Most of the contributors were African scholars and intellectuals, primarily from French-speaking areas. European and American intellectuals also contributed. (The journal was originally published in French; later an English edition was also published; at present, the journal has articles in both English and French.) *Présence Africaine* also sponsored conferences of African intellectuals and began publishing their books.

In the late 1940s and throughout the 1950s, African intellectuals in London and Paris returned to Africa to engage in the nationalist struggle. It is significant that many of these men later became prominent political leaders in the new African states. Without going into individual detail, this pattern is illustrated in Figure 12.

2. SECOND-GENERATION INTELLECTUALS

The second generation of postwar intellectuals generally received their university education abroad but returned to Africa at about the time of independence or shortly thereafter. These younger men have been more concerned with the problems of nation-building than with the fight against colonialism. Most returned to African universities, which were building considerable strength at this time (see Module 42), rather than to political activity. Consequently, in

FIGURE 12
FIRST-GENERATION AFRICAN INTELLECTUALS WITH POLITICAL ROLES

Name	Country	Primary intellectual focus	Primary political role
1. Jomo Kenyatta	Kenya	Ethnography	Prime Minister
2. Dr. K. A. Busia	Ghana	Sociology	Prime Minister
3. Dr. Kwame Nkrumah	Ghana	Philosophy	Former President
4. Dr. Joseph Danquah	Ghana	Ethnography	Former opposition leader
5. Boubou Hama	Niger	History	President of the National Assembly
6. Mbonu Ojike	Nigeria	Social change	Former minister in Eastern Region
7. Dr. Nnamdi Azikiwe	Nigeria	History	Former President
8. Obafemi Awalowo	Nigeria	Jurisprudence	Commissioner of Finance
9. Aminu Kano	Nigeria	Islamic studies	Commissioner of Communications
10. Mamadou Dia	Senegal	Economics	Former Prime Minister
11. Gabriel d'Arboussier	Senegal	Social thought	Ambassador
12. Abdoulaye Ly	Senegal	History	Founder of party (PRA)
13. Léopol Senghor	Senegal	Philosophy	President
14. Bernard Dadié	Ivory Coast	Literature	Minister of Information
15. Mabika Kalanda	Congo-Kinshasa	Ethnography	Former Foreign Minister
16. Fodeba Keita	Guinea	Literature	Minister of Interior
17. Ahmadou Hampaté Ba	Mali	History	Former Minister of Culture
18. Fily Dabo Sissoko	Mali	Literature	Former deputy
19. Julius Nyerere	Tanzania	Philosophy	President

the one-party state systems which developed in Africa, a major issue was the relationship of social thought, within a university context, to the political goals and expediencies of the state. During the crises of nation-building which were to emerge, a category of professors, called "leaders of thought" in English-speaking Africa, began to take a more or less active role in wrestling with the problems of adapting inherited political systems to the realities of African life and with questions regarding the role of African culture and pluralism. They have founded intellectual journals based in Africa, and have been prolific writers. Not surprisingly, there have been occasional tensions between the second-generation intellectuals and the governments of the day.

The pattern of second-generation social thought may be illustrated in brief by a comparison of three individuals: Ali Mazrui of Kenya, W. E. (Kofi) Abraham of Ghana, and B. J. Dudley of Nigeria.

Mazrui obtained his doctorate at Oxford in political theory; Abraham, a logician, was the first African scholar elected to All Souls, Oxford; Dudley received his doctorate from London. All returned to Africa in the early 1960s, with appointments at Makerere, Legon, and Ibadan universities, respectively. All have been prolific, not only in their scholarly writings (see *Bibliography*) but in journals of opinion as well. Mazrui has been a regular contributor to the Kampala-based journal *Transition* (whose editor, Rajat Neogy, was jailed in early 1969, and later released, for publishing materials considered to be critical of the Uganda government). Dudley was a co-founder of a leading Nigerian journal *Nigerian Opinion* and has been a regular contributor to that journal. Abraham was an active contributor to party publications during the Nkrumah regime and was intimately involved with certain chapters of what is perhaps Nkrumah's major work, *Consciencism* (1964). All three individuals have been under pressure at various times from the government in power. In short, the second generation of intellectuals have tended to assume positions of leadership within the African universities and to become involved with the basic issues of nation-building.

3. THIRD-GENERATION INTELLECTUALS

The third postwar generation of intellectuals are the students presently enrolled in African universities. For the most part, they will not receive university education abroad and have grown up (over the past ten years) in African states which were independent but facing the full range of problems in nation-building. Such problems have come to include bureaucratic corruption, a slowing down of economic development, an increased significance of interethnic tensions in national life, and the continuing power of European economic interests in Africa. During 1968, student protest at such conditions resulted in riots, strikes, or disturbances temporarily closing down the major universities in Senegal, Upper Volta, Ivory Coast, Ethiopia, U.A.R., Tunisia, Algeria, Morocco,

South Africa, Kenya, and Madagascar. Student journals (as well as faculty journals) exist in most African universities.

It is ironic, perhaps, that in these student protests three generations of African intellectual elites have confronted each other. In Ghana, where some of the bitterest demonstrations were held, led by "third-generation" students, the present head-of-state (Dr. Busia) is a former "first-generation" professor of sociology, and many of the university personnel in Ghana are "second-generation" intellectuals (including W. E. Abraham, who has been released from jail and is back at the University in Legon).

It is not the purpose of this module to analyze the nature of the generational conflict, but merely to caution against an avoidance of the issues which are involved. Each generation has come to engage its intellectual energies with different issues. To the extent that differences exist as to what are the priority issues, there will continue to be ardent debate. Unlike many other countries where the generation gap represents vastly different life styles, in Africa the three-generation debate is taking place within an intellectual framework which is common to all participants. The wealth of literature in social thought which is coming out of these debates may be an important contribution to world intellectual history. (For further discussion of journals and newspapers, see the article by Panofsky and Koester in the *Guide to Resources*; for background on modern African thought see Wauthier, 1964 and July, 1967.)

92

Urban Design and Architecture

ARCHITECTURE REFERS TO THE FULL RANGE of structures built by man, from rudimentary shelters to grain elevators and skyscrapers. Their arrangement in space and interrelationship in form and function as part of the urban scene represents urban design. This, however, also involves a scale which extends beyond simple clusters of buildings to include the patterning of activity areas (residential, commercial, industrial, etc.) within the city. At this scale, urban design represents a major component of urban or town planning. Both of these scales of urban design—individual structures and clusters of related buildings, and the broader patterns of urban "ecology"—will be discussed in this module with regard to their distinctive developments in the African context. To an increasing extent, African cities and modern architecture are having an impact on international patterns of the building arts.

1. BUILDINGS AND ARCHITECTURE

Many of the traditional residential structures in rural Africa achieved an attractive and distinctive form which reflected a close adjustment to the local environment and available materials and technology. Nearly all were simple structures built with various combinations of grass, thatch, clay, and mud, with reinforcements of wood branches, wattle, and occasionally woven basketry. In the more centralized societies, political and religious buildings were much larger and more imposing structures—the stone cities of Kush; the massive churches, palaces, and stelae of Ethiopia (see Bidder, 1960); the palaces of the Yoruba kings (see Ojo, 1966); the mosques of Timbuktu and Jenne (see Prussin, 1968).

In those areas where pre-colonial urbanization existed, urban architectural style often represented a dense clustering of much the same type of house which existed in rural areas. Thus the typical Yoruba town consisted of compact groups of compounds densely packed near the Oba's palace in the center of the urban area. Each compound generally consisted of a rectangular clay and laterite structure surrounding a central court, which was rimmed with a terrace and protective "awning." The compound consisted of several rooms to house the extended family and was fairly cool and comfortable. In the Islamic urban areas, however, buildings followed the form of Middle Eastern houses—rectangular in shape, sometimes with two stories, built with mud generally reinforced with branches or palm fronds. The flat roofs with low parapets provided airy terraces where, in the cool evenings, the family could gather together. Large portions of such cities as Ibadan, Kano, and Mombasa still consist of structures very much like those in which the local people have lived for generations. The major concession to "modern" architectural materials has often been the adoption of corrugated iron, "tin" or aluminum roofs, and the widespread use of cement.

Most of the larger cities in Africa, however, especially those designated by Mabogunje (*Essays*, chap. 17) as "colonial" and "European," and major portions of the "rejuvenated traditional" towns, are composed (at least in the central areas and wealthier suburbs) of Western European or European-influenced buildings. During the early colonial period, most construction was derived from nineteenth-century European architecture. It was plain and practical but too often ugly and unsuited to the local environment.

Since World War II, however, a remarkable development of contemporary architecture has transformed the urban scene in Africa. Every major European architectural office is represented in Africa; often these firms work closely with local architects and designers, creating an effective blend between African and Western forms and styles. Such groups have produced some of the freshest and most attractive solutions to tropical architecture and urban design, especially in the construction of major public buildings. The degree to which these structures and styles have been accepted by Africans has suggested to many observers a high degree of commonality between traditional African forms and contemporary European forms, especially with respect to simplification, economy of decoration, and functional orientation. African students who move from simple huts to the modern Le Corbusier-like buildings at the major universities (some of which, like Ahmadu Bello in northern Nigeria, have large architectural degree-programs) appear to make the shift easily. Furthermore, it is remarkable how aesthetically pleasing and comfortable many of these modern buildings are on the African landscape.

Some of the outstanding examples of modern architecture in Africa include hotels such as the Ambassador in Accra, the Pan-Afric in Nairobi, the Kilimanjaro in Dar es Salaam, and the Premier in Ibadan; the University College Hospital in Ibadan (designed by a Chicago firm); and nearly all the major African universities. The University of Ibadan, largely designed by the British firm of Maxwell Fry in conjunction with local architects, is particularly attractive. The careful attention to ventilation through the use of louvered vents and concrete sun-screens has produced a remarkably airy and cool atmosphere. In addition, light colors are used in the concrete and the grillwork. Some of the more recently constructed faculty residences are especially well designed. Huge screened-in porches surround spacious living and dining rooms, from which they are separated by sliding glass doors. These houses tend to remain cool, even during the day, without air conditioning (which is available in the bedrooms and study). (For further discussion of trends in architecture, see Kulterman, 1969.)

2. URBAN DESIGN AND TOWN PLANNING

Town planning is both a practical necessity in Africa and an aesthetic challenge. As noted in Modules 45, 46, and 47, most large African cities are growing at rates which are among the highest in the world. Planning is necessary to ensure that transportation, sewage, health, shopping, and residential facilities are available. Such planning is occurring both within African metropolitan government circles and by contract with European firms.

The Institute of Tropical Architecture in London, for example, is working closely on at least two major town-planning schemes in Africa: the Agege suburb of Lagos, Nigeria, and the Gezira township in Sudan. Indigenous sociologists and geographers as well as engineers and architects work together to design the urban infrastructure and provide the cost-accounting which will both be acceptable to the local people and within the financial means of the government. Published town-planning reports are available for many major cities in Africa, such as Kano (see Trevallion, 1966), Kaduna (see Lock, 1967), and Kampala. The Tema project in Ghana, one of the earliest (begun in the 1950s) and most imaginative town-planning schemes, has come to fruition. Since Accra is not a good ocean port, the nearby site of Tema was selected and developed, virtually from nothing, into a modern, well-planned, combination residential, industrial, and port town (see Amarteifio *et al.*, 1966).

The large cities in French-speaking Africa, to an even greater extent than in English-speaking Africa, are modern and well designed. They tend to be laid out in a gridlike symmetry which is reminiscent of Paris or Washington D.C., the first planned city in the United States. In several French-speaking areas, the "traditional" cities have been bulldozed down to make room for a more gridlike reconstruction as modern cities (for example, the Hausa town of Tahoua in Niger Republic).

In other areas, however, the traditional towns have remained standing in immediate proximity to the "new cities," often providing an aesthetic reminder of the cultural dualism of modern Africa. The old and new cities of Fez, Casablanca, and Marrakesh (in Morocco), and those of Kano, Sokoto, and Ibadan (in Nigeria) represent a pattern which is not unique to Africa (it is perhaps best illustrated by Istanbul, Turkey) but which has become characteristic of many cities in Africa.

The growth of modern airports, which are usually several miles outside of town, has resulted in the mushrooming of modern supporting complexes (including new hotels, clinics, shopping districts, tourist facilities, etc.). These developments have provided an aesthetic and practical challenge. The airport and supporting complex of Dakar is perhaps one of the most beautiful in the world, overlooking warm beaches and linked by a modern highway to the city of Dakar. The airport in Lagos has precipitated the development of a wealthy and modern supporting complex.

In summary, the growth of towns and cities in Africa has often resulted in the overcrowding and shanty-towns which are described in Module 47. It has also, however, resulted in some of the most imaginative architecture and urban design observable in the modern world.

93
___

Visual Arts and Music

THE BEST IN CONTEMPORARY AFRICAN ART AND MUSIC represents a striking blend of traditional African styles and motifs with a variety of external influences, primarily Western and Islamic. At the same time, however, there has been a proliferation of poor "imitation" art, often crudely executed and highly commercialized (such as the airport curios which have been imported in increasing numbers to Europe and America). In this module, some attention will be given to both of these distinctive features of contemporary African art and music.

1. CONTEMPORARY VISUAL ART IN AFRICA

Traditional African sculpture played an important role in liberating "modern art" from its nineteenth-century naturalism. Although the social meaning deriving from its functional use was neglected, traditional African interpretations of form and expression powerfully influenced such outstanding Western artists as Picasso, Braque, Klee, Roualt, Modigliani, Derain, and Vlaminck. Today, many African artists have become increasingly part of a cosmopolitan world of modern art, working with both universal genres and distinctly African themes. (For a list of over 300 African artists working in 25 countries, see E. S. Brown, 1966.)

In the period just prior to the late 1950s, there appeared to be an aesthetic lull in African art. Traditional art seemed to be "fossilizing," as traditional carvers either became carpenters or joined together in cooperatives to produce curios for Western tourists. As noted in the excellent volume by Ulli Beier, an Austrian refugee who has encouraged the growth of contemporary African art through his many workshops, this commercialized art is

> hideous because it is carried out without conviction or care and simply repeats the empty forms of tradition. In many areas the carvers have become completely cynical and specialize in forging antiquities (Beier, 1968).

The spirit of optimism and confidence which preceded independence, however, generated an enthusiastic rebirth of African art, first in the form of bright and colorful "popular art," and then in what Beier calls "the coming of the intellectual African artist." Popular art (within the African context) produced the oddly attractive cement lions on Yoruba houses and the elaborate concrete and wooden grillwork on homes and public buildings, elaborate paintings and murals throughout Africa, and the renewed attention to textile design and embroidery. The "intellectual African artist" on the other hand has produced some of the world's finest contemporary art in nearly every medium. Even tourist art in certain areas has begun to evolve away from empty imitation of "traditional" art and toward original and interesting forms. One good example is the appearance of the tremendously diverse and non-serialized carvings of the Makonde, a group who migrated from Mozambique to Tanzania (mainly Dar es Salaam) to work for the tourist shops (see Stout, 1967).

An outstanding artists' colony has developed in the city of Oshogbo (Nigeria), largely focused at the Mbari Mbayo Club. Beier, who played a major role in Oshogbo, describes in detail the incredible range of art and artists to emerge in this area. In his *Contemporary Art in Africa* (1968) there are descriptions and illustrations of the intricate and surrealistic gouaches and etchings of Twins Seven-Seven (one of the best known of the Oshogbo artists), the beadwork and mosaics of Jimoh Buraimoh, the sensitive and sophisticated oil paintings of Muraina Oyelemi, the gentle and decorative aluminum reliefs of Ashiru Olatunde, and the enchanting cement sculpture of the Oshun Shrine (produced in large part by Suzanne Wenger, an Austrian artist who has lived in Nigeria since 1950, and who, having become deeply absorbed into Yoruba culture, is now a priestess of Obatala, the Yoruba creator god). The enormous individualism in the art produced in Oshogbo alone illustrates how difficult it is to speak of African artists in general terms.

Beier also describes similar developments elsewhere in Africa, particularly the successful art school founded by Frank McEwan in Salisbury. A key factor in the creative excellence of the Oshogbo, Salisbury, and a few other schools, was the method of "teaching." Only minimal formal training was given. Instead, the African artists received materials, a place to work, limited financial encouragement, attention, and — perhaps most important — solitude (see Crowley, in Carter and Paden, 1969).

It is appropriate to conclude this section with one further quote from Beier (p. 14):

> The African artist has refused to be fossilized. . . . The African artist does not hesitate to adopt new materials, be inspired by foreign art, look for a different role in society. New forms, new styles and new personalities are emerging everywhere and this contemporary African art is rapidly becoming as rich and as varied as were the more rigid artistic conventions of several generations ago.

2. CONTEMPORARY MUSIC IN AFRICA

As in the other arts, contemporary music in Africa is emerging as a blend of traditional and modern influences. Much of this music is becoming known in the United States through record albums and visiting African performers. Thus, the songs of South African vocalist Miriam Makeba (RCA Victor), the Afro-percussion of Olatunji (Columbia), and even the innovative chorale music of the *Missa Luba* (Philips), sung by Congolese of the Luba ethnic group, are all readily available. The visiting performances of the Ballets Africaines or the Ghana Dancers (under the direction of Master Drummer Dr. Nketia) are known through both live performances and television coverage.

In Africa itself, however, there is an extremely broad range of musical innovation. This seems to be occurring in three distinct contexts: (1) the universities, (2) the churches, (3) the night clubs.

In the African universities, both through formal disciplines and through informal improvisation, there is a broad range of experimentation. At Makerere University (Uganda) recently, the first all-African "grand opera" (as distinguished from traditional folk opera, as among the Yoruba) was presented. It was composed, directed, and performed by Africans. At the University of Ghana, Legon there have been two decades of experimentation with synthesizing West Indian calypso, West African high life, and European classical music forms. The solo guitar improvisation of musician-scholars such as Onyena or Wiredu are clearly precursors of baroque jazz in this country.

In the churches of Africa, musical innovation has occurred largely in the Zionist and independency churches (see Module 51). Traditional drumming is used in some of the European imported hymns, which are modified almost beyond recognition. The *Missa Luba* and *Missa Bantu* of the Congo are Roman Catholic masses performed to African rhythm (both are available on Philips records). It should be mentioned that Islamic liturgies (called *Ishirinya*) have also been modified to African musical style. This is noticeable throughout the entire Sudanic belt.

The night clubs of Africa are world famous for their high life. This blend of jazz, calypso, and African traditional music is found in the many clubs which have mushroomed in every African city. Dozens of small-scale African recording companies turn out albums by name-bands which are avidly collected by young urban men and women.

In all three of these contexts (university, churches, clubs) there is an experimentation not only with musical forms (e.g., rhythm, harmony, scale, pitch) but with instrumentation as well. The electric guitar and the saxophone have joined with the full range of tonal drums and beaded calabashes to express the dynamism of the new Africa. (A regular column on contemporary African music, written by Alan Merriam, appeared in *Africa Report* prior to its editorial changes in late 1969, providing reviews and listings of records and books on African music; see also Merriam's *African Music on LP: An Annotated Discography*, published in 1970.)

Afro-American
Linkages

Africa and
Afro-American Identity

As discussed in Turner (*Essays*, chap. 30), there has been a wide variety of interpretations and feelings about Africa by black people in America. The shifts in feeling over time are particularly important and are likely to increase in intensity in the future.

1. INTELLECTUAL AND LITERARY INTERPRETATIONS

Increasingly in the twentieth century, Afro-American writers and intellectuals have tried to come to grips with the question of Africa and black identity. W. E. B. DuBois, who did his Ph.D. dissertation at Harvard in the late nineteenth century on the topic of the slave trade, later came to write extensively about the place of Africa in the modern world (see, for example, *The World and Africa*, 1965, originally published in 1946), and the relationship of Afro-Americans to Africa. His early position suggested that Afro-Americans were neither African nor American, but a unique amalgamation of the two cultures. While he did not espouse a "return to Africa," many of his mature years were spent in support of the nationalist movements and the Pan-African efforts in Africa. In his last years he took up residence in Ghana under the Nkrumah regime. (DuBois wrote three autobiographies in the course of his long life: see 1921, 1940, 1968.)

The intellectual career of Richard Wright is parallel to that of DuBois in many ways. He felt initially that Afro-Americans were neither African nor American, but a blend of both cultures. He too later took up residence in Ghana.

363

His interpretation of Africa is contained in a volume entitled *Black Power* (1954) which is an honest account of his difficulties as well as satisfactions in adjusting to African society.

The career of James Baldwin took him into "self-imposed exile" in Paris in the middle and late 1950s at precisely the time when many of the African intellectuals in Paris were involved in the negritude movement. Although Baldwin had close contacts with the circle of *Présence Africaine* writers and intellectuals, he did not become involved in the ideology of negritude. In some of his essays (e.g., *Nobody Knows My Name*, 1961) Baldwin records his impressions of the Paris African writers. In the early 1960s, Baldwin visited Africa for the first time, and the experience seems to have had a profound, if subtle, impact on his writing (see *The Fire Next Time*, 1963). In his most recent novel (*Tell Me How Long the Train's Been Gone*, 1968), Baldwin's protagonist is an Afro-American actor who recalls through interior monologue not only his own ghetto childhood but also his reverence for the beauty, mystery, and warmth of Africa—the distant motherland.

Among contemporary writers and intellectuals there are a wide range of references to Africa. Pulitzer-Prize-winning poet Gwendolyn Brooks seems to question the relevance of Senegalese poet Senghor to the life and death issues of the Chicago ghetto (see *In the Mecca*, 1968). Others, such as Samuel Allen and Mercer Cook, have been actively engaged in the translation of French-speaking African writers for American readers.

In the late 1950s, the *Présence Africaine* literary group in Paris gave impetus to the creation of the American Society of African Culture (AMSAC), located in New York. AMSAC has sponsored conferences to explore the relationship of Afro-American culture to African culture, and many of these conferences have been published in book form (see *Africa Seen by American Negroes*, 1958; and *The American Negro Writer and His Roots*, 1960). AMSAC also publishes a journal, *African Forum*, which deals with a full range of political, social, and literary issues. (For a recent assessment of "The Militant Black Writer in Africa and the United States," see Cook and Henderson, 1969; for an assessment of the "Sentiments of Negro American Leaders on Africa from 1800 to 1950," see Hill and Kilson, 1969.)

2. AFRICA AND BLACK CONSCIOUSNESS AT THE POPULAR LEVEL

Perhaps the most significant shift of perspectives on Africa in the 1960s has been the way in which Africa has become a reference point for the ordinary black American and is no longer the exclusive purview of the Afro-American intellectual. The manifestations of this shift have taken political, social, and cultural forms. Part of this shift has been directly due to the new role that Africa has assumed within the global context. Negative and pejorative images are being replaced by positive associations. According to C. Eric Lincoln:

> Many Negroes for whom Africa seemed as remote as the planet Jupiter now find themselves exhilarated and encouraged by the emergence of black national states in the once "dark" continent. But they also find themselves strangely threatened, for the African may leave his American brother behind as the only remaining symbol of racial inferiority, of the socially and politically *declassé* "Black Man" left in the world (Lincoln, 1961, pp. 9–10).

The result of this new image of Africa, together with the frustration at the slow pace of "integration" within the American context, led in 1966 to the emergence of "black power" as a new self-image and strategy, and to the interpretation of the situation of black people in America as a distinct type of colonialism (see Carmichael and Hamilton, 1967). The influence of Africa as a source of identity in the black-power era remains to be seen. "Afro" fashions, hair styles, mannerisms, and even the changing of names and the use of Swahili slogans have become especially evident in the younger elements of the black community.

In terms of the mass media, magazines such as *Ebony* and the *Negro Digest,* which have always covered Africa from a more-or-less middle-class point of view, have been joined by journals such as the *Liberator,* which seeks to reconstruct black nationalism in radical form within the United States. The *Liberator* differs from many earlier Afro-American journals in being frank in its dislike for those contemporary African leaders (such as the late Tom Mboya of Kenya) who have taken a nonrevolutionary approach to the "liberation" of black people in America. Interestingly, the *Black Panther Journal* (which is an organ of the party) differs from many of the black-nationalist approaches by stressing the solidarity of all oppressed groups rather than just black groups. In this, there seems to have been a conscious adaptation of the Nkrumah model of coalition behavior (which is distinctive partly for its emphasis on cooperation between ideologically radical forces, whatever their skin color). The letters from Eldridge Cleaver (writing from Africa) to Stokely Carmichael in *Ramparts* (September and October, 1969) focus precisely on the issue of "class" solidarity *vs.* "racial" solidarity.

Finally, it should be mentioned that television programs by Afro-Americans (especially in the northern urban areas) such as *Black Journal, For Blacks Only,* and *Our People* seem to devote a significant share of their time to the question of Afro-American interpretations of Africa. Such programming is explicitly directed to the average black person in America.

3. AFRICA AND AMERICAN BLACK-MUSLIM IDENTITIES

In 1913 a black man from North Carolina, Timothy Drew, moved to Newark, changed his name to Noble Drew Ali, and established a Moorish Science Temple.

During the years of World War I, Moorish Science attracted approximately 30,000 followers among the black communities of various northern cities. Such adherents changed their names to Muslim names, and adopted symbols to identify themselves as Muslim "Asiatics." The stress on *Moorish* identity (they insisted on being called "Moors") is interesting particularly because the Moors (as found in Morocco and Mauritania) are a mixture of light-skinned Berber peoples and dark-skinned African peoples. The Moorish Science temples declined in the 1930s after the death of Noble Drew Ali.

The vacuum left by Moorish Science was soon to be filled by the Nation of Islam. In 1930 W. D. Fard, who never publicly identified his country of origin, settled in Detroit and founded a Temple of Islam. By the time he "disappeared" four years later, the mantle of leadership had fallen on a young man who had moved to Detroit from Georgia in the 1920s—Elijah Muhammad (Elijah Poole). By 1960 the Nation of Islam (or "Black Muslims" as they came to be called) had approximately 100,000 members in 69 temples (mosques) in twenty-seven states (see Lincoln, 1961). The stress within the Nation of Islam is on black solidarity, and the rejection of Christianity as the religion of the white man. The ultimate goal of Elijah Muhammad is the repatriation of all American blacks to Africa. (For details of the Nation of Islam, see Essien-Udom, 1962.)

The best-known disciple of Elijah Muhammad was Malcolm X, who was minister of Temple 7 in Harlem. The writings of Malcolm X clearly stress the importance of Africa to black identity in America. Thus, in a speech at Harvard:

> We must stress the cultural roots of our forefathers, that will lend dignity and make the black man cease to be ashamed of himself. We have to teach our people something about our cultural roots. We have to teach them something of their glorious civilizations before they were kidnapped by your grandfathers and brought over to this country. Once our people are taught about the glorious civilization that existed on the African continent, they won't be ashamed of who they are. We will reach back and link ourselves to those roots, and this will make the feeling of dignity come into us; we will feel that as we lived in times gone by, we can in like manner today. If we had civilizations, cultures, societies, and nations hundreds of years ago, before you came and kidnapped us and brought us here, so we can have the same today. The restoration of our cultural roots and history will restore dignity to the black people in this country (Malcolm X, 1968, p. 142).

At another lecture at Harvard, he told the predominantly white audience: "The only way you can really understand the black man in America and the changes in his heart and mind is to fully understand the heart and mind of the black man on the African continent" (Malcolm X, 1968, p. 168).

The first visit of Malcolm X to Africa on his return from Mecca in spring, 1964, is recorded in his autobiography (1966). He was clearly overwhelmed by the positive reception he received in the various African countries. The split between Malcolm X and Elijah Muhammad (which led Malcolm X to establish a counterpart organization in New York) was partly over the issue of the appropriate relationship between Afro-American Muslims, the international world of Islam, and the black peoples of the African continent. Malcolm X appeared to be moving away from a purely racist point of view and away from the back-to-Africa dreams of Elijah Muhammad, toward closer cooperation with Muslim communities of whatever color throughout the world (while at the same time calling for more black-nationalist activity in the U.S.). The reaction of Eldridge Cleaver (who is a supporter of Malcolm X rather than Elijah Muhammad) to this ideological matter is found in *Soul on Ice* (1968) and *Post Prison Writings and Speeches* (1969).

4. AFRO-AMERICAN IDENTITY AND AFRICAN STUDIES

The demand for black-studies programs in American educational institutions has raised the question of the relationship of African studies to Afro-American studies and black studies. A whole series of questions arise from this issue which are currently being debated within the university community (see Easum, 1969; Kilson, 1969; the Harvard University *Report of the Faculty Committee on African and Afro-American Studies,* 1969; and the proceedings of the Yale Symposium on *Black Studies in the University,* edited by Robinson *et al.,* 1969). The issues are being resolved in many different ways, depending on local needs and circumstances. This module will not attempt answers but will try to summarize some of the questions.

1. If Afro-American studies are to be related to African studies, what aspects of African studies should be stressed? Should it be the pre-Western empires and states? The confrontation between Europe and Africa? The slave trade? The rise of contemporary culture in Africa?

2. What African languages, if any, should be taught in American schools? Only those with a written literature, such as Amharic? Those with a political vocabulary of racial confrontation, such as Swahili in East Africa or Zulu in South Africa? Those from West Africa, such as Yoruba or Twi, where most Afro-Americans originated? Or those languages such as Hausa and Arabic, which are among the largest language groups in Africa? (For a discussion of the rationale for studying Swahili, see Ron Karenga, in Robinson, 1969, p. 54.)

3. In what ways can Afro-Americans ensure that they will have a part in the inquiry into their historical roots? (The early work of W. L. Hansberry, Rayford Logan, and Elliott Skinner is well known and has been important in the reassessment of African history and culture.) What should be the relationship between nationalist mythology and historical reality in black studies? (See Kilson, in Robinson, 1969, for problems of the intellectual validity of black studies.) Does the younger generation of Afro-American scholars who are now working in African studies (such as Sylvester Whitaker, James Gibbs, Martin Kilson, I. K.

Sundiata, John Willis, William Brown, and Joseph Harris) have any special responsibility to the development of cultural identity within the Afro-American community?

The answers to these questions will be based in part on certain intellectual considerations and principles. In many cases, however, the issues will probably be resolved by political expediency, which has so often characterized black-white relations in the United States.

95

Africa and Afro-American Social Change

THE EMERGENCE OF AFRICAN-BASED IDENTITIES in contemporary America (discussed in Module 94) is clearly part of the larger process of social change. This module will discuss some of the Afro-American organizations and movements which are both a product of social change and are engaged in social change. A number of movements have come and gone (or were transformed): The National Movement for the Establishment of a Forty-Ninth State, The National Union of People of African Descent, the Peace Movement of Ethiopia, the United Africa National Movement. Others are emerging at the present time (e.g., the Organization of Afro-American Unity, formed by the late Malcolm X). On the American political spectrum some of these movements have been radical, some moderate, and some conservative. It is interesting that, since the Civil War, most of the back-to-Africa movements have been supported by the Ku Klux Klan and similar "white citizens" groups. In this module we will discuss three topics: (1) the back-to-Africa movement, (2) contemporary Afro-American organizations and movements, and (3) the impact of Africa on the emergence of Afro-American leadership. This module will not discuss the important topic of Afro-American religious movements in relationship to Africa.

1. THE BACK-TO-AFRICA MOVEMENT IN AMERICA

The back-to-Africa movement of the nineteenth century, which focused on the return of freed slaves to the newly created state of Liberia (meaning "Liberty") has been discussed briefly in Module 29. It was mentioned that many of the Afro-Americans in Liberia (or Americo-Liberians, as they formerly called themselves) seemed to reflect a disdain for the "pagan" Africans which led to intensive Afro-American missionary efforts among the African peoples as well as to the almost complete separation of the Americo-Liberian community from the interior "Protectorate" Africans. In short, the Liberian experiment was deemed a return to a physical homeland but not to a cultural homeland.

In the 1920s a second major back-to-Africa movement gained momentum through the efforts of Marcus Garvey (see Cronon, 1955). Garvey was a Jamaican, who, in 1914, conceived the idea of a Universal Negro Improvement Association (UNIA) which would remove all American Negroes to an independent African state. In 1916, Garvey came to New York and from that base toured 38 states, preaching his manifesto of return to Africa. By the summer of 1919 Garvey was able to claim two million adherents in 30 branches across the country. Race relations in the United States at that time were at a critical stage. Black veterans were returning from service duty, yet within the first year after the war more than 70 Negroes were lynched. In the summer of 1919 there were 25 race riots in cities across the country (in Chicago 38 were killed and 537 injured). The support among segments of the black community for a withdrawal from the America in the 1920s was strong and visible. Within this context Garvey was heard when he said:

> We shall now organize the 400,000,000 Negroes of the world into a vast organization to plant the banner of freedom on the great continent of Africa. . . . If Europe is for the Europeans, then Africa shall be for the black peoples of the world (quoted in Lincoln, 1961, p. 59).

In 1920, at the first international convention of the UNIA, Garvey was elected provisional president of the African Republic, and millions of dollars were subscribed by followers to the various commercial enterprises which were established to achieve the end of return to Africa—especially the Black Star Steamship Line. Arrangements were made with the government of Liberia for 100,000 Garvey followers to settle in Liberia in 1924. The American government stepped in at this point: pressure was put on the Liberian government to withdraw the offer (the land was instead leased to Firestone Rubber Company), and in 1925 Garvey was jailed for "using the mails to defraud." In 1927 he was deported (since he was not an American citizen), and he died in London in 1940. The movement dissipated after the imprisonment of Garvey.

The influence of Garvey, however, has continued to be felt. His writings were collected and published by his wife (see *The Philosophy of Marcus Garvey*, 1967). Malcolm X recounts in his autobiography how his father (before his murder in Michigan) had been a Garvey follower and recruiter in the Midwest. The back-to-Africa movement of Elijah Muhammad and the Nation of Islam (see Module 94) seems to have derived some impetus from the Garvey movement.

2. CONTEMPORARY AFRO-AMERICAN ORGANIZATIONS

Although there are certain contemporary Afro-American organizations which espouse return-to-Africa (such as the Black Hebrews, who have recently experimented with settlement in Liberia), the majority clearly do not. The more radical of the contemporary groups espouse complete separation and the creation of a sovereign black state in the southern part of the United States—"The Republic of New Africa" (see Robert Sherrill, 1969). Other groups, such as the Black Panther Party, are seeking a drastic return of "all power to the people" within a reformed multiracial United States (see Gene Marine, 1969; Eldridge Cleaver, 1968). Other groups, such as major segments of the Student Non-Violent Co-ordinating Committee (SNCC) and of the Congress of Racial Equality (CORE) seem to be advocating cultural pluralism and ethnic restratification within the present constitutional framework (for SNCC, see H. Rap Brown, 1969; for CORE, see Floyd McKissick, 1969). By contrast, the Urban League (see Whitney Young, 1969); the National Association for the Advancement of Colored People (NAACP); the Southern Christian Leadership Conference (see Martin Luther King, Jr. 1968); and more specifically Africa-oriented groups such as Crossroads Africa (see James Robinson, 1968) are clearly dedicated to the integration of black and white people in America. It may be useful to comment on several of the less well-known organizations in more detail.

The Republic of New Africa (RNA) developed as a concept and then as an organization during the ten-year "exile" (1959–69) in Africa and elsewhere of Robert F. Williams, formerly president of the NAACP in Monroe, North Carolina. The stated purpose (Sherrill, 1969) of the organization is to gain voting control in five southern states—Mississippi, Alabama, Louisiana, Georgia, and South Carolina—through lawful means (where possible), i.e., the return-migration of northern black people to the South and the exercise of voting control in local elections. The RNA has formally petitioned the U.S. government to give them $400 billion (in reparations) to help in the development of the five states in the Republic of New Africa.

The Black Panther Party (BPP) was formed in 1966 in San Francisco by Huey P. Newton and Bobby Seale. The original ten-point program is still the core of the movement and is intended as a manifesto for black people in America: (1) freedom for blacks to determine the destiny of the black community; (2) full employment; (3) housing fit for human beings; (4) black men exempt from military service; (5) decent education; (6) an end to the "robbery by the white racist businessmen of black people in their community"; (7) an end to police brutality; (8) release of black people from jail on the grounds that they were tried by white juries; (9) trial by jury of peers—i.e., persons of same socioeconomic and racial background; (10) a reaffirmation, word-for-word, of the U.S. Declaration of Independence. In the 1968 national election the BPP joined in coalition with white and Spanish-speaking ("brown") caucus groups to form the Peace and Freedom Party. Since 1966, a number of the Black Panthers have been jailed, and Eldridge Cleaver, minister of information for the party, has served as chief spokesman (see Cleaver, 1967 and 1968). Cleaver left the United States in 1968 and has been living in Algeria.

The literature on SNCC, CORE, Urban League, NAACP, and other such groups is readily available and will not be summarized in this module. In most cases there is not an explicit statement of intended relationship with the new African states, but in several cases this is only the distinction between nationalism which is spiritual and nationalism which is based on particular geographic areas. With the newer organizations, the existence of independent Africa forms a homeland, whether in fact or in imagination. Significantly, three of the most prominent leaders of Afro-American organizations (Carmichael, Cleaver, Williams) have taken up residence in Africa after skirmishes with the law in the United States. Almost all of the leaders mentioned above have traveled in Africa.

3. PATTERNS OF AFRO-AMERICAN LEADERSHIP

The black leadership in contemporary America represents all points on the political spectrum, both in terms of socioeconomic policy and in terms of race-relations policy. One of the possible impacts of modern Africa on the Afro-American community has been to legitimate a full range of black leadership styles. In Africa from 1960 to 1963 there was often bitter tension between the leaders of the "conservative" states (Monrovia group) and leaders of the "radical" states (Casablanca group). In 1963 both groups agreed to join together in the Organization of African Unity. Whether the causal linkage is direct or indirect, this pattern seems to have had some impact on the relations between Afro-American organizations and leaders in the United States (for example, the coalition behavior of black groups in Chicago vis-à-vis the construction trade unions).

As a way of dramatizing the idea of variation in leadership styles (or ideology) it might be possible to compare some of the Afro-American leaders mentioned here and in Module 94 with some of the African leaders. The similarities of certain sets are striking, but it is more as a basis of discussion than as an exercise in social science that the following parallels are suggested. (1) Julius Nyerere (president of Tanzania) and the late Martin Luther King, Jr. (SCLC)—both are intellectual and religious men representing nonviolence and racial cooperation; (2) Félix Houphouet-Boigny (president of Ivory Coast) and Whitney Young (Urban League)—both are pragmatic on matters of working within the existing capitalist economic system; (3) Jomo Kenyatta (president of Kenya) and W.E.B. Du Bois—both are scholars and have written extensively about their own cultures, yet both have been militantly active in liberation; (4) Sékou Touré (president of Guinea) and Eldridge Cleaver (BPP) — both are young and militant but emphasize radical ideology rather than skin color, and both are Muslim; (5) Léopold Senghor (president of Senegal) and James Baldwin — both are writers and essayists concerned with problems of identity, yet both retain close personal relations with the white world; (6) Kwame Nkrumah (former president of Ghana) and the late Malcolm X — both were early leaders in "liberation" but focused on ideology rather than race; (7) Nnamdi Azikiwe (former president of Nigeria) and Roy Wilkins (NAACP) — both have been long-time proponents of economic self-help and use legal channels to achieve their ends, both are concerned with racial equality and harmony; (8) the late Patrice Lumumba (president of Congo-Kinshasa) and H. Rap Brown (SNCC) — both are young and articulate, refusing to compromise with the Establishment, their authority based on skill in protest rather than the wielding of power; (9) Obafemi Awolowo (Nigeria) and Floyd McKissick (CORE) — both are constitutional lawyers and are concerned to use law to restructure society; (10) Kenneth Kaunda (president, Zambia) and the Reverend Ralph Abernathy (SNCC) — both are religious and espouse nonviolence in pursuit of justice and liberation and thus bear a similar relationship to Nyerere and King.

A number of other parallels — or modifications of those discussed — might be suggested. In all cases multiple criteria exist for drawing comparisons: background, occupation, socioeconomic policies, race-relations policy, religious characteristics, intellectual propensities, age similarities, etc.

4. CONCLUSIONS

The impact of Africa on Afro-American social change has been noticeable in many areas in the twentieth century: in the Garvey movement, in the Nation of Islam (Black Muslims), and in the full range of organizations and leadership styles which have emerged in contemporary America. There are a number of ways in which Africa might influence the future of social change in America: (1) the basic question of cultural co-existence *vs.* separation of black people in white America may partly be determined by African attitudes; (2) the ways in which Afro-American affairs may become political issues in Africa once African states achieve greater economic and political strength (at present, the annual budget of New York is greater than the combined budgets of the Black African states); (3) the ways in which a fuller understanding of the cultural richness of the African heritage might influence the attitudes of both white and black America; (4) the change in world bipolarity patterns which would result from a "United States of Africa." There are some who might argue that the future of America rests partly in African hands.

96

African Interpretations of Multiracial America

THE IMPACT OF AFRICA on the Americas (as discussed in Modules 30, 94, and 95) has been considerable, although it will be the task of future historians to sift and judge the subtleties of this impact. Part of the impact has been the political symbolism of Africa: within fifteen years nearly forty African states were able to cast off colonialism and attain their freedom. Part of the impact has been the cultural symbolism of Africa: the rejection of complete assimilation into European civilization and the assertion of the validity of the African heritage. Part of the impact has been the symbolism of leadership styles: the legitimation of a variety of types of black leadership. Future developments in Africa may do much to influence both white and black America. In this module we will try to assess the attitudes of black Africans toward both black and white America.

1. AFRICAN STUDENTS IN AMERICA: INTERPRETATIONS

At the moment there are several thousand African students studying in the United States. In the past, although the numbers were fewer, African graduates returned home to become prominent in all aspects of national development. Many have recorded their impressions of the United States in various written forms. The autobiography of former president Nkrumah of Ghana (1957) contains chapters on his experience at Lincoln University and his work in this country after his graduation. The collected speeches of former president Azikiwe of Nigeria (1961) include many given to various audiences in America both as a student at Lincoln University and later. He stresses his respect for the "democratic experiment" in America but is essentially concerned about the potentially constructive relationship between Africa and Afro-Americans.

One of the more literary-minded students writing about America is the Nigerian author (and current editor of the journal *Black Orpheus*) J. P. Clark, who wrote *America Their America* (1964) on the basis of his graduate experience at Princeton University. The book expresses what might be described as "culture shock" both at the values and behavior of mainstream white America and at the anomie of Harlem.

One of the few African students who has focused his graduate research on black-white relations within the United States is E. U. Essien-Udom, who is currently chairman of the Department of Political Science at the University of Ibadan (Nigeria). Working out of the University of Chicago, he undertook a major study of the Nation of Islam ("Black Muslims"), which was later published as *Black Nationalism—A Search for Identity in America* (1962). Although he is not Muslim, his sympathetic yet scholarly approach to the subject has made this book the major work to date on religious-syncretistic black nationalism in America.

A comment on the attitudes of African students toward multiracial America is the frequent phenomenon of their own reorientation from ethnic or national identities to an African identity (see Klineberg and Zavalloni, 1969), comparable perhaps to the emergence of an African identity among African students in Paris after World War II (see N'Diaye, 1962). This new-found African identity may be partly attributable to the structure and perceptions of American society, which seem to foster a sense of black/white distinctiveness on the part of African students.

2. AFRICAN STATESMEN: INTERPRETATIONS

A large number of African statesmen have visited the United States, either through private auspices or on official business at the United Nations or in Washington, D.C. A central characteristic of most African leaders has been their reluctance to "get involved" in the internal politics of the United States (at least publicly), since they are required to work with whatever government is in power. However, even on the official level there are three major themes which seem to characterize the observations of such leaders: their opposition to racism in any form (white or black), their opposition to colonialism and imperialism in any form, and their priority need to further the economic development of their respective countries. Thus, they tend to be critical of racist elements in the United States and of those aspects of United States foreign policy which appear to be imperialistic; yet they admire the level of economic development which has been achieved by the United States. The innovative and dynamic aspects of American technology, combined with the considerable scope of American financial resources, are frequently regarded in sharp contrast to those of the European states (including Britain and France).

Several of the African leaders, however, have been more verbal in their comments on American society—both black and white. One of the most recent episodes was the confrontation of the late Tom Mboya (minister of economic planning and development in Kenya) with portions of the black community in Harlem on March 18, 1969, over the issue of "back-to-Africa" movements. Earlier in the year, the Kenya parliament had debated the issue of unrestricted migration for black Americans who wished to return to Africa. It was decided that Afro-Americans would have to go through the same procedure as any other would-be citizens (including those from other African states). In his presentation of the reasons for the position taken by the Kenya government, Mboya expressed his own view that Afro-Americans might help Africa more by fighting racism and economic oppression in this country than by retreating to Africa. A bitter controversy developed at the Harlem meeting and has continued since that time. (See, for example, the July, 1969, issue of the *Liberator;* Mboya elaborates his views in his article in the *New York Times Magazine,* July 13, 1969.)

This controversy, however, should be seen within the broader context of Mboya's perception of America:

> I have seen black ghettos in America. I have seen individuals living under degrading conditions. Black poverty is more outrageous in America than in my own country because it is surrounded by unparalleled wealth. Thus, for black America the problem of equality looms larger than the problem of development; but they are similar in that the achievement of both requires massive institutional changes. . . . Africans are highly conscious of the plight of black America, and they will be suspicious of the intentions of American foreign policy until they are convinced that the goal of American domestic policy is social justice for all (Mboya, 1969, p. 30).

In contrast to Mboya's attitude toward unrestricted Afro-American migration to Africa has been that of the former president of Ghana, Kwame Nkrumah. Although his ten years' experience in this country may have given him a more detailed backlog of perceptions and grievances, his major criticism has been against the "capitalist" system itself. In many of his later books (e.g., see *Neo-Colonialism*, 1965) he came to identify American capital with international finance, and international finance with the continued domination of the African economic and political systems by the West. During his regime a large number of Afro-Americans were encouraged to migrate to Ghana.

3. THE AFRICAN "COMMON MAN": INTERPRETATIONS

Most Africans have had no opportunity to visit the United States. Their interpretations of the United States are usually based on two sources: the news media within Africa and Americans (both black and white) they meet or have heard about in Africa. The news media, particularly radio, extend to all parts of Africa, and broadcasting is increasingly conducted in both European and vernacular languages. The ordinary African has an opportunity to listen regularly to international news from many points of view, including items regarding the United States. In northern Nigeria, for example, a farmer with a transistor radio might listen (in Hausa) to radio Nigeria, radio Cairo, the French and British overseas broadcasting services, and any of several broadcasts from surrounding countries (e.g., Dahomey, Niger, Chad, or Cameroon). Most of these broadcasting services would carry news about the United States, but the net result is frequently a series of conflicting interpretations.

Perhaps the major source of interpretations becomes first- , or second- , or third-hand observations of those Americans who, for some reason, are in Africa. Historically, Americans in Africa have represented many different interests (see Clendenen, *et al.*, 1966). The largest category has probably been American missionaries. Many of these missionaries are from evangelical sects (e.g., Jehovah's Witnesses). Nearly all of them are white, and many are from the southern part of the United States. Such missionaries are usually dedicated to life-time work in Africa, speak the local languages, may disapprove of local customs, and appear to convey (whether intended or not) a subtle type of "separate but equal" racism (or at best paternalism).

A second category of Americans in Africa are those who have some connection with the American government. This includes embassy personnel, A.I.D. personnel, and the Peace Corps. There seems to be a marked difference in the perception by ordinary Africans of A.I.D. (Agency for International Development) technicians and Peace Corps volunteers. The A.I.D. technicians tend to remain isolated from the African community, and in fact seem to prefer to set up "little Americas." Their salaries are usually several times higher than those of their African counterparts. Many of the A.I.D. technicians seem to come from the American Midwest, and usually have two-year commitments to work in Africa. This image of affluent, middle-aged, technically oriented, homogeneous, ethnocentric America is sharply offset by the Peace Corps volunteers, most of whom are recent college graduates, primarily from the East or West Coasts of America, ethnically integrated, getting salaries comparable to their African counterparts, and who pride themselves on speaking local languages, eating local foods, and learning local customs.

A third category of Americans is a mélange of businessmen (of whom there are relatively few in Africa), foundation executives, visiting scholars, and ordinary tourists.

It is important to note that until recently most Americans who visited Africa were white, and African perceptions of them probably corroborated the general image of "Europeans." In the post-colonial period (that is, since the independence of Ghana in 1957) a number of Afro-Americans have gone to Africa in a variety of capacities. Several have been U.S. ambassadors (e.g., in Ghana, Senegal, and Upper Volta); a number have been involved in Peace Corps administration or consular service; a fairly large group have been in business or publishing; and the Peace Corps and academic groups have been heavily represented by Afro-Americans. Although it is extremely difficult to generalize, it is probably true to say that most ordinary Africans regard Afro-Americans as Americans first and black men second. Skin color is used less frequently in Africa as a means of categorizing people than language and/or culture. Since Afro-Americans are perceived as culturally and linguistically American, they have tended to be labeled "American."

In short, there is probably a great deal of confusion or mixed imagery regarding social and political developments in America, yet at the same time there is a great deal of insight regarding the full range of race relations between Americans.

Study Questions

Study Questions:
Africa and the Modern World

THE FOLLOWING STUDY QUESTIONS are both analytical and judgmental. A student should have a clear overview of Africa's role in the modern world but should also be willing to identify and discuss the values and moral implications involved in each of the major issues.

1. What are the major concepts of supranationalism? Are they identified with particular African spokesmen? With different periods in time? What kind of regionalism emerged during the colonial period? Why did the French break up their two large federations (in West and Equatorial Africa)? How does the legacy of economic regionalism affect patterns of interstate cooperation and conflict? What factors do you feel are most important in interstate economic integration (e.g., infrastructural linkage, common currency, free flow of raw materials/manpower/goods, telecommunications, free flow of capital, etc.)? What effect would a suprastate regional market have on investment priorities and location of industry? Is Pan-Africanism primarily an ideological and political program, or is it an economic program? What would be the differences between these two approaches? Has ideology changed? Has it increased or diminished in effect since independence? What has been the role of the OAU in the post-independence period? What are the prospects for political federation in Africa? For economic union? What are the major advantages of economic union? Are there any disadvantages? Why do you feel it has been so difficult to establish economic (or political) unions in Africa? What are the prospects for a United States of Africa?

2. What has been the impact of Africa on the United Nations as an organization? Do you think that very small states should be allowed to have voting status equal to large states in the General Assembly? In what alternative ways might small African states have a voice in world affairs? Do you think that African states will be willing to give up sovereignty some day to merge into a United States of Africa? What would be the difference in impact on world affairs if the African states spoke with a single voice?

3. What is meant by neocolonialism? What are the advantages and disadvantages to Africa of close economic links with Europe? What is the general state of relations between the African states and their former metropoles? How important was President de Gaulle to the close links between France and most of the French-speaking states? What has been the fate of states which have cut back contact with their former metropoles (e.g., Mali, Guinea, Ghana)?

4. To what extent has Soviet–United States competition carried over into Africa? What might be the strategic significance, if any, of Africa in such East-West competition? What types of trade relations have developed between the United States and Africa? Why has Communism made little headway in the internal politics of most African states? How does "African socialism" as an ideology affect Soviet and/or American relations with Africa? To what extent has the Sino-Soviet conflict been carried over into Africa?

5. Does it make any sense to lump African states together with other poor, ex-colonial, nonwhite countries and refer to them as the "Third World"? Do the components of the Third World have any common interests? Is the racial criterion (i.e., "nonwhite") more or less important than the economic (i.e., "poor") criterion or the political (i.e., "ex-colonial") criterion? How serious is the potential conflict between Asians and black Africans in Africa? What would likely be the role of India or Pakistan if such a conflict were to develop?

6. Does it make political, economic, or cultural sense to include North Africa with the rest of Africa for purposes of political analysis? Are the North African states more likely to act as "Arab states" or as "African states" on international political issues? How is the Islamic linkage likely to affect African attitudes toward the Middle East crisis?

7. What are the white South African arguments *against* majority rule? Against any form of black political participation? What is the philosophy of apartheid? Have African resistance movements been possible in South Africa? What are the various means of decolonization in Portuguese Africa (including the possibility of rapid change in Portugal itself)? Does the United States (through NATO) support the Portuguese effort to repress African nationalists? What courses of action were open to Britain when faced with the rebellion of white Rhodesia? In what way, if at all, is the potential for conflict in southern Africa similar to the Middle East crisis?

8. Which of the arts in Africa have made the most significant contributions to world civilization? Is the contemporary form of most African arts—i.e., a synthesis of modern and traditional forms—turning out to be a dilution or an enhancement of African creative genius? Is there anything distinctive or unique about African urban design? Why has West Africa (both French- and English-speaking) produced a disproportionate share of African writers? Which languages should African writers use in their literature, poetry, drama, music? Are there any thematic differences between writers using French and those using English as a vehicle of expression?

9. What has been Africa's role in the creation of an Afro-American identity? To what extent do Afro-Americans consider Africa their homeland? What parallels, if any, can be identified between developments in Africa and those among the Afro-American population of the United States during the past two decades? What kind of role might African studies play in the growth of Afro-American studies? Is there a difference between Afro-American studies and black studies? What has been the African contribution to culture in the United States? What are the pros and cons of a back-to-Africa philosophy?

10. What kinds of interpretations of the United States have been made by African students studying in this country? What types of relationships have Africans in the United States had with Afro-Americans. To what extent is the concept of "diaspora" appropriate to a description of African/Afro-American linkages? What have been the African reactions to the variety of problems and proposed solutions regarding the position of Afro-Americans in the United States?

EPILOGUE

Social Science And Africa

98

Africa and the Concept of Social Science

THE CONCEPT OF SOCIAL SCIENCE is discussed by Paden (Essays, chap. 31) in terms of basic concepts, priorities of research, methods of data collection, methods of data analysis, and problems of research in Africa. It will be the purpose of Modules 98, 99, and 100 to summarize some of the social-science research which has been done in Africa, to indicate some of the research currently going on in Africa, and to examine the frontiers of future research. While research frontiers may not be of immediate interest in an introductory course on Africa, they may serve to indicate the areas of concern and ignorance within the social sciences, and perhaps to challenge younger people to consider committing their own intellectual resources to the problems ahead.

1. THE IDEA OF SOCIAL SCIENCE

Social science is primarily a process which seeks to record observations about human behavior and to discover the interrelationships between various kinds of human behavior. These two functions are often called *data collection* and *data analysis*. Much of the training in social science requires attention to *methods* of collection and analysis, since objectivity can be claimed only if the procedures by which data are collected and analyzed are made clear and explicit. The credibility of conclusions in social science is based partly on the credibility of the procedures followed. This does not mean that proper procedures will always result in proper conclusions. The sequence of procedures is basically the same as in the natural sciences: a problem is identified, hypotheses are proposed and tested, and conclusions are drawn.

One of the most difficult aspects of cross-cultural studies is the identification of meaningful problems rather than just the transfer of problems which are relevant in a Western context to a non-Western context. The entire intellectual structure of the three volumes of *The African Experience* implies the existence of a series of problems or areas of inquiry. A student who has gone through the materials in the *Syllabus* and *Essays* volumes should be able to do several things. First, he should be able to identify the range of issue selection, i.e., he should know what was not included as well as what was included. Second, he should be able to discuss the types of data sources which are available on all the major topics (for example, much of the existing data at the moment on the early empires of the Western Sudan depend on a handful of Arabic manuscripts; the evidence for the civilization of Nok depends mainly on terracotta heads dug up by archaeologists; the evidence for the skin color of the early Egyptians rests largely on some frescos along the Nile Valley). Third, he should be able to identify the way in which inferences regarding general conclusions are drawn from specific instances (e.g., conclusions regarding marriage patterns in Africa from a sample of about 90 ethnic societies). Finally, he should be able to recognize, both here and in the *Essays,* when the authors are giving personal judgments and when they are presenting "facts." It will be noted that this volume is not intended to be a presentation of social-science *findings* on Africa. This volume is designed primarily for *teaching* purposes, and part of the teaching process should be to encourage the student to *discover* the problems for himself. Hopefully, the study-question sections will help in this process.

In this discovery process, certain concepts may be useful to the student. For example, the idea of a *system* is fundamental in social science. A system refers to the processes by which entities are interactive within a context, so that a change in one entity will produce a change in another. This concept of system may help the student to see African societies and empires not only as isolated interactive universes in their own right but also as entities within larger systems of international trade and interurban linkages. European or Arab contact with Black Africa usually implies some type of larger system. One of the most obvious examples of a system is the so-called "triangle trade," in which European powers of the eighteenth century bought slaves in Africa in exchange for manufactured goods and traded the slaves in the New World for raw materials (from which they produced more manufactured goods).

There are many different levels of universes (i.e., systems) which might be useful for an analysis of contemporary Africa; one which has been stressed in this syllabus has been the emergence of national systems, i.e., the establishment of linkages between the various elements within a country so that there is an interactive effect. At the same time, the African states are being linked up to a variety of international systems, including one which might be called "Pan-African." The future development of a Pan-African system will depend very much on the technical and infrastructural linkages which are being forged bit by bit, but also on the development of a common identity and some degree of value congruence (see Module 57).

2. METHODS OF DATA COLLECTION

There is no fixed number of techniques which qualify as appropriate methods of data collection. Data may be inferred from a fragment of pottery, from a radiocarbon dating, from an autobiographical book by an African leader, or from the price of yams in the Ibadan market. The student should be able to judge what kinds of data are appropriate to particular problems.

The five techniques of data collection mentioned by Paden, however, seem to represent the major methods of contemporary social science. In most re-search circumstances a combination of methods would be used, i.e., the so-called "multimethod" approach.

a. Participant Observation

Clearly a major type of data is that generated by participants in the activity under observation. When O'Brien writes about the United Nations in the Congo (1962) he is drawing on his experience as a member of the United Nations team in the Congo. When Kenyatta writes about initiation rites in Kikuyu society (1964) he is writing as a participant. When a young Ghanaian student named Emmanuel Hevi writes about *The Dragon's Embrace* (1967) he is drawing on his own experiences as a student in China.

The three examples above, however, also illustrate the major problem of participant observation: the fact that a participant often has an "ax to grind." Thus, certain guidelines are necessary both to evaluate the existing participant-observation literature and to encourage future studies. (Such guidelines as well as other types of participation, are discussed by Paden; also see Bruyn, 1966; Ellis, 1969; Bowen, 1964; Powdermaker, 1966.)

b. Interviews

The process of interviewing is basic in social science. Since scholars are seldom able to participate in the events which interest them, they try to talk with persons who have participated in such events. There are several different types of in-terviews in social science: open-ended, closed, in-depth, retrospective, etc. The idea of oral-history interviews is discussed by Vansina (1961). The type of in-terview selected will depend on one's research problem (see Dexter, 1970).

c. Survey Research

Students are probably familiar with the Gallup polls or the Roper surveys in the United States, which through scientific sampling and closed-answer ques-tionnaires are able to assess social attitudes of a large population. There are a few such survey units in Africa (e.g., Marco Surveys in East Africa). While most surveys are inquiries into attitude patterns, some, such as census enumerations, are more concerned with demographic patterns. At present the OAU (work-ing with Columbia University) is collecting in Addis Ababa the computer cards of all of the aggregate data surveys which have been conducted in Africa.

d. Documentary Analysis

Most African states have national archives which contain the hundreds of thousands of documents which the colonial and independent governments of these countries have generated over the years. In addition, some national ar-chives also have private papers which have been donated. Such documents are providing data on a whole range of problems. (For a listing and evaluation of archives in Africa, see, Dadzie and Strickland, 1965.)

e. Experimental Techniques

Particularly in the field of psychology (see Wickert, 1967), experiments are important in getting some types of immediate and firsthand observations (see Segall, 1969). Such techniques are not yet widely used in Africa, but the use of Thematic Apperception Tests (see Cohen, 1970) and dream-recall analysis (see Robert LeVine, 1966) have been reported on.

3. METHODS OF DATA ANALYSIS

In Paden, two major modes of analysis are discussed: comparative analysis (focused on the study of similarities and dissimilarities of units which are regarded as sharing certain common systems-properties) and developmental analysis (basically the study of change over time—the historical approach). Although each is distinctive in emphasis, the two are frequently combined. Both are susceptible to quantitative analysis and theory-building.

The technology of data analysis is becoming increasingly complex, primarily in response to the need for dealing with increasingly complex data (which in turn stems partly from the increased magnitude of the research questions posed). This has led to a slow but increasing emphasis on the development and use of quantitative techniques in African research and a growing involvement with computer analysis. Although there is still a relative scarcity of statistical data on Africa, the amount that has become available in recent years or that can be obtained through field research is sufficient to present a major challenge to quantitative research on Africa. Quantitative analysis and the use of computers are, of course, dependent upon the quality of the input of data and on the programming and interpretive skills of the people involved in the analysis. Nevertheless, computer-based techniques of analysis permit an examination of complex research problems which has hitherto been impossible and thus supply an essential component of the "toolkit" of social science. (For a discussion of computer technology as it relates to problems of national integration research in Africa, see Morrison *et al.*, 1970; and Hopkins, 1969.)

99

Conducting Social Research
in Africa

A DISCUSSION OF THE WAYS in which social research has been conducted in Africa may indicate both strengths and weaknesses of the present state of knowledge about Africa (see introduction to the *Bibliography*).

1. A HISTORY OF SOCIAL RESEARCH IN AFRICA

Social-science research, as mentioned earlier, is a process of problem selection, hypothesis formation and testing, and the drawing of conclusions. In the past this process was often less rigorous than that required by contemporary standards. Some of the earliest scholars who recorded observations about social patterns and historical developments in Africa were Arabs such as Ibn Battuta (*The Travels of Ibn Battuta*, 1958, translated by Gibb), Moorish Africans such as Leo Africanus (*The History and Description of Africa*, 1896, translated by John Pory in 1600), and various Europeans, such as the Portuguese navigators and explorers. By the sixteenth century, the empires of the Central Sudan all had scribes and scholars who were able to record history in written form. (For a later example, see Arnett, 1929, a translation of Muhammad Bello, *Infaq al-Maisur*, a history of the Fulani and other Sudanic peoples.)

With the increase in Western contact, especially in the nineteenth century, there were a large number of European scholar-explorers such as Barth (*Travels and Discoveries in North and Central Africa*, 1968); Denham, Clapperton, and Oudney (*Narrative of Travels and Discoveries in Northern and Central Africa in the Years 1822, 1823, 1824*, 1966); and Lander. Such scholars were interested in geographical as well as ethnographic data, but very clearly exemplify the problems of ethnocentrism in cross-cultural research. As mentioned in Rowe (*Essays*, chap. 9) by the turn of the twentieth century a number of African Christian writers had emerged as historians of their own peoples, e.g., Samuel Johnson, J. H. Soga.

In the early twentieth century, certain colonial administrator-scholars continued the tradition of recording observations, but came to focus on social patterns. They also began extensive translations of Arabic material. Men such as Palmer (*Sudanese Memoirs*, 1928); Marty (a twelve-volume set of studies on Islam in West Africa, from 1915 to the late 1920s); Rattray (*Ashanti Law and Constitution*, 1929); Delafosse (*Les Noirs de l'Afrique*, 1941); and many others began to provide a foundation for modern African studies. (Much of this early material has subsequently been re-evaluated by African and European scholars.)

In the interwar period, and subsequently, a new breed of scholar—the anthropologist—was attracted to Africa. Englishmen such as Evans-Pritchard (1940) and Radcliffe-Brown (1935), who had worked with Malinowski in London, began to provide a new framework for cross-cultural analysis—the structure/function approach—and began to generate a series of detailed ethnographic case studies. At the same time, Frenchmen such as Balandier (who worked primarily among the Fang of Gabon) and Mercier (who worked in urban centers in Senegal) approached their studies from a more sociological and geographical tradition, but essentially used the case-study method. American anthropologists such as Herskovits (who as early as 1930 was writing about the "culture areas of Africa") were distinctive in trying to get past the colonial framework in viewing African society and in trying to place African cultures within a historical and global perspective.

In the postwar period, new administrator-scholars continued the tradition of scholarship in the fields of linguistics and social history (e.g., Frenchmen such as Alexandre, Froelich, Cornevin, and Deschamps, and Englishmen such as Arnott, Parsons, Muffett, and Kirk-Greene). During this same period, an increasing number of African scholars were writing historical and ethnographic accounts. Men such as Kofi Busia (1951) of Ghana, Jomo Kenyatta (1964) of Kenya, Kenneth Dike (1956) of Nigeria, and Amadou Hampate Ba (1962) of Mali wrote accounts of particular aspects of their own ethnic socieites or areas.

With independence, African scholars such as W. E. Abraham (*The Mind of Africa,* 1962) of Ghana, Cheikh Anta Diop (*The Cultural Unity of Negro Africa,* 1962) of Senegal, Ali Mazrui (*Towards a Pax Africana,* 1967) of Kenya, Joseph Ki-Zerbo (*Le Monde africain noir: Histoire et civilisation,* 1963) of Upper Volta, and others began to *reinterpret* in a fundamental way their African cultural experience.

In the mid-1950s, two developments of major importance occurred: first, new universities were established in Africa, and these began to shift the bases of academic pursuit to the African countries; and, second, a number of scholars from disciplines other than anthropology began to do research in Africa. At the same time, institutes of African studies were emerging throughout the world.

By the mid-1960s, another significant pattern had developed: African scholars primarily based in the African universities were beginning to undertake postgraduate research themselves in significant numbers and to publish such research. Such relatively young African scholars as Cheikh Tidiane Sy (Senegal), Saburi Biobaku (Nigeria), Ade J. F. Ajayi (Nigeria), E. A. Ayandele (Nigeria), Bethwell Ogot (Kenya), Adu Boahen (Ghana), Bernard Chidzero (Central Africa), Stanislas Adotevi (Dahomey), Isaria Kimambo (Tanzania), and Memel Fote (Ivory Coast) are focusing primarily on African history. Other young scholars such as B. J. Dudley, Akin Mabogunje, T. M. Yesufu, H. M. A. Onitiri, Victor Uchendu, Abdalla Bujra, Fatou Sow, and many others are working mainly in the contemporary social sciences.

2. AFRICAN RESEARCH INSTITUTES

By 1960, the "big four" universities in sub-Saharan Africa were as follows: University of Dakar (Senegal); University of Ghana (in Legon near Accra); University of Ibadan (Nigeria); and Makerere University (Kampala, Uganda). Since 1960, a number of institutes of higher learning have been transformed into national universities (e.g., Fourah Bay College, Sierra Leone; and the University Colleges of Nairobi and Dar es Salaam), and almost every remaining African country has established a national university (see Module 42).

Within these university communities, a number of research institutes have developed. At Ibadan, the Institute of African Studies (dealing primarily with the arts, languages, humanities, and archaeology) and the Nigerian Institute of Social and Economic Research (NISER, dealing with political, social, and economic development) were built into major research coordinating bodies. In Ghana, the Institute of African Studies at Legon came to focus primarily on historical and cultural research. The Institut Fondamental de l'Afrique Noire (IFAN) at Dakar sponsored both social science and natural science research, and has generated a series of IFAN centers in almost all of the French-speaking African states. The Institute of Social Research at Makerere, the larger East African Institute of Social and Economic Development, and the University of East Africa social-science conferences have come to encourage and support a full range of social research in East Africa.

More recently, the Economic Commission for Africa, located in Addis Ababa, Ethiopia, has come to serve as a "bank" for social-science data (including census data) from all parts of Africa. At the moment, computer facilities are being set up in Addis Ababa to accommodate the vast accumulation of data. The Haile Selassie I University in Addis Ababa may eventually come to be a major research center, in part because of its proximity to the ECA data sources. Another activity in Addis Ababa has been the Organization of African Unity (OAU) project in developing an *Encyclopedia Africana.* This project was originally started in Ghana, but after 1966 was transferred to the OAU. The two immediate projects are to create an encyclopedia of African biography and an encyclopedia of African country profiles.

3. PROBLEMS OF SOCIAL RESEARCH IN AFRICA

One of the major difficulties of social research in Africa has been the language problem. Anthropologists usually learned the language of the group with which they were living. But the problem becomes magnified when the focus of research is on multilingual urban areas or multilingual national contexts. Three different types of solutions have emerged: team research (particularly in cooperation with indigenous scholars) rather than individual research, research by indigenous scholars who are multilingual, and greater use of interpreters.

A second problem of research has been the relative lack of background or related studies upon which a scholar can build. Often it becomes necessary to engage in basic demographic, linguistic, and historical research before a particular contemporary problem can be dealt with. Many scholars are addressing themselves to this dearth of demographic, linguistic, and historical studies and are also engaged in re-evaluation and interpretation of much of the scholarly literature that came out of the colonial era.

A continuing problem is the lack of finances for major research in all areas. It is clear that if archaeological excavation were to become a high priority within the new African states, many of the existing gaps in our knowledge about the pre-colonial empires and movements of peoples could be significantly narrowed. But such research is extremely expensive. In Module 100, the question of research priorities will be discussed. For further discussion of research problems in Africa, see Paden (*Essays,* chap. 31).

100

Research Frontiers in Africa

THERE HAVE BEEN SEVERAL VOLUMES published within the past five years that deal with the question of research priorities in Africa. *The African World* (Lystad, 1965), prepared under the auspices of the African Studies Association, is a survey of social research in three broad areas: Historical and Socio-Cultural Studies, Physico-Biological Studies, and Psycho-Cultural Studies. *Expanding Horizons in African Studies* (Carter and Paden, 1969) consists of interpretive essays by scholars who assess the future directions of both disciplinary and inter-disciplinary research in Africa. In addition, more specific assessments of research priorities appear regularly in such publications as the *African Studies Bulletin, Rural Africana,* and *African Urban Notes.* As reviews of existing research, these surveys and statements broadly outline the accomplishments of the social and natural sciences in the African contexts. But as blueprints for the future, they have increasingly come to reflect the priorities which are now clearly being established by the governments and academic leaders in the new African states. Indeed, a major watershed in African research has been reached as the African states themselves take the initiative in shaping the patterns and priorities of future research.

1. COORDINATION OF SOCIAL-SCIENCE RESEARCH IN AFRICA

One of the most important developments regarding the conduct of social-science research in Africa has been the establishment of "clearing houses" in Africa (both governmental agencies—usually ministries of interior—and university committees) which screen proposed research and set research priorities. American or European scholars wishing to do research in Africa must generally obtain permission from these offices before entering the country. Proposed projects are evaluated with respect to existing priorities, potential contributions to government or university programs, degree of political sensitivity, and other factors considered relevant to the country concerned. After permission is received, the applicant is usually given an associate status in some form with the national university; certain amenities (perhaps an office or typing facilities); and an easier access to documents, archives, and offices of the government. In return, the researcher may assume some university obligations (lectures, seminar participation) and makes an agreement to deposit copies of all publications deriving from the proposed research in the university or government libraries.

This new pattern of research clearance and coordination has been developed for several reasons. First, some expatriate researchers in the past have taken advantage of the good will and cooperation of the African governments, taking up large amounts of time interviewing government officials without a reciprocal contribution to the African countries involved. Locally conducted research led to publications which were not available locally. Frequently, work of potential benefit to the African countries was buried in relatively inaccessible academic journals or university libraries in America and Europe.

A second factor has been African sensitivity to interference in the internal affairs of African states. Some researchers in Africa have either directly or indirectly contributed to intelligence reports for American or European governments. On occasion, some have been found to be working directly for foreign governments. This has created much anger and suspicion in the African countries. In recent years, there has been an attempt in African states to monitor all social-science research and, in particular, to undertake closer scrutiny of foreign researchers working within a country. There is still an understandable residue of suspicion which periodically reaches serious proportions.

But probably the most important factor shaping the research atmosphere in Africa is the increasing need to channel research of all kinds into areas which could potentially benefit the African countries. Many countries have already established statements on national research priorities which are beginning to influence not only the patterns of approval of foreign research projects but also the types of projects being proposed. In many ways, this development parallels the growing emphasis on relevant or "action-oriented" social-science research in the United States—research which is directed toward major contemporary problems and issues. The result is that the African states have more effective control of research carried on within their boundaries than ever before. Priorities have been established, along with procedures for approval and association, and research has begun to conform more closely to the most important needs of the African states. (The African viewpoint on social-science research is clearly exemplified by Dr. Zake, minister of education and acting attorney-general in Uganda; see Carter and Paden, 1969.) It should be mentioned that research in South Africa and the Portuguese colonies is quite a different problem. Very few American scholars are allowed into these areas.

2. THE PATTERN OF RESEARCH PRIORITIES

The preceding discussion should not imply that theoretical research in Africa has been sacrificed in the establishment of practical national priorities. Many have noted that there is nothing so practical as good theory. The major research frontiers in African studies, therefore, lie in the close association between theoretical and practical orientations, with the focal points of this association increasingly being established by African scholars and leaders to suit their particular contexts.

In very broad terms it seems likely that the social sciences will continue to concentrate upon problems of social change (including education and urbanization), economic development (especially in the rural areas), and national integration; the natural sciences will focus on the question of environmental control and resource utilization, in keeping with national priorities in economic development; and the arts and humanities will concern themselves primarily with the preservation of cultural heritages and with the new syntheses of art forms which are emerging in modern Africa. Special priorities, combining various disciplines, may emerge in particular countries. Such joint research has already begun, for example, with respect to the resettlement of Africans on formerly European farmland in Kenya, the integration of legal systems in Ethiopia, and the problems of national reconstruction in Nigeria (growing out of the Nigeria-Biafra conflict). In a broader sense, the national development plans of each country have already become blueprints for research needs and concentration.

There have been dozens of conferences and meetings in Africa which have been concerned with the establishment of priorities. Many of these have been held under the auspices of the Organization of African Unity and the Economic Commission for Africa and have been directed toward continent-wide priorities. Recently, for example, a joint committee composed of the African Development Bank, the International Bank for Reconstruction and Development (The World Bank), the United Nations Development Program, and the Economic Commission for Africa was established to deal with development priorities in transportation, power resources, and communications.

In *Expanding Horizons* (Carter and Paden, 1969), major research priorities within the individual social-science disciplines are explored by a wide range of contributors. To take just a few examples, Victor Uchendu (anthropology) stresses the need for cultural studies within *national* contexts rather than the use of the ethnic society alone as the unit of analysis. Ali Mazrui (political science) underscores the sensitivity of many political topics in contemporary Africa but notes the need for further examination of the problems of national integration, particularly the role of ethnic groups in helping or hindering unity. Isaria Kimambo (history) calls for an emphasis on local histories, particularly through the examination of oral traditions. Remi Clignet (sociology) stresses the need for systematic urban studies, and Peter Gould (geography) notes the important geographical research needed in development planning and in the study of modernization and change. There is also a concern expressed by Sterling Stuckey (history) that Afro-American studies be included in African studies, particularly with respect to the psychological effects of racial oppression. In general, the consensus of the volume is that social-science research about Africa should be interdisciplinary, since the concepts and methods involved are so clearly overlapping, and that the criterion of relevance to contemporary African problems, as they are identified by the African states themselves, should be clearly recognized. (Apart from the social sciences, interpretations of frontiers and priorities for the arts and humanities, natural sciences and technology, and the professions — law, education, administration — are also discussed.)

Nearly all the modules in this syllabus point to gaps in our knowledge about Africa. The selection of 100 module topics clearly conveys the kinds of priorities which the authors consider important for students of Africa in this country. These may or may not be the same as *research* priorities which are being worked out by social scientists (of whatever color or nationality) and by the variety of host communities in Africa. If the objectives of this syllabus are achieved, however, the reader should be able to perceive a variety of intellectual frontiers in a study of the African experience.

Although there are no separate study questions to Modules 98, 99, and 100 ("Social Science and Africa"), this may be one of the most controversial, yet fundamental, segments in the syllabus. Students and teachers might assess together some of the following matters: What have been some of the past distortions in the perception of Africa by Westerners? By Arabs? By Africans? Does social science have any claim to "objectivity"? Is a particular technique of data collection — e.g., interview *vs.* participant observation — likely to produce differences in social-science "conclusions" regarding social patterns in Africa? What should be the units of social-science analysis in Africa? Individuals? Ethnic groups? Racial groups? Urban centers? National states? The continent as a whole? Who should set research priorities in Africa? Why? What priorities would *you* (the reader) like to see established? Who should be allowed to do research in Africa? How might such research be organized in the social sciences?

In the arts and humanities? In the natural sciences? In the professional schools? Is there such a thing as "the African experience"? Is there such a thing as "the black experience"? Are they the same thing?

APPENDIX A

The *Essays* as Text: Keying in the *Syllabus* and *Bibliography*

TEACHERS WHO USE THE *Essays* as a text, may wish to arrange the *Syllabus* to follow the text. Although both are basically parallel in structure, a number of modules may be brought in as background to more than one essay. In order to illustrate this possible use of the modules, we list the *Essays* below in order, and suggest some of the relevant modules. Furthermore, in order to stress that the modules are intended to be guides to further reading, we suggest one or two introductory books (including case studies) from the *Bibliography*.

Volume I, *Essays* (chapters)	Volume II, *Syllabus* (modules)	Volume III, *Bibliography* (introductory references): + = single case study; ++ = volume includes several case studies
1. Introduction to the African Experience (Soja)	1. African Society, History and Social Change	Bohannan, *Africa and the Africans* (1964) Davidson, *Africa in History* (1968) Davidson, *The African Genius* (1969) Herskovits, *The Human Factor in Changing Africa* (1962)

Volume I, *Essays* (chapters)	Volume II, *Syllabus* (modules)	Volume III, *Bibliography* (introductory references): + = single case study; ++ = volume includes several case studies
	2. Nation-Building and the Modern World	++Coleman & Rosberg, *Political Parties and National Integration in Tropical Africa* (1964)
		Wallerstein, *Africa: The Politics of Unity* (1967)
		Mazrui, *Towards a Pax Africana* (1967)
2. The African Setting (Soja and Paden)	17. Continental Origins and Physical Character	Ady, *Africa: A Regional Economic Atlas* (1965)
		de Blij, *A Geography of Sub-Saharan Africa* (1964)
	18. The Evolution of Man in Africa	Howell & Bourlière, *African Ecology and Human Evolution* (1966)
		Bishop & Clarke, *Background to Evolution in Africa* (1966)
	74. Population Pressure and Social Factors in Development	++Brass *et al.*, *The Demography of Tropical Africa* (1968)
	78. Emergent Patterns of Regionalism	++Hazlewood, *African Integration and Disintegration* (1967)

Volume I, *Essays* (chapters)	Volume II, *Syllabus* (modules)	Volume III, *Bibliography* (introductory references): + = single case study; ++ = volume includes several case studies
3. Traditional Society in Africa (Cohen)	3. The African Ethnic Mosaic	Greenberg, *The Languages of Africa* (1963–66) Murdock, *Africa—Its People and Their Culture History* (1959)
	4. The Nature of Ethnicity	Shibutani & Kwan, *Ethnic Stratification* (1965)
	5. On the Concept of "Tribe"	++Helm, *Essays on the Problem of Tribe* (1968)
	6. The Changing Nature of Ethnic Boundaries	++Cohen & Middleton, *From Tribe to Nation in Africa* (1969)
	7. Modern Variants of Ethnicity	++Kuper & Smith, *Pluralism in Africa* (1969)
	8. Family and Kinship	++Radcliffe-Brown and Forde, *African Systems of Kinship and Marriage* (1950) Goody, *Comparative Studies in Kinship* (1969)
	9. Traditional Political Systems	++Cohen & Middleton, *Comparative Political Systems* (1967)

Volume I, *Essays* (chapters)	Volume II, *Syllabus* (modules)	Volume III, *Bibliography* (introductory references): + = single case study; ++ = volume includes several case studies
	16. Study Questions: African Society and Culture	++Ottenberg & Otten-berg, *Cultures and Societies of Africa*, (1960) ++Gibbs, *Peoples of Africa* (1965)
4. Traditional Eco-nomic Systems (Dalton)	10. Traditional Economic Systems	++Bohannan & Dalton, *Markets in Africa* (1962)
	70. Agricultural Reorgani-zation	Dumont, *False Start in Africa* (1966) Yudelman, *Africans on the Land* (1964)
5. Language Systems and Literature (Berry)	11. Language and Lin-guistic Systems	Greenberg, *The Lan-guages of Africa* (1963–66)
	12. Literature and Oral Tradition	Vansina, *Oral Tradition* (1961)
	49. New Modes of Communication	Fishman, *et al., Language Problems of Developing Nations* (1968)
	90. Contemporary African Literature	Cartey, *Whispers from a Continent* (1969) Wauthier, *The Literature and Thought of Modern Africa* (1964)

Volume I, *Essays* (chapters)	Volume II, *Syllabus* (modules)	Volume III, *Bibliography* (introductory references): + = single case study; ++ = volume includes several case studies
6. Conceptual Systems in Africa (Albert)	13. Conceptual Systems and Religion	++Forde, *African Worlds* (1965) ++Fortes & Dieterlen, *African Systems of Thought* (1965)
	21. The Impact of Islam in Africa	Trimingham, *The Influence of Islam upon Africa* (1968) ++Lewis, *Islam in Tropical Africa* (1966)
	51. Innovation, Synthesis, and Independency	Barrett, *Schism and Renewal in Africa* (1968)
7. Visual Art in Africa (Willett)	14. Visual Arts	Fagg, *The Art of Western Africa* and *The Art of Central Africa* (both 1967) ++Biebuyck, *Tradition and Creativity in Tribal Art* (1969)
	93. Visual Arts and Music	Beier, *Contemporary Art in Africa* (1968)
8. Ethnomusicology in Africa (Wachsmann)	15. Traditional Music	Jones, *Studies in African Music* (1961) Merriam, *African Music on LP* (1970)

Volume I, *Essays* (chapters)	Volume II, *Syllabus* (modules)	Volume III, *Bibliography* (introductory references): + = single case study; ++ = volume includes several case studies
	93. Visual Arts and Music	East, *African Theatre* (1970)
9. Major Themes in African History (Rowe)	36. Study Questions: Perspectives on the Past	Ajayi & Espie, *A Thousand Years of West African History* (1965)
		Davidson, *A History of East and Central Africa* (1967)
		++Collins, *Problems in African History* (1968)
	19. Ecological Adaptation and Diffusion of Agriculture	Oliver & Fage, *A Short History of Africa* (1962)
	20. Early Culture and State Formation	+Shinnie, *Meroe, a Civilization of the Sudan* (1967)
10. Empires and State Formation (Holden)	21. The Impact of Islam in Africa	Trimingham, *Islam in West Africa* (1959)
		Trimingham, *Islam in East Africa* (1965)
		++ Kritzeck and Lewis, *Islam in Africa* (1969)
	22. Empires of the Western Sudan	Bovill, *The Golden Trade of the Moors* (1958)
		Davidson, *The Growth of African Civilization: A History of West Africa 1000–1800* (1969)

Volume I, *Essays* (chapters)	Volume II, *Syllabus* (modules)	Volume III, *Bibliography* (introductory references): + = single case study; ++ = volume includes several case studies
	23. Coastal States of East Africa	Sutton, *The East African Coast* (1966) +Oliver & Mathew, *History of East Africa* (1963)
	24. States of the Central Sudan	+Johnston, *The Fulani Empire of Sokoto* (1967) +M. G. Smith, *Government in Zazzau* (1960)
	25. Indigenous Kingdoms of East and Central Africa	Vansina, *Kingdoms of the Savanna* (1968) Ranger, *Aspects of Central African History* (1968) Ogot & Kiernan *Zamani* (1968)
	26. Forest States of West Africa	++Forde & Kaberry, *West African Kingdoms* (1967)
11. West Africa and the Afro-Americans (Hammond)	27. Early Western Contact	Curtin, *The Image of Africa* (1963)
	28. Origins and Growth of the Slave Trade	Mannix & Cowley, *Black Cargoes* (1962) Davidson, *The African Slave Trade* (1961) Curtin, *The Atlantic Slave Trade: A Census* (1969)

Volume I, *Essays* (chapters)	Volume II, *Syllabus* (modules)	Volume III, *Bibliography* (introductory references): + = single case study; ++ = volume includes several case studies
	29. Abolition and States for Freed Slaves	+Peterson, *Province of Freedom* (1969) +Liebenow, *Liberia: The Evolution of Privilege* (1969)
	30. The African Legacy in the New World	Herskovits, *The New World Negro* (1966)
12. Race and Resistance in South Africa (Mbata)	31. White and Black Migrations in Southern Africa	Wilson & Thompson, *The Oxford History of South Africa*, Vol. I (1969)
	32. African Reactions to European Settlement	Omer-Cooper, *The Zulu Aftermath* (1966) Feit, *African Opposition in South Africa* (1967)
	88. Race Relations in Southern Africa	van den Berghe, *Race and Racism* (1967) Simons and Simons, *Class and Colour in South Africa 1850–1950* (1969)
	89. Politics and Race in South Africa	Carter, *The Politics of Inequality* (1952) Carter *et al.*, *South Africa's Transkei* (1967)

Volume I, *Essays* (chapters)	Volume II, *Syllabus* (modules)	Volume III, *Bibliography* (introductory references): + = single case study; ++ = volume includes several case studies
13. The Impact of Colonialism (Crowder)	33. The Scramble for Africa	Robinson & Gallagher, *Africa and the Victorians* (1961) Roberts, *History of French Colonial Policy, 1870–1925* (1963)
	34. African Resistance and Reaction	++Mazrui & Rotberg, *The Traditions of Protest in Black Africa, 1886–1966* (1970) +Ranger, *Revolt in Southern Rhodesia, 1896–97* (1967)
	35. The Nature of Colonial Systems	Crowder, *West Africa Under Colonial Rule* (1968) Lugard, *The Dual Mandate in British Tropical Africa* (1965)
14. Major Themes in Social Change (van den Berghe)	37. Concepts of Social Change and Modernization	Finkle & Gable, *Political Development and Social Change* (1966) ++Wallerstein, *Social Change, The Colonial Situation* (1966)
	38. Social Change and Modernization in Africa	++Bascom & Herskovits, *Continuity and Change in African Cultures* (1962) van den Berghe, *Africa—Social Problems of Change and Conflict* (1965)

Volume I, *Essays* (chapters)	Volume II, *Syllabus* (modules)	Volume III, *Bibliography* (introductory references): + = single case study; ++ = volume includes several case studies
	53. Study Questions: Processes of Change	Lloyd, *Africa in Social Change* (1967)
15. Personality and Change (LeVine)	39. The Concept of African Personality	Abraham, *The Mind of Africa* (1962)
	40. Characteristics of African Personality	++Wickert, *Readings in African Psychology* (1967)
	41. Personality and Social Change	LeVine, *Dreams and Deeds* (1966) Fanon, *Black Skin, White Masks* (1967)
16. Education and Elite Formation (Clignet)	42. Educational Systems in Africa	Sasnett & Sepmeyer, *Educational Systems of Africa* (1966)
	43. Education and Elite Recruitment	+Clignet & Foster, *The Fortunate Few* (1966)
	44. The New Elites of Africa	++Lloyd, *The New Elites of Tropical Africa* (1966)
17. Urbanization and Change (Mabogunje)	45. The Development of Urban Society	++Miner, *The City in Modern Africa* (1967) +Lloyd, Mabogunje, & Awe, *The City of Ibadan* (1967)
	46. The Nature of Urban Life	Little, *West African Urbanization* (1965)
	47. Problems of Urbanization	++Breese, *The City in Newly Developing Countries* (1969)

Volume I, *Essays* (chapters)	Volume II, *Syllabus* (modules)	Volume III, *Bibliography* (introductory references): + = single case study; ++ = volume includes several case studies
18. Communications and Change (Soja)	48. Spatial Aspects of Transportation and Communications	+Soja, *The Geography of Modernization in Kenya* (1968) +Riddell, *The Spatial Dynamics of Moderniza-tion in Sierra Leone: Struc-ture, Diffusion and Re-sponse* (1970)
	49. New Modes of Com-munication	UNESCO, *World Com-munications* (1966) Pye, *Communications and Political Development* (1963)
19. Religion and Change (Fabian)	50. The Impact of Christianity	++Baeta, *Christianity in Tropical Africa* (1968) Beetham, *Christianity and the New Africa* (1967)
	51. Innovation, Synthesis and Independency	Barrett, *Schism and Re-newal in Africa* (1968)
	52. Islamic Reformation Movements	+Abun-Nasr, *The Tijaniyya—A Sufi Order in the Modern World* (1965)
	13. Conceptual Systems and Religion	++Forde, *African Worlds—Studies in the Cosmological Ideas and Social Values of African Peoples* (1965) ++Fortes & Dieterlen, *African Systems of Thought* (1965)

Volume I, *Essays* (chapters)	Volume II, *Syllabus* (modules)	Volume III, *Bibliography* (introductory references): + = single case study; ++ = volume includes several case studies
20. African Concepts of Nationhood (Paden)	54. Concepts of Nationalism	+Dia, *The African Nations and World Solidarity* (1962)
	55. Patterns of African Nationalism	Hodgkin, *Nationalism in Colonial Africa* (1965)
	56. Independence	++Legum, *Africa: A Handbook to the Continent* (1966) Wallerstein, *The Politics of Independence* (1961)
	60. The Role of Ideology in Nation-Building	Apter, *Ideology and Discontent* (1964) ++Emerson & Kilson, *The Political Awakening of Africa* (1965)
	77. Concepts of Supra-nationalism	Legum, *Pan-Africanism a Short Political Guide* (1962) ++AMSAC, *Pan-Africanism Reconsidered* (1962)
21. Patterns of Nation-Building (Zolberg)	76. Study Questions: Consolidation of Nation-States	Ake, *A Theory of Political Integration* (1967) ++Carter, *National Unity and Regionism in Eight African States* (1966) ++Deutsch & Foltz, *Nation-Building* (1966)
	57. Interethnic Integration	++Cohen & Middleton, *From Tribe to Nation in Africa* (1969)

Volume I, *Essays* (chapters)	Volume II, *Syllabus* (modules)	Volume III, *Bibliography* (introductory references): + = single case study; ++ = volume includes several case studies
	58. Mass-Elite Integration	LeVine, V. *Political Leadership in Africa* (1967)
	59. Territorial Integration and Boundaries	++Hazlewood, *African Integration and Disintegration* (1967) ++Widstrand, *African Boundary Problems* (1969)
	60. The Role of Ideology in Nation-Building	Zolberg, *Creating Political Order — The Party States of West Africa* (1966)
22. Political Systems Development (C. Young)	61. Types of Civilian Regimes	++Coleman & Rosberg, *Political Parties and National Integration in Tropical Africa* (1964)
	62. Institutions and Bureaucracy	Adu, *The Civil Service in the New African States* (1962)
	63. Participation and Mobilization	++MacKenzie & Robinson, *Five Elections in Africa* (1960)
	64. Elite Instability and Military Rule	++Welch, *Soldier and State in Africa* (1970)
	65. The Implications of Nigeria-Biafra	++Melson & Wolpe, *Communalism and Modernization in Nigeria* (1970)
23. Legal Systems Development (R. Young)	66. Legal Systems in Africa	++Kuper & Kuper, *African Law — Adaptation and Development* (1965)
	67. The Integration of Legal Systems	++Sawyerr, *East African Law and Social Change* (1967)

Volume I, *Essays* (chapters)	Volume II, *Syllabus* (modules)	Volume III, *Bibliography* (introductory references): + = single case study; ++ = volume includes several case studies
	68. The Development of Constitutional Law	Peaslee, *Constitutions of Nations, Volume I, Africa* (1965)
24. Economic Systems Development (Rivkin)	69. An Assessment of Resources	Hance, *The Geography of Modern Africa* (1964)
	70. Agricultural Reorganization	Dumont, *False Start in Africa* (1966) ++de Wilde *et al., Experiences with Agricultural Development in Tropical Africa* (1967)
	71. The Industrialization Process	Ewing, *Industry in Africa* (1968) United Nations, *Industrial Development in Africa* (1967)
	72. Planning for Development	+Stolper, *Planning Without Facts* (1966)
	73. Development of Economic Systems	Robson, *Economic Integration in Africa* (1969) Robson & Lury, *The Economies of Africa* (1969) Kamarck, *The Economics of African Development* (1967)
25. Developments in Technology (Kliphardt)	74. Population Pressure and Social Factors in Development	+Caldwell & Okonjo, *The Population of Tropical Africa* (1968) Adelman & Morris, *Society, Politics, and Economic Development, A Quantitative Approach* (1967)

Volume I, *Essays* (chapters)	Volume II, *Syllabus* (modules)	Volume III, *Bibliography* (introductory references): + = single case study; ++ = volume includes several case studies
	75. Technology and Nation-Building	Hunter, *The Best of Both Worlds* (1967)
	92. Urban Design and Architecture	Kultermann, *New Architecture in Africa* (1963)
		Kultermann, *New Directions in African Architecture* (1969)
		+Lock, *Kaduna* (1967)
26. African International Relations (Mazrui)	77. Concepts of Supra-nationalism	Mazrui, *Towards a Pax Africana* (1967)
	78. Emergent Patterns of Regionalism	++Rothchild, *The Politics of Integration* (1968)
		Welch, *Dream of Unity: Pan-Africanism and Political Unification in West Africa* (1966)
	79. Pan-Africanism and Continental Unity	Green & Seidman, *Unity or Poverty: the Economics of Pan-Africanism* (1968)
		Legum, *Pan-Africanism A Short Political Guide* (1962)
	80. International Organizations in Africa	Zartman, *International Relations in the New Africa* (1966)
	81. Africa at the United Nations	Hovet, *Africa in the United Nations* (1963)
	82. Africa and the Former Metropoles	Okigbo, *Africa and the Common Market* (1967)
		Mazrui, *The Anglo-African Commonwealth* (1967)

Volume I, *Essays* (chapters)	Volume II, *Syllabus* (modules)	Volume III, *Bibliography* (introductory references): + = single case study; ++ = volume includes several case studies
	83. Africa and the United States	Emerson, *Africa and United States Policy* (1967)
	84. Africa and the Communist Bloc	Morison, *The USSR and Africa* (1964)
	97. Study Questions: Africa and the Modern World	Wallerstein, *Africa — The Politics of Unity* (1967) Nielsen, *The Great Powers and Africa* (1969)
27. Africa and the Islamic World (Abu-Lughod)	85. Africa and the Third World	Mazrui, *On Heroes and Uhuru-Worship* (1967)
	86. Africa and the Middle East	Kerekes, *The Arab Middle East and Muslim Africa* (1961)
	21. The Impact of Islam in Africa	Trimingham, *The Influence of Islam upon Africa* (1968) ++Lewis, *Islam in Tropical Africa* (1966)
28. Confrontation in Southern Africa (Carter)	87. The Remnants of Colonialism	Abshire and Samuels, *Portuguese Africa — A Handbook* (1969) Nkrumah, *Neo-Colonialism, the Last Stage of Imperialism* (1965)
	88. Race Relations in Southern Africa	van den Berghe, *Race and Racism — A Comparative Perspective* (1967)
	89. Politics and Race in South Africa	Carter, *et al., South Africa's Transkei* (1967)

Volume I, *Essays* (chapters)	Volume II, *Syllabus* (modules)	Volume III, *Bibliography* (introductory references): + = single case study; ++ = volume includes several case studies
	32. African Reactions to European Settlement	+Omer-Cooper, *The Zulu Aftermath* (1966)
29. Contemporary African Literature (Cartey)	90. Contemporary African Literature	Cartey, *Whispers from a Continent* (1969)
	91. Contemporary Social Thought	Wauthier, *The Literature and Thought of Modern Africa* (1964)
	12. Literature and Oral Tradition	+Johnston, *A Selection of Hausa Stories* (1966)
30. Afro-American Perspectives (Turner)	94. Africa and Afro-American Identity	++AMSAC, *Africa Seen by American Negroes* (1958) Hill & Kilson, *Apropos of Africa* (1969) +Essien-Udom, *Black Nationalism — A Search for Identity in America* (1962)
	95. Africa and Afro-American Social Change	++Robinson *et al, Black Studies in the University* (1969) +Cronon, *Black Moses* (1955) +Malcolm X, *The Autobiography of Malcolm X* (1965)
	96. African Interpretations of Multiracial America	Clark, *America Their America* (1964)

Volume I, *Essays* (chapters)	Volume II, *Syllabus* (modules)	Volume III, *Bibliography* (introductory references): + = single case study; ++ = volume includes several case studies
31. Social Science and Africa (Paden)	98. Africa and the Concept of Social Science	Galtung, *Theory and Methods of Social Research* (1967) Bruyn, *The Human Perspective in Sociology* (1966)
	99. Conducting Social Research in Africa	Cohen & Naroll, *Handbook of Methodology in Cultural Anthropology* (1970) +Vansina and Mauny, *The Historian in Tropical Africa* (1964)
	100. Research Frontiers in Africa	++Carter & Paden, *Expanding Horizons* (1969) ++Lystad, *The African World* (1965) ++Bown & Crowder, *The Proceedings of the First International Congress of Africanists* (1964)

APPENDIX B

Chronology
of African History

THIS CHRONOLOGICAL SUMMARY has been designed to include all the major dates mentioned in this syllabus as well as supplementary dates to provide a broad overview of African history. The supplementary materials have been drawn primarily from Basil Davidson, *Africa in History: Themes and Outlines* (New York: The Macmillan Company, 1968) and from the chronologies included in *A History of East and Central Africa To The Late Nineteenth Century* (New York: Doubleday and Company, 1969) and *The Growth of African Civilization: A History of West Africa* (London: Longmans, 1966; Garden City, N.Y.: Doubleday, Anchor Books, 1969) by the same author.

5000 B.C.–500 B.C.	***Spread of Agriculture in Africa***
5000–2000	Sahara sufficiently moist to support both agriculture and pastoralism
c. 4000	Cereal agriculture in Lower Nile Valley and the Fayum Depression
3500	Neolithic culture exists in Algeria/Niger border region
c. 2000	Desert conditions established in Sahara. Gradual movement of agricultural peoples southward from the Sahara
c. 1000	Agriculture developed in parts of the Sudanic belt (probably begun much earlier)
	Agriculturists appear in various localities from Kenya south to Zambia and southern Angola
500	Agriculture develops in the forest lands of West Africa

413

3500	***Early State Formation in Nile Valley***
3200	Pharaoh Menes unites Lower and Upper Egypt. Pharaonic Egypt begins
1525	Egyptian conquest of Nubia
1000	First trans-Saharan crossings by chariots and carts drawn by horses and/or donkeys occurs (c. 500 B.C. Berber chariots traversing Sahara by routes from Morocco to the Senegal River and from Tunisia to the middle Niger River region)
814	Phoenicians found Carthage
730	Hyksos rule of Egypt continues until c. 570 B.C.
c. 700	Foundation of *Kingdom of Kush* with its capital at Napata
c. 550	Capital of Kushite Kingdom (Napata) moved to *Merowe*
500 B.C.–A.D. 700	***Early Iron Age Developments:*** Further spread of iron-working and agriculture; beginnings of Bantu migrations; growth of trans-Saharan trade
500 B.C.	Expansion of Kushite Kingdom of Merowe on the Middle Nile (flourishing trading empire reached its peak from mid-third century B.C. to the early Christian era)
	Ancestors of Amharic people from southern Arabia have settled in northern Ethiopia
448 B.C.	Herodotus writes that Phoenicians under King Necho circumnavigate the African continent
c. 250 B.C.	*The Nok Culture.* Iron-working in West Africa south of the Sahara. Trans-Saharan trade continues
146 B.C.	Rome destroys Carthage. End of Third Punic War
100 B.C.	Iron-working in Zambezi River Basin
	Camels first introduced into trans-Saharan trade
23 B.C.	Petronius leads Roman invasion of Nubia

10 B.C.	First Roman penetration into southern Libya

A.D. 100   *Kingdom of Axum,* in northern Ethiopian Highlands, is the nucleus of a rapidly expanding empire. Its principal port of Adulis receives ships from Egypt and India and conducts trade with the Indian Ocean complex. Trade expands along East Coast

Egyptian and Arab traders visit the East Coast. Trade and purchase of various products such as African ivory and tortoise-shells

Alexandrian Greek writes the *Periplus of the Erythrian Sea* (c. A.D. 120), which provides earliest references to peoples inhabiting the East African Coast

A.D. 200   Diffusion of iron-working and agriculture across Central and East Africa

A.D. 320   Earliest Iron Age villages in the *Zimbabwe* area. Gradual spread of early Iron Age cultures in areas south and east of the Zambezi River Basin

A.D. 400   Indonesians from Java and Sumatra have settled in Madagascar and visited the East Coast. Introduce banana, coconut, and outrigger canoe

C. A.D. 325   Axum destroys Kushite Kingdom of Merowe. Ezana, the ruler of Axum, converts to *Coptic Christianity*

A.D. 543   Foundations of first Christian states in Nubia on Middle Nile

A.D. 700–1000   ***Period of Migrations, Diffusion, and Regional Development:*** Later Iron Age developments and continued Bantu migrations into eastern, central and southern Africa; beginnings of Islamic period in northern and Sudanic Africa; early period of state formation in Western Sudan; long-range trading patterns firmly established in several areas

700   Growth and expansion of Christian civilization in Nubia (Northern Sudan) after the emergence of states in the mid-sixth century

700	Iron Age peoples of the *Bantu* language group inhabit settlements in many areas of East and Central Africa (migrations begun many centuries earlier)
	Demographic movements across the Limpopo River. Proliferation of Bantu languages in areas of southern Africa
	Early developments in *Swahili culture* and Swahili language. Coastal settlements involved in Indian Ocean trade
	Iron Age techniques utilized in Katanga region along with early copper mining
	Trading state of *Ghana* develops in Western Sudan. Stimulates increased North African and Berber trans-Saharan trade (Note: initial growth here probably began much earlier)
	Islamic penetration and expansion in North Africa following the death (A.D. 632) of the Prophet Muhammad
800	Muslim Berber merchants initiate Islamic penetration of Western Sudan
	Ghana state increases trans-Saharan trade in gold and salt
c. 850	Sefuwa dynasty founds early *Kanem* state to the east of Lake Chad
900	Iron Age cultures in southern Zambia and Malawi
943	Arab geographer-historian, Al-Mas'udi, writes about his travels to the East Coast
A.D. 1000–1400	***First Period of Extensive State Formation in Sub-Saharan Africa:*** Built upon earlier states and long-distance trading patterns; Muslim states in Sudanic belt, Maghrib, and Iberian Peninsula
1000	Ivory and gold trade between Central Africa and East Coast. Imports of Indian cottons, beads, and various other commodities
	Important East Coast trading city-states include Kilwa, Pemba, Zanzibar, and those of the Banadir Coast (Somali coast)

Ghana empire at peak of its power. Extensive trading links with North Africa and the Mediterranean world

Founding and growth of urban centers of Timbuktu, Jenne, and Gao on Niger River

Kanem state expands in Lake Chad region. Founding of early *Hausa* kingdoms in the Sudanic belt and *Yoruba* states in the forest lands

1054   *Almoravid Berbers* invade the trading center of Audaghost and disrupt Ghana empire's trans-Saharan trade links

Muslim states created in Morocco and Spain (1062–1147) following Almoravid invasion of North Africa

Bani Hillal invasions of Tunisia and eastern Algeria

Foundation of Songhai state around the trading center of Gao

1076   Almoravid Berbers attack Ghana and invade its capital, Kumbi Saleh

1100   Later Iron Age on plateau south of the Zambezi River Basin associated with Karanga peoples

c. 1100   Conclusion of Shirazi migrations southward from Persian Gulf area and Banadir Coast. Main coastal city-states are Pemba, Mafia, Mogadishu, and Kilwa

1135   Collapse of Almoravid control in the Western Sudan

c. 1200   *City-state of Kilwa* dominates trade and politics on the east coast. City-state of Kisimani on Mafia Island challenges Kilwa hegemony

City-states of Kilwa and Mogadishu trade with settlements in Central Africa for ivory, gold, and copper

State formation appears in southern Uganda

1235   Sundiata establishes Keita dynasty in Mandinka state of Kangaba, defeats Susu overlords, and founds Mali empire

1255	Mansa Uli continues to expand the commercial prosperity of the *Mali empire* until his death in 1270
1290	Decline of *Almohad*-created Muslim state in Maghrib and Spain
c. 1300	*Wolof* kingdoms appear in Senegal
1312	Mansa Musa assumes Mali throne and increases territorial domain of the Mali empire. Makes pilgrimage to Mecca in 1324–25
1331	Moroccan historian, Ibn Battuta, visits east coast city-states of Kilwa, Mombasa and Mogadishu
c. 1331	Early state formation in Malawi
1375	Sunni Suleiman-Mar, ruler of *Gao*, extends the early Songhai state's commercial power over the middle Niger River region
	First map of West Africa is drawn in Majorca
A.D. 1400–1700	***Continued State Formation and Early European Contacts:*** **Portuguese contacts; beginnings of the slave trade**
1400	Songhai army from Gao destroys Niani, capital of the declining Mali empire. Malian commercial hegemony declines
	Hausa and Yoruba states are powerful. Trans-Saharan trade with the Maghrib. Trade links with the Niger River region expand
	Coastal city-states continue their commercial prosperity. Individual city-states wax and wane depending on the volume of trade along East African coast
	Urban centers of Timbuktu and Jenne in the Western Sudan are nodal points of regional trade and Muslim learning
c. 1400	*Karanga* south of the Zambezi River Basin establish powerful kingdoms
	Ntemi chieftainships diffuse throughout northern and western Tanzania
	Rulers of the *Chwezi Dynasty* consolidate several polities in southern Uganda

1434   *Portuguese*, followed by other Europeans,
                first trade along the Senegambian
                coast of West Africa

c. 1450   Matope expands early *Mwenemutapa* (later
                corrupted to Monomotapa) state until
                his death c. 1480

1465   Sunni Ali becomes ruler of Gao and builds
                Songhai's overlordship of the middle
                Niger river region

                Muhammad Rumfa, first powerful Muslim
                ruler of Kano, rules until 1499

1473   Portuguese sail to Bight of Benin.
                First Christian *missionaries* arrive

1482   Portuguese construct *Elmina* fort on the
                Accra plains (Ghana coast)

                Kongo state dominates the coastal states
                of Central Africa

1487   Bartolemeu Dias reaches the Cape of Good
                Hope. Portuguese contact with East
                Africa begins

1493   Askia Muhammad rules Songhai empire until
                his death in 1528

1498   Vasco da Gama reaches Mombasa and returns
                to Portugal in 1499. Continued
                Portuguese presence on east coast

c. 1500   *Changamire* state is formed and grows
                rapidly as the kingdom of Mwenemutapa
                declines in late sixteenth century

                State formation in southern Uganda.
                Kingdom of *Bunyoro-Kitara* emerges.
                Period of *Luo* migrations from the
                southern Sudan

1505   Portuguese overrun coastal city-states of
                Kilwa and *Mombasa* and attempt to control
                coastal trade

c. 1505   Chieftainships of Undi, Karanga, and Mwase
                (*Malawi* peoples) resist early Portuguese
                penetration

1507	Battle of Garni-Kiyala. Ruler of *Bornu*, Mai Idris Katakarmabe, defeats Kanem
c. 1510	Expansion of trade between middle Niger and forest regions. *Jenne* expands
1519	Mahmud Kati of Timbuktu completes his *Tarikh al-Fattash*
c. 1520	*Chronicle of Kilwa* written in Arabic
	State formation in Katanga region and Congo grasslands. *Luba* and *Lunda* states become powerful after c. 1500
1534	Malian ambassador reaches Portugal
1541	First Portuguese expedition to Ethiopia
c. 1550	Kingdom of Gonja (Northern Ghana) founded by Mandinka invaders from Mali empire
1553	English reach *Kingdom of Benin*
1559	Denianke rulers established in Futa Toro (Guinea)
1575	Katsina, leading Hausa state, rebels against overlordship of Songhai
1580	Mai Idris Alooma is ruler of *Bornu* and establishes powerful state before his death in 1617
1585	East coast city-states resist Portuguese control
c. 1585	Portuguese penetrate the (later) state of Mwenemutapa and establish colonies along the Zambezi River
1587	Zimba invade city-state of Kilwa
1591	Moroccan army crosses Sahara and invades Songhai. Collapse of Songhai empire
1593	Portuguese build Fort Jesus at Mombasa
1600	Kingdom of Gonja wars against neighboring Dagomba states (Northern Ghana)
1629	Portuguese defeat Mwenemutapa armies. Decline of (later) Mwenemutapa empire
c. 1630	*Bunyoro* state powerful. Expansion of *Buganda* state in Interlacustrine region

	Kamba people trade with city-state of Mombasa
1650	*Oyo* empire expands over other Yoruba states and Dahomey
	Formation of state in Dahomey
	Expansion of trading state of Denkyira in Elmina hinterland (Coastal Ghana)
	Establishment of trading city-states in Niger Delta
1652	Dutch East India Company anchors at Table Bay in Capetown, South Africa
	State formation in Congo grasslands. Kingdoms of Kongo and Ndongo decline from Portuguese penetration and *Atlantic slave trade*
	Omani forces fight Portuguese along east coast
1657	First slaves arrive in Capetown from Java and Madagascar
1659	French colonize St. Louis in Senegal
1685	Increased slave trade attributed to large-scale sugar and tobacco plantations on the Caribbean islands
1693	Changamire drives Portuguese from Zimbabwe area
1698	Mazrui leads Omani forces against Portuguese at Mombasa. Portuguese defeat marks the end of their domination of the east coast
A.D. 1700–1884	**Period of Transition and Widespread Disruption:** Intensification of slave trade and European contacts; conflicts between African states and with Europeans; major shifts in power balance (e.g., forest against Sudanic states in West Africa; white against black in South Africa)
1700	Osei Tutu militarily expands *Ashanti* state from capital at Kumasi (c. 1680)

1712	Bambara state of Segu expands under Mamari Kulibali (1712–55)
1725	Establishment of Imamate of Fouta Jallon (Guinea)
1750	Formation of Bemba and Lozi kingdoms in Zambia
1753	Bambara state of Kaarta founded
	Niger delta city-states increase trading with Europeans on coast
1776	Foundation of Imamate of Futa Toro
	French land at Kilwa on east coast. Slave trade expands
1790	Beginning of so-called *Kaffir wars* that inter-mittantly continue until 1830s in South Africa
1791	Foundation of Freetown (*Sierra Leone*) as base for freed slaves
1804	Seyyid Said, ruler of Oman, expands power along east coast
	Fulani wars and conquest of Hausaland (1804–1810)
	Church Missionary Society arrives in Freetown
1806	First British-Ashanti clash. Ashanti controls its territories successfully
1807	British officially abolish slave trade. Denmark and France follow
1808	Sierra Leone becomes a British Colony
1817	Foundation of Bathurst (Gambia)
1818	*Shaka* of the Zulu defeats Ndwandwe. Beginning of the *Wars of Wandering*
1821	Dahomey fights Oyo
	First settlement of freed slaves in Liberia
1827	British clash again with Ashanti armies. British are defeated and retreat toward coast
	Fourah Bay Institution established in Freetown (Sierra Leone)

1831	Foundation of Basutoland by Mosheshwe (after 1825)
1836	*Great Trek.* One-fourth of Cape Colony's Afrikaner population migrates northward across the Orange and Fish rivers
1837	Matabele attack Kololo in Barotseland
1840	*Kabaka* Suna rules powerful Buganda state
	Matabele established in Changamire lands. Extend control over surrounding chieftainships
	Establishment of Omani Court under Seyyid Said in Zanzibar. Growth of Sultanate of Zanzibar as a dominant power in East Africa. Clove plantations develop based upon slave labor. Arab and Swahili traders penetrate far into interior
	Kazembe state powerful in Katanga. Trades with East Coast through Nyamwezi and Swahili traders
1843	Holy Ghost Fathers establish missions in Senegal
	Liberia becomes independent republic
1856	Kabaka Mutesa succeeds Suna in Buganda. Makes first contacts with British explorers
	Extension of *Yao* power in southern Tanzania and Malawi
1865	Formation of Ngoni states in Malawi
1866	Holy Ghost Fathers establish missions in Angola and Congo
1876	*Mirambo* of Unyamwezi, in north-central Tanganyika, consolidates control of interior trade
1878	White Fathers begin missionary activity in Tanganyika and Uganda
1881	Mahdi Muhamad Ahmad Ibn Abdullah leads Muslim Reformation in the Eastern Sudan
A.D. 1884–1945	***The European "Scramble for Africa" and the Colonial Period***
1884–85	Congress of Berlin on the European partition of Africa. Beginning of *colonial period*

1892	Society of Jesus begins missionary work in the Congo
1897	Matabele and Mashona revolts in Southern Rhodesia
1897	British conquer Benin
1898	French armies defeat *Samory Touré* at Sikasso. Conclusion of series of wars that began with Samory's victory over French at Nafadie (1885)
1899	Anglo-Boer War (1899–1902)
	Joint rule established in Sudan by Britain and Egypt
1901	British annex Ashanti as a crown colony. Conclusion of Ashanti wars of resistance (1900–1901)
1904	Herero and Nama *risings* against Germans in South-West Africa
1905	Maji Maji *rebellion* against German colonial administration in Tanganyika. Rising ends in 1907
1906–7	Zulu rebellion in South Africa
1908	Congo Free State becomes colony under rule of Belgian parliament after 24 years of personal rule by King Leopold II
1910	Union of South Africa becomes independent territory within British Commonwealth
1912	Foundation of *African National Congress* (originally South African Native Congress) in South Africa
1914	Society of the One Almighty God founded in Uganda
	British amalgamate Lagos colony with protectorates in Northern and Southern Nigeria
1914–18	*World War I.* Many Africans participate as soldiers. Some fighting in Africa (mainly German colonies)
1919	*Trusteeships* set up under League of Nations: Cameroons and Togo divided between Britain and France, South-West Africa to South Africa, Ruanda-Urundi to Belgium, and German East Africa (Tanganyika) to Britain

1920	Foundation of Destour Party (Tunisia)
1921	Young Kikuyu Association founded by Harry Thuku (Kenya)
1923–24	Southern Rhodesia becomes self-governing colony under British Crown; Northern Rhodesia becomes British protectorate
1935	Fascist Italy invades Ethiopia; resistance continues until 1939
1936	Establishment of Natives Representatives Council in South Africa
1941	Italians driven out of Ethiopia
1944	Foundation of ANC Youth League in South Africa
A.D. 1945–1956	***The Rise of African Nationalism and the Drive toward Independence***
1945	League of Nations mandates become *Trust Territories* under the United Nations (South Africa refuses to withdraw mandate from South-West Africa)
	Sixth Pan-Africanist Congress meets in Manchester, England
1946	Rassemblement Démocratique Africain (RDA) founded in Bamako, Mali (then French Soudan)
1948	Independents d'Outre-mer (IOM) founded
	Afrikaner Nationalist Party comes to power in South Africa
1951	First general elections held in Gold Coast; *Kwame Nkrumah* becomes first black African head of government under colonial rule
1952	*Mau Mau rebellion* officially recognized by British government to have begun in Kenya; Emergency lasts to 1960
	Naguib leads Free Officer's *coup d'etat* in Egypt
1952–53	Federation established between Southern Rhodesia, Northern Rhodesia, and Nyasaland
1953	Sudan granted self-government by Britain and Egypt
1954	Beginning of Algerian war against French rule

1954	Gamal Abdul Nasser becomes president of Egypt
A.D. 1956–1970	***African Independence and the Era of Nation-Building*** (Complete tables showing dates of independence and patterns of regime instability are given in the *Syllabus*, Modules 56 and 64)
1956	Sudan, Tunisia, and Morocco become independent
1957	*Ghana,* under Kwame Nkrumah, becomes first independent state in Black Africa and first black-ruled state in British Commonwealth
	Mouvement Socialiste Africain (MSA) established
1958	Military government takes over in *coup d'état* in Sudan
	First Conference of Independent African States meets in Accra
	French referendum for its African colonies. Only Guinea opts for immediate independence and discontinues affiliation with France
	Parti Regroupement Africain (PRA) formed
1960	Somali Republic, Nigeria, Congo-Leopoldville, Cameroon, Togo, Malagasy Republic, Mauritania, Senegal, Mali, Upper Volta, Niger, Dahomey, Ivory Coast, Chad, Central African Republic, Gabon, and Congo-Brazzaville become independent
	Anti-Portuguese rebellion begins in Angola
	Many Africans are killed after police panic over peaceful demonstration against pass laws in Sharpeville, South Africa
	Katanga demands secession from Congo-Leopoldville after army mutiny begins first Congo crisis; internal turmoil and civil war in parts of country
	Senegal secedes from Mali Federation
	Abortive coup in Ethiopia
1961	Sierra Leone and Tanganyika become independent

W. E. B. DuBois invited to Ghana as Director of Encyclopaedia Africana project

1962   Rwanda, Burundi, Algeria, and Uganda become independent

FRELIMO is established in Mozambique; major anti-Portuguese rebellion begins

1963   Independence of Kenya

Organization of African Unity founded in Addis Ababa

Anti-Portuguese activity begins in Portuguese Guinea

Katanga secession ended after occupation by U.N. troops

W. E. B. DuBois (born 1868) dies in Ghana and is buried in Accra

Major problem of secession arises in Southern Sudan

President Olympio assassinated in Togo (replaced by Grunitsky); also coup in Dahomey

Transkei established as first *Bantustan* in South Africa

1964   Malawi, Zambia, and Zanzibar become independent; revolution in Zanzibar leads to formation of union with Tanganyika as Tanzania

New Congo crisis develops; leadership reshuffled; Belgian and American paratroops dropped in Kisangani (formerly Stanleyville); major crisis lasts into 1965, with thousands killed

First International Conference of Africanists (Accra)

African Development Bank established

Malcolm X visits Africa

Nationwide strike in Nigeria

Successful coup in Gabon ousts M'Ba, but he is restored after French intervention

Civilian government restored in Sudan

1965   Gambia independent

1965   *Unilateral Declaration of Independence* by white
            minority government in Southern Rhodesia
            (under Ian Smith)

            Coup in Algeria (Boumedienne replaces ben
            Bella)

            Coup in Dahomey

            Meeting of OAU in Accra

1966   Botswana and Lesotho become independent

            Major period of instability throughout Africa;
            successful coups occur in Burundi, Central
            African Republic, Dahomey, Upper Volta, and
            Ghana (which ousts Kwame Nkrumah); riots
            over language policy occur in Mauritania;
            Obote seizes all power in Uganda, ousts Presi-
            dent Mutesa (the kabaka of Buganda), and
            state of emergency begins in Buganda (lasting
            until 1968)

            UN declares South African control over South-
            West Africa illegal

            First Nigerian coup against civilian regime
            (January); Prime Minister Balewa, the minister
            of finance, and the prime ministers of the
            Western and Northern regions are assassi-
            nated; commanding officer Aguiyi-Ironsi, who
            was not involved in the planning or execution
            of the coup, heads military government

            After period when many Ibos have been killed
            in the north, a second coup is staged by
            northern troops in July; Aguiyi-Ironsi seized
            and killed; Yakubu Gowon assumes command;
            large scale migration of Ibos out of north
            begins

1967   *Arusha Declaration* introduced; becomes basic
            policy guideline in Tanzania under its major
            author, President Julius Nyerere

            Eastern Region of Nigeria secedes on May 31,
            declaring itself the independent republic of
            Biafra; full-scale war breaks out; federal
            troops invade Eastern Region and Eastern

troops successfully seize Mid-West Region; federal government regains control of Mid-West later in year

East African Community established in Kampala, comprising Kenya, Uganda, and Tanzania; several other states express interest in creating larger economic union

Coups take place in Togo and Sierra Leone

Second International Conference of Africanists (Dakar)

1968 Swaziland, Equatorial Guinea, and Mauritius become independent

Coups occur in Congo-Brazzaville, Mali, and Sierra Leone (the latter resulting in restoration of civilian government); civil government restored in Dahomey

United Nations General Assembly declares South-West Africa should henceforth be called *Namibia;* resolves to take effective action to eliminate South African control; South Africa completes blueprints for full incorporation of South-West Africa as its fifth province

Stability and peace return to previously turbulent Congo-Kinshasa (under President Mobutu) and to the Horn of Africa (after detente between leaders of Somali Republic, Kenya, and Ethiopia over Somali irridentism)

1969 Two African leaders are assassinated: Tom Mboya in Nairobi and Eduardo Mondlane, leader of the Mozambique liberation movement, in Dar es Salaam

Pan-African Cultural Conference held in Algiers

Coups in Somali Republic, Sudan, and Libya

Ghana restored to civilian rule in national election; K. A. Busia assumes leadership

Miss Angie Brooks (Liberia) elected President of U.N. General Assembly

Several major conflicts in Africa continue: the Nigeria-Biafra civil war, anti-Portuguese

1969   rebellions in Angola, Mozambique, and Guinea-
                       Bassa; the Rhodesian situation; French troops
                       sent into Chad. (*Note:* the civil war in Nigeria
                       was officially ended in January, 1970)

APPENDIX C
Guide to Pronunciation of African Names

THIS APPENDIX is designed to guide the user of the *Syllabus* in the pronunciation of African words and other terms relevant to African studies. The guide stresses widely accepted standards of American pronunciation, although an attempt is made in nearly every case to give a pronunciation which is as close as possible to the language the word is derived from. Major exceptions occur, however, particularly when American English has no equivalent sound (as for Arabic gutturals, the click in Xhosa, or some French nasalized sounds) or when an alternate pronunciation has become widely established (e.g., beginning Uganda with *yoo* rather than *oo*, as is demanded in Bantu languages). The guide therefore is aimed at acceptable standards of pronunciation rather than linguistic precision.

The form of pronunciations given contains no special symbols or marks, but attempts to follow consistent rules which are outlined below. Accented syllables are capitalized.

a = short *a* as in *apart*
ah = broader sound as in *odd*
ee = long *e* as in *bee*
eh = shorter *e* as in *egg*
igh = long *i* as in *high*
i = short *i* as in *ill*
oh = long *o* as in *old*
oo = long *oo* as in *food*

In addition, there are certain African words that require pronunciations that are not familiar in American English. These include, for example, the voiced consonants *m* and *n*, as in *Mboya* or *Nkrumah*. These sounds are given as *mm* and *nn*. The *mm* should be pronounced something like the sound in "*mm* good," not with a preceding vowel sound (that is, not *em*-Boya or *im*-Boya). Similarly, *Nkrumah* should not begin with the sound *in* or *en*. Somewhat related is the form *ny,* as in *Nyerere:* this should be pronounced as a single consonant, perhaps as in *canyon,* not as *nigh.*

African language experts are likely to find several examples in this guide with which they disagree. We have chosen to make the guide as simple and as useful as possible and have therefore sacrificed some linguistic precision to permit greater ease of use by a general American audience.

Abako	ah-BAH-koh	almoravid	el-more-AH-vid
Abboud	ah-BOOD	Al-Qayrawani,	el-KARE-a-wah-
Abeokuta	ab-bee-o-KOO-tah	Ibn Avi Zayd	nee, i-ben ah-vee
Abidjan	ah-bee-JAHN		zah-EED
abirru	a-BEE-roo	Amharic	am-HAH-rick
Abuja	a-BOO-jah	Anas, Malik	ah-NAHS,
Accra	ack-RAH	Ibn	mah-LEEK i-ben
Achebe,	a-CHEH-bee,	Angola	ang-GO-lah
Chinua	CHIN-oo-ah	Ankole	ang-KOH-leh
Addis Ababa	AD-dis AH-bah-	apartheid	a-PART-hate
	bah	Arewa	a-RAY-wah
Adulis	a-DYOO-liss	Armah, Ayi	ARM-mah, AH-yee
Afars and Issas	A-farz and EE-sahz	Kwei	KWAY
Afrikaans	a-fri-KAHNS	Arusha	a-ROO-sha
Afrikaner	a-fri-KAH-ner	Asantehene	a-sont-a-HEE-nee
Agege	a-GAY-geh	Ashanti	a-SHON-tee
Agni	ON-yee	Ashiru	a-SHEE-roo
Aguiyi-Ironsi	a-GWEE-yee	assimilado	ah-see-mee-LAH-
	i-RON-see		doh
Ahidjo,	ah-HEED-jo,	Aswan	ASS-wahn
Ahmadou	ah-mah-du	Aughrabies	aw-GRAH-beez
Ahmadiyya	ah-mah-DEE-yah	Falls	
Ahmad,	AH-mahd, GOO-	Awolowo	a-WOL-oh-woh
Ghulum	loom	Axum	OX-soom
Akan	AH-kahn	Azikiwe,	a-ZEEK-a-way,
aladura	ah-lah-DOO-rah	Nnamdi	NAM-dee
Al-Azhar	el-a-ZHAR		
Al-Azhari,	el-a-ZAHR-hee,	Baganda	bah-GAHN-dah
Ismail	ISH-may-eel	Bagirmi	buh-GEAR-mee
Algeria	al-JEER-ree-yah	Bahr el Ghazal	bar-el-ga-ZAHL
Al-hajj	el-HODGE	Bakongo	bah-KONG-go
Ali, Sunni	AH-lee, SOO-nee	Balari	bah-LAH-ree
alkali	al-KAHL-lee	Balewa,	buh-LAY-wah,
al-Kanemi,	el-kah-NEE-mee,	Abubakar	ah-boo-BAH-kar
Shehu	SHAY-hoo	Tafawa	ta-FAH-wah
Allah	AH-lah	Bambara	bahm-BAH-rah
		Bamileke	bam-a-LEE-kee

Banda	BAN-duh	Changamire	chong-a-MEER-eh
Bangala	bang-GAH-lah	Chwezi	CHWAY-zee
Bantu	BAHN-too	Congo-Kin-	KONG-go kin-
Baoule	BAH-oh-lay	shasa	SHAH-sah
Batetele	bah-teh-TAY-lay	Congo-Kor-	KONG-go core-
Baya	BAH-yah	dofanian	doh-FAN-ee-in
Bello, Ahmadu	BELL-oh, ah-mah-du	Coptic	KOP-tick
Bemba	BEM-bah	Creole	KREE-ohl
Bete	BAY-tay	Cunene River	koo-NAY-neh
Benin	beh-NEEN		
Benue	BEH-new-way	Dacko, David	DACK-oh
Berber	BURR-burr	Daddah,	DAH-dah, MOOK-
Biafra	bee-AH-frah	Moktar Ould	tar OOLD
bidonvilles	bee-dohn-VEEL	Dahomey	dah-HOME-ee
Birni Gazar-	BEER-nee gah-	Dakar	dak-KAR
gamo	ZAHR-ga-moh	dar-al-islam	dar-el-iss-LAHM
Bito	BEE-toh	Dar es Salaam	dar-ess-sah-LAHM
Bodele depres-	bo-DAY-lay	Daura	DOW-rah
sion		Dia, Mamadou	DEE-ah, MOM-ah-
			doo
Boer	BORE	Dingiswayo	ding-iss-WHY-oh
Bokassa	bo-KAH-sah	Dinka	DINK-ah
bori	BORE-ree	Diola	dee-OH-lah
Bornu	bore-NOO	Diop	DEE-op
Botswana	buh-TSWAH-nah	Diori, Hamani	dee-OAR-ree,
Buganda	boo-GAHN-dah		hah-MAH-nee
Bulawayo	boo-lah-WHY-oh	Djerma	JERM-ah
Bunyoro	boon-YORE-oh	Djibouti	jib-BOO-tee
Buraimoh,	boo-RYE-moh,	Dorobo	DORE-oh-ba
Jimoh	JEE-moh	Douala	doo-AH-lah
Burundi	boo-ROON-dee	Durban	DER-bin
Bushongo	boo-SHONG-go		
Busia, Kofi	boo-SEE-ah, KOH-	Edea	eh-DAY-ah
	fee	Edo	ED-doh
Bwanba	BWAHM-bah	Ekwensi,	eh-KWEN-see,
		Cyprian	SIP-ree-in
Caliphate	KAY-lif-ate	Elmina	el-MEE-nah
Cameroon	kam-ah-ROON	Enugu	eh-NOO-goo
Carthage	KAR-thidge	Erythrian Sea	eh-ri-THREE-in
Casablanca	cass-ah-BLANK-ah	Ethiopia	eeth-ee-OH-pee-ah
Ceuta	SAY-oo-tah	Ewe	EV-vay
Chagga	CHOG-ah	Ewondo	eh-WON-doh
Chewa	CHAY-wah		
Changa	CHONG-ah	Fang	FONG

Fanon, Frantz	fa-NOHN	Ijebu	i-JEH-boo
Fanti	FAHN-tee	Ila	EE-lah
Fernando Po	fur-NAN-doh POH	Ilesha	i-LESH-ah
		imam	ee-MAHM
Fon	FAHN	interlacustrine	in-ter-lah-CUSS-trin
Fourah Bay	FOO-rah BAY		
Fouta Jallon	FOO-tah JAH-lon	Ironsi (see Aguiyi-Ironsi)	
Fulani	foo-LAH-nee		
		Iru	EE-roo
Gabon	ga-BONE	Ishirinya	ish-er-RIN-ya
Gambia	GAM-bee-ah	Itsekiri	check-KEER-ee
Ganda	GAHN-dah		
Gao	GA-oh	Jawara, Dauda	ja-WAH-rah, DOW-dah
Garun Gabas	ga-ROON ga-BAHS	Jenne	JEN-nee
Gerawa	je-RAH-wah	jihad	JEE-hod
Ghana	GAH-nah	Jinja	JIN-jah
Gobir	go-BEER	Jos	JOSS
Gondwanaland	gon-DWAH-nah-land		
		kaaba	KAH-bah
Gowon, Yakubu	go-WAHN, yah-koo-boo	kabaka	kah-BOCK-ah
		Kaduna	kah-DOON-ah
Guinea	GI-nee	Kainji	kah-EEN-jee
		Kairawan	KAY-roo-wahn
hadith	had-DEETH	Kalahari	kah-lah-HAH-ree
hajj	HODGE	Kambundu	kam-BOON-doo
Hadza	HA-tsa	Kamba	KOM-bah
Hamitic	ha-MITT-ick	Kanawa	kah-NAH-wah
Hanbali	hon-BAH-lee	Kanem	KAH-nem
Hanafi	HON-ah-fee	Kangaba	kahn-GAH-bah
Hama, Boubou	HOM-ah, boo-boo	Kankan	kahn-kahn
haram	hah-RAM	Kano	KAH-noh
Hottentot	HOT-in-tot	Kano, Aminu	KAH-noh, ah-MEE-noo
Hausa	HOW-sah		
Houphouet-Boigny	hoo-fway-bwah-NYEE	Kanuri	kah-NOO-ree
		Kariba	kah-REE-bah
Hima	HEE-mah	Kasavubu, Joseph	kass-a-VOO-boo
Hutu	HOO-too		
		Katanga	ka-TANG-gah
Ibadan	i-BAH-din	Katsina	kat-SIN-ah
Ibibio	i-BIB-ee-oh	Kaunda, Kenneth	kah-OON-dah
Ibn Battuta	i-ben-bah-TOO-tah		
Ibo	EE-boh		
Ife	EE-fay		

Kayibanda, Gregoire — kah-yee-BAHN-dah, greg-WAHR

Keïta, Modibo — KAY-tah, moh-DEE-boh

Kenya — KEN-yah

Kenyatta, Jomo — ken-YAH-tah, JOE-moh

Khalil, Sidi — kah-LEEL, see-dee

Khama, Seretse — KAH-mah, seh-RET-see

Khartoum — kar-TOOM

Khoisan — koy-sonn

Kikuyu — ki-KOO-yoo

Kilimanjaro — ki-lee-mon-JAR-oh

Kilwa — KILL-wah

Kimbangu, Simon — kim-BONG-goo, see-MOHN

Kinshasa — kin-SHAH-sah

Kitara — ki-TAH-rah

Kisangani — kee-sahng-GAH-nee

Kom — KAHM

Kongo — KONG-go

Kongolo — kong-GO-loh

Konkoure — kahn-KOO-ray

Kumasi — koo-MAH-see

Lagos — LAY-gohs

La Guma, Alex — lah GOO-mah

Lamizana — lah-mee-ZAH-nah

Lamu — LAH-moo

Lango — LANG-goh

Laye, Camera — LIGH, KAHM-rah

Legon — LAY-gahn

Lenshina, Alice — len-SHEE-nah

Lesotho — leh-SOOT-oh

Liberia — lye-BEER-ee-yah

Libreville — LEE-bra-veel

Libya — LIB-ee-ah

Lifiquane — lee-fee-KAH-neh

Limba — LIM-bah

Limpopo — lim-POH-poh

Lingala — ling-GAH-lah

Lozi — LOH-zee (LOH-tsee)

Louvanium — loo-VAH-nee-um

Luba — LOO-bah

Lubumbashi — loo-boom-BAH-shee

Luganda — loo-GAHN-dah

Lugbara — loog-BAH-rah

Luhya — LOO-yah

Lumumba, Patrice — luh-MOOM-bah, pah-TREESE

Lunda — LOON-dah

Luo — LOO-oh

Lusaka — loo-SAH-kah

Luxor — LUX-ore

ma'aji — MAH-ah-jee

Maga, Hubert — MAH-gah, hoo-bear

M'Ba, Leon — mm-BAH, lay-ohn

Mboya, Tom — mm-BOY-ah

Mbundu — mm-BOON-doo

Mbuti Pygmies — mm-BOO-tee PIG-meez

Madagascar — mad-dah-GAS-kar

Mafia — MAH-fee-yah

Maghrib — MAH-grib

Maguzawa — mah-goo-ZAH-wah

Mahdi — MAH-dee

Maiduguri — my-DOO-gah-ree

Makarikari Salt Flats — ma-KAH-ree-KAH-ree

Makerere — ma-KARE-rare-ee

Malagasy Republic (Fr. Malgache) — ma-lah-GAH-see (mal-GOSH)

Malawi — ma-LAH-wee

Mali — MAH-lee

Maliki — ma-LEE-kee

Malindi — ma-LIN-dee

mallam — MAHL-lum

Mande — MAN-dee

Mandingo	man-DING-go	Muwatta	moo-WATT-ah
Mandinka	man-DINK-ah	Mwenemutapa	mweh-neh-moo-TAH-pah
Mansa Musa	MAN-sah MOO-sah		
Margai, Milton	mar-GUY	Nairobi	nigh-ROH-bee
Marrakesh	mah-rah-KESH	Namibia	na-MIB-ee-ah
Masai	mah-SIGH	Napata	NAP-a-tah
Matabele	mah-tah-BELL-ee	Ndongo	nn-DONG-oh
Mau Mau	mao-mao	ngola	nn-GO-lah
Mauritania	maw-ri-TAY-nee-yah	Ngoni	nn-GO-nee
		Ngugi, James	nn-GOO-gee
Mende	MEN-dee	Niane	nee-AH-nay
Menelik	MEN-eh-lick	Niass, Ibrahim	NEE-os, eeb-RAH-heem
Merowe	MEH-roh-way		
Mfecane	mm-feh-KAH-neh	Niger	NIGH-jer (Fr. NEE-zhair)
Mobutu, Joseph	moh-BOO-too		
		Nigeria	nigh-JEER-ee-yah
Mogadishu	moh-gah-DISH-oo	Nketia	nn-keh-TEE-yah
Mombasa	mom-BAH-sah	Nkrumah, Kwame	nn-KROO-mah, KWAH-mee
Mongo	MONG-go		
Monomotapa	moh-no-mo-TOP-ah	Nkomo, Joshua	nn-KOH-moh
Morocco	moh-ROCK-oh	Nok	NOCK
Mossi	MOH-see	Nsukka	nn-SOO-kah
Mouride	moo-REED	Nubia	NOO-bee-yah
Mouridiyya	moo-ree-DEE-yah	Nuer	NOO-air
Mondlane, Eduardo	mond-LON-eh, eh-DWAHR-doh (mond-LANE)	Nyakibanda	nyah-kee-BON-dah
		Nyakyusa	nyah-KYOO-sah
Mozambique	moh-zam-BEEK	Nyamwezi	nyam-WAY-zee
Mphalele, Ezekiel	mm-fah-LAY-leh, eh-ZEE-kee-yul	Nyanja	NYAHN-jah
		Nyasaland	NIGH-ass-a-land (NYAH-sah-land)
Mrima	mm-REE-mah		
Mtetwa	mm-TET-wah	Nyerere, Julius	nyeh-REH-ree
Muganda	moo-GAHN-dah	Nzima	nn-ZEE-mah
Muhammad	moo-HAHM-id		
Muhammad, Askia	moo-HAHM-id, ass-KEY-ah	Oba	OH-buh
		Obatala	oh-bah-TAH-lah
Muhirua, Andre	moo-HEE-roo-ah, on-DRAY	Obote, Apollo Milton	oh-BOAT-tay
Mukhtasar	mook-TASS-are	Odinga, Oginga	oh-DING-ah, oh-GING-ah
Mutum Nijeriya	moo-TOOM nee-JEER-ee-ah		
		Okovango	oh-koh-VANG-oh

Swamps	
Olatunji	oh-lah-TOON-jee
Olduvai	ohl-doo-VIGH
Omani	oh-MAH-nee
Opobo	oh-POH-boh
Oshogbo	oh-SHOHG-boh
Oshun shrine	OH-shoon
Oyelemi, Muraina	oh-yeh-LEH-mee, moo-RIGH-nah
Oyo	OY-oh
Oyono, Ferdinand	oy-OH-noh
Pate	PAH-tay
Pemba	PEM-bah
Principe Island	PRIN-see-pee
Qadir, Abdul	kah-DEER, OB-dool
Qadiriyya	kah-dah-REE-yah
Que Que	KWAY-kway
Quran	KORE-ahn
Rano	RAH-noh
Rio Muni	REE-oh MYOO-nee
Risala	ree-SAH-lah
Ruanda	roo-AHN-dah
Rubadiri, David	roo-bah-DEER-ee
Rundi	ROON-dee
Rwanda	roo-AHN-dah
Sahara	sah-HAH-rah
Said, Seyyid	sah-EED, SAY-id
Salisbury	SAWLS-burr-ee
Sandawe	sahn-DAH-way
Sango (ethnic group)	SANG-go
Sango (Yoruba deity)	SHANG-go
Sankore	san-KORE-eh
São Tome	SOW TOH-may

Sara	SAH-rah
Shaka	SHAH-kah
Selassie I, Haile	seh-LAH-see, HIGH-lee
Sembène, Ousmane	Sem-BEN, oos-man
Senegal	SEH-neh-gahl
Senghor, Leopold	SAHN-gore, LAY-oh-pold
Serere	seh-RARE
shahada	sha-HAH-dah
Shafi	SHAH-fee
shari'a	shah-REE-yah
Shermarke, A. A.	shirr-MAR-kay
Shirawa	sheer-AH-wah
Shirazi	shee-RAH-zee
Shiroro	shee-ROH-roh
Simba	SIM-bah
Sierra Leone	see-EH-ra lee-OHN
Sithole, Ndabaningi	sit-TOH-leh, nn-dah-bah-NING-gee
Sofala	soh-FAH-lah
Soglo	SOH-glow
Sokoto	SOH-kuh-toh
Somali	so-MAH-lee
Songhai	SONG-guy
Soninke	soh-NING-kay
Sotho	SOO-toh
Soyinka, Wole	shoy-INK-ah, WOH-lay
Sudan	soo-DAN
Sudd	SOOD
Sundiata	soon-dee-AH-tah
Sufi	SOO-fee
Sullubawa	soo-loo-BAH-wah
Swahili	swah-HEE-lee
Swaziland	SWAH-zee-land
Tahoua	TAH-hoo-wah

Tallensi	ta-LEN-see	Urundi	oo-ROON-dee
Tana Valley	TAH-nah	Uzama	oo-ZAH-mah
Tananarive	ta-nah-na-REEVE	Verwoerd	fair-VOORT
Tanzania	tan-za-NEE-yah	Vorster	FOR-stir
Tarkwa	TAR-kwah		
Tassili	TASS-il-ee	Wa-Benzi	wah-BEN-zee
Tema	TEH-mah	Waday	wah-DIGH
Temne	TEM-nee	wadi	WAH-dee
Thebes	THEEBZ	waziri	wah-ZEE-ree
Tijani, Ahmad	tid-JAH-nee,	Witwatersrand	vit-VAH-ters-
	AH-mahd		rahnd
Tijaniyya	tid-jah-NEE-yah	Wolof	WAH-luff
Timbuktu	tim-buck-TOO	Xhosa	KOH-sah
Togo	TOH-goh		
Tombalbaye,	tom-bahl-BIGH-	Yaku	YAH-ku
François	yeh, frahn-	Yoruba	YORE-roo-bah
	SWAH	Yaméogo,	yah-mee-
Touré, Samory	TOO-ray, SAM-	Maurice	OH-goh
	oh-ree	Yao	YOW
Touré, Sékou	TOO-ray, SAY-koo	Youlou,	YOO-loo,
Transkei	trans-KIGH	Fulbert	fool-BEAR
Transvaal	trans-VAHL		
Tswana	TSWAH-nah	Zakat	ZAH-kaht
Tunisia	too-NEE-zha	Zambezi	zam-BEE-zee
Tutsi	TOOT-see	Zambia	ZAM-bee-yah
Tutuola, Amos	too-too-OH-lah	Zanaki	za-NAH-kee
Twi	CHWEE	Zande	ZAN-dee
		Zanzibar	ZAN-zi-bar
Ubangi-Shari	oo-BANG-gee-	Zaria	ZAH-ree-yah
	SHAH-ree	Zazzau	ZAZZ-zow
Uganda	yoo-GAHN-dah	Zimbabwe	zim-BAH-bweh
	(oo-GAHN-dah)	Zinj	ZINJ
Ujamaa	oo-jah-MAH	Zomba	ZAHM-bah
ulama	OO-la-mah	Zulhajj	zool-HODGE
umma	OO-mah	Zulu	ZOO-loo

DATE DUE

7/6			
DEC 8 1972			